A BIT OF BULL FROM JOHN BULL

January, in the year of our Lord 2009

Dear readers,

I was taken to see my first England match by my late father in May 1977 when the national team squeezed home 2–1 against Northern Ireland in a Home International at Belfast's Windsor Park. My Dad had previously taken time out from work to follow the fortunes of the host nation at the 1966 World Cup, including the final itself. His football programme forms part of the back cover. I have remained an 'interested observer' in the fluctuating fortunes of the England team ever since.

Here follows a few little bits about this wondrous publication. Every match contained herein is a 'friendly', unless otherwise stated. To describe any international fixture as a 'friendly' is in itself dubious, as players' careers were frequently on the line in these 'amicable' contests. All individuals marked with a nice star were selected as captain for the occasion. Also, to the dismay of any of you pedantic people in book-reading land, I have merely stuck to numbers 1 to 11 for all the matches, even though there were instances where squad numbers were used instead, such as the 1966 World Cup final when Peters was No.16 and Hunt was No.21. I haven't bothered to detail which clubs that the opposing players represent nor even who the substitutes or goalscorers were. This anti-foreigner omission will no doubt be raised for discussion at the United Nations General Assembly, but let's face it folks, this is a book which acts as a statistical reminder of England's journey from a team full of potential in 1946 through to a team in 2006 full of, er potential too. If only the potential was more frequently realised, as you will certainly discover! Incidentally, if you have a manic desire to discover the names of all the opposing substitutes, who scored for the opposition, and when, then feel free to visit www.englandstats.com where you will be treated to a vast array of more statistics for your pleasure. I have already been there and done that, so it is only right and proper that I do that website the courtesy of mentioning them. I also made use of the following website for portions of my appendices: www.englandfootballonline.com ,so again one must give credit where credit is due.

Regrettably, ladies and gentlemen, boys and girls, I myself am playing in the non-level playing field of the celebrity-driven book trade. In view of this, I felt the need to recruit a celeb to provide the foreword, but obviously without success. I sent emails to Ian Wright, Alvin Martin, Stan Collymore, Mike Ingham, and John Inverdale, but clearly they were too precious to offer a preface. Mike 'Porky' Parry pledged to do so, but he did not keep his promise. Let us thus kneel down, bow our heads and pray as I throw this book at the mercy of the merciless book wholesalers and retailers in the hope that this majestic offering is granted its rightful place on numerous book shelves in retail outlets throughout England's green and pleasant land. Otherwise, the author too will remain full of potential that isn't realised, just like the national team! Now be off with you, kind reader, and avail yourself of all the fabulous matches from yesteryear. If you don't want to know the scores, then look away now.

Kind regards to you all

This little preface was lovingly brought to your attention by a talented genius.

ABOUT THE PUBLISHERS

If you are desperately trying to get a foot in the door and get your book into the public domain, you could do worse than submit a sample of it to ourselves, preferably on a disc and/or in PDF format. We are Parkbench Publications, PO Box 1081, Belfast, BT1 9EP. Unlike most publishers, we will not put your sample to the bottom of a pile and then glance at it several weeks later. You will receive a quick decision and your project will be afforded the respect that it deserves, which is uncommon amongst the major publishing houses that will not entertain you unless you have a cookery programme on Channel Four or appear regularly in OK magazine.

Alternatively, you can waste time circulating samples to the major publishing houses and wait literally months for their standard, tiresome 'good luck elsewhere' replies.

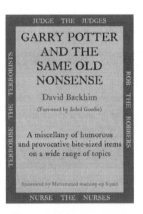

Northern Ireland 2 ENGLAND 7; in Belfast; Saturday 28th September 1946 (Home International)

1	Russell	1	Swift	(Man City)
2	Gorman	2	Scott	(Arsenal)
3	Aherne	3	Hardwick*	(Middlesbrough)
4	Carey	4	Wright	(Wolves)
5	Vernon	5	Franklin	(Stoke City)
6	Douglas	6	Cockburn	(Man Utd)
7	Cochrane	7	Finney	(Preston North End)
8	McAlindon	8	Carter	(Sunderland)
9	McMorran	9	Lawton	(Chelsea)
10	Doherty	10	Mannion	(Middlesbrough)
11	Lockhart	11	Langton	(Blackburn)

Crowd: 57,111

England scorers: Carter, Mannion (3), Finney, Lawton, Langton

Comments: England scored twice in the first 10 minutes, but only led 3–2 at half-time. Then 4 goals in the last half hour decided the issue. This was Walter Winterbottom's first match as manager.

Republic of Ireland 0 ENGLAND 1; in Dublin; Monday 30th September 1946

1	Breen	1	Swift	(Man City)
2	Gorman	2	Scott	(Arsenal)
3	Hayes	3	Hardwick*	(Middlesbrough)
4	Carey	4	Wright	(Wolves)
5	Martin	5	Franklin	(Stoke City)
6	Walsh	6	Cockburn	(Man Utd)
7	O'Flanagan	7	Finney	(Preston North End)
8	Coad	8	Carter	(Sunderland)
9	Unknown	9	Lawton	(Chelsea)
10	Stevenson	10	Mannion	(Middlesbrough)
11	Eglington	11	Langton	(Blackburn)

Crowd: 32,000

England scorer: Finney

Comments: The great Tom Finney had now scored twice in his first two internationals. His winner came less than ten minutes from the end.

ENGLAND 3 Wales 0; at Maine Road;
Wednesday 13th November 1946 (Home International)

1 Swift	(Man City)	1 Sidlow	
2 Scott	(Arsenal)	2 Sherwood	
3 Hardwick*	(Middlesbrough)	3 Hughes	
4 Wright	(Wolves)	4 Witcomb	
5 Franklin	(Stoke City)	5 Jones	
6 Cockburn	(Man Utd)	6 Burgess	
7 Finney	(Preston North End)	7 Jones	
8 Carter	(Sunderland)	8 Powell	
9 Lawton	(Chelsea)	9 Richards	
10 Mannion	(Middlesbrough)	10 Powell	
11 Langton	(Blackburn)	11 Edwards	

Crowd: 59,121

England scorers: Mannion (2), Lawton

Comments: North-east legend Wilf Mannion had now scored five times in his first three matches as England marched into a 3–0 lead by half-time in this Home International fixture.

ENGLAND 8 Holland 2; at Huddersfield;
Wednesday 27th November 1946

1 Swift	(Man City)	1 Kraak	
2 Scott	(Arsenal)	2 Potharst	
3 Hardwick*	(Middlesbrough)	3 van der Linden	
4 Wright	(Wolves)	4 Paauwe	
5 Franklin	(Stoke City)	5 Vermeer	
6 Johnston	(Blackpool)	6 de Vroet	
7 Finney	(Preston North End)	7 Drager	
8 Carter	(Sunderland)	8 Wilkes	
9 Lawton	(Chelsea)	9 Roosen	
10 Mannion	(Middlesbrough)	10 Smit	
11 Langton	(Blackburn)	11 Bergman	

Crowd: 32,435

England scorers: Lawton (4), Carter (2), Mannion, Finney

Comments: Lawton netted 4 times as England stormed into a 6–1 interval lead. This was supposed to be a friendly. England's only friendly gesture was when Hardwick missed a penalty!

ENGLAND 1 Scotland 1; at Wembley;
Saturday 12th April 1947 (Home International)

1 Swift	(Man City)	1 Miller
2 Scott	(Arsenal)	2 Young
3 Hardwick*	(Middlesbrough)	3 Shaw
4 Wright	(Wolves)	4 Macauley
5 Franklin	(Stoke City)	5 Woodburn
6 Johnston	(Blackpool)	6 Forbes
7 Matthews	(Stoke City)	7 Smith
8 Carter	(Sunderland)	8 McLaren
9 Lawton	(Chelsea)	9 Delaney
10 Mannion	(Middlesbrough)	10 Steel
11 Mullen	(Wolves)	11 Pearson

Crowd: 98,250

England scorer: Carter

Comments: The first clash against the 'auld enemy' in almost a decade ended in stalemate after Raich Carter's equaliser cancelled out Scotland's half-time lead. This was Jimmy Mullen's debut.

ENGLAND 3 France 0; at Highbury;
Saturday 3rd May 1947

1 Swift	(Man City)	1 Darui
2 Scott	(Arsenal)	2 Swiatek
3 Hardwick*	(Middlesbrough)	3 Marche
4 Wright	(Wolves)	4 Cuissard
5 Franklin	(Stoke City)	5 Gregoire
6 Lowe	(Aston Villa)	6 Prouff
7 Finney	(Preston North End)	7 Vaast
8 Carter	(Sunderland)	8 Tempowski
9 Lawton	(Chelsea)	9 Bongiorni
10 Mannion	(Middlesbrough)	10 Heisserer
11 Langton	(Blackburn)	11 Lechantre

Crowd: 54,389

England scorers: Finney, Mannion, Carter

Comments: The home team scored all their goals in the second-half to secure victory in Eddie Lowe's debut appearance. Tom Finney reclaimed the No. 7 jersey from Stanley Matthews.

Switzerland 1 ENGLAND 0; in Zurich;
Sunday 18th May 1947

1	Ballabio	1	Swift	(Man City)
2	Gyger	2	Scott	(Arsenal)
3	Steffan	3	Hardwick*	(Middlesbrough)
4	Belli	4	Wright	(Wolves)
5	Eggimann	5	Franklin	(Stoke City)
6	Bocquet	6	Lowe	(Aston Villa)
7	Tamini	7	Matthews	(Blackpool)
8	Fink	8	Carter	(Sunderland)
9	Bickel	9	Lawton	(Chelsea)
10	Amado	10	Mannion	(Middlesbrough)
11	Fatton	11	Langton	(Blackburn)

Crowd: 34,000

Comments: Fatton scored just before the half-hour mark for victory in this friendly. Stanley Matthews (now recruited by Blackpool) regained the No. 7 jersey from Tom Finney.

Portugal 0 ENGLAND 10; in Lisbon;
Sunday 25th May 1947

1	Azevedo	1	Swift	(Man City)
2	Cardoso	2	Scott	(Arsenal)
3	Fereira	3	Hardwick*	(Middlesbrough)
4	Amaro	4	Wright	(Wolves)
5	Feliciano	5	Franklin	(Stoke City)
6	Moreira	6	Lowe	(Aston Villa)
7	Correia	7	Matthews	(Blackpool)
8	Araujo	8	Mortensen	(Blackpool)
9	Peyroteo	9	Lawton	(Chelsea)
10	Travacos	10	Mannion	(Middlesbrough)
11	de Carvalho	11	Finney	(Preston North End)

Crowd: 65,000

England scorers: Lawton (4), Mortensen (4), Finney, Matthews

Comments: Stan Mortensen netted four times on his debut. Tommy Lawton scored the first of his four goals after just 17 seconds – England's fastest-ever goal.

Belgium 2 ENGLAND 5; in Brussels;
Sunday 21st September 1947

1	Daenen	1	Swift	(Man City)
2	Aernaudts	2	Scott	(Arsenal)
3	Pannaye	3	Hardwick*	(Middlesbrough)
4	Coppens	4	Ward	(Derby County)
5	Henriet	5	Franklin	(Stoke City)
6	Massay	6	Wright	(Wolves)
7	Lemberechts	7	Matthews	(Blackpool)
8	Mermans	8	Mortensen	(Blackpool)
9	de Cleyn	9	Lawton	(Chelsea)
10	Anoul	10	Mannion	(Middlesbrough)
11	Thirifays	11	Finney	(Preston North End)

Crowd: 54,326

England scorers: Lawton (2), Mortensen, Finney (2)

Comments: This time Tommy Lawton had to wait more than thirty seconds to open his goals account! Tim Ward made his debut in another emphatic friendly victory for England.

Wales 0 ENGLAND 3; in Cardiff;
Saturday 18th October 1947 (Home International)

1	Sidlow	1	Swift	(Man City)
2	Lambert	2	Scott	(Arsenal)
3	Barnes	3	Hardwick*	(Middlesbrough)
4	Powell	4	Taylor	(Liverpool)
5	Jones	5	Franklin	(Stoke City)
6	Burgess	6	Wright	(Wolves)
7	Thomas	7	Matthews	(Blackpool)
8	Powell	8	Mortensen	(Blackpool)
9	Lowrie	9	Lawton	(Chelsea)
10	Jones	10	Mannion	(Middlesbrough)
11	Edwards	11	Finney	(Preston North End)

Crowd: 55,000

England scorers: Finney, Mortensen, Lawton

Comments: All the visitors' goals came in the first half-hour of this fixture. Phil Taylor made his debut. For the second successive game, the same three men scored for England.

ENGLAND 2 Northern Ireland 2; at Goodison Park; Wednesday 5th November 1947 (Home International)

1	Swift	(Man City)	1	Hinton	
2	Scott	(Arsenal)	2	Martin	
3	Hardwick*	(Middlesbrough)	3	Carey	
4	Taylor	(Liverpool)	4	Walsh	
5	Franklin	(Stoke City)	5	Vernon	
6	Wright	(Wolves)	6	Farrell	
7	Matthews	(Blackpool)	7	Cochrane	
8	Mortensen	(Blackpool)	8	Smyth	
9	Lawton	(Notts County)	9	Walsh	
10	Mannion	(Middlesbrough)	10	Doherty	
11	Finney	(Preston North End)	11	Eglington	

Crowd: 67,980

England scorers: Mannion, Lawton

Comments: In this remarkable match, the home team scored twice in the last 10 minutes to take the lead, only for Peter Doherty to equalise in the last minute. Mannion had earlier missed a penalty.

ENGLAND 4 Sweden 2; at Highbury; Wednesday 19th November 1947

1	Swift	(Man City)	1	Lindberg	
2	Scott	(Arsenal)	2	Nordahl	
3	Hardwick*	(Middlesbrough)	3	Nilsson	
4	Taylor	(Liverpool)	4	Andersson	
5	Franklin	(Stoke City)	5	Nordahl	
6	Wright	(Wolves)	6	Emanuelsson	
7	Finney	(Preston North End)	7	Martensson	
8	Mortensen	(Blackpool)	8	Gren	
9	Lawton	(Notts County)	9	Nordahl	
10	Mannion	(Middlesbrough)	10	Liedholm	
11	Langton	(Blackburn)	11	Nilsson	

Crowd: 44,282

England scorers: Mortensen (3), Lawton (Pen)

Comments: Mortensen found the back of the net inside the last five minutes to ensure a home win, thereby helping himself to his second hat-trick in his first year of international football.

Scotland 0 ENGLAND 2; in Glasgow;
Saturday 10th April 1948 (Home International)

1	Black	1	Swift	(Man City)
2	Govan	2	Scott	(Arsenal)
3	Shaw	3	Hardwick*	(Middlesbrough)
4	Campbell	4	Wright	(Wolves)
5	Young	5	Franklin	(Stoke City)
6	Macauley	6	Cockburn	(Man Utd)
7	Delaney	7	Matthews	(Blackpool)
8	Combe	8	Mortensen	(Blackpool)
9	Thornton	9	Lawton	(Notts County)
10	Steel	10	Pearson	(Man Utd)
11	Liddell	11	Finney	(Preston North End)

Crowd: 135,376

England scorers: Finney, Mortensen

Comments: Tom Finney opened the lead for England just before the interval and then Stan Mortensen sealed a win in the second half. Stan Pearson made his debut in front of a huge crowd.

Italy 0 ENGLAND 4; in Turin;
Sunday 16th May 1948

1	Bacigalupo	1	Swift*	(Man City)
2	Ballarin	2	Scott	(Arsenal)
3	Eliani	3	Howe	(Derby County)
4	Annovazzi	4	Wright	(Wolves)
5	Parola	5	Franklin	(Stoke City)
6	Grezar	6	Cockburn	(Man Utd)
7	Menti	7	Matthews	(Blackpool)
8	Loik	8	Mortensen	(Blackpool)
9	Gabetto	9	Lawton	(Notts County)
10	Mazzola	10	Mannion	(Middlesbrough)
11	Carapellese	11	Finney	(Preston North End)

Crowd: 58,000

England scorers: Mortensen, Lawton, Finney (2)

Comments: Jack Howe won his first cap and England went home happy thanks to a second-half double from Finney to add to the first-half efforts from the prolific Lawton and Mortensen.

Denmark 0 ENGLAND 0; in Copenhagen;
Sunday 26th September 1948

1 Nielsen	1 Swift*	(Man City)
2 Hansen	2 Scott	(Arsenal)
3 Hansen	3 Aston	(Man Utd)
4 Ploger	4 Wright	(Wolves)
5 Praest	5 Franklin	(Stoke City)
6 Praest	6 Cockburn	(Man Utd)
7 Jensen	7 Matthews	(Blackpool)
8 Jensen	8 Hagan	(Sheffield United)
9 Pilmark	9 Lawton	(Notts County)
10 Ornvold	10 Shackleton	(Sunderland)
11 Petersen	11 Langton	(Preston North End)

Crowd: 41,000

Comments: Jack Aston and Len Shackleton won their first caps for the away team whilst James Hagan made his only appearance for England in this scoreless draw.

Northern Ireland 2 ENGLAND 6; in Belfast;
Saturday 9th October 1948 (Home International)

1 Smyth	1 Swift	(Man City)
2 Carey	2 Scott	(Arsenal)
3 Martin	3 Howe	(Derby County)
4 Walsh	4 Wright*	(Wolves)
5 Vernon	5 Franklin	(Stoke City)
6 Farrell	6 Cockburn	(Man Utd)
7 O'Driscoll	7 Matthews	(Blackpool)
8 McAlindon	8 Mortensen	(Blackpool)
9 Walsh	9 Milburn	(Newcastle Utd)
10 Tully	10 Pearson	(Man Utd)
11 Eglington	11 Finney	(Preston North End)

Crowd: 53,629

England scorers: Matthews, Mortensen (3), Milburn, Pearson

Comments: This match was delicately poised at 1–0 to England at the interval before Mortensen registered a second-half hat-trick. Debutant Jackie Milburn also contributed a goal.

ENGLAND 1 Wales 0; at Villa Park;
Wednesday 10th November 1948 (Home International)

1	Swift	(Man City)	1	Hughes
2	Scott	(Arsenal)	2	Barnes
3	Aston	(Man Utd)	3	Sherwood
4	Ward	(Derby County)	4	Paul
5	Franklin	(Stoke City)	5	Jones
6	Wright*	(Wolves)	6	Burgess
7	Matthews	(Blackpool)	7	Jones
8	Mortensen	(Blackpool)	8	Powell
9	Milburn	(Newcastle Utd)	9	Ford
10	Shackleton	(Sunderland)	10	Morris
11	Finney	(Preston North End)	11	Clarke

Crowd: 67,770

England scorer: Finney

Comments: Laurie Scott had to leave the field due to an injury and England played the last 65 minutes with 10 men. This handicap didn't stop Tom Finney from scoring just before half-time.

ENGLAND 6 Switzerland 0; at Highbury;
Thursday 2nd December 1948

1	Ditchburn	(Tottenham)	1	Corrodi
2	Ramsey	(Southampton)	2	Gyger
3	Aston	(Man Utd)	3	Bocquet
4	Wright*	(Wolves)	4	Lanz
5	Franklin	(Stoke City)	5	Eggimann
6	Cockburn	(Man Utd)	6	Lusenti
7	Matthews	(Blackpool)	7	Bickel
8	Rowley	(Man Utd)	8	Amado
9	Milburn	(Newcastle Utd)	9	Tamini
10	Haines	(West Brom)	10	Bader
11	Hancocks	(Wolves)	11	Fatton

Crowd: 48,000

England scorers: Haines (2), Hancocks (2), Rowley, Milburn

Comments: England gained revenge for a loss 18 months earlier. John Haines scored twice in the first-half on his debut and never played again. John Hancocks also scored twice on his debut.

ENGLAND 1 Scotland 3; at Wembley;
Saturday 9th April 1949 (Home International)

1	Swift	(Man City)	1	Cowan
2	Aston	(Man Utd)	2	Young
3	Howe	(Derby County)	3	Cox
4	Wright*	(Wolves)	4	Evans
5	Franklin	(Stoke City)	5	Woodburn
6	Cockburn	(Man Utd)	6	Aitken
7	Matthews	(Blackpool)	7	Waddell
8	Mortensen	(Blackpool)	8	Mason
9	Milburn	(Newcastle Utd)	9	Houliston
10	Pearson	(Man Utd)	10	Steel
11	Finney	(Preston North End)	11	Reilly

Crowd: 98,188

England scorer: Milburn

Comments: Jackie Milburn's goal fifteen minutes from time was merely a consolation as Scotland were already out of sight, having dished out a spanking in this Home International fixture.

Sweden 3 ENGLAND 1; in Stockholm;
Friday 13th May 1949

1	Svensson	1	Ditchburn	(Tottenham)
2	Nordahl	2	Shimwell	(Blackpool)
3	Nilsson	3	Aston	(Man Utd)
4	Rosen	4	Wright*	(Wolves)
5	Leander	5	Franklin	(Stoke City)
6	Andersson	6	Cockburn	(Man Utd)
7	Johnsson	7	Finney	(Preston North End)
8	Gren	8	Mortensen	(Blackpool)
9	Jeppson	9	Bentley	(Chelsea)
10	Carlsson	10	Rowley	(Man Utd)
11	Backvall	11	Langton	(Preston North End)

Crowd: 37,500

England scorer: Finney

Comments: For the second successive match, England found themselves three goals in arrears. The unfortunate debutant Eddie Shimwell never played again after this latest debacle.

Norway 1 ENGLAND 4; in Oslo;
Wednesday 18th May 1949

1 Torgersen	1 Swift	(Man City)
2 Spydevold	2 Ellerington	(Southampton)
3 Karlsen	3 Aston	(Man Utd)
4 Andersen	4 Wright*	(Wolves)
5 Svenssen	5 Franklin	(Stoke City)
6 Andersen	6 Dickinson	(Portsmouth)
7 Nordahl	7 Finney	(Preston North End)
8 Arnesen	8 Morris	(Derby County)
9 Andresen	9 Mortensen	(Blackpool)
10 Dahlen	10 Mannion	(Middlesbrough)
11 Thoresen	11 Mullen	(Wolves)

Crowd: 32,874

England scorers: Mullen, Finney, Spydevold (OG), Morris

Comments: John Morris scored on his debut in this friendly contest as the visitors returned to winning ways. It was also a happy first cap for Billy Ellerington and Jimmy Dickinson.

France 1 ENGLAND 3; in Paris;
Sunday 22nd May 1949

1 Vignal	1 Williams	(Wolves)
2 Grilla	2 Ellerington	(Southampton)
3 Salva	3 Aston	(Man Utd)
4 Jonquet	4 Wright*	(Wolves)
5 Mindonnet	5 Franklin	(Stoke City)
6 Hon	6 Dickinson	(Portsmouth)
7 Gabet	7 Finney	(Preston North End)
8 Cuissard	8 Morris	(Derby County)
9 Quenolle	9 Rowley	(Man Utd)
10 Batteux	10 Mannion	(Middlesbrough)
11 Moreel	11 Mullen	(Wolves)

Crowd: 61,308

England scorers: Morris (2), Wright

Comments: John Morris scored a late goal to ensure an away triumph after France had took the lead in the first minute. Even Billy Wright was able to register his first goal for his country.

ENGLAND 0 Republic Of Ireland 2; at Goodison Park; Wednesday 21st September 1949

1	Williams	(Wolves)	1	Godwin
2	Mozley	(Derby County)	2	Carey
3	Aston	(Man Utd)	3	Aherne
4	Wright*	(Wolves)	4	Walsh
5	Franklin	(Stoke City)	5	Martin
6	Dickinson	(Portsmouth)	6	Moroney
7	Harris	(Portsmouth)	7	Corr
8	Morris	(Derby County)	8	Farrell
9	Pye	(Wolves)	9	Walsh
10	Mannion	(Middlesbrough)	10	Desmond
11	Finney	(Preston North End)	11	O'Connor

Crowd: 51,487

Comments: Peter Harris and Bert Mozley made their first appearances as England succumbed to the Irish. Meanwhile, this would be Jesse Pye's only cap after England's latest setback.

Wales 1 ENGLAND 4; in Cardiff; Saturday 15th October 1949 (Home International/World Cup qualifier)

1	Sidlow	1	Williams	(Wolves)
2	Barnes	2	Mozley	(Derby County)
3	Sherwood	3	Aston	(Man Utd)
4	Paul	4	Wright*	(Wolves)
5	Jones	5	Franklin	(Stoke City)
6	Burgess	6	Dickinson	(Portsmouth)
7	Griffiths	7	Finney	(Preston North End)
8	Lucas	8	Mortensen	(Blackpool)
9	Ford	9	Milburn	(Newcastle Utd)
10	Scrine	10	Shackleton	(Sunderland)
11	Edwards	11	Hancocks	(Wolves)

Crowd: 60,000

England scorers: Mortensen, Milburn (3)

Comments: 'Wor' Jackie Milburn recorded his first England hat-trick after the visitors had led 3–0 at the interval. This match at Ninian Park was a World Cup qualifier and a 'Home International'.

ENGLAND 9 Northern Ireland 2; at Maine Road;
Wednesday 16th November 1949 (Home International/World Cup qualifier)

1	Streten	(Luton Town)	1	Kelly
2	Mozley	(Derby County)	2	Feeney
3	Aston	(Man Utd)	3	McMichael
4	Watson	(Sunderland)	4	Bowler
5	Franklin	(Stoke City)	5	Vernon
6	Wright*	(Wolves)	6	McCabe
7	Finney	(Preston North End)	7	Cochrane
8	Mortensen	(Blackpool)	8	Smyth
9	Rowley	(Man Utd)	9	Brennan
10	Pearson	(Man Utd)	10	Tully
11	Froggatt	(Portsmouth)	11	McKenna

Crowd: 70,000

England scorers: Rowley (4), Froggatt, Pearson (2), Mortensen (2)

Comments: Red Devils' Jack Rowley and Stan Pearson scored six goals between them as England put the visitors to the sword. This was another Home International and World Cup qualifier.

ENGLAND 2 Italy 0; at White Hart Lane;
Wednesday 30th November 1949

1	Williams	(Wolves)	1	Moro
2	Ramsey	(Tottenham)	2	Bertuccelli
3	Aston	(Man Utd)	3	Giovannini
4	Watson	(Sunderland)	4	Annovazzi
5	Franklin	(Stoke City)	5	Parola
6	Wright*	(Wolves)	6	Piccinini
7	Finney	(Preston North End)	7	Boniperti
8	Mortensen	(Blackpool)	8	Lorenzi
9	Rowley	(Man Utd)	9	Amadei
10	Pearson	(Man Utd)	10	Martino
11	Froggatt	(Portsmouth)	11	Carapellese

Crowd: 71,797

England scorers: Rowley, Wright

Comments: Rowley and Wright scored in quick succession in the final quarter of this friendly as England maintained their fine post-war form against Italy, the reigning world champions.

Scotland 0 ENGLAND 1; in Glasgow;
Saturday 15th April 1950 (Home International/World Cup qualifier)

1	Cowan	1	Williams	(Wolves)
2	Young	2	Ramsey	(Tottenham)
3	Cox	3	Aston	(Man Utd)
4	McColl	4	Wright*	(Wolves)
5	Woodburn	5	Franklin	(Stoke City)
6	Forbes	6	Dickinson	(Portsmouth)
7	Waddell	7	Finney	(Preston North End)
8	Moir	8	Mannion	(Middlesbrough)
9	Bauld	9	Mortensen	(Blackpool)
10	Steel	10	Bentley	(Chelsea)
11	Liddell	11	Langton	(Bolton Wanderers)

Crowd: 133,000

England scorer: Bentley

Comments: Bentley's first goal for his country in the second half earned England maximum points in the Home International Championship. England also qualified for the World Cup finals.

Portugal 3 ENGLAND 5; in Lisbon;
Sunday 14th May 1950

1	de Oliveira	1	Williams	(Wolves)
2	Mendes	2	Ramsey	(Tottenham)
3	Carvalho	3	Aston	(Man Utd)
4	Batista	4	Wright*	(Wolves)
5	Antunes	5	Jones	(Liverpool)
6	Ferreira	6	Dickinson	(Portsmouth)
7	Carvalho	7	Milburn	(Newcastle Utd)
8	Vasques	8	Mortensen	(Blackpool)
9	Ben David	9	Bentley	(Chelsea)
10	Travacos	10	Mannion	(Middlesbrough)
11	Pereira	11	Finney	(Preston North End)

Crowd: 65,000

England scorers: Finney (4), Mortensen

Comments: Bill Jones made his debut as England embarked on another Portuguese goals frenzy. The 'Preston Plumber' Tom Finney helped himself to four goals, including two penalties.

Belgium 1 ENGLAND 4; in Brussels;
Thursday 18th May 1950

	Belgium		England	
1	Meert	1	Williams	(Wolves)
2	Vaillant	2	Ramsey	(Tottenham)
3	Anoul	3	Aston	(Man Utd)
4	van der Auwera	4	Wright*	(Wolves)
5	Carre	5	Jones	(Liverpool)
6	Mees	6	Dickinson	(Portsmouth)
7	van Looy	7	Milburn	(Newcastle Utd) replaced by Mullen
8	D'Aguilar	8	Mortensen	(Blackpool)
9	Mermans	9	Bentley	(Chelsea)
10	de Hert	10	Mannion	(Middlesbrough)
11	Mordant	11	Finney	(Preston North End)

Crowd: 55,854

England scorers: Mullen, Mortensen, Mannion, Bentley

Comments: Jimmy Mullen became England's first-ever substitute, replacing the injured Milburn. He then equalised after England had trailed 1–0 at half-time in this last World Cup rehearsal.

ENGLAND 2 Chile 0; in Rio de Janeiro;
Sunday 25th June 1950 (World Cup finals)

	England			Chile
1	Williams	(Wolves)	1	Livingstone
2	Ramsey	(Tottenham)	2	Farias
3	Aston	(Man Utd)	3	Roldan
4	Wright*	(Wolves)	4	Alvarez
5	Hughes	(Liverpool)	5	Busquet
6	Dickinson	(Portsmouth)	6	Carvalho
7	Finney	(Preston North End)	7	Mananes
8	Mannion	(Middlesbrough)	8	Cremaschi
9	Bentley	(Chelsea)	9	Robledo
10	Mortensen	(Blackpool)	10	Munoz
11	Mullen	(Wolves)	11	Diaz

Crowd: 29,703

England scorers: Mortensen, Mannion

Comments: One goal in each half secured a win in this Pool 2 group match. Laurie Hughes collected his first cap in this fixture. Regrettably this was the peak of England's World Cup.

ENGLAND 0 USA 1; in Belo Horizonte; Thursday 29th June 1950 (World Cup finals)

1	Williams	(Wolves)	1	Borghi
2	Ramsey	(Tottenham)	2	Keough
3	Aston	(Man Utd)	3	Maca
4	Wright*	(Wolves)	4	McIlvenny
5	Hughes	(Liverpool)	5	Colombo
6	Dickinson	(Portsmouth)	6	Bahr
7	Finney	(Preston North End)	7	Wallace
8	Mannion	(Middlesbrough)	8	Pariani
9	Bentley	(Chelsea)	9	Gaetjens
10	Mortensen	(Blackpool)	10	Souza
11	Mullen	(Wolves)	11	Souza

Crowd: 10,151

Comments: A Gaetjens goal before half-time delivered the mother of all shocks. The USA may have become a superpower, but in soccer, it was a minnow. This was an embarrassment.

ENGLAND 0 Spain 1; in Rio de Janeiro; Sunday 2nd July 1950 (World Cup finals)

1	Williams	(Wolves)	1	Ramallets
2	Ramsey	(Tottenham)	2	Alonso
3	Eckersley	(Blackburn)	3	Parra
4	Wright*	(Wolves)	4	Gonzalvo
5	Hughes	(Liverpool)	5	Gonzalvo
6	Dickinson	(Portsmouth)	6	Puchades
7	Matthews	(Blackpool)	7	Basora
8	Mortensen	(Blackpool)	8	Igoa
9	Milburn	(Newcastle Utd)	9	Zarra
10	Baily	(Tottenham)	10	Panizo
11	Finney	(Preston North End)	11	Gainza

Crowd: 74,462

Comments: A goal from Zarra just after the break decided this issue. Having drawn a blank for the second successive group match, England's Brazil World Cup adventure was finished.

Northern Ireland 1 ENGLAND 4; in Belfast;
Saturday 7th October 1950 (Home International)

1	Kelly		1	Williams	(Wolves)
2	Gallogly		2	Ramsey	(Tottenham)
3	McMichael		3	Aston	(Man Utd)
4	Blanchflower		4	Wright*	(Wolves)
5	Vernon		5	Chilton	(Man Utd)
6	Cush		6	Dickinson	(Portsmouth)
7	Campbell		7	Matthews	(Blackpool)
8	Crossan		8	Mannion	(Middlesbrough)
9	McMorran		9	Lee	(Derby County)
10	Brennan		10	Baily	(Tottenham)
11	McKenna		11	Langton	(Bolton Wanderers)

Crowd: 50,000

England scorers: Baily (2), Lee, Wright

Comments: Jack Lee scored on his only outing while the away team needed two late goals to settle this contest. Allenby Chilton also made his debut in this Home International fixture.

ENGLAND 4 Wales 2; at Roker Park;
Wednesday 15th November 1950 (Home International)

1	Williams	(Wolves)		1	Hughes
2	Ramsey*	(Tottenham)		2	Barnes
3	Smith	(Arsenal)		3	Sherwood
4	Watson	(Sunderland)		4	Paul
5	Compton	(Arsenal)		5	Daniel
6	Dickinson	(Portsmouth)		6	Lucas
7	Finney	(Preston North End)		7	Griffiths
8	Mannion	(Middlesbrough)		8	Allen
9	Milburn	(Newcastle Utd)		9	Ford
10	Baily	(Tottenham)		10	Allchurch
11	Medley	(Tottenham)		11	Clarke

Crowd: 59,137

England scorers: Baily (2), Mannion, Milburn

Comments: Eddie Baily's first-half double put England on the way to a win, but it took a last minute goal from Milburn to make sure of another Home International win against Wales.

ENGLAND 2 Yugoslavia 2; at Highbury;
Wednesday 22nd November 1950

1	Williams	(Wolves)	1	Beara
2	Ramsey*	(Tottenham)	2	Stankovic
3	Eckersley	(Blackburn)	3	Colic
4	Watson	(Sunderland)	4	Cajkovski
5	Compton	(Arsenal)	5	Horvat
6	Dickinson	(Portsmouth)	6	Djajic
7	Hancocks	(Wolves)	7	Ognjanov
8	Mannion	(Middlesbrough)	8	Mitic
9	Lofthouse	(Bolton Wanderers)	9	Zivanovic
10	Baily	(Tottenham)	10	Bobek
11	Mullen	(Tottenham)	11	Vukas

Crowd: 60,000

England scorer: Lofthouse (2)

Comments: Debutant Nat Lofthouse gave the home team a 2–0 lead but they were pegged back. This would be the last cap for Leslie Compton, John Hancocks, and for Willie Watson.

ENGLAND 2 Scotland 3; at Wembley;
Saturday 14th April 1951 (Home International)

1	Williams	(Wolves)	1	Cowan
2	Ramsey	(Tottenham)	2	Young
3	Eckersley	(Blackburn)	3	Cox
4	Johnston	(Blackpool)	4	Evans
5	Froggatt	(Portsmouth)	5	Woodburn
6	Wright*	(Wolves)	6	Redpath
7	Matthews	(Blackpool)	7	Waddell
8	Mannion	(Middlesbrough)	8	Johnstone
9	Mortensen	(Blackpool)	9	Reilly
10	Hassall	(Huddersfield Town)	10	Steel
11	Finney	(Preston North End)	11	Liddell

Crowd: 98,000

England scorers: Hassall, Finney

Comments: Harold Hassall became the latest debutant to score a goal as he gave England the lead. Scotland then scored the next 3 goals. England played the last 80 minutes with 10 men.

ENGLAND 2 Argentina 1; at Wembley; Wednesday 9th May 1951

1 Williams	(Wolves)	1 Rugilo
2 Ramsey	(Tottenham)	2 Colman
3 Eckersley	(Blackburn)	3 Filgueiras
4 Wright*	(Wolves)	4 Faina
5 Taylor	(Fulham)	5 Pescia
6 Cockburn	(Man Utd)	6 Yacono
7 Finney	(Preston North End)	7 Boye
8 Mortensen	(Blackpool)	8 Bravo
9 Milburn	(Newcastle Utd)	9 Labruna
10 Hassall	(Huddersfield Town)	10 Loustau
11 Metcalfe	(Huddersfield Town)	11 Mendez

Crowd: 99,000

England scorers: Mortensen, Milburn

Comments: Argentina took an early lead, but were overtaken by 2 late goals. This was back in the days when a game against Argentina was a 'friendly'. Taylor and Metcalfe made their debut.

ENGLAND 5 Portugal 2; at Goodison Park; Saturday 19th May 1951

1 Williams	(Wolves)	1 de Oliveira
2 Ramsey*	(Tottenham)	2 Mendes
3 Eckersley	(Blackburn)	3 das Neves
4 Nicholson	(Tottenham)	4 Canario
5 Taylor	(Fulham)	5 Antunes
6 Cockburn	(Man Utd)	6 Ferreira
7 Finney	(Preston North End)	7 Patalino
8 Pearson	(Blackpool)	8 Travacos
9 Milburn	(Newcastle Utd)	9 Ben David
10 Hassall	(Huddersfield Town)	10 Caiado
11 Metcalfe	(Huddersfield Town)	11 Pereira

Crowd: 52,686

England scorers: Nicholson, Milburn (2), Finney, Hassall

Comments: Bill Nicholson scored after thirty seconds of his debut and never played for England again! The home side had now netted 20 times against Portugal in three post-war matches.

ENGLAND 2 France 2; at Highbury;
Wednesday 3rd October 1951

1 Williams	(Wolves)	1 Vignal	
2 Ramsey	(Tottenham)	2 Grillon	
3 Willis	(Tottenham)	3 Salva	
4 Wright*	(Wolves)	4 Firoud	
5 Chilton	(Man Utd)	5 Jonquet	
6 Cockburn	(Man Utd)	6 Bonifaci	
7 Finney	(Preston North End)	7 Alpsteg	
8 Mannion	(Middlesbrough)	8 Baratte	
9 Milburn	(Newcastle Utd)	9 Grumellon	
10 Hassall	(Huddersfield Town)	10 Flamion	
11 Medley	(Tottenham)	11 Doye	

Crowd: 57,603

England scorers: Firoud (OG), Medley

Comments: All four goals came in the first half. Arthur Willis collected his only cap from this match, while it was also the last cap for Allenby Chilton, Henry Cockburn, and Wilf Mannion.

Wales 1 ENGLAND 1; in Cardiff;
Saturday 20th October 1951 (Home International)

1 Shortt		1 Williams	(Wolves)
2 Barnes		2 Ramsey	(Tottenham)
3 Sherwood		3 Smith	(Arsenal)
4 Paul		4 Wright*	(Wolves)
5 Daniel		5 Barrass	(Bolton Wanderers)
6 Burgess		6 Dickinson	(Portsmouth)
7 Foulkes		7 Finney	(Preston North End)
8 Kinsey		8 Thompson	(Aston Villa)
9 Ford		9 Lofthouse	(Bolton Wanderers)
10 Allchurch		10 Baily	(Tottenham)
11 Clarke		11 Medley	(Tottenham)

Crowd: 60,000

England scorer: Baily

Comments: Both goals arrived in the first ten minutes as Wales finally earned their first post-war Home International point against England. Barrass and Thompson won their first caps.

ENGLAND 2 Northern Ireland 0; at Villa Park;
Wednesday 14th November 1951 (Home International)

1	Merrick	(Birmingham City)	1	Uprichard
2	Ramsey	(Tottenham)	2	Graham
3	Smith	(Arsenal)	3	McMichael
4	Wright*	(Wolves)	4	Dickson
5	Barrass	(Bolton Wanderers)	5	Vernon
6	Dickinson	(Portsmouth)	6	McCourt
7	Finney	(Preston North End)	7	Bingham
8	Sewell	(Sheffield Wed)	8	Smyth
9	Lofthouse	(Bolton Wanderers)	9	McMorran
10	Phillips	(Portsmouth)	10	McIlroy
11	Medley	(Tottenham)	11	McKenna

Crowd: 57,889

England scorer: Lofthouse (2)

Comments: Gil Merrick kept a clean sheet on his debut while Jackie Sewell and Leslie Phillips earned their first caps too. Lofthouse scored towards the end of each half to secure two points.

ENGLAND 2 Austria 2; at Wembley;
Wednesday 28th November 1951

1	Merrick	(Birmingham City)	1	Zeman
2	Ramsey	(Tottenham)	2	Rockl
3	Eckersley	(Blackburn)	3	Happl
4	Wright*	(Wolves)	4	Hanappi
5	Froggatt	(Portsmouth)	5	Ocwirk
6	Dickinson	(Portsmouth)	6	Brinek
7	Milton	(Arsenal)	7	Melchior
8	Broadis	(Man City)	8	Gernhardt
9	Lofthouse	(Bolton Wanderers)	9	Huber
10	Baily	(Tottenham)	10	Stojaspal
11	Medley	(Tottenham)	11	Korner

Crowd: 100,000

England scorers: Ramsey (Pen), Lofthouse

Comments: All the goals came after the interval, with the hosts opening the scoring with a penalty and Austria ending the scoring with a penalty. Ivor Broadis and Arthur Milton made their debut.

Scotland 1 ENGLAND 2; in Glasgow;
Saturday 5th April 1952 (Home International)

1 Brown	1 Merrick	(Birmingham City)
2 Young	2 Ramsey	(Tottenham)
3 McNaught	3 Garrett	(Blackpool)
4 Scoular	4 Wright*	(Wolves)
5 Woodburn	5 Froggatt	(Portsmouth)
6 Redpath	6 Dickinson	(Portsmouth)
7 Smith	7 Finney	(Preston North End)
8 Johnstone	8 Broadis	(Man City)
9 Reilly	9 Lofthouse	(Bolton Wanderers)
10 McMillan	10 Pearson	(Man Utd)
11 Liddell	11 Rowley	(Man Utd)

Crowd: 134,504

England scorer: Pearson (2)

Comments: Stan Pearson recorded two first-half goals on his return to the England team. The home team could only manage a late consolation. Tom Garrett made his debut in this victory.

Italy 1 ENGLAND 1; in Florence;
Sunday 18th May 1952

1 Moro	1 Merrick	(Birmingham City)
2 Giovannini	2 Ramsey	(Tottenham)
3 Manente	3 Garrett	(Blackpool)
4 Mari	4 Wright*	(Wolves)
5 Ferrario	5 Froggatt	(Portsmouth)
6 Piccinini	6 Dickinson	(Portsmouth)
7 Boniperti	7 Finney	(Preston North End)
8 Pandolfini	8 Broadis	(Man City)
9 Piola	9 Lofthouse	(Bolton Wanderers)
10 Amadei	10 Pearson	(Man Utd)
11 Cappello	11 Elliott	(Burnley)

Crowd: 60,000

England scorer: Broadis

Comments: Broadis scored his first international goal inside the first five minutes but Italy equalised in the second half. This was Billy Elliott's first England match and Pearson's last.

Austria 2 ENGLAND 3; in Vienna;
Sunday 25th May 1952

1	Musil	1	Merrick	(Birmingham City)
2	Rockl	2	Ramsey	(Tottenham)
3	Happl	3	Eckersley	(Blackburn)
4	Schleger	4	Wright*	(Wolves)
5	Ocwirk	5	Froggatt	(Portsmouth)
6	Brinek	6	Dickinson	(Portsmouth)
7	Melchior	7	Finney	(Preston North End)
8	Hanappi	8	Sewell	(Sheffield Wed)
9	Dienst	9	Lofthouse	(Bolton Wanderers)
10	Huber	10	Baily	(Tottenham)
11	Haummer	11	Elliott	(Burnley)

Crowd: 64,000

England scorers: Lofthouse (2), Sewell

Comments: England led twice in the first half but had to settle for 2–2 at the interval. Eventually Nat Lofthouse scored a late winner in this end of season friendly.

Switzerland 0 ENGLAND 3; in Zurich;
Wednesday 28th May 1952

1	Preiss	1	Merrick	(Birmingham City)
2	Kernan	2	Ramsey	(Tottenham)
3	Bocquet	3	Eckersley	(Blackburn)
4	Schmidhauser	4	Wright*	(Wolves)
5	Eggimann	5	Froggatt	(Portsmouth)
6	Neukom	6	Dickinson	(Portsmouth)
7	Ballaman	7	Allen	(West Brom)
8	Hugi	8	Sewell	(Sheffield Wed)
9	Bader	9	Lofthouse	(Bolton Wanderers)
10	Pasteur	10	Baily	(Tottenham)
11	Fatton	11	Finney	(Preston North End)

Crowd: 33,000

England scorers: Sewell, Lofthouse (2)

Comments: England had the same duo of goalscorers from their previous friendly with Lofthouse adding a second-half brace to Sewell's early effort. Ronnie Allen made his debut in this triumph.

Northern Ireland 2 ENGLAND 2; in Belfast;
Saturday 4th October 1952 (Home International)

1	Uprichard	1	Merrick	(Birmingham City)
2	Cunningham	2	Ramsey	(Tottenham)
3	McMichael	3	Eckersley	(Blackburn)
4	Blanchflower	4	Wright*	(Wolves)
5	Dickson	5	Froggatt	(Portsmouth)
6	McCourt	6	Dickinson	(Portsmouth)
7	Bingham	7	Finney	(Preston North End)
8	D'Arcy	8	Sewell	(Sheffield Wed)
9	McMorran	9	Lofthouse	(Bolton Wanderers)
10	McIlroy	10	Baily	(Tottenham)
11	Tully	11	Elliott	(Burnley)

Crowd: 58,000

England scorers: Lofthouse, Elliott

Comments: The prolific Nat Lofthouse scored in the first minute and Billy Elliott equalised in the last minute in this extraordinary encounter. Charlie Tully netted twice for the home team.

ENGLAND 5 Wales 2; at Wembley;
Wednesday 12th November 1952 (Home International)

1	Merrick	(Birmingham City)	1	Shortt
2	Ramsey	(Tottenham)	2	Stitfall
3	Smith	(Arsenal)	3	Sherwood
4	Wright*	(Wolves)	4	Paul
5	Froggatt J	(Portsmouth)	5	Daniel
6	Dickinson	(Portsmouth)	6	Burgess
7	Finney	(Preston North End)	7	Foulkes
8	Froggatt R	(Sheffield Wed)	8	Davies
9	Lofthouse	(Bolton Wanderers)	9	Ford
10	Bentley	(Chelsea)	10	Allchurch
11	Elliott	(Burnley)	11	Clarke

Crowd: 94,094

England scorers: Finney, Lofthouse (2), Froggatt J, Bentley

Comments: England scored twice in the first ten minutes and led 3–1 at the interval. Redfearn Froggatt made his debut whilst older brother Jack was amongst the scorers.

ENGLAND 5 Belgium 0; at Wembley;
Wednesday 26th November 1952

1	Merrick	(Birmingham City)	1	Boogaerts
2	Ramsey	(Tottenham)	2	Dirickx
3	Smith	(Arsenal)	3	van Brandt
4	Wright*	(Wolves)	4	Mees
5	Froggatt J	(Portsmouth)	5	Carre
6	Dickinson	(Portsmouth)	6	Maertens
7	Finney	(Preston North End)	7	Lemberechts
8	Bentley	(Chelsea)	8	van der Auwera
9	Lofthouse	(Bolton Wanderers)	9	Mermans
10	Froggatt R	(Sheffield Wed)	10	Coppens
11	Elliott	(Burnley)	11	Straetmans

Crowd: 68,333

England scorers: Elliott (2), Lofthouse (2), Froggatt R

Comments: This time it was Redfearn Froggatt who helped himself to a goal in this goals spree. Billy Elliott may have netted twice but he was never chosen to play for England again.

ENGLAND 2 Scotland 2; at Wembley;
Saturday 18th April 1953 (Home International)

1	Merrick	(Birmingham City)	1	Farm
2	Ramsey	(Tottenham)	2	Young
3	Smith	(Arsenal)	3	Cox
4	Wright*	(Wolves)	4	Docherty
5	Barrass	(Bolton Wanderers)	5	Brennan
6	Dickinson	(Portsmouth)	6	Cowie
7	Finney	(Preston North End)	7	Wright
8	Broadis	(Man City)	8	Johnstone
9	Lofthouse	(Bolton Wanderers)	9	Reilly
10	Froggatt R	(Sheffield Wed)	10	Steel
11	Froggatt J	(Portsmouth)	11	Liddell

Crowd: 97,000

England scorer: Broadis (2)

Comments: The goals were shared between Broadis and Lawrie Reilly, with the latter snatching a late equaliser for the visitors. This would be the last cap for Malcolm Barrass and Lionel Smith.

Argentina 0 ENGLAND 0; in Buenos Aires;
Sunday 17th May 1953

1	Musimessi	1	Merrick	(Birmingham City)
2	Dellacha	2	Ramsey	(Tottenham)
3	Garcia	3	Eckersley	(Blackburn)
4	Gutierrez	4	Wright*	(Wolves)
5	Lombardo	5	Johnston	(Blackpool)
6	Mourino	6	Dickinson	(Portsmouth)
7	Cecconato	7	Finney	(Preston North End)
8	Cruz	8	Broadis	(Man City)
9	Grillo	9	Lofthouse	(Bolton Wanderers)
10	Lacasia	10	Taylor	(Man Utd)
11	Micheli	11	Berry	(Man Utd)

Crowd: 80,000

Comments: This big occasion was something of a damp squib as the event was abandoned due to a waterlogged pitch after 36 minutes. Johnny Berry and Tommy Taylor won their first caps.

Chile 1 ENGLAND 2; in Santiago;
Sunday 24th May 1953

1	Livingstone	1	Merrick	(Birmingham City)
2	Farias	2	Ramsey	(Tottenham)
3	Nunez	3	Eckersley	(Blackburn)
4	Alvarez	4	Wright*	(Wolves)
5	Rojas	5	Johnston	(Blackpool)
6	Cortes	6	Dickinson	(Portsmouth)
7	Carrasco	7	Finney	(Preston North End)
8	Cremaschi	8	Broadis	(Man City)
9	Melendez	9	Lofthouse	(Bolton Wanderers)
10	Munoz	10	Taylor	(Man Utd)
11	Diaz	11	Berry	(Man Utd)

Crowd: 56,398

England scorers: Taylor, Lofthouse

Comments: All the goals came after the interval as Taylor opened the scoring with his first goal for England and then Lofthouse doubled the away team's advantage in this friendly fixture.

Uruguay 2 ENGLAND 1; in Montevideo; Sunday 31st May 1953

1	Maspoli	1	Merrick	(Birmingham City)
2	Gonzalez	2	Ramsey	(Tottenham)
3	Martinez	3	Eckersley	(Blackburn)
4	Andrade	4	Wright*	(Wolves)
5	Carballo	5	Johnston	(Blackpool)
6	Cruz	6	Dickinson	(Portsmouth)
7	Abbadie	7	Finney	(Preston North End)
8	Schiaffino	8	Broadis	(Man City)
9	Miguez	9	Lofthouse	(Bolton Wanderers)
10	Perez	10	Taylor	(Man Utd)
11	Cabrera	11	Berry	(Man Utd)

Crowd: 66,072

England scorer: Taylor

Comments: Walter Winterbottom chose the same team for the third successive South American outing, but Tommy Taylor's goal was merely a very late consolation for the visitors.

USA 3 ENGLAND 6; in New York; Monday 8th June 1953

1	Moore	1	Ditchburn	(Tottenham)
2	Keough	2	Ramsey	(Tottenham)
3	Milne	3	Eckersley	(Blackburn)
4	Springthorpe	4	Wright*	(Wolves)
5	Decker	5	Johnston	(Blackpool)
6	Bahr	6	Dickinson	(Portsmouth)
7	Schultz	7	Finney	(Preston North End)
8	Connelly	8	Broadis	(Man City)
9	McLaughlin	9	Lofthouse	(Bolton Wanderers)
10	Atheneos	10	Froggatt R	(Sheffield Wed)
11	Chachurian	11	Froggatt J	(Portsmouth)

Crowd: 7,271

England scorers: Broadis, Lofthouse (2), Finney (2), Froggatt R

Comments: For 40 minutes this match was scoreless and then England proceeded to avenge their humiliation of 1950. In spite of this, neither of the Froggatts would play for England again.

Wales 1 ENGLAND 4; in Cardiff;
Saturday 10th October 1953 (Home International/World Cup qualifier)

1	Howells	1	Merrick	(Birmingham City)
2	Barnes	2	Garrett	(Blackpool)
3	Sherwood	3	Eckersley	(Blackburn)
4	Paul	4	Wright*	(Wolves)
5	Daniel	5	Johnston	(Blackpool)
6	Burgess	6	Dickinson	(Portsmouth)
7	Foulkes	7	Finney	(Preston North End)
8	Davies	8	Quixall	(Sheffield Wed)
9	Charles	9	Lofthouse	(Bolton Wanderers)
10	Allchurch	10	Wilshaw	(Wolves)
11	Clarke	11	Mullen	(Wolves)

Crowd: 61,000

England scorers: Wilshaw (2), Lofthouse(2)

Comments: England posted another routine win over Wales, although Ivor Allchurch had scored first. Dennis Wilshaw scored twice on his debut, while Albert Quixall collected his first cap.

ENGLAND 4 FIFA 4; at Wembley;
Wednesday 21st October 1953

1	Merrick	(Birmingham City)	1	Zemen	(Austria)
2	Ramsey	(Tottenham)	2	Navarro	(Argentina)
3	Eckersley	(Blackburn)	3	Hanappi	(Austria)
4	Wright*	(Wolves)	4	Cajkovski	(Yugoslavia)
5	Ufton	(Charlton Athletic)	5	Posipal	(West Germany)
6	Dickinson	(Portsmouth)	6	Ocwirk	(Austria)
7	Matthews	(Blackpool)	7	Boniperti	(Italy)
8	Mortensen	(Blackpool)	8	Kubala	(Spain)
9	Lofthouse	(Bolton Wanderers)	9	Nordahl	(Sweden)
10	Quixall	(Sheffield Wed)	10	Vukas	(Yugoslavia)
11	Mullen	(Wolves)	11	Zebec	(Yugoslavia)

Crowd: 96,000

England scorers: Mortensen, Mullen (2), Ramsey(Pen)

Comments: The Blackpool towers, Matthews and Mortensen, were recalled for this match to mark the 90th anniversary of the English FA. Derek Ufton earned his only cap in this goals spree.

ENGLAND 3 Northern Ireland 1; at Goodison Park; Wednesday 11th November 1953 (Home International/World Cup qualifier)

1	Merrick	(Birmingham City)	1	Smyth
2	Rickaby	(West Brom)	2	Graham
3	Eckersley	(Blackburn)	3	McMichael
4	Wright*	(Wolves)	4	Blanchflower
5	Johnston	(Blackpool)	5	Dickson
6	Dickinson	(Portsmouth)	6	Cush
7	Matthews	(Blackpool)	7	Bingham
8	Quixall	(Sheffield Wed)	8	McIlroy
9	Lofthouse	(Bolton Wanderers)	9	Simpson
10	Hassall	(Bolton Wanderers)	10	McMorran
11	Mullen	(Wolves)	11	Lockhart

Crowd: 70,000

England scorers: Hassall (2), Lofthouse

Comments: The Bolton duo of Hassall and Lofthouse ensured victory in a match that doubled up as a Home International and a World Cup qualifier. Stan Rickaby collected his only England cap.

ENGLAND 3 Hungary 6; at Wembley; Wednesday 25th November 1953

1	Merrick	(Birmingham City)	1	Grosics
2	Ramsey	(Tottenham)	2	Buzansky
3	Eckersley	(Blackburn)	3	Lantos
4	Wright*	(Wolves)	4	Bozsik
5	Johnston	(Blackpool)	5	Lorant
6	Dickinson	(Portsmouth)	6	Zakarias
7	Matthews	(Blackpool)	7	Budai
8	Taylor	(Blackpool)	8	Kocsis
9	Mortensen	(Blackpool)	9	Hidegkuti
10	Sewell	(Sheffield Wed)	10	Puskas
11	Robb	(Tottenham)	11	Czibor

Crowd: 100,000

England scorers: Sewell, Mortensen, Ramsey (Pen)

Comments: Puskas and his team destroyed England's unbeaten stint at Wembley with mouth-watering soccer. Eckersley, Johnston, Mortensen, Ramsey, Robb and Taylor never played again.

Scotland 2 ENGLAND 4; in Glasgow;
Saturday 3rd April 1954 (Home International/World Cup qualifier)

1	Farm	1	Merrick	(Birmingham City)
2	Haughney	2	Staniforth	(Huddersfield Town)
3	Cox	3	Byrne	(Man Utd)
4	Evans	4	Wright*	(Wolves)
5	Brennan	5	Clarke	(Tottenham)
6	Aitken	6	Dickinson	(Portsmouth)
7	Mackenzie	7	Finney	(Preston North End)
8	Johnstone	8	Broadis	(Newcastle Utd)
9	Henderson	9	Allen	(West Brom)
10	Brown	10	Nicholls	(West Brom)
11	Ormond	11	Mullen	(Wolves)

Crowd: 134,544

England scorers: Broadis, Nicholls, Allen, Mullen

Comments: With a 1–1 half-time stalemate, Johnny Nicholls scored on his debut to give England the lead. They then went on to win and earn a place at the World Cup finals in Switzerland.

Yugoslavia 1 ENGLAND 0; in Belgrade;
Sunday 16th May 1954

1	Beara	1	Merrick	(Birmingham City)
2	Stankovic	2	Staniforth	(Huddersfield Town)
3	Crnkovic	3	Byrne	(Man Utd)
4	Cajkovski	4	Wright*	(Wolves)
5	Milovanov	5	Owen	(Luton Town)
6	Boskov	6	Dickinson	(Portsmouth)
7	Milutinovic	7	Finney	(Preston North End)
8	Mitic	8	Broadis	(Newcastle Utd)
9	Vukas	9	Allen	(West Brom)
10	Bobek	10	Nicholls	(West Brom)
11	Dvornic	11	Mullen	(Wolves)

Crowd: 60,000

Comments: It took a very late goal to break the deadlock as the visitors warmed up for the World Cup tournament. Syd Owen made his debut while Nicholls collected the last of his two caps.

Hungary 7 ENGLAND 1; in Budapest;
Sunday 23rd May 1954

1	Grosics		1	Merrick	(Birmingham City)
2	Buzansky		2	Staniforth	(Huddersfield Town)
3	Lantos		3	Byrne	(Man Utd)
4	Bozsik		4	Wright*	(Wolves)
5	Lorant		5	Owen	(Luton Town)
6	Zakarias		6	Dickinson	(Portsmouth)
7	Toth		7	Harris	(Portsmouth)
8	Kocsis		8	Sewell	(Sheffield Wed)
9	Hidegkuti		9	Jezzard	(Fulham)
10	Puskas		10	Broadis	(Newcastle Utd)
11	Czibor		11	Finney	(Preston North End)

Crowd: 92,000

England scorer: Broadis

Comments: By the time that Ivor Broadis scored, the away team were already six goals in arrears. Bedford Jezzard made his debut as England got whipped again by a superb Hungary.

ENGLAND 4 Belgium 4 [After extra time]; in Basle;
Thursday 17th June 1954 (World Cup finals)

1	Merrick	(Birmingham City)	1	Gernaey
2	Staniforth	(Huddersfield Town)	2	Dries
3	Byrne	(Man Utd)	3	van Brandt
4	Wright*	(Wolves)	4	Huysmans
5	Owen	(Luton Town)	5	Carre
6	Dickinson	(Portsmouth)	6	Mees
7	Matthews	(Blackpool)	7	Mermans
8	Broadis	(Newcastle Utd)	8	Houf
9	Lofthouse	(Bolton Wanderers)	9	Coppens
10	Taylor	(Man Utd)	10	Anoul
11	Finney	(Preston North End)	11	van den Bosch

Crowd: 29,000

England scorers: Broadis (2), Lofthouse (2)

Comments: This match went to extra-time, after it was drawn 3–3 at 90 minutes. It ended a draw with no penalties taken. England had now leaked eleven goals in their last two outings.

Switzerland 0 ENGLAND 2; in Berne;
Sunday 20th June 1954 (World Cup finals)

1	Parlier	1	Merrick	(Birmingham City)
2	Neury	2	Staniforth	(Huddersfield Town)
3	Bocquet	3	Byrne	(Man Utd)
4	Kernen	4	McGarry	(Huddersfield Town)
5	Eggimann	5	Wright*	(Wolves)
6	Bigler	6	Dickinson	(Portsmouth)
7	Antenen	7	Finney	(Preston North End)
8	Vonlanthen	8	Broadis	(Newcastle Utd)
9	Meier	9	Taylor	(Man Utd)
10	Ballamann	10	Wilshaw	(Wolves)
11	Fatton	11	Mullen	(Wolves)

Crowd: 43,119

England scorers: Mullen, Wilshaw

Comments: Mullen opened the scoring against the hosts just before half-time and then never played for England again! Bill McGarry made his debut as England collected maximum points.

ENGLAND 2 Uruguay 4; in Basle;
Saturday 26th June 1954 (World Cup finals)

1	Merrick	(Birmingham City)	1	Maspoli
2	Staniforth	(Huddersfield Town)	2	Martinez
3	Byrne	(Man Utd)	3	Santamaria
4	McGarry	(Huddersfield Town)	4	Andrade
5	Wright*	(Wolves)	5	Varela
6	Dickinson	(Portsmouth)	6	Cruz
7	Matthews	(Blackpool)	7	Abbadie
8	Broadis	(Newcastle Utd)	8	Ambrois
9	Lofthouse	(Bolton Wanderers)	9	Miguez
10	Wilshaw	(Wolves)	10	Schiaffino
11	Finney	(Preston North End)	11	Borges

Crowd: 50,000

England scorers: Lofthouse, Finney

Comments: This would be the last cap for Gil Merrick and for Ivor Broadis as England bowed out of the World Cup at the quarter-finals, thanks mainly to two goals either side of half-time.

Northern Ireland 0 ENGLAND 2; in Belfast; Saturday 2nd October 1954 (Home International)

1 Uprichard	1 Wood	(Man Utd)
2 Montgomery	2 Foulkes	(Man Utd)
3 McMichael	3 Byrne	(Man Utd)
4 Blanchflower	4 Wheeler	(Bolton Wanderers)
5 Dickson	5 Wright*	(Wolves)
6 Peacock	6 Barlow	(West Brom)
7 Bingham	7 Matthews	(Blackpool)
8 Blanchflower	8 Revie	(Man City)
9 Simpson	9 Lofthouse	(Bolton Wanderers)
10 McIlroy	10 Haynes	(Fulham)
11 McParland	11 Pilkington	(Burnley)

Crowd: 59,000

England scorers: Haynes, Revie

Comments: Johnny Haynes and Don Revie scored on their debuts in quick succession late in this match. Barlow, Foulkes, Pilkington, and Wheeler all just played this once for England.

ENGLAND 3 Wales 2; at Wembley; Wednesday 10th November 1954 (Home International)

1 Wood	(Man Utd)	1 King
2 Staniforth	(Huddersfield United)	2 Williams
3 Byrne	(Man Utd)	3 Sherwood
4 Phillips	(Portsmouth)	4 Paul
5 Wright*	(Wolves)	5 Daniel
6 Slater	(Wolves)	6 Sullivan
7 Matthews	(Blackpool)	7 Tapscott
8 Bentley	(Chelsea)	8 Ford
9 Allen	(West Brom)	9 Charles
10 Shackleton	(Sunderland)	10 Allchurch
11 Blunstone	(Chelsea)	11 Clarke

Crowd: 89,789

England scorer: Bentley (3)

Comments: Bentley's hat-trick came in the last 20 minutes, including a late winner. This was tough on John Charles who scored twice for Wales. Blunstone and Slater won their first caps.

ENGLAND 3 West Germany 1; at Wembley;
Wednesday 1st December 1954

1 Williams	(Wolves)	1 Herkenrath
2 Staniforth	(Huddersfield United)	2 Posipal
3 Byrne	(Man Utd)	3 Kohlmeyer
4 Phillips	(Portsmouth)	4 Erhardt
5 Wright*	(Wolves)	5 Liebrich
6 Slater	(Wolves)	6 Harpers
7 Matthews	(Blackpool)	7 Kaufhold
8 Bentley	(Chelsea)	8 Pfeiffer
9 Allen	(West Brom)	9 Seeler
10 Shackleton	(Sunderland)	10 Derwall
11 Finney	(Preston North End)	11 Beck

Crowd: 100,000

England scorers: Bentley, Allen, Shackleton

Comments: Ronnie Allen and Len Shackleton both scored and never played for England again. This win over the world champions was also the last cap for Len Phillips and Ron Staniforth.

ENGLAND 7 Scotland 2; at Wembley;
Saturday 2nd April 1955 (Home International)

1 Williams	(Wolves)	1 Martin
2 Meadows	(Man City)	2 Cunningham
3 Byrne	(Man Utd)	3 Haddock
4 Armstrong	(Chelsea)	4 Docherty
5 Wright*	(Wolves)	5 Davidson
6 Edwards	(Man Utd)	6 Cumming
7 Matthews	(Blackpool)	7 Mackenzie
8 Revie	(Man City)	8 Johnstone
9 Lofthouse	(Bolton Wanderers)	9 Reilly
10 Wilshaw	(Wolves)	10 McMillan
11 Blunstone	(Chelsea)	11 Ring

Crowd: 96,847

England scorers: Wilshaw (4), Lofthouse (2), Revie

Comments: Ken Armstrong and James Meadows won their only caps in this rout. It was also the debut of Duncan Edwards. This annihilation was due to 3 second-half goals from Wilshaw.

France 1 ENGLAND 0; in Paris;
Sunday 15th May 1955

1 Remetter	1 Williams	(Wolves)
2 Bieganski	2 Sillett	(Chelsea)
3 Marche	3 Byrne	(Man Utd)
4 Penverne	4 Flowers	(Wolves)
5 Jonquet	5 Wright*	(Wolves)
6 Louis	6 Edwards	(Man Utd)
7 Ujlaki	7 Matthews	(Blackpool)
8 Glovacki	8 Revie	(Man City)
9 Kopa	9 Lofthouse	(Bolton Wanderers)
10 Bliard	10 Wilshaw	(Wolves)
11 Vincent	11 Blunstone	(Chelsea)

Crowd: 54,696

Comments: Ron Flowers and Peter Sillett collected their first caps but the visitors were sunk by a penalty from Kopa shortly before the interval at the Stade de Colombes in this friendly.

Spain 1 ENGLAND 1; in Madrid;
Wednesday 18th May 1955

1 Ramallets	1 Williams	(Wolves)
2 Matito	2 Sillett	(Chelsea)
3 Garay	3 Byrne	(Man Utd)
4 Campanal	4 Dickinson	(Portsmouth)
5 Mauri	5 Wright*	(Wolves)
6 Zarraga	6 Edwards	(Man Utd)
7 Mano	7 Matthews	(Blackpool)
8 Paya	8 Bentley	(Chelsea)
9 Kubala	9 Lofthouse	(Bolton Wanderers)
10 Riala	10 Quixall	(Sheffield Wed)
11 Gento	11 Wilshaw	(Wolves)

Crowd: 125,000

England scorer: Bentley

Comments: Bentley gave the away team the lead with a goal just before the interval. However Rial equalised just after the hour mark as this match at the Bernabeu ended a draw.

Portugal 3 ENGLAND 1; in Oporto;
Sunday 22nd May 1955

1 Pereira	1 Williams	(Wolves)
2 Caldeira	2 Sillett	(Chelsea)
3 Carvalho	3 Byrne	(Man Utd)
4 Pedroto	4 Dickinson	(Portsmouth)
5 Passos	5 Wright*	(Wolves)
6 Juca	6 Edwards	(Man Utd)
7 Dimas	7 Matthews	(Blackpool)
8 Matateu	8 Bentley	(Chelsea)
9 Aguas	9 Lofthouse	(Bolton Wanderers) replaced by Quixall
10 Travacos	10 Wilshaw	(Wolves)
11 Pedro	11 Blunstone	(Chelsea)

Crowd: 52,000

England scorer: Bentley

Comments: Roy Bentley opened the scoring again in his last match, but 2 late goals for the hosts decided this friendly. Quixall in his last match replaced an injured Lofthouse before half-time.

Denmark 1 ENGLAND 5; in Copenhagen;
Sunday 2nd October 1955

1 Henriksen	1 Baynham	(Luton Town)
2 Andersen	2 Hall	(Birmingham City)
3 Nielsen	3 Byrne	(Man Utd)
4 Jensen	4 McGarry	(Huddersfield Town)
5 Brogger	5 Wright*	(Wolves)
6 Olesen	6 Dickinson	(Portsmouth)
7 Hansen	7 Milburn	(Newcastle Utd)
8 Jacobsen	8 Revie	(Man City)
9 Andersen	9 Lofthouse	(Bolton Wanderers)
10 Lundberg	10 Bradford	(Bristol Rovers)
11 Pedersen	11 Finney	(Preston North End)

Crowd: 50,000

England scorers: Revie (2), Lofthouse (2), Bradford

Comments: Geoff Bradford scored the final goal in this rout in his only England outing. The away team already led 3–0 at half-time. Ron Baynham and Jeff Hall also collected their first caps.

Wales 2 ENGLAND 1; in Cardiff;
Saturday 22nd October 1955 (Home International)

1	Kelsey	1	Williams	(Wolves)
2	Williams	2	Hall	(Birmingham City)
3	Sherwood	3	Byrne	(Man Utd)
4	Charles M	4	McGarry	(Huddersfield Town)
5	Charles J	5	Wright*	(Wolves)
6	Paul	6	Dickinson	(Portsmouth)
7	Tapscott	7	Matthews	(Blackpool)
8	Kinsey	8	Revie	(Man City)
9	Ford	9	Lofthouse	(Bolton Wanderers)
10	Allchurch	10	Wilshaw	(Wolves)
11	Jones	11	Finney	(Preston North End)

Crowd: 60,000

England scorer: Charles J (OG)

Comments: Wales finally recorded their first post-war victory against England. Derek Tapscott and Cliff Jones had scored immediately before half-time to give Wales a two-nil lead.

ENGLAND 3 Northern Ireland 0; at Wembley;
Wednesday 2nd November 1955 (Home International)

1	Baynham	(Luton Town)	1	Uprichard
2	Hall	(Birmingham City)	2	Cunningham
3	Byrne	(Man Utd)	3	Graham
4	Clayton	(Blackburn)	4	Blanchflower
5	Wright*	(Wolves)	5	McCavana
6	Dickinson	(Portsmouth)	6	Peacock
7	Finney	(Preston North End)	7	Bingham
8	Haynes	(Fulham)	8	McIlroy
9	Jezzard	(Fulham)	9	Coyle
10	Wilshaw	(Wolves)	10	Tully
11	Perry	(Blackpool)	11	McParland

Crowd: 62,000

England scorers: Wilshaw (2), Finney

Comments: There would be no Home International upset this time, although the hosts had to wait until the second half to record their 3 goals. Ronnie Clayton and Bill Perry won their first caps.

ENGLAND 4 Spain 1; at Wembley;
Wednesday 30th November 1955

1 Baynham	(Luton Town)	1 Cedron
2 Hall	(Birmingham City)	2 Guillamon
3 Byrne	(Man Utd)	3 Garay
4 Clayton	(Blackburn)	4 Campanal
5 Wright*	(Wolves)	5 Mauri
6 Dickinson	(Portsmouth)	6 Maguregui
7 Finney	(Preston North End)	7 Gonzalez
8 Atyeo	(Bristol City)	8 Paya
9 Lofthouse	(Bolton Wanderers)	9 Arieta
10 Haynes	(Fulham)	10 Domenech
11 Perry	(Blackpool)	11 Collar

Crowd: 95,550

England scorers: Atyeo, Perry (2), Finney

Comments: John Atyeo opened the scoring on his debut. Tom Finney had earlier missed a penalty, before adding to the goals. The Spanish could only muster a late consolation in this friendly.

Scotland 1 ENGLAND 1; in Glasgow;
Saturday 14th April 1956 (Home International)

1 Younger	1 Matthews	(Coventry City)
2 Parker	2 Hall	(Birmingham City)
3 Hewie	3 Byrne	(Man Utd)
4 Evans	4 Dickinson	(Portsmouth)
5 Young	5 Wright*	(Wolves)
6 Glen	6 Edwards	(Man Utd)
7 Leggat	7 Finney	(Preston North End)
8 Johnstone	8 Taylor	(Man Utd)
9 Reilly	9 Lofthouse	(Bolton Wanderers)
10 McMillan	10 Haynes	(Fulham)
11 Smith	11 Perry	(Blackpool)

Crowd: 132,817

England scorer: Haynes

Comments: Johnny Haynes scored in the dying seconds to rescue a point for the visitors after Graham Leggat had given Scotland the lead. Reg Matthews made his debut between the sticks.

ENGLAND 4 Brazil 2; at Wembley; Wednesday 9th May 1956

1	Matthews	(Coventry City)		1	Gilmar
2	Hall	(Birmingham City)		2	Djalma Santos
3	Byrne	(Man Utd)		3	Pavao
4	Clayton	(Blackburn)		4	Zozimo
5	Wright*	(Wolves)		5	Nilton Santos
6	Edwards	(Man Utd)		6	Dequinha
7	Matthews	(Blackpool)		7	Didi
8	Atyeo	(Bristol City)		8	Paulinho
9	Taylor	(Man Utd)		9	Alvaro
10	Haynes	(Fulham)		10	Gino
11	Grainger	(Sheffield United)		11	Canhoteiro

Crowd: 97,000

England scorer: Taylor (2), Grainger (2)

Comments: England scored twice in the first ten minutes. Brazil scored twice in the first ten minutes of the second half. Gilmar saved two penalties, and Grainger scored twice on his debut!

Sweden 0 ENGLAND 0; in Stockholm; Wednesday 16th May 1956

1	Svensson		1	Matthews	(Coventry City)
2	Johansson		2	Hall	(Birmingham City)
3	Axbom		3	Byrne	(Man Utd)
4	Svensson		4	Clayton	(Blackburn)
5	Gustavsson		5	Wright*	(Wolves)
6	Parling		6	Edwards	(Man Utd)
7	Berndtsson		7	Berry	(Man Utd)
8	Lofgren		8	Atyeo	(Bristol City)
9	Ekstrom		9	Taylor	(Man Utd)
10	Lindskog		10	Haynes	(Fulham)
11	Sandberg		11	Grainger	(Sheffield United)

Crowd: 35,000

Comments: Johnny Berry collected his fourth and final cap from this outing. He was one of four 'Busby babes' selected for this end of season friendly fixture.

Finland 1 ENGLAND 5; in Helsinki;
Sunday 20th May 1956

1 Hurri	1 Wood	(Man Utd)
2 Pajunen	2 Hall	(Birmingham City)
3 Sommarberg	3 Byrne	(Man Utd)
4 Lintamo	4 Clayton	(Blackburn)
5 Lehtinen	5 Wright*	(Wolves)
6 Jalava	6 Edwards	(Man Utd)
7 Peltonen	7 Astall	(Birmingham City)
8 Hiltunen	8 Haynes	(Fulham)
9 Pahlman	9 Taylor	(Man Utd) replaced by Lofthouse
10 Lahtinen	10 Wilshaw	(Wolves)
11 Forsgren	11 Grainger	(Sheffield United)

Crowd: 20,177

England scorers: Wilshaw, Haynes, Astall, Lofthouse (2)

Comments: Gordon Astall became the latest England player to score on his debut while Nat Lofthouse bagged a pair of goals, having come on as a substitute for Tommy Taylor.

West Germany 1 ENGLAND 3; in Berlin;
Saturday 26th May 1956

1 Herkenrath	1 Matthews	(Coventry City)
2 Retter	2 Hall	(Birmingham City)
3 Juskowiak	3 Byrne	(Man Utd)
4 Schlienz	4 Clayton	(Blackburn)
5 Wewers	5 Wright*	(Wolves)
6 Mai	6 Edwards	(Man Utd)
7 Waldner	7 Astall	(Birmingham City)
8 Morlock	8 Haynes	(Fulham)
9 Walter	9 Taylor	(Man Utd)
10 Walter	10 Wilshaw	(Wolves)
11 Schafer	11 Grainger	(Sheffield United)

Crowd: 95,000

England scorers: Edwards, Grainger, Haynes

Comments: Duncan Edwards gave the away team a half-time lead, which they then twice added to before Walter scored a late consolation for the world champions in this friendly contest.

Northern Ireland 1 ENGLAND 1; in Belfast;
Saturday 6th October 1956 (Home International)

1	Gregg		1	Matthews	(Coventry City)
2	Cunningham		2	Hall	(Birmingham City)
3	McMichael		3	Byrne	(Man Utd)
4	Blanchflower		4	Clayton	(Blackburn)
5	Blanchflower		5	Wright*	(Wolves)
6	Casey		6	Edwards	(Man Utd)
7	Bingham		7	Matthews	(Blackpool)
8	McIlroy		8	Revie	(Man City)
9	Jones		9	Taylor	(Man Utd)
10	McAdams		10	Wilshaw	(Wolves)
11	McParland		11	Grainger	(Sheffield United)

Crowd: 58,420

England scorer: Matthews

Comments: Stanley Matthews and then Jimmy McIlroy both scored in the opening ten minutes and then the match ended in stalemate as the hosts earned a rare point against England.

ENGLAND 3 Wales 1; at Wembley;
Wednesday 14th November 1956 (Home International)

1	Ditchburn	(Tottenham)		1	Kelsey
2	Hall	(Birmingham City)		2	Sherwood
3	Byrne	(Man Utd)		3	Hopkins
4	Clayton	(Blackburn)		4	Harrington
5	Wright*	(Wolves)		5	Daniel
6	Dickinson	(Portsmouth)		6	Sullivan
7	Matthews	(Blackpool)		7	Medwin
8	Brooks	(Tottenham)		8	Charles.M
9	Finney	(Preston North End)		9	Charles. J
10	Haynes	(Fulham)		10	Allchurch
11	Grainger	(Sheffield United)		11	Jones

Crowd: 93,796

England scorers: Haynes, Brooks, Finney

Comments: John Charles scored again against England, giving Wales an early lead. The hosts then replied with 3 goals in the second half, including a goal for another debutant, John Brooks.

ENGLAND 3 Yugoslavia 0; at Wembley;
Wednesday 28th November 1956

1	Ditchburn	(Tottenham)	1	Beara	
2	Hall	(Birmingham City)	2	Belin	
3	Byrne	(Man Utd)	3	Stankovic	
4	Clayton	(Blackburn)	4	Tasic	
5	Wright*	(Wolves)	5	Horvat	
6	Dickinson	(Portsmouth)	6	Boskov	
7	Matthews	(Blackpool)	7	Rajkov	
8	Brooks	(Tottenham)	8	Conc	
9	Finney	(Preston North End)	9	Toplak	
10	Haynes	(Fulham) replaced by Taylor	10	Vukas	
11	Blunstone	(Chelsea)	11	Zebek	

Crowd: 75,000

England scorers: Brooks, Taylor (2)

Comments: Brooks gave England an early lead, but it took 2 second-half efforts from Taylor to decide the outcome. Tommy Taylor had replaced the injured Johnny Haynes after half an hour.

ENGLAND 5 Denmark 2; at Molineux;
Wednesday 5th December 1956 (World Cup qualifier)

1	Ditchburn	(Tottenham)	1	Drengsgaard	
2	Hall	(Birmingham City)	2	Larsen	
3	Byrne	(Man Utd)	3	Nielsen	
4	Clayton	(Blackburn)	4	Nielsen	
5	Wright*	(Wolves)	5	Hansen	
6	Dickinson	(Portsmouth)	6	Olesen	
7	Matthews	(Blackpool)	7	Hansen	
8	Brooks	(Tottenham)	8	Petersen	
9	Taylor	(Man Utd)	9	Nielsen	
10	Edwards	(Man Utd)	10	Jensen	
11	Finney	(Preston North End)	11	Hansen	

Crowd: 54,000

England scorers: Taylor (3), Edwards (2)

Comments: Only 3 men scored the 7 goals. Ove Bech Nielsen opened the scoring. Tommy Taylor then recorded a hat-trick before his fellow 'red devil' Duncan Edwards netted the last 2 goals.

ENGLAND 2 Scotland 1; at Wembley;
Saturday 6th April 1957 (Home International)

1 Hodgkinson	(Sheffield United)	1 Younger
2 Hall	(Birmingham City)	2 Caldow
3 Byrne	(Man Utd)	3 Hewie
4 Clayton	(Blackburn)	4 McColl
5 Wright*	(Wolves)	5 Young
6 Edwards	(Man Utd)	6 Docherty
7 Matthews	(Blackpool)	7 Collins
8 Thompson	(Preston North End)	8 Fernie
9 Finney	(Preston North End)	9 Reilly
10 Kevan	(West Brom)	10 Mudie
11 Grainger	(Sunderland)	11 Ring

Crowd: 97,520

England scorers: Kevan, Edwards

Comments: Tommy Ring scored in the first minute for Scotland, but their hearts were broke by a late winner from Edwards, after debutant Derek Kevan had notched a second-half equaliser.

ENGLAND 5 Republic Of Ireland 1; at Wembley;
Wednesday 8th May 1957 (World Cup qualifier)

1 Hodgkinson	(Sheffield United)	1 Kelly
2 Hall	(Birmingham City)	2 Donovan
3 Byrne	(Man Utd)	3 Cantwell
4 Clayton	(Blackburn)	4 Farrell
5 Wright*	(Wolves)	5 Mackey
6 Edwards	(Man Utd)	6 Saward
7 Matthews	(Blackpool)	7 Ringstead
8 Atyeo	(Bristol City)	8 Whelan
9 Taylor	(Man Utd)	9 Curtis
10 Haynes	(Fulham)	10 Fitzsimons
11 Finney	(Preston North End)	11 Haverty

Crowd: 52,000

England scorers: Taylor (3), Atyeo (2)

Comments: Tommy Taylor recorded a first-half hat-trick as England stormed into a 4–0 interval lead. This was a World Cup qualifier, and England were en route to the finals in Sweden.

Denmark 1 ENGLAND 4; in Copenhagen;
Wednesday 15th May 1957 (World Cup qualifier)

1 Drengsgaard	1 Hodgkinson	(Sheffield United)
2 Amdisen	2 Hall	(Birmingham City)
3 Nielsen	3 Byrne	(Man Utd)
4 Nielsen	4 Clayton	(Blackburn)
5 Hansen	5 Wright*	(Wolves)
6 Olesen	6 Edwards	(Man Utd)
7 Hansen	7 Matthews	(Blackpool)
8 Jensen J	8 Atyeo	(Bristol City)
9 Jensen E	9 Taylor	(Man Utd)
10 Jensen A	10 Haynes	(Fulham)
11 Hansen	11 Finney	(Preston North End)

Crowd: 35,000

England scorers: Haynes, Taylor (2), Atyeo

Comments: John Jensen gave the hosts a brief lead, but three second half goals ensured that England would be playing at the World Cup finals. This was the last cap for Stanley Matthews.

Republic Of Ireland 1 ENGLAND 1; in Dublin;
Sunday 19th May 1957 (World Cup qualifier)

1 Godwin	1 Hodgkinson	(Sheffield United)
2 Dunne	2 Hall	(Birmingham City)
3 Cantwell	3 Byrne	(Man Utd)
4 Nolan	4 Clayton	(Blackburn)
5 Hurley	5 Wright*	(Wolves)
6 Saward	6 Edwards	(Man Utd)
7 Ringstead	7 Finney	(Preston North End)
8 Whelan	8 Atyeo	(Bristol City)
9 Curtis	9 Taylor	(Man Utd)
10 Fitzsimons	10 Haynes	(Fulham)
11 Haverty	11 Pegg	(Man Utd)

Crowd: 50,000

England scorer: Atyeo

Comments: In this final qualifying match, the hosts took an early lead, but John Atyeo scored in the last minute, and then he never won another cap. It was also the only cap for David Pegg.

Wales 0 ENGLAND 4; in Cardiff;
Saturday 19th October 1957 (Home International)

1	Kelsey	1	Hopkinson	(Bolton Wanderers)
2	Williams	2	Howe	(West Brom)
3	Hopkins	3	Byrne	(Man Utd)
4	Harrington	4	Clayton	(Blackburn)
5	Charles	5	Wright*	(Wolves)
6	Bowen	6	Edwards	(Man Utd)
7	Hewitt	7	Douglas	(Blackburn)
8	Hewitt	8	Kevan	(West Brom)
9	Charles	9	Taylor	(Man Utd)
10	Allchurch	10	Haynes	(Fulham)
11	Jones	11	Finney	(Preston North End)

Crowd: 58,000

England scorers: Hopkins (OG), Haynes (2), Finney

Comments: Two goals in each half contributed to this emphatic win. Bryan Douglas, Eddie Hopkinson and Don Howe made their debuts while Billy Wright's 86th cap was a world record.

ENGLAND 2 Northern Ireland 3; at Wembley;
Wednesday 6th November 1957 (Home International)

1	Hopkinson	(Bolton Wanderers)	1	Gregg
2	Howe	(West Brom)	2	Keith
3	Byrne	(Man Utd)	3	McMichael
4	Clayton	(Blackburn)	4	Blanchflower
5	Wright*	(Wolves)	5	Blanchflower
6	Edwards	(Man Utd)	6	Peacock
7	Douglas	(Blackburn)	7	Bingham
8	Kevan	(West Brom)	8	McCrory
9	Taylor	(Man Utd)	9	Simpson
10	Haynes	(Fulham)	10	McIlroy
11	A'Court	(Liverpool)	11	McParland

Crowd: 42,000

England scorers: A'Court, Edwards

Comments: The visitors were already 2–0 ahead when Alan A'Court scored on his debut. The goal from Edwards was just a consolation as Northern Ireland recorded a rare but famous win.

ENGLAND 4 France 0; at Wembley;
Wednesday 27th November 1957

1	Hopkinson	(Bolton Wanderers)	1	Abbes	
2	Howe	(West Brom)	2	Zitouni	
3	Byrne	(Man Utd)	3	Kaelbel	
4	Clayton	(Blackburn)	4	Domingo	
5	Wright*	(Wolves)	5	Tylinski	
6	Edwards	(Man Utd)	6	Bollini	
7	Douglas	(Blackburn)	7	Wisnieski	
8	Robson	(West Brom)	8	Ujlaki	
9	Taylor	(Man Utd)	9	Douis	
10	Haynes	(Fulham)	10	Piantoni	
11	Finney	(Preston North End)	11	Vincent	

Crowd: 64,349

England scorers: Taylor (2), Robson (2)

Comments: Robson scored twice on his debut, but this happy occasion was the last England match for Roger Byrne, Duncan Edwards, and Tommy Taylor. 3 months later they were all killed.

Scotland 0 ENGLAND 4; in Glasgow;
Saturday 19th April 1958 (Home International)

1	Younger	1	Hopkinson	(Bolton Wanderers)
2	Parker	2	Howe	(West Brom)
3	Haddock	3	Langley	(Fulham)
4	McColl	4	Clayton	(Blackburn)
5	Evans	5	Wright*	(Wolves)
6	Docherty	6	Slater	(Wolves)
7	Herd	7	Douglas	(Blackburn)
8	Murray	8	Charlton	(Man Utd)
9	Mudie	9	Kevan	(West Brom)
10	Forrest	10	Haynes	(Fulham)
11	Ewing	11	Finney	(Preston North End)

Crowd: 127,874

England scorers: Douglas, Kevan (2), Charlton

Comments: 2 goals in each half sealed the win. Bryan Douglas scored his first England goal, Jim Langley won his first cap, and Bobby Charlton won his first cap and scored his first goal.

ENGLAND 2 Portugal 1; at Wembley;
Wednesday 7th May 1958

1	Hopkinson	(Bolton Wanderers)	1	Gomes
2	Howe	(West Brom)	2	Mendes
3	Langley	(Fulham)	3	Gaspar
4	Clayton	(Blackburn)	4	Graca
5	Wright*	(Wolves)	5	Arcanjo
6	Slater	(Wolves)	6	Torres
7	Douglas	(Blackburn)	7	Duarte
8	Charlton	(Man Utd)	8	Coluna
9	Kevan	(West Brom)	9	Augusto
10	Haynes	(Fulham)	10	Rocha
11	Finney	(Preston North End)	11	da Silva

Crowd: 72,000

England scorer: Charlton (2)

Comments: Bobby Charlton (a survivor of the Munich air tragedy) scored in each half as an unchanged England team warmed up for the World Cup with yet another win over Portugal.

Yugoslavia 5 ENGLAND 0; in Belgrade;
Sunday 11th May 1958

1	Beara	1	Hopkinson	(Bolton Wanderers)
2	Crnkovic	2	Howe	(West Brom)
3	Sijakovic	3	Langley	(Fulham)
4	Krstic	4	Clayton	(Blackburn)
5	Zebec	5	Wright*	(Wolves)
6	Boskov	6	Slater	(Wolves)
7	Petakovic	7	Douglas	(Blackburn)
8	Veselinovic	8	Charlton	(Man Utd)
9	Milutinovic	9	Kevan	(West Brom)
10	Sekularac	10	Haynes	(Fulham)
11	Pasic	11	Finney	(Preston North End)

Crowd: 55,000

Comments: 4 weeks before their first World Cup match, England conceded 4 second half-goals as their hosts proceeded to humiliate them. This was Langley's last cap.

USSR 1 ENGLAND 1; in Moscow;
Sunday 18th May 1958

1	Yashin	1	McDonald	(Burnley)
2	Ogonkov	2	Howe	(West Brom)
3	Krizhevsky	3	Banks	(Bolton Wanderers)
4	Kuznetsov	4	Clamp	(Wolves)
5	Voinov	5	Wright*	(Wolves)
6	Netto	6	Slater	(Wolves)
7	Apukhtin	7	Douglas	(Blackburn)
8	Ivanov	8	Robson	(West Brom)
9	Streltsov	9	Kevan	(West Brom)
10	Falin	10	Haynes	(Fulham)
11	Ilyin	11	Finney	(Preston North End)

Crowd: 102,000

England scorer: Kevan

Comments: England and Russia peculiarly played a friendly 3 weeks before their World Cup match. Tommy Banks, Eddie Clamp, and Colin McDonald all earned their first caps in this draw.

ENGLAND 2 USSR 2; in Gothenburg;
Sunday 8th June 1958 (World Cup finals)

1	McDonald	(Burnley)	1	Yashin
2	Howe	(West Brom)	2	Kesarev
3	Banks	(Bolton Wanderers)	3	Krizhevsky
4	Clamp	(Wolves)	4	Kuznetsov
5	Wright*	(Wolves)	5	Voinov
6	Slater	(Wolves)	6	Tsarev
7	Douglas	(Blackburn)	7	Ivanov
8	Robson	(West Brom)	8	Ivanov
9	Kevan	(West Brom)	9	Simonyan
10	Haynes	(Fulham)	10	Salnikov
11	Finney	(Preston North End)	11	Ilyin

Crowd: 49,348

England scorers: Kevan, Finney (Pen)

Comments: The Russians craftily made five changes which paid off as they took a 2–0 lead in the second half. It took a late penalty from the veteran Finney to earn England a precious point.

ENGLAND 0 Brazil 0; in Gothenburg;
Wednesday 11th June 1958 (World Cup finals)

1 McDonald	(Burnley)	1	Gilmar
2 Howe	(West Brom)	2	de Sordi
3 Banks	(Bolton Wanderers)	3	Bellini
4 Clamp	(Wolves)	4	Pecanha
5 Wright*	(Wolves)	5	Santos
6 Slater	(Wolves)	6	Dino Sani
7 Douglas	(Blackburn)	7	Didi
8 Robson	(West Brom)	8	Joel
9 Kevan	(West Brom)	9	Mazola
10 Haynes	(Fulham)	10	Vava
11 A'Court	(Liverpool)	11	Zagallo

Crowd: 40,895

Comments: Colin McDonald kept a clean sheet as England held the eventual winners to a scoreless draw. Walter Winterbottom's team had now drawn their last three consecutive matches.

ENGLAND 2 Austria 2; in Boras;
Sunday 15th June 1958 (World Cup finals)

1 McDonald	(Burnley)	1	Szanwald
2 Howe	(West Brom)	2	Kollman
3 Banks	(Bolton Wanderers)	3	Swoboda
4 Clamp	(Wolves)	4	Hanappi
5 Wright*	(Wolves)	5	Happl
6 Slater	(Wolves)	6	Koller
7 Douglas	(Blackburn)	7	Kozlicek
8 Robson	(West Brom)	8	Senekowitsch
9 Kevan	(West Brom)	9	Buzek
10 Haynes	(Fulham)	10	Korner
11 A'Court	(Liverpool)	11	Kozlicek

Crowd: 16,800

England scorers: Haynes, Kevan

Comments: Yet again England had to come from behind twice in order to rescue a point. This was Eddie Clamp's last match. England now had to play the USSR in a group play-off in 2 days' time.

ENGLAND 0 USSR 1; in Gothenburg;
Tuesday 17th June 1958 (World Cup finals)

1	McDonald	(Burnley)	1	Yashin
2	Howe	(West Brom)	2	Kesarev
3	Banks	(Bolton Wanderers)	3	Krizhevsky
4	Clayton	(Blackburn)	4	Kuznetsov
5	Wright*	(Wolves)	5	Voinov
6	Slater	(Wolves)	6	Tsarev
7	Brabrook	(Chelsea)	7	Apukhtin
8	Broadbent	(Wolves)	8	Ivanov
9	Kevan	(West Brom)	9	Simonyan
10	Haynes	(Fulham)	10	Falin
11	A'Court	(Liverpool)	11	Ilyin

Crowd: 23,182

Comments: Peter Brabrook and Peter Broadbent were both thrown in at the deep end in this crucial tie. In the event a toothless England bowed out of the World Cup without having won a match.

Northern Ireland 3 ENGLAND 3; in Belfast;
Saturday 4th October 1958 (Home International)

1	Gregg	1	McDonald	(Burnley)
2	Keith	2	Howe	(West Brom)
3	Graham	3	Banks	(Bolton Wanderers)
4	Blanchflower	4	Clayton	(Blackburn)
5	Cunningham	5	Wright*	(Wolves)
6	Peacock	6	McGuinness	(Man Utd)
7	Bingham	7	Brabrook	(Chelsea)
8	Cush	8	Broadbent	(Wolves)
9	Casey	9	Charlton	(Man Utd)
10	McIlroy	10	Haynes	(Fulham)
11	McParland	11	Finney	(Preston North End)

Crowd: 58,000

England scorers: Charlton (2), Finney

Comments: It was déjà vu as the visitors had to equalise 3 times to earn a point in this Home International. Wilf McGuinness won his 1st cap. England were now 7 matches without a win!

ENGLAND 5 USSR 0; at Wembley;
Wednesday 22nd October 1958

1	McDonald	(Burnley)	1	Beliayev
2	Howe	(West Brom)	2	Kesarev
3	Shaw	(Sheffield United)	3	Maslyonkin
4	Clayton	(Blackburn)	4	Kuznetsov
5	Wright*	(Wolves)	5	Voinov
6	Slater	(Wolves)	6	Tsarev
7	Douglas	(Blackburn)	7	Metreveli
8	Charlton	(Man Utd)	8	Ivanov
9	Lofthouse	(Bolton Wanderers)	9	Simonyan
10	Haynes	(Fulham)	10	Mamedov
11	Finney	(Preston North End)	11	Ilyin

Crowd: 100,000

England scorers: Haynes (3), Charlton (Pen), Lofthouse

Comments: A recalled Nat Lofthouse sealed this win after Johnny Haynes had scored a hat-trick which was revenge for their World Cup exit. This was the last outing for the great Tom Finney.

ENGLAND 2 Wales 2; at Villa Park;
Wednesday 26th November 1958 (Home International)

1	McDonald	(Burnley)	1	Kelsey
2	Howe	(West Brom)	2	Williams
3	Shaw	(Sheffield United)	3	Hopkins
4	Clayton	(Blackburn)	4	Crowe
5	Wright*	(Wolves)	5	Charles
6	Flowers	(Wolves)	6	Bowen
7	Clapton	(Arsenal)	7	Medwin
8	Broadbent	(Wolves)	8	Ward
9	Lofthouse	(Bolton Wanderers)	9	Tapscott
10	Charlton	(Man Utd)	10	Allchurch
11	A'Court	(Liverpool)	11	Woosnam

Crowd: 41,581

England scorer: Broadbent (2)

Comments: Once more England came from behind twice to salvage a dismal draw. Colin McDonald, Nat Lofthouse, Alan A'Court, and debutant Dan Clapton never played for England again.

ENGLAND 1 Scotland 0; at Wembley;
Saturday 11th April 1959 (Home International)

1 Hopkinson	(Bolton Wanderers)	1	Brown
2 Howe	(West Brom)	2	Mackay
3 Shaw	(Sheffield United)	3	Caldow
4 Clayton	(Blackburn)	4	Docherty
5 Wright*	(Wolves)	5	Evans
6 Flowers	(Wolves)	6	Mackay
7 Douglas	(Blackburn)	7	Leggat
8 Broadbent	(Wolves)	8	Collins
9 Charlton	(Man Utd)	9	Herd
10 Haynes	(Fulham)	10	Dick
11 Holden	(Bolton Wanderers)	11	Ormond

Crowd: 98,329

England scorer: Charlton

Comments: Charlton's goal just before the hour mark settled this game in which Albert Holden made his debut. The captain, Billy Wright, collected his one hundredth cap in this grudge match.

ENGLAND 2 Italy 2; at Wembley;
Wednesday 6th May 1959

1 Hopkinson	(Bolton Wanderers)	1	Buffon
2 Howe	(West Brom)	2	Robotti
3 Shaw	(Sheffield United)	3	Castelletti
4 Clayton	(Blackburn)	4	Zaglio
5 Wright*	(Wolves)	5	Bernasconi
6 Flowers	(Wolves)	6	Segato
7 Bradley	(Man Utd)	7	Mariani
8 Broadbent	(Wolves)	8	Gratton
9 Charlton	(Man Utd)	9	Brighenti
10 Haynes	(Fulham)	10	Galli
11 Holden	(Bolton Wanderers)	11	Petris

Crowd: 92,000

England scorers: Charlton, Bradley

Comments: Warren Bradley scored on his debut to give England a 2–0 half-time lead. However, Walter Winterbottom's team had to settle for a draw in this end of season friendly fixture.

Brazil 2 ENGLAND 0; in Rio de Janeiro;
Wednesday 13th May 1959

1	Gilmar	1 Hopkinson	(Bolton Wanderers)
2	Santos	2 Howe	(West Brom)
3	Bellini	3 Armfield	(Blackpool)
4	Pecanha	4 Clayton	(Blackburn)
5	Santos	5 Wright*	(Wolves)
6	Dino Sani	6 Flowers	(Wolves)
7	Didi	7 Deeley	(Wolves)
8	Julinho	8 Broadbent	(Wolves)
9	Henrique	9 Charlton	(Man Utd)
10	Pele	10 Haynes	(Fulham)
11	Canhoteiro	11 Holden	(Bolton Wanderers)

Crowd: 160,000

Comments: Jimmy Armfield and Warren Deeley won their first caps in front of the biggest-ever crowd for an England match. No fewer than four Wolves' players were named in the line-up.

Peru 4 ENGLAND 1; in Lima;
Sunday 17th May 1959

1	Asca	1 Hopkinson	(Bolton Wanderers)
2	Flemming	2 Howe	(West Brom)
3	Fernandez	3 Armfield	(Blackpool)
4	Andrade	4 Clayton	(Blackburn)
5	de la Vega	5 Wright*	(Wolves)
6	Benitez	6 Flowers	(Wolves)
7	Montalvo	7 Deeley	(Wolves)
8	Loayza	8 Greaves	(Chelsea)
9	Joya	9 Charlton	(Man Utd)
10	Carrasco	10 Haynes	(Fulham)
11	Seminario	11 Holden	(Bolton Wanderers)

Crowd: 50,306

England scorer: Greaves

Comments: The great Jimmy Greaves scored on his debut as he would do for every team he played for. However, England trailed 4–0 at half-time. This was Deeley's last international appearance.

Mexico 2 ENGLAND 1; in Mexico City;
Sunday 24th May 1959

1	Carbajal	1	Hopkinson	(Bolton Wanderers)
2	Bosco	2	Howe	(West Brom)
3	del Muro	3	Armfield	(Blackpool)
4	Jauregui	4	Clayton	(Blackburn)
5	Cardenas	5	Wright*	(Wolves)
6	Flores	6	McGuinness	(Man Utd) replaced by Flowers
7	del Aguila	7	Holden	(Bolton Wanderers) replaced by Bradley
8	Reyes	8	Greaves	(Chelsea)
9	Gonzalez	9	Kevan	(West Brom)
10	Ponce	10	Haynes	(Fulham)
11	Arellano	11	Charlton	(Man Utd)

Crowd: 83,000

England scorer: Kevan

Comments: Mexico came from behind to secure victory. Bradley and Flowers came on as second-half substitutes for Holden and McGuinness. The latter two never played for England again.

USA 1 ENGLAND 8; in Los Angeles;
Thursday 28th May 1959

1	Ottoboni	1	Hopkinson	(Bolton Wanderers)
2	Farquhar	2	Howe	(West Brom)
3	Cinowitz	3	Armfield	(Blackpool)
4	Bachmeier	4	Clayton	(Blackburn)
5	Evans	5	Wright*	(Wolves)
6	Traina	6	Flowers	(Wolves)
7	Cameron	7	Bradley	(Man Utd)
8	Murphy	8	Greaves	(Chelsea)
9	Carson	9	Kevan	(West Brom)
10	Looby	10	Haynes	(Fulham)
11	Zerhusen	11	Charlton	(Man Utd)

Crowd: 13,000

England scorers: Bradley, Flowers (2), Charlton (3), Kevan, Haynes

Comments: England trailed for half an hour before the floodgates opened. Billy Wright and Warren Bradley won their last caps in this annihilation in front of a very small crowd.

Wales 1 ENGLAND 1; in Cardiff;
Saturday 17th October 1959 (Home International)

1 Kelsey	1 Hopkinson	(Bolton Wanderers)
2 Williams	2 Howe	(West Brom)
3 Hopkins	3 Allen	(Stoke City)
4 Crowe	4 Clayton*	(Blackburn)
5 Sullivan	5 Smith	(Birmingham City)
6 Nurse	6 Flowers	(Wolves)
7 Medwin	7 Connelly	(Burnley)
8 Moore	8 Greaves	(Chelsea)
9 Woosnam	9 Clough	(Middlesbrough)
10 Allchurch	10 Charlton	(Man Utd)
11 Jones	11 Holliday	(Middlesbrough)

Crowd: 62,000

England scorer: Greaves

Comments: Both goals came in the first half as England again failed to beat Wales. England had 5 debutants, namely Tony Allen, Brian Clough, John Connelly, Edwin Holliday and Trevor Smith.

ENGLAND 2 Sweden 3; at Wembley;
Wednesday 28th October 1959

1 Hopkinson	(Bolton Wanderers)	1 Nyholm
2 Howe	(West Brom)	2 Bergmark
3 Allen	(Stoke City)	3 Axbom
4 Clayton*	(Blackburn)	4 Jonsson
5 Smith	(Birmingham City)	5 Johansson
6 Flowers	(Wolves)	6 Parling
7 Connelly	(Burnley)	7 Berndtsson
8 Greaves	(Chelsea)	8 Thillberg
9 Clough	(Middlesbrough)	9 Simonsson
10 Charlton	(Man Utd)	10 Borjesson
11 Holliday	(Middlesbrough)	11 Salomonsson

Crowd: 72,000

England scorers: Connelly, Charlton

Comments: The home team led 1–0 at half-time, only for Sweden to score the next three goals. As a result of this setback, Clough, Hopkinson, and Smith never played for England again.

ENGLAND 2 Northern Ireland 1; at Wembley;
Wednesday 18th November 1959 (Home International)

1	Springett	(Sheffield Wed)		1	Gregg
2	Howe	(West Brom)		2	Keith
3	Allen	(Stoke City)		3	McMichael
4	Clayton*	(Blackburn)		4	Blanchflower
5	Brown	(West Ham Utd)		5	Cunningham
6	Flowers	(Wolves)		6	Peacock
7	Connelly	(Burnley)		7	Bingham
8	Haynes	(Fulham)		8	Crossan
9	Baker	(Hibernian)		9	Cush
10	Parry	(Bolton Wanderers)		10	McIlroy
11	Holliday	(Middlesbrough)		11	McParland

Crowd: 60,000

England scorers: Baker, Parry

Comments: Ron Springett saved a penalty on his debut. Ken Brown also won his only cap, while both goals came from the debutants, Joe Baker and Ray Parry. The latter scored in the last minute.

Scotland 1 ENGLAND 1; in Glasgow;
Tuesday 19th April 1960 (Home International)

1	Haffey		1	Springett	(Sheffield Wed)
2	Mackay		2	Armfield	(Blackpool)
3	Caldow		3	Wilson	(Huddersfield Town)
4	Cumming		4	Clayton*	(Blackburn)
5	Evans		5	Slater	(Wolves)
6	McCann		6	Flowers	(Wolves)
7	Leggat		7	Connelly	(Burnley)
8	Young		8	Broadbent	(Wolves)
9	St John		9	Baker	(Hibernian)
10	Law		10	Parry	(Bolton Wanderers)
11	Weir		11	Charlton	(Man Utd)

Crowd: 129,783

England scorer: Charlton (Pen)

Comments: Bobby Charlton's penalty at the start of the second half cancelled out Leggat's earlier effort. Ray Wilson made his debut while Broadbent, Parry, and Slater never won another cap.

ENGLAND 3 Yugoslavia 3; at Wembley;
Wednesday 11th May 1960

1 Springett	(Sheffield Wed)	1 Soskic
2 Armfield	(Blackpool)	2 Durkovic
3 Wilson	(Huddersfield Town)	3 Jusufi
4 Clayton*	(Blackburn)	4 Zanetic
5 Swan	(Sheffield Wed)	5 Zebec
6 Flowers	(Wolves)	6 Perusic
7 Douglas	(Blackburn)	7 Liposinovic
8 Haynes	(Fulham)	8 Jerkovic
9 Baker	(Hibernian)	9 Sekularac
10 Greaves	(Chelsea)	10 Galic
11 Charlton	(Man Utd)	11 Kostic

Crowd: 60,000

England scorers: Douglas, Greaves, Haynes

Comments: It took a late goal from Johnny Haynes to earn England a draw. Peter Swan earned his first cap whilst the skipper, Ronnie Clayton, played for the 35th and last time for the home team.

Spain 3 ENGLAND 0; in Madrid;
Sunday 15th May 1960

1 Ramallets	1 Springett	(Sheffield Wed)
2 Perez	2 Armfield	(Blackpool)
3 Gracia	3 Wilson	(Huddersfield Town)
4 Verges	4 Robson	(West Brom)
5 Garay	5 Swan	(Sheffield Wed)
6 Segarra	6 Flowers	(Wolves)
7 Pereda	7 Brabrook	(Chelsea)
8 Martinez	8 Haynes*	(Fulham)
9 di Stefano	9 Baker	(Hibernian)
10 Peiro	10 Greaves	(Chelsea)
11 Gento	11 Charlton	(Man Utd)

Crowd: 77,000

Comments: Martinez scored twice as the hosts led 3–0 at half-time in this end of season friendly. Peter Brabrook made his last appearance, against a team that included the great Alfredo di Stefano.

Hungary 2 ENGLAND 0; in Budapest;
Sunday 22nd May 1960

1 Grosics	1 Springett	(Sheffield Wed)
2 Matrai	2 Armfield	(Blackpool)
3 Dalnoki	3 Wilson	(Huddersfield Town)
4 Bundzsak	4 Robson	(West Brom)
5 Sipos	5 Swan	(Sheffield Wed)
6 Kotasz	6 Flowers	(Wolves)
7 Sandor	7 Douglas	(Blackburn)
8 Gorocs	8 Haynes*	(Fulham)
9 Albert	9 Baker	(Hibernian)
10 Dunai	10 Viollet	(Man Utd)
11 Rakosi	11 Charlton	(Man Utd)

Crowd: 90,000

Comments: For the fourth time this year, England failed to win, but with no Puskas playing, they were not routed by Hungary for a change. Dennis Viollet won his first cap in this friendly defeat.

Northern Ireland 2 ENGLAND 5; in Belfast;
Saturday 8th October 1960 (Home International)

1 Gregg	1 Springett	(Sheffield Wed)
2 Keith	2 Armfield	(Blackpool)
3 Elder	3 McNeil	(Middlesbrough)
4 Blanchflower	4 Robson	(West Brom)
5 Forde	5 Swan	(Sheffield Wed)
6 Peacock	6 Flowers	(Wolves)
7 Bingham	7 Douglas	(Blackburn)
8 McIlroy	8 Greaves	(Chelsea)
9 McAdams	9 Smith	(Tottenham)
10 Dougan	10 Haynes*	(Fulham)
11 McParland	11 Charlton	(Man Utd)

Crowd: 60,000

England scorers: Smith, Greaves (2), Charlton, Douglas

Comments: It took two late goals from Douglas and the prolific Greaves to settle this match. Bobby Smith started the goals avalanche on his debut. It was also the first cap for Mick McNeil.

Luxembourg 0 ENGLAND 9; in Luxembourg City; Wednesday 19th October 1960 (World Cup qualifier)

1 Stendebach	1 Springett	(Sheffield Wed)
2 Brenner	2 Armfield	(Blackpool)
3 Hoffmann	3 McNeil	(Middlesbrough)
4 Mertl	4 Robson	(West Brom)
5 Brosius	5 Swan	(Sheffield Wed)
6 Jahn	6 Flowers	(Wolves)
7 Schmit	7 Douglas	(Blackburn)
8 Cirelli	8 Greaves	(Chelsea)
9 May	9 Smith	(Tottenham)
10 Konter	10 Haynes*	(Fulham)
11 Bauer	11 Charlton	(Man Utd)

Crowd: 5,500

England scorers: Charlton (3), Greaves (3), Smith (2), Haynes

Comments: The away team were given shooting practice in this World Cup qualifier. Charlton and Greaves duly obliged with a pair of hat-tricks. Not all World Cup matches would be this simple.

ENGLAND 4 Spain 2; at Wembley; Wednesday 26th October 1960

1 Springett	(Sheffield Wed)	1 Ramallets
2 Armfield	(Blackpool)	2 Alfonso
3 McNeil	(Middlesbrough)	3 Gracia
4 Robson	(West Brom)	4 Ruiz Sosa
5 Swan	(Sheffield Wed)	5 Santamaria
6 Flowers	(Wolves)	6 Verges
7 Douglas	(Blackburn)	7 Mateos
8 Greaves	(Chelsea)	8 del Sol
9 Smith	(Tottenham)	9 di Stefano
10 Haynes*	(Fulham)	10 Suarez
11 Charlton	(Man Utd)	11 Gento

Crowd: 85,000

England scorers: Greaves, Douglas, Smith (2)

Comments: Jimmy Greaves scored inside two minutes but it needed a brace from Bobby Smith in the final half hour to enable England to avenge their friendly defeat from May.

ENGLAND 5 Wales 1; at Wembley;
Wednesday 23rd November 1960 (Home International)

1	Hodgkinson	(Sheffield United)	1	Kelsey
2	Armfield	(Blackpool)	2	Harrington
3	McNeil	(Middlesbrough)	3	Williams
4	Robson	(West Brom)	4	Crowe
5	Swan	(Sheffield Wed)	5	Nurse
6	Flowers	(Wolves)	6	Baker
7	Douglas	(Blackburn)	7	Medwin
8	Greaves	(Chelsea)	8	Woosnam
9	Smith	(Tottenham)	9	Leek
10	Haynes*	(Fulham)	10	Vernon
11	Charlton	(Man Utd)	11	Jones

Crowd: 65,000

England scorers: Greaves (2), Charlton, Smith, Haynes

Comments: The lethal Greaves again scored inside two minutes and then added the final goal as England finally recorded a win over Wales. This would be Alan Hodgkinson's last England cap.

ENGLAND 9 Scotland 3; at Wembley;
Saturday 15th April 1961 (Home International)

1	Springett	(Sheffield Wed)	1	Haffey
2	Armfield	(Blackpool)	2	Shearer
3	McNeil	(Middlesbrough)	3	Caldow
4	Robson	(West Brom)	4	Mackay
5	Swan	(Sheffield Wed)	5	McNeill
6	Flowers	(Wolves)	6	McCann
7	Douglas	(Blackburn)	7	Macleod
8	Greaves	(Chelsea)	8	Law
9	Smith	(Tottenham)	9	St John
10	Haynes*	(Fulham)	10	Quinn
11	Charlton	(Man Utd)	11	Wilson

Crowd: 97,350

England scorers: Robson, Greaves (3), Douglas, Smith (2), Haynes (2)

Comments: Trailing 3–0 at half-time, Scotland scored twice at the start of the second half, but then England went into a goals frenzy. Bannockburn was avenged by this humiliation of the Scots.

ENGLAND 8 Mexico 0; at Wembley;
Wednesday 10th May 1961

1	Springett	(Sheffield Wed)	1	Mota
2	Armfield	(Blackpool)	2	Pena
3	McNeil	(Middlesbrough)	3	Sepulveda
4	Robson	(West Brom)	4	Jauregui
5	Swan	(Sheffield Wed)	5	Portugal
6	Flowers	(Wolves)	6	Cardenas
7	Douglas	(Blackburn)	7	del Aguila
8	Kevan	(West Brom)	8	Reyes
9	Hitchens	(Aston Villa)	9	Gonzalez
10	Haynes*	(Fulham)	10	Flores
11	Charlton	(Man Utd)	11	Mercado

Crowd: 77,000

England scorers: Hitchens, Charlton (3), Robson, Douglas (2), Flowers (Pen)

Comments: Free-scoring England could only manage eight this time! Gerry Hitchens scored within two minutes of his first start. 4 goals were scored in each half. This would be Kevan's last cap.

Portugal 1 ENGLAND 1; in Lisbon;
Sunday 21st May 1961 (World Cup qualifier)

1	Pereira	1	Springett	(Sheffield Wed)
2	Goulart	2	Armfield	(Blackpool)
3	da Conceicao	3	McNeil	(Middlesbrough)
4	Mendes	4	Robson	(West Brom)
5	Figueiredo	5	Swan	(Sheffield Wed)
6	Cruz	6	Flowers	(Wolves)
7	Pinto	7	Douglas	(Blackburn)
8	Santana	8	Greaves	(Chelsea)
9	Pinto	9	Smith	(Tottenham)
10	Coluna	10	Haynes*	(Fulham)
11	Gomes Cavem	11	Charlton	(Man Utd)

Crowd: 65,000

England scorer: Flowers

Comments: This World Cup qualifier had been scoreless at half-time, but it required a late equaliser from Ron Flowers to earn the away team a draw. Portugal were no longer a pushover!

Italy 2 ENGLAND 3; in Rome;
Wednesday 24th May 1961

1	Buffon	1	Springett	(Sheffield Wed)
2	Losi	2	Armfield	(Blackpool)
3	Castelletti	3	McNeil	(Middlesbrough)
4	Bolchi	4	Robson	(West Brom)
5	Salvadore	5	Swan	(Sheffield Wed)
6	Trapattoni	6	Flowers	(Wolves)
7	Mora	7	Douglas	(Blackburn)
8	Lojacono	8	Greaves	(Chelsea)
9	Brighenti	9	Hitchens	(Aston Villa)
10	Sivori	10	Haynes*	(Fulham)
11	Corso	11	Charlton	(Man Utd)

Crowd: 90,000

England scorers: Hitchens (2), Greaves

Comments: Jimmy Greaves netted a late winner as England again got the better of the Italians. Greaves would soon be playing club football in Italy, although his stay was short-lived.

Austria 3 ENGLAND 1; in Vienna;
Saturday 27th May 1961

1	Fraydl	1	Springett	(Sheffield Wed)
2	Trubrig	2	Armfield	(Blackpool)
3	Stotz	3	Angus	(Burnley)
4	Strobl	4	Miller	(Burnley)
5	Hanappi	5	Swan	(Sheffield Wed)
6	Koller	6	Flowers	(Wolves)
7	Nemec	7	Douglas	(Blackburn)
8	Hof	8	Greaves	(Chelsea)
9	Buzek	9	Hitchens	(Aston Villa)
10	Senekowitsch	10	Haynes*	(Fulham)
11	Rafreider	11	Charlton	(Man Utd)

Crowd: 90,726

England scorer: Greaves

Comments: Burnley duo John Angus and Brian Miller were drafted in for what would be their only international appearance as England suffered their first defeat in twelve promising months.

ENGLAND 4 Luxembourg 1; at Highbury;
Thursday 28th September 1961 (World Cup qualifier)

1	Springett	(Sheffield Wed)	1	Steffen	
2	Armfield*	(Blackpool)	2	Brenner	
3	McNeil	(Middlesbrough)	3	Hoffmann	
4	Robson	(West Brom)	4	Zambon	
5	Swan	(Sheffield Wed)	5	Brosius	
6	Flowers	(Wolves)	6	Konter	
7	Douglas	(Blackburn)	7	Dimmer	
8	Fantham	(Sheffield Wed)	8	Cirelli	
9	Pointer	(Burnley)	9	Hoffmann	
10	Violett	(Man Utd)	10	Schneider	
11	Charlton	(Man Utd)	11	Schmit	

Crowd: 33,409

England scorers: Pointer, Violett, Charlton (2)

Comments: Luxembourg were less generous this time as England took more than half an hour to open their goals account. Ray Pointer scored on his debut, while Violett scored in his last outing.

Wales 1 ENGLAND 1; in Cardiff;
Saturday 14th October 1961 (Home International)

1	Kelsey	1	Springett	(Sheffield Wed)
2	Harrington	2	Armfield	(Blackpool)
3	Williams S	3	Wilson	(Huddersfield Town)
4	Charles	4	Robson	(West Brom)
5	Charles	5	Swan	(Sheffield Wed)
6	Crowe	6	Flowers	(Wolves)
7	Jones	7	Connelly	(Burnley)
8	Woosnam	8	Douglas	(Blackburn)
9	Ward	9	Pointer	(Burnley)
10	Allchurch	10	Haynes*	(Fulham)
11	Williams G	11	Charlton	(Man Utd)

Crowd: 61,566

England scorer: Douglas

Comments: Graham Williams gave the home team the lead on the half hour, only for Bryan Douglas to level the scores just before the interval. Both teams had to settle for a point.

ENGLAND 2 Portugal 0; at Wembley;
Wednesday 25th October 1961 (World Cup qualifier)

1 Springett	(Sheffield Wed)	1	Pereira
2 Armfield	(Blackpool)	2	Goulart
3 Wilson	(Huddersfield Town)	3	da Conceicao
4 Robson	(West Brom)	4	Perides
5 Swan	(Sheffield Wed)	5	Soares
6 Flowers	(Wolves)	6	Lucas
7 Connelly	(Burnley)	7	Yauca
8 Douglas	(Blackburn)	8	Eusebio
9 Pointer	(Burnley)	9	Pinto
10 Haynes*	(Fulham)	10	Coluna
11 Charlton	(Man Utd)	11	Gomes Cavem

Crowd: 100,000

England scorers: Connelly, Pointer

Comments: Both goals came in the first ten minutes as England earned a place at the 1962 World Cup finals. Losing at Wembley would become a regular habit for the great Eusebio.

ENGLAND 1 Northern Ireland 1; at Wembley;
Wednesday 22nd November 1961 (Home International)

1 Springett	(Sheffield Wed)	1	Hunter
2 Armfield	(Blackpool)	2	Magill
3 Wilson	(Huddersfield Town)	3	Elder
4 Robson	(West Brom)	4	Blanchflower
5 Swan	(Sheffield Wed)	5	Neill
6 Flowers	(Wolves)	6	Nicholson
7 Douglas	(Blackburn)	7	Bingham
8 Byrne	(Crystal Palace)	8	Barr
9 Crawford	(Ipswich Town)	9	McAdams
10 Haynes*	(Fulham)	10	McIlroy
11 Charlton	(Man Utd)	11	McLaughlin

Crowd: 30,000

England scorer: Charlton

Comments: It was Northern Ireland's turn to score a late goal against England as Jimmy McIlroy earned the visitors a Home International point after Bobby Charlton gave the hosts an early lead.

ENGLAND 3 Austria 1; at Wembley;
Wednesday 4th April 1962

1	Springett	(Sheffield Wed)		1	Fraydl
2	Armfield	(Blackpool)		2	Trubrig
3	Wilson	(Huddersfield Town)		3	Stotz
4	Anderson	(Sunderland)		4	Hasenkopf
5	Swan	(Sheffield Wed)		5	Oslansky
6	Flowers	(Wolves)		6	Koller
7	Connelly	(Burnley)		7	Knoll
8	Hunt	(Liverpool)		8	Hof
9	Crawford	(Ipswich Town)		9	Buzek
10	Haynes*	(Fulham)		10	Fiala
11	Charlton	(Man Utd)		11	Rafreider

Crowd: 50,000

England scorers: Crawford, Flowers, Hunt

Comments: Stan Anderson won his first cap, while Roger Hunt scored on his debut. Ray Crawford had given England an early lead on his second and last appearance.

Scotland 2 ENGLAND 0; in Glasgow;
Saturday 18th April 1962 (Home International)

1	Brown		1	Springett	(Sheffield Wed)
2	Hamilton		2	Armfield	(Blackpool)
3	Caldow		3	Wilson	(Huddersfield Town)
4	Crerand		4	Anderson	(Sunderland)
5	McNeill		5	Swan	(Sheffield Wed)
6	Baxter		6	Flowers	(Wolves)
7	Scott		7	Douglas	(Blackburn)
8	White		8	Greaves	(Tottenham)
9	St John		9	Smith	(Tottenham)
10	Law		10	Haynes*	(Fulham)
11	Wilson		11	Charlton	(Man Utd)

Crowd: 132,441

Comments: Two Rangers' players (Davie Wilson and then Eric Caldow from the penalty spot) scored at the start and end of this match as Scotland atoned for their 9–3 embarrassment of last year.

ENGLAND 3 Switzerland 1; at Wembley; Wednesday 9th May 1962

1 Springett	(Sheffield Wed)	1 Permunian	
2 Armfield	(Blackpool)	2 Rosch	
3 Wilson	(Huddersfield Town)	3 Tachella	
4 Robson	(West Brom)	4 Grobety	
5 Swan	(Sheffield Wed)	5 Schneiter	
6 Flowers	(Wolves)	6 Weber	
7 Connelly	(Burnley)	7 Antenen	
8 Greaves	(Tottenham)	8 Vonlanthen	
9 Hitchens	(Inter Milan)	9 Eschmann	
10 Haynes*	(Fulham)	10 Allemann	
11 Charlton	(Man Utd)	11 Durr	

Crowd: 30,000

England scorers: Flowers, Hitchens, Connelly

Comments: All the goals were scored in the first forty minutes. In spite of this pre-World Cup warm-up success, Bobby Robson and Peter Swan did not play for England again.

Peru 0 ENGLAND 4; in Lima; Sunday 20th May 1962

1 Bazan	1 Springett	(Sheffield Wed)	
2 Fleming	2 Armfield	(Blackpool)	
3 Donayre	3 Wilson	(Huddersfield Town)	
4 Guzman	4 Moore	(West Ham Utd)	
5 de la Vega	5 Norman	(Tottenham)	
6 Grimaldo	6 Flowers	(Wolves)	
7 Zegarra	7 Douglas	(Blackburn)	
8 Nieri	8 Greaves	(Tottenham)	
9 Lobaton	9 Hitchens	(Inter Milan)	
10 Zevallos	10 Haynes*	(Fulham)	
11 Montalvo	11 Charlton	(Man Utd)	

Crowd: 32,565

England scorers: Flowers (Pen), Greaves (3)

Comments: For the second successive match, all the goals came in the first forty minutes. Three goals in 15 minutes for Greaves made this a happy debut for Bobby Moore and Maurice Norman.

ENGLAND 1 Hungary 2; in Rancagua;
Thursday 31st May 1962 (World Cup finals)

1	Springett	(Sheffield Wed)	1	Grosics	
2	Armfield	(Blackpool)	2	Matrai	
3	Wilson	(Huddersfield Town)	3	Sarosi	
4	Moore	(West Ham Utd)	4	Solymosi	
5	Norman	(Tottenham)	5	Mesoely	
6	Flowers	(Wolves)	6	Sipos	
7	Douglas	(Blackburn)	7	Sandor	
8	Greaves	(Tottenham)	8	Rakosi	
9	Hitchens	(Inter Milan)	9	Albert	
10	Haynes*	(Fulham)	10	Tichy	
11	Charlton	(Man Utd)	11	Fenyvesi	

Crowd: 7,938

England scorer: Flowers (Pen)

Comments: A really puny crowd figure didn't do justice to this big occasion as England again succumbed to their bogey team. A Flowers penalty put England level but only for about a minute!

ENGLAND 3 Argentina 1; in Rancagua;
Saturday 2nd June 1962 (World Cup finals)

1	Springett	(Sheffield Wed)	1	Roma	
2	Armfield	(Blackpool)	2	Cap	
3	Wilson	(Huddersfield Town)	3	Paez	
4	Moore	(West Ham Utd)	4	Navarro	
5	Norman	(Tottenham)	5	Marzolini	
6	Flowers	(Wolves)	6	Sacchi	
7	Douglas	(Blackburn)	7	Rattin	
8	Greaves	(Tottenham)	8	Oleniak	
9	Peacock	(Middlesbrough)	9	Sosa	
10	Haynes*	(Fulham)	10	Sanfilippo	
11	Charlton	(Man Utd)	11	Belen	

Crowd: 9,794

England scorers: Flowers (Pen), Charlton, Greaves

Comments: For once England did themselves proud as they sailed into a 3–0 lead halfway through the second half. Alan Peacock made his debut in front of another tiny crowd.

ENGLAND 0 Bulgaria 0; in Rancagua;
Thursday 7th June 1962 (World Cup finals)

1 Springett	(Sheffield Wed)	1 Naidenov
2 Armfield	(Blackpool)	2 Dimov
3 Wilson	(Huddersfield Town)	3 Jetchev
4 Moore	(West Ham Utd)	4 Kostov
5 Norman	(Tottenham)	5 Dimitrov
6 Flowers	(Wolves)	6 Kovachev
7 Douglas	(Blackburn)	7 Kostov
8 Greaves	(Tottenham)	8 Velichkov
9 Peacock	(Middlesbrough)	9 Asparukhov
10 Haynes*	(Fulham)	10 Kolev
11 Charlton	(Man Utd)	11 Dermendjev

Crowd: 5,700

Comments: Not for the first time, England failed to overcome a less fancied team in a World Cup match. The attendance figure was appalling again. How did Chile ever get awarded a World Cup?!

ENGLAND 1 Brazil 3; in Vina del Mar;
Sunday 10th June 1962 (World Cup finals)

1 Springett	(Sheffield Wed)	1 Gilmar
2 Armfield	(Blackpool)	2 Santos
3 Wilson	(Huddersfield Town)	3 Oliveira
4 Moore	(West Ham Utd)	4 Zozimo
5 Norman	(Tottenham)	5 Santos
6 Flowers	(Wolves)	6 Zito
7 Douglas	(Blackburn)	7 Didi
8 Greaves	(Tottenham)	8 Garrincha
9 Hitchens	(Inter Milan)	9 Vava
10 Haynes*	(Fulham)	10 Amarildo
11 Charlton	(Man Utd)	11 Zagallo

Crowd: 17,736

England scorer: Hitchens

Comments: Hitchens scored in his last match as England drew level at half-time in this quarter-final. This was Johnny Haynes's last cap too as Brazil cruised towards a second World Cup.

ENGLAND 1 France 1; at Hillsborough;
Wednesday 3rd October 1962 (European Championship)

1	Springett	(Sheffield Wed)	1	Bernard
2	Armfield*	(Blackpool)	2	Wendling
3	Wilson	(Huddersfield Town)	3	Lerond
4	Moore	(West Ham Utd)	4	Chorda
5	Norman	(Tottenham)	5	Synakowski
6	Flowers	(Wolves)	6	Ferrier
7	Hellawell	(Birmingham City)	7	Robuschi
8	Crowe	(Wolves)	8	Bonnel
9	Charnley	(Blackpool)	9	Kopa
10	Greaves	(Tottenham)	10	Goujon
11	Hinton	(Wolves)	11	Sauvage

Crowd: 35,380

England scorer: Flowers (Pen)

Comments: Yet another Flowers penalty cancelled out France's half-time lead in the first leg of this contest. Ray Charnley, Chris Crowe, Mike Hellawell, and Alan Hinton were all new recruits.

Northern Ireland 1 ENGLAND 3; in Belfast;
Saturday 20th October 1962 (Home International)

1	Irvine	1	Springett	(Sheffield Wed)
2	Magill	2	Armfield*	(Blackpool)
3	Elder	3	Wilson	(Huddersfield Town)
4	Blanchflower	4	Moore	(West Ham Utd)
5	Neill	5	Labone	(Everton)
6	Nicholson	6	Flowers	(Wolves)
7	Humphries	7	Hellawell	(Birmingham City)
8	Barr	8	Hill	(Bolton Wanderers)
9	McMilliam	9	Peacock	(Middlesbrough)
10	McIlroy	10	Greaves	(Tottenham)
11	Bingham	11	O'Grady	(Huddersfield Town)

Crowd: 55,000

England scorers: Greaves, O'Grady (2)

Comments: After Hubert Barr equalised just after the hour mark, the debutant Michael O'Grady scored two quick goals to secure a win. First caps were also awarded to Fred Hill and Brian Labone.

ENGLAND 4 Wales 0; at Wembley;
Wednesday 21st November 1962 (Home International)

1 Springett	(Sheffield Wed)	1 Millington
2 Armfield*	(Blackpool)	2 Williams
3 Shaw	(Sheffield United)	3 Sear
4 Moore	(West Ham Utd)	4 Hennessey
5 Labone	(Everton)	5 Nurse
6 Flowers	(Wolves)	6 Lucas
7 Connelly	(Burnley)	7 Jones
8 Hill	(Bolton Wanderers)	8 Allchurch
9 Peacock	(Middlesbrough)	9 Leek
10 Greaves	(Tottenham)	10 Vernon
11 Tambling	(Chelsea)	11 Medwin

Crowd: 27,500

England scorers: Connelly, Peacock (2), Greaves

Comments: Two goals in each half were the perfect send-off in Walter Winterbottom's last match. It was also the last cap for Fred Hill and Graham Shaw, as well as the debut of Bobby Tambling.

France 5 ENGLAND 2; in Paris;
Wednesday 27th February 1963 (European Championship)

1 Bernard	1 Springett	(Sheffield Wed)
2 Wendling	2 Armfield*	(Blackpool)
3 Lerond	3 Henry	(Tottenham)
4 Rodzik	4 Moore	(West Ham Utd)
5 Synakowski	5 Labone	(Everton)
6 Herbin	6 Flowers	(Wolves)
7 Wisnieski	7 Connelly	(Burnley)
8 Bonnel	8 Tambling	(Chelsea)
9 Goujon	9 Smith	(Tottenham)
10 Douis	10 Greaves	(Tottenham)
11 Coussou	11 Charlton	(Man Utd)

Crowd: 23,986

England scorers: Smith, Tambling

Comments: England were 3–0 behind at half-time before briefly pulling the lead back to 3–2 in Alf Ramsey's first match as the manager. It was also the only cap for Ron Henry.

ENGLAND 1 Scotland 2; at Wembley;
Saturday 6th April 1963 (Home International)

1	Banks	(Leicester City)	1	Brown
2	Armfield*	(Blackpool)	2	Hamilton
3	Byrne	(Liverpool)	3	Caldow
4	Moore	(West Ham Utd)	4	Mackay
5	Norman	(Tottenham)	5	Ure
6	Flowers	(Wolves)	6	Baxter
7	Douglas	(Blackburn)	7	Henderson
8	Greaves	(Tottenham)	8	White
9	Smith	(Tottenham)	9	St John
10	Melia	(Liverpool)	10	Law
11	Charlton	(Man Utd)	11	Wilson

Crowd: 98,606

England scorer: Douglas

Comments: The 9–3 drubbing seemed to galvanise the Scots. This time, Jim Baxter scored twice past new goalie, Gordon Banks, to give the Scots an interval lead. Douglas replied with a late goal.

ENGLAND 1 Brazil 1; at Wembley;
Wednesday 8th May 1963

1	Banks	(Leicester City)	1	Gilmar
2	Armfield*	(Blackpool)	2	Lima
3	Wilson	(Huddersfield Town)	3	Eduardo
4	Milne	(Liverpool)	4	Dias
5	Norman	(Tottenham)	5	Rildo
6	Moore	(West Ham Utd)	6	Zequinha
7	Douglas	(Blackburn)	7	Mengalvio
8	Greaves	(Tottenham)	8	Dorval
9	Smith	(Tottenham)	9	Coutinho
10	Eastham	(Arsenal)	10	Amarildo
11	Charlton	(Man Utd)	11	Pepe

Crowd: 92,000

England scorer: Douglas

Comments: Bryan Douglas scored a late equaliser as George Eastham and Gordon Milne made their debuts. This was the first time in 25 years that nobody from Wolves was in the starting line-up!

Czechoslovakia 2 ENGLAND 4; in Bratislava;
Wednesday 29th May 1963

1 Schrojf	1 Banks	(Leicester City)
2 Lala	2 Shellito	(Chelsea)
3 Pluskal	3 Wilson	(Huddersfield Town)
4 Popluhar	4 Milne	(Liverpool)
5 Novak	5 Norman	(Tottenham)
6 Kvasnak	6 Moore*	(West Ham Utd)
7 Masopust	7 Paine	(Southampton)
8 Stibranyi	8 Greaves	(Tottenham)
9 Scherer	9 Smith	(Tottenham)
10 Kadraba	10 Eastham	(Arsenal)
11 Masek	11 Charlton	(Man Utd)

Crowd: 50,000

England scorers: Greaves (2), Smith, Charlton

Comments: Greaves scored the first and last goals and England scored the first two and last two goals as they returned to winning ways. Terry Paine and Ken Shellito won their first caps.

East Germany 1 ENGLAND 2; in Leipzig;
Sunday 2nd June 1963

1 Fritzsche	1 Banks	(Leicester City)
2 Urbanczyk	2 Armfield*	(Blackpool)
3 Heine	3 Wilson	(Huddersfield Town)
4 Krampe	4 Milne	(Liverpool)
5 Kaiser	5 Norman	(Tottenham)
6 Liebrecht	6 Moore	(West Ham Utd)
7 Nachtigall	7 Paine	(Southampton)
8 Frenzel	8 Hunt	(Liverpool)
9 Ducke	9 Smith	(Tottenham)
10 Noldner	10 Eastham	(Arsenal)
11 Ducke	11 Charlton	(Man Utd)

Crowd: 90,000

England scorers: Hunt, Charlton

Comments: Roger Hunt equalised on half-time and Bobby Charlton scored twenty minutes from time to secure this friendly win as England travelled behind the iron curtain.

Switzerland 1 ENGLAND 8; in Basle;
Wednesday 5th June 1963

1	Stettler	1	Springett	(Sheffield Wed)
2	Grobety	2	Armfield*	(Blackpool)
3	Schneiter	3	Wilson	(Huddersfield Town)
4	Tacchella	4	Kay	(Everton)
5	Weber	5	Moore	(West Ham Utd)
6	Leimgruber	6	Flowers	(Wolves)
7	Allemann	7	Douglas	(Blackburn)
8	Odermatt	8	Greaves	(Tottenham)
9	Kuhn	9	Byrne	(West Ham Utd)
10	Bertschi	10	Melia	(Liverpool)
11	Pottier	11	Charlton	(Man Utd)

Crowd: 47,588

England scorers: Charlton (3), Byrne (2), Douglas, Kay, Melia

Comments: The visitors scored five times in the second half. Tony Kay and James Melia both scored and never played again. This friendly win was also the last cap for Bryan Douglas.

Wales 0 ENGLAND 4; in Cardiff;
Saturday 12th October 1963 (Home International)

1	Hollins	1	Banks	(Leicester City)
2	Williams	2	Armfield*	(Blackpool)
3	Williams	3	Wilson	(Huddersfield Town)
4	Hennessey	4	Milne	(Liverpool)
5	England	5	Norman	(Tottenham)
6	Burton	6	Moore	(West Ham Utd)
7	Allchurch	7	Paine	(Southampton)
8	Vernon	8	Greaves	(Tottenham)
9	Davies	9	Smith	(Tottenham)
10	Allchurch	10	Eastham	(Arsenal)
11	Jones	11	Charlton	(Man Utd)

Crowd: 48,350;

England scorers: Smith (2), Greaves, Charlton

Comments: Bobby Smith gave the away team an early lead, but the final three goals did not arrive until the final quarter of this Home International match, as Wales got trounced in the end.

ENGLAND 2 Rest Of The World 1; at Wembley;
Wednesday 23rd October 1963

1 Banks	(Leicester City)	1 Yashin	(USSR)
2 Armfield*	(Blackpool)	2 Santos	(Brazil)
3 Wilson	(Huddersfield Town)	3 Popluhar	(Czechoslovakia)
4 Milne	(Liverpool)	4 Schnellinger	(West Germany)
5 Norman	(Tottenham)	5 Pluskal	(Czechoslovakia)
6 Moore	(West Ham Utd)	6 Masopust	(Czechoslovakia)
7 Paine	(Southampton)	7 Kopa	(France)
8 Greaves	(Tottenham)	8 Law	(Scotland)
9 Smith	(Tottenham)	9 di Stefano	(Spain)
10 Eastham	(Arsenal)	10 Eusebio	(Portugal)
11 Charlton	(Man Utd)	11 Gento	(Spain)

Crowd: 100,000

England scorers: Paine, Greaves

Comments: This epic gathering commemorated the centenary of the English FA. Denis Law equalised eight minutes from time only for Jimmy Greaves to snatch a last-minute winner.

ENGLAND 8 Northern Ireland 3; at Wembley;
Wednesday 20th November 1963 (Home International)

1 Banks	(Leicester City)	1 Gregg
2 Armfield*	(Blackpool)	2 Magill
3 Thomson	(Wolves)	3 Parke
4 Milne	(Liverpool)	4 Harvey
5 Norman	(Tottenham)	5 Neill
6 Moore	(West Ham Utd)	6 McCullough
7 Paine	(Southampton)	7 Bingham
8 Greaves	(Tottenham)	8 Humphries
9 Smith	(Tottenham)	9 Wilson
10 Eastham	(Arsenal)	10 Crossan
11 Charlton	(Man Utd)	11 Hill

Crowd: 55,000

England scorers: Paine (3), Greaves (4), Smith

Comments: Greaves and Paine went on the rampage, although England only led 4–3 at half-time. Gregg and Bingham never played for Northern Ireland again, while this was Bobby Smith's last cap.

Scotland 1 ENGLAND 0; in Glasgow;
Saturday 11th April 1964 (Home International)

1	Forsyth	1	Banks	(Leicester City)
2	Hamilton	2	Armfield*	(Blackpool)
3	Kennedy	3	Wilson	(Huddersfield Town)
4	Greig	4	Milne	(Liverpool)
5	McNeill	5	Norman	(Tottenham)
6	Baxter	6	Moore	(West Ham United)
7	Henderson	7	Paine	(Southampton)
8	White	8	Hunt	(Liverpool)
9	Gilzean	9	Byrne	(West Ham Utd)
10	Law	10	Eastham	(Arsenal)
11	Wilson	11	Charlton	(Man Utd)

Crowd: 133,245

Comments: Alan Gilzean scored with less than twenty minutes to go as Scotland recorded their third consecutive win over the 'Auld Enemy' in the Home International Championships.

ENGLAND 2 Uruguay 1; at Wembley;
Wednesday 6th May 1964

1	Banks	(Leicester City)	1	Taibo
2	Cohen	(Fulham)	2	Martinez
3	Wilson	(Huddersfield Town)	3	Diaz
4	Milne	(Liverpool)	4	Cincunegui
5	Norman	(Tottenham)	5	Pereira
6	Moore*	(West Ham Utd)	6	Pavoni
7	Paine	(Southampton)	7	Flores
8	Greaves	(Tottenham)	8	Cortes
9	Byrne	(West Ham Utd)	9	Spencer
10	Eastham	(Arsenal)	10	Gil
11	Charlton	(Man Utd)	11	Pintos

Crowd: 55,000

England scorer: Byrne (2)

Comments: Johnny Byrne scored either side of half-time to give England a 2–0 lead. Uruguay grabbed a late consolation. This was the first international appearance for George Cohen.

Portugal 3 ENGLAND 4; in Lisbon;
Sunday 17th May 1964

1 Pereira	1 Banks	(Leicester City)
2 Festa	2 Cohen	(Fulham)
3 de Figueiredo	3 Wilson	(Huddersfield Town)
4 Lucas	4 Milne	(Liverpool)
5 Cruz	5 Norman	(Tottenham)
6 Coluna	6 Moore*	(West Ham Utd)
7 Pinto	7 Thompson	(Liverpool)
8 Pinto	8 Greaves	(Tottenham)
9 Eusebio	9 Byrne	(West Ham Utd)
10 Torres	10 Eastham	(Arsenal)
11 Simoes	11 Charlton	(Man Utd)

Crowd: 40,000

England scorers: Byrne (3), Charlton

Comments: The home team led 1–0 and 3–2 but hat-trick hero Johnny Byrne hit a late winner for the visitors. This was the first international outing for Peter Thompson.

Republic Of Ireland 1 ENGLAND 3; in Dublin;
Sunday 24th May 1964

1 Dwyer	1 Waiters	(Blackpool)
2 Dunne	2 Cohen	(Fulham)
3 Cantwell	3 Wilson	(Huddersfield Town)
4 Strahan	4 Milne	(Liverpool)
5 Browne	5 Flowers	(Wolves)
6 McGrath	6 Moore*	(West Ham Utd)
7 Giles	7 Thompson	(Liverpool)
8 McEvoy	8 Greaves	(Tottenham)
9 Bailham	9 Byrne	(West Ham Utd)
10 Ambrose	10 Eastham	(Arsenal)
11 Haverty	11 Charlton	(Man Utd)

Crowd: 45,000

England scorers: Eastham, Byrne, Greaves

Comments: Although Strahan reduced the lead to 2–1 shortly before the interval, Jimmy Greaves sealed the win ten minutes after the break. Tony Waiters won his first cap in between the sticks.

USA 0 ENGLAND 10; in New York;
Wednesday 27th May 1964

1 Schwart	1 Banks	(Leicester City)	
2 Borodiak	2 Cohen	(Fulham)	
3 Racz	3 Thomson	(Wolves)	
4 Rick	4 Bailey	(Charlton Athletic)	
5 Garcia	5 Norman	(Tottenham)	
6 Horvath	6 Flowers*	(Wolves)	
7 Chyzowych	7 Paine	(Southampton)	
8 Noha	8 Hunt	(Liverpool)	
9 Mate	9 Pickering	(Everton)	
10 Murphy	10 Eastham	(Arsenal) replaced by Charlton	
11 Wild	11 Thompson	(Liverpool)	

Crowd: 5,062

England scorers: Hunt (4), Pickering (3), Paine (2), Charlton

Comments: Fred Pickering recorded a hat-trick on his debut. Roger Hunt went one better and scored four times. It was also the first cap for Mike Bailey in front of a tiny crowd.

Brazil 5 ENGLAND 1; in Rio de Janeiro;
Saturday 30th May 1964

1 Gilmar	1 Waiters	(Blackpool)
2 Torres	2 Cohen	(Fulham)
3 Brito	3 Wilson	(Huddersfield Town)
4 Dias	4 Milne	(Liverpool)
5 Camargo	5 Norman	(Tottenham)
6 Rildo	6 Moore*	(West Ham Utd)
7 Julinho	7 Thompson	(Liverpool)
8 Gerson	8 Greaves	(Tottenham)
9 Vava	9 Byrne	(West Ham Utd)
10 Pele	10 Eastham	(Arsenal)
11 Rinaldo	11 Charlton	(Man Utd)

Crowd: 77,000

England scorer: Greaves

Comments: Brazil only led 1–0 at half-time and Greaves equalised at the start of the second half. Thereafter the floodgates opened, with Pele scoring Brazil's third and decisive goal.

Portugal 1 ENGLAND 1; in Sao Paulo;
Thursday 4th June 1964

1	Americo	1	Banks	(Leicester City)
2	Festa	2	Thomson	(Wolves)
3	Baptista	3	Wilson	(Everton)
4	da Silva	4	Flowers	(Wolves)
5	Gomes	5	Norman	(Tottenham)
6	Medes	6	Moore*	(West Ham Utd)
7	Coluna	7	Paine	(Southampton)
8	Pinto	8	Greaves	(Tottenham)
9	Torres	9	Byrne	(West Ham Utd)
10	Eusebio	10	Hunt	(Liverpool)
11	Peres	11	Thompson	(Liverpool)

Crowd: 25,000

England scorer: Hunt

Comments: The Portuguese took the lead just before half-time but still they couldn't beat England. This was the second fixture in the Brazil Jubilee Tournament for Alf Ramsey's team.

Argentina 1 ENGLAND 0; in Rio de Janeiro;
Saturday 6th June 1964

1	Carrizo	1	Banks	(Leicester City)
2	Delgado	2	Thomson	(Wolves)
3	Vidal	3	Wilson	(Everton)
4	Simeone	4	Milne	(Liverpool)
5	Rattin	5	Norman	(Tottenham)
6	Vieytez	6	Moore*	(West Ham Utd)
7	Onega	7	Thompson	(Liverpool)
8	Rendo	8	Greaves	(Tottenham)
9	Prospitti	9	Byrne	(West Ham Utd)
10	Rojas	10	Eastham	(Arsenal)
11	Telch	11	Charlton	(Man Utd)

Crowd: 15,000

Comments: England bowed out of this Brazilian tournament without a win, though their cause was not helped by having to play Argentina two days after drawing with Portugal.

Northern Ireland 3 ENGLAND 4; in Belfast; Saturday 3rd October 1964 (Home International)

1 Jennings	1 Banks	(Leicester City)
2 Magill	2 Cohen	(Fulham)
3 Elder	3 Thomson	(Wolves)
4 Harvey	4 Milne	(Liverpool)
5 Neill	5 Norman	(Tottenham)
6 McCullough	6 Moore *	(West Ham Utd)
7 Best	7 Paine	(Southampton)
8 Crossan	8 Greaves	(Tottenham)
9 Wilson	9 Pickering	(Everton)
10 McLaughlin	10 Charlton	(Man Utd)
11 Braithwaite	11 Thompson	(Liverpool)

Crowd: 58,000

England scorers: Pickering, Greaves (3)

Comments: The away team led 4–0 inside 25 minutes only for the hosts to score three times inside 15 minutes early in the second half. England held on in the last quarter for another bizarre win.

ENGLAND 2 Belgium 2; at Wembley; Wednesday 21st October 1964

1 Waiters	(Blackpool)	1 Nicolay	
2 Cohen	(Fulham)	2 Heylens	
3 Thomson	(Wolves)	3 Viebiest	
4 Milne	(Liverpool)	4 Plaskie	
5 Norman	(Tottenham)	5 Cornelis	
6 Moore*	(West Ham Utd)	6 Sulon	
7 Thompson	(Liverpool)	7 Jurion	
8 Greaves	(Tottenham)	8 Vermeyen	
9 Pickering	(Everton)	9 van Himst	
10 Venables	(Chelsea)	10 Vandenberg	
11 Hinton	(Notts Forest)	11 Puis	

Crowd: 39,321

England scorers: Pickering, Hinton

Comments: England came from behind twice on the debut of Terry Venables. Pickering scored for the third consecutive match and never played again! Milne also never played for England again.

ENGLAND 2 Wales 1; at Wembley;
Wednesday 18th November 1964 (Home International)

1	Waiters	(Blackpool)	1	Millington
2	Cohen	(Fulham)	2	Williams
3	Thomson	(Wolves)	3	Williams
4	Bailey	(Charlton Athletic)	4	Hennessey
5	Flowers*	(Wolves)	5	England
6	Young	(Sheffield Wed)	6	Hole
7	Thompson	(Liverpool)	7	Rees
8	Hunt	(Liverpool)	8	Davies
9	Wignall	(Notts Forest)	9	Davies
10	Byrne	(West Ham Utd)	10	Allchurch
11	Hinton	(Notts Forest)	11	Jones

Crowd: 40,000

England scorer: Wignall (2)

Comments: Frank Wignall scored twice on his debut to give England a 2–0 lead. Cliff Jones scored a late reply. It was also the only cap for Gerry Young and the last outing for Bailey and Hinton.

Holland 1 ENGLAND 1; in Amsterdam;
Wednesday 9th December 1964

1	Graafland	1	Waiters	(Blackpool)
2	Flinkevleugel	2	Cohen	(Fulham)
3	Israel	3	Thomson	(Wolves)
4	Schrijvers	4	Mullery	(Tottenham)
5	Veldhoen	5	Norman	(Tottenham)
6	Muller	6	Flowers*	(Wolves)
7	Fransen	7	Thompson	(Liverpool)
8	Nuninga	8	Greaves	(Tottenham)
9	van Nee	9	Wignall	(Notts Forest)
10	Bouwmeester	10	Venables	(Chelsea)
11	Mouljin	11	Charlton	(Man Utd)

Crowd: 60,000

England scorer: Greaves

Comments: Greaves snatched a late equaliser on the debut of Alan Mullery. This would be the last appearance for no fewer than five players: Norman, Thomson, Venables, Waiters, and Wignall.

ENGLAND 2 Scotland 2; at Wembley;
Saturday 10th April 1965 (Home International)

1 Banks	(Leicester City)	1 Brown
2 Cohen	(Fulham)	2 Hamilton
3 Wilson	(Everton)	3 McCreadie
4 Stiles	(Man Utd)	4 Crerand
5 Charlton J	(Leeds United)	5 McNeill
6 Moore*	(West Ham Utd)	6 Greig
7 Thompson	(Liverpool)	7 Henderson
8 Greaves	(Tottenham)	8 Collins
9 Bridges	(Chelsea)	9 St John
10 Byrne	(West Ham Utd)	10 Law
11 Charlton R	(Man Utd)	11 Wilson

Crowd: 98,199

England scorers: Charlton R, Greaves

Comments: The hosts led 2–0 but Denis Law and then Ian St John pulled Scotland level. This was the final cap for Johnny Byrne but the debut for Barry Bridges, Jack Charlton and Nobby Stiles.

ENGLAND 1 Hungary 0; at Wembley;
Wednesday 5th May 1965

1 Banks	(Leicester City)	1 Gelei
2 Cohen	(Fulham)	2 Matrai
3 Wilson	(Everton)	3 Meszoly
4 Stiles	(Man Utd)	4 Sarosi
5 Charlton	(Leeds United)	5 Nagy
6 Moore*	(West Ham Utd)	6 Sipos
7 Paine	(Southampton)	7 Gorocs
8 Greaves	(Tottenham)	8 Varga
9 Bridges	(Chelsea)	9 Bene
10 Eastham	(Arsenal)	10 Nogradi
11 Connelly	(Man Utd)	11 Fenyvesi

Crowd: 70,000

England scorer: Greaves

Comments: Jimmy Greaves scored inside the first twenty minutes as England finally exorcised the demons of Hungary and the spirits of 1953 and 1954.

Yugoslavia 1 ENGLAND 1; in Belgrade; Sunday 9th May 1965

1	Soskic	1	Banks	(Leicester City)
2	Durkovic	2	Cohen	(Fulham)
3	Jusufi	3	Wilson	(Everton)
4	Becejac	4	Stiles	(Man Utd)
5	Vasovic	5	Charlton	(Leeds United)
6	Popovic	6	Moore*	(West Ham Utd)
7	Lukaric	7	Paine	(Southampton)
8	Zambata	8	Greaves	(Tottenham)
9	Kovacevic	9	Bridges	(Chelsea)
10	Galic	10	Ball	(Blackpool)
11	Dzajic	11	Connelly	(Man Utd)

Crowd: 60,000

England scorer: Bridges

Comments: Both goals came in the first quarter of this end of season friendly as Barry Bridges cancelled out the home team's earlier effort. Alan Ball won his first cap in this engagement.

West Germany 0 ENGLAND 1; in Nurenberg; Wednesday 12th May 1965

1	Tilkowski	1	Banks	(Leicester City)
2	Piontek	2	Cohen	(Fulham)
3	Hottges	3	Wilson	(Everton)
4	Schulz	4	Flowers	(Wolves)
5	Sieloff	5	Charlton	(Leeds United)
6	Lorenz	6	Moore*	(West Ham Utd)
7	Thielen	7	Paine	(Southampton)
8	Kramer	8	Ball	(Blackpool)
9	Rodekamp	9	Jones	(Sheffield United)
10	Overath	10	Eastham	(Arsenal)
11	Hornig	11	Temple	(Everton)

Crowd: 65,000

England scorer: Paine

Comments: Terry Paine scored just before half-time to decide this friendly match. Mick Jones made his debut while Derek Temple won his only cap against the formidable West Germans.

Sweden 1 ENGLAND 2; in Gotherburg;
Sunday 16th May 1965

1 Arvidsson	1 Banks	(Leicester City)
2 Rosander	2 Cohen	(Fulham)
3 Wing	3 Wilson	(Everton)
4 Mild	4 Stiles	(Man Utd)
5 Bergmark	5 Charlton	(Leeds United)
6 Nordqvist	6 Moore*	(West Ham Utd)
7 Eriksson	7 Paine	(Southampton)
8 Larsson	8 Ball	(Blackpool)
9 Simonsson	9 Jones	(Sheffield United)
10 Carlsson	10 Eastham	(Arsenal)
11 Persson	11 Connelly	(Man Utd)

Crowd: 18,975

England scorer: Ball, Connelly

Comments: Alan Ball gave the visitors an early lead and then John Connelly restored the lead twenty minutes from time as England continued to gather pre-World Cup momentum.

Wales 0 ENGLAND 0; in Cardiff;
Saturday 2nd October 1965 (Home International)

1 Sprake	1 Springett	(Sheffield Wed)
2 Rodrigues	2 Cohen	(Fulham)
3 Green	3 Wilson	(Everton)
4 Hennessey	4 Stiles	(Man Utd)
5 England	5 Charlton J	(Leeds United)
6 Hole	6 Moore*	(West Ham Utd)
7 Rees	7 Paine	(Southampton)
8 Vernon	8 Greaves	(Tottenham)
9 Davies	9 Peacock	(Leeds United)
10 Allchurch	10 Charlton R	(Man Utd)
11 Reece	11 Connelly	(Man Utd)

Crowd: 30,000

Comments: Ron Springett returned to the starting line-up and duly collected a clean sheet. However, Gary Sprake did likewise, so the away team had to settle for a share of the points.

ENGLAND 2 Austria 3; at Wembley;
Wednesday 20th October 1965

1	Springett	(Sheffield Wed)	1	Fraydl
2	Cohen	(Fulham)	2	Sara
3	Wilson	(Everton)	3	Frank
4	Stiles	(Man Utd)	4	Stamm
5	Charlton J	(Leeds United)	5	Ludescher
6	Moore*	(West Ham Utd)	6	Ullmann
7	Paine	(Southampton)	7	Hasil
8	Greaves	(Tottenham)	8	Fritsch
9	Bridges	(Chelsea)	9	Buzek
10	Charlton R	(Man Utd)	10	Flogel
11	Connelly	(Man Utd)	11	Macek

Crowd: 65,000

England scorers: Charlton R, Connelly

Comments: England led twice thanks to two Red Devils, but Fritsch scored twice in the last twenty minutes to inflict a defeat. This was the last international appearance for Barry Bridges.

ENGLAND 2 Northern Ireland 1; at Wembley;
Wednesday 10th November 1965 (Home International)

1	Banks	(Leicester City)	1	Jennings
2	Cohen	(Fulham)	2	Magill
3	Wilson	(Everton)	3	Elder
4	Stiles	(Man Utd)	4	Harvey
5	Charlton J	(Leeds United)	5	Neill
6	Moore*	(West Ham Utd)	6	Nicholson
7	Thompson	(Liverpool)	7	McIlroy
8	Baker	(Arsenal)	8	Crossan
9	Peacock	(Leeds United)	9	Irvine
10	Charlton R	(Man Utd)	10	Dougan
11	Connelly	(Man Utd)	11	Best

Crowd: 70,000

England scorers: Baker, Peacock

Comments: Both teams were deadlocked at 1–1 at the interval. It took a goal from Alan Peacock twenty minutes from time to secure a win. The hero, Peacock, never played for England again.

Spain 0 ENGLAND 2; in Madrid;
Wednesday 8th December 1965

1	Iribar	1	Banks	(Leicester City)	
2	Reija	2	Cohen	(Fulham)	
3	Olivella	3	Wilson	(Everton)	
4	Sanchis	4	Stiles	(Man Utd)	
5	Glaria	5	Charlton J	(Leeds United)	
6	Zoco	6	Moore*	(West Ham Utd)	
7	Ufarte	7	Ball	(Blackpool)	
8	Adelardo	8	Hunt	(Liverpool)	
9	Ansola	9	Baker	(Arsenal) replaced by Hunter	
10	Martinez	10	Eastham	(Arsenal)	
11	Lapetra	11	Charlton R	(Man Utd)	

Crowd: 30,000

England scorers: Baker, Hunt

Comments: Joe Baker gave England an early lead and then had to be replaced by Norman Hunter who thus won his first cap. Roger Hunt increased the lead just short of the hour mark.

ENGLAND 1 Poland 1; at Goodison Park;
Wednesday 5th January 1966

1	Banks	(Leicester City)	1	Szeja	
2	Cohen	(Fulham)	2	Gmoch	
3	Wilson	(Everton)	3	Brejza	
4	Stiles	(Man Utd)	4	Oslizlo	
5	Charlton	(Leeds United)	5	Rewilak	
6	Moore*	(West Ham Utd)	6	Suski	
7	Ball	(Blackpool)	7	Schmidt	
8	Hunt	(Liverpool)	8	Wilim	
9	Baker	(Arsenal)	9	Galeczka	
10	Eastham	(Arsenal)	10	Sadek	
11	Harris	(Burnley)	11	Kowalik	

Crowd: 48,000

England scorer: Moore

Comments: The Poles took the lead shortly before half-time before the skipper scored his first England goal fifteen minutes from the end. This was the only appearance for Gordon Harris.

ENGLAND 1 West Germany 0; at Wembley;
Wednesday 23rd February 1966

1 Banks	(Leicester City)	1	Tilkowski
2 Cohen	(Fulham)	2	Lutz
3 Newton	(Blackburn) replaced by Wilson	3	Schulz
4 Moore*	(West Ham Utd)	4	Weber
5 Charlton J	(Leeds United)	5	Lorenz
6 Hunter	(Leeds United)	6	Beckenbauer
7 Ball	(Blackpool)	7	Szymaniak
8 Hunt	(Liverpool)	8	Kramer
9 Stiles	(Man Utd)	9	Held
10 Hurst	(West Ham Utd)	10	Netzer
11 Charlton R	(Man Utd)	11	Hornig

Crowd: 75,000

England scorer: Stiles

Comments: Nobby Stiles scored the only goal just before half-time. Geoff Hurst won his first cap, and the Germans would get acquainted with him again in July! Keith Newton also made his debut.

Scotland 3 ENGLAND 4; in Glasgow;
Saturday 2nd April 1966 (Home International)

1 Ferguson	1 Banks	(Leicester City)
2 Greig	2 Cohen	(Fulham)
3 Gemmell	3 Newton	(Blackburn)
4 Murdoch	4 Stiles	(Man Utd)
5 McKinnon	5 Charlton J	(Leeds United)
6 Baxter	6 Moore*	(West Ham Utd)
7 Johnstone	7 Ball	(Blackpool)
8 Law	8 Hunt	(Liverpool)
9 Wallace	9 Charlton R	(Man Utd)
10 Bremner	10 Hurst	(West Ham Utd)
11 Johnston	11 Connelly	(Man Utd)

Crowd: 123,052

England scorers: Hurst, Hunt (2), Charlton R

Comments: England were always in control, leading 2–0, 3–1, and 4–2. Willie Johnston's 2 second half goals were in vain. Only John Greig and Denis Law had played for Scotland in the same fixture a year ago.

ENGLAND 2 Yugoslavia 0; at Wembley; Wednesday 4th May 1966

1 Banks	(Leicester City)	1 Soskic
2 Armfield*	(Blackpool)	2 Cuzzi
3 Wilson	(Everton)	3 Jeftic
4 Peters	(West Ham Utd)	4 Becejac
5 Charlton J	(Leeds United)	5 Rasovic
6 Hunter	(Leeds United)	6 Vasovic
7 Paine	(Southampton)	7 Samardzic
8 Greaves	(Tottenham)	8 Melic
9 Charlton R	(Man Utd)	9 Musovic
10 Hurst	(West Ham Utd)	10 Skoblar
11 Tambling	(Chelsea)	11 Dzajic

Crowd: 55,000

England scorers: Greaves, Charlton R

Comments: Both goals were scored before the interval as England maintained their impressive pre-World Cup form. Martin Peters collected his first cap, while Bobby Tambling won his last one.

Finland 0 ENGLAND 3; in Helsinki; Sunday 26th June 1966

1 Halme	1 Banks	(Leicester City)
2 Makipaa	2 Armfield*	(Blackpool)
3 Aho	3 Wilson	(Everton)
4 Kautonen	4 Peters	(West Ham Utd)
5 Kanerva	5 Charlton J	(Leeds United)
6 Kilponen	6 Hunter	(Leeds United)
7 Kumpulampi	7 Callaghan	(Liverpool)
8 Makela	8 Hunt	(Liverpool)
9 Hyvarinen	9 Charlton R	(Man Utd)
10 Laine	10 Hurst	(West Ham Utd)
11 Hyttinen	11 Ball	(Blackpool)

Crowd: 12,899

England scorers: Peters, Hunt, Charlton J

Comments: Jack Charlton and Martin Peters scored their first England goals, while Ian Callaghan collected his first cap, and the captain Jimmy Armfield made his last appearance in this easy win.

Norway 1 ENGLAND 6; in Oslo;
Wednesday 29th June 1966

1 Andersen	1 Springett	(Sheffield Wed)
2 Johansen	2 Cohen	(Fulham)
3 Mathisen	3 Byrne	(Liverpool)
4 Pedersen	4 Stiles	(Man Utd)
5 Stakset	5 Flowers	(Wolves)
6 Thorsen	6 Moore*	(West Ham Utd)
7 Stavrum	7 Paine	(Southampton)
8 Nilsen	8 Greaves	(Tottenham)
9 Sunde	9 Charlton	(Man Utd)
10 Johansen	10 Hunt	(Liverpool)
11 Berg	11 Connelly	(Man Utd)

Crowd: 29,500

England scorers: Greaves (4), Connelly, Moore

Comments: Norway took a very early lead only to find themselves 5–1 in arrears at the interval. In spite of this goals bonanza, Gerry Byrne, Ron Flowers, and Ron Springett never won another cap.

Denmark 0 ENGLAND 2; in Copenhagen;
Sunday 3rd July 1966

1 Nielsen	1 Bonetti	(Chelsea)
2 Hansen	2 Cohen	(Fulham)
3 Hartwig	3 Wilson	(Everton)
4 Petersen	4 Stiles	(Man Utd)
5 Boel	5 Charlton	(Leeds United)
6 Moller	6 Moore*	(West Ham Utd)
7 Hansen	7 Ball	(Blackpool)
8 Olsen	8 Greaves	(Tottenham)
9 Enoksen	9 Hurst	(West Ham Utd)
10 Sondergaard	10 Eastham	(Arsenal)
11 le Fevre	11 Connelly	(Man Utd)

Crowd: 32,000

England scorers: Charlton, Eastham

Comments: The vistors scored a goal in each half. George Eastham sealed the win just after the hour mark, but never played for England again. Peter Bonetti kept a clean sheet on his debut.

Poland 0 ENGLAND 1; in Chorzow;
Tuesday 5th July 1966

1	Szeja	1	Banks	(Leicester City)
2	Strzalkowski	2	Cohen	(Fulham)
3	Brejza	3	Wilson	(Everton)
4	Anczok	4	Stiles	(Man Utd)
5	Winkler	5	Charlton J	(Leeds United)
6	Gmoch	6	Moore*	(West Ham Utd)
7	Suski	7	Ball	(Blackpool)
8	Galeczka	8	Greaves	(Tottenham)
9	Lubanski	9	Charlton R	(Man Utd)
10	Liberda	10	Hunt	(Liverpool)
11	Kowalik	11	Peters	(West Ham Utd)

Crowd: 93,000

England scorer: Hunt

Comments: Roger Hunt scored the only goal inside the first quarter of an hour. This looked very much like the team that Alf Ramsey would use for the imminent World Cup in England itself.

ENGLAND 0 Uruguay 0; at Wembley;
Monday 11th July 1966 (World Cup finals)

1	Banks	(Leicester City)	1	Mazurkiewicz
2	Cohen	(Fulham)	2	Troche
3	Wilson	(Everton)	3	Manicera
4	Stiles	(Man Utd)	4	Goncalvez
5	Charlton J	(Leeds United)	5	Caetano
6	Moore*	(West Ham Utd)	6	Cortes
7	Ball	(Blackpool)	7	Rocha
8	Greaves	(Tottenham)	8	Perez
9	Charlton R	(Man Utd)	9	Ubinas
10	Hunt	(Liverpool)	10	Viera
11	Connelly	(Man Utd)	11	Silva

Crowd: 87,148

Comments: Ironically, England began the World Cup finals by failing to score at Wembley for the first time since 1938. John Connelly (who replaced Martin Peters) never played for England again.

ENGLAND 2 Mexico 0; at Wembley;
Saturday 16th July 1966 (World Cup finals)

1 Banks	(Leicester City)	1	Calderon
2 Cohen	(Fulham)	2	Pena
3 Wilson	(Everton)	3	Hernandez
4 Stiles	(Man Utd)	4	Chaires
5 Charlton J	(Leeds United)	5	del Muro
6 Moore*	(West Ham Utd)	6	Jauregui
7 Paine	(Southampton)	7	Diaz
8 Greaves	(Tottenham)	8	Nunez
9 Charlton R	(Man Utd)	9	Borja
10 Hunt	(Liverpool)	10	Reyes
11 Peters	(West Ham Utd)	11	Padilla

Crowd: 92,570

England scorers: Charlton R, Hunt

Comments: It took the home team more than half an hour to open their goals account, but this was a morale-boosting win. Terry Paine (who replaced Alan Ball) never played for England again.

ENGLAND 2 France 0; at Wembley;
Wednesday 20th July 1966 (World Cup finals)

1 Banks	(Leicester City)	1	Arbour
2 Cohen	(Fulham)	2	Djorkaeff
3 Wilson	(Everton)	3	Bosquier
4 Stiles	(Man Utd)	4	Herbert
5 Charlton J	(Leeds United)	5	Artelesa
6 Moore*	(West Ham Utd)	6	Budzinski
7 Callaghan	(Liverpool)	7	Herbin
8 Greaves	(Tottenham)	8	Bonnel
9 Charlton R	(Man Utd)	9	Gondet
10 Hunt	(Liverpool)	10	Simon
11 Peters	(West Ham Utd)	11	Hausser

Crowd: 98,270

England scorer: Hunt (2)

Comments: For the second match running England took the lead just before half time and again secured both points fifteen minutes from the end. Roger Hunt was the hero of the hour (and a half).

ENGLAND 1 Argentina 0; at Wembley;
Saturday 23rd July 1966 (World Cup finals)

1	Banks	(Leicester City)	1	Roma
2	Cohen	(Fulham)	2	Ferreiro
3	Wilson	(Everton)	3	Marzolini
4	Stiles	(Man Utd)	4	Rattin
5	Charlton J	(Leeds United)	5	Perfumo
6	Moore*	(West Ham Utd)	6	Albrecht
7	Ball	(Blackpool)	7	Onega
8	Hurst	(West Ham Utd)	8	Solari
9	Charlton R	(Man Utd)	9	Artime
10	Hunt	(Liverpool)	10	Gonzalez
11	Peters	(West Ham Utd)	11	Maz

Crowd: 90,584

England scorer: Hurst

Comments: Hurst replaced the injured Greaves and scored a late goal to clinch a quarter-final win. Rattin was sent off in an ill-tempered match. Alf Ramsey described the opposition as "animals".

ENGLAND 2 Portugal 1; at Wembley;
Tuesday 26th July 1966 (World Cup finals)

1	Banks	(Leicester City)	1	Pereira
2	Cohen	(Fulham)	2	Festa
3	Wilson	(Everton)	3	Baptista
4	Stiles	(Man Utd)	4	Carlos
5	Charlton J	(Leeds United)	5	Conceicao
6	Moore*	(West Ham Utd)	6	Graca
7	Ball	(Blackpool)	7	Coluna
8	Hurst	(West Ham Utd)	8	Augusto
9	Charlton R	(Man Utd)	9	Eusebio
10	Hunt	(Liverpool)	10	Torres
11	Peters	(West Ham Utd)	11	Simoes

Crowd: 94,493

England scorer: Charlton R (2)

Comments: Bobby Charlton appeared to have clinched victory ten minutes from time, but Eusebio then scored from a penalty. Nevertheless, England held on and were through to the final.

ENGLAND 4 West Germany 2 [After extra time]; at Wembley; Saturday 30th July 1966 (World Cup FINAL)

1	Banks	(Leicester City)	1	Tilkowski
2	Cohen	(Fulham)	2	Hottges
3	Wilson	(Everton)	3	Schnellinger
4	Stiles	(Man Utd)	4	Beckenbauer
5	Charlton J	(Leeds United)	5	Schulz
6	Moore*	(West Ham Utd)	6	Weber
7	Ball	(Blackpool)	7	Haller
8	Hurst	(West Ham Utd)	8	Held
9	Charlton R	(Man Utd)	9	Seeler
10	Hunt	(Liverpool)	10	Overath
11	Peters	(West Ham Utd)	11	Emmerich

Crowd: 96,924

England scorers: Peters, Hurst (3)

Comments: Martin Peters got booked and scored, but a late equaliser from Weber almost spoiled the party. In the event, this was the Hurst cup final, assisted by a 'helpful' Russian linesman.

Northern Ireland 0 ENGLAND 2; in Belfast; Thursday 20th October 1966 (European Championship)

1	Jennings	1	Banks	(Leicester City)
2	Parke	2	Cohen	(Fulham)
3	Elder	3	Wilson	(Everton)
4	Todd	4	Stiles	(Man Utd)
5	Harvey	5	Charlton J	(Leeds United)
6	McCullough	6	Moore*	(West Ham Utd)
7	Ferguson	7	Ball	(Everton)
8	Crossan	8	Hurst	(West Ham Utd)
9	Irvine	9	Charlton R	(Man Utd)
10	Dougan	10	Hunt	(Liverpool)
11	Best	11	Peters	(West Ham Utd)

Crowd: 48,600

England scorers: Hunt, Peters

Comments: The new world champions were unchanged for the fourth consecutive match and they secured both points in this Home International with a goal in each half.

ENGLAND 0 Czechoslovakia 0; at Wembley;
Wednesday 2nd November 1966

1	Banks	(Leicester City)	1	Viktor
2	Cohen	(Fulham)	2	Lala
3	Wilson	(Everton)	3	Horvath
4	Stiles	(Man Utd)	4	Popluhar
5	Charlton J	(Leeds United)	5	Taborsky
6	Moore*	(West Ham Utd)	6	Galeta
7	Ball	(Everton)	7	Kvasnak
8	Hurst	(West Ham Utd)	8	Vesely
9	Charlton R	(Man Utd)	9	Szikora
10	Hunt	(Liverpool)	10	Schmidt
11	Peters	(West Ham Utd)	11	Adamec

Crowd: 75,000

Comments: The home team may have failed to score, but Gordon Banks collected his eleventh clean sheet in his last fifteen appearances. The solid defence deserves much credit for this.

ENGLAND 5 Wales 1; at Wembley;
Wednesday 16th November 1966 (European Championship)

1	Banks	(Leicester City)	1	Millington
2	Cohen	(Fulham)	2	Green
3	Wilson	(Everton)	3	Williams
4	Stiles	(Man Utd)	4	Hennessey
5	Charlton J	(Leeds United)	5	England
6	Moore*	(West Ham Utd)	6	Hole
7	Ball	(Everton)	7	Rees
8	Hurst	(West Ham Utd)	8	Davies W
9	Charlton R	(Man Utd)	9	Davies R
10	Hunt	(Liverpool)	10	Jones
11	Peters	(West Ham Utd)	11	Jarvis

Crowd: 75,380

England scorers: Hurst (2), Charlton R, Hennessey (OG), Charlton J

Comments: Although Wyn Davies reduced the lead to 2–1, England scored again before half-time and twice after the interval. Both Charlton brothers contributed to the goals avalanche.

ENGLAND 2 Scotland 3; at Wembley;
Saturday 15th April 1967 (European Championship)

	England			Scotland
1	Banks	(Leicester City)	1	Simpson
2	Cohen	(Fulham)	2	Gemmell
3	Wilson	(Everton)	3	McCreadie
4	Stiles	(Man Utd)	4	Greig
5	Charlton J	(Leeds Utd)	5	McKinnon
6	Moore*	(West Ham Utd)	6	Baxter
7	Ball	(Everton)	7	Wallace
8	Greaves	(Tottenham)	8	Bremner
9	Charlton R	(Man Utd)	9	McCalliog
10	Hurst	(West Ham Utd)	10	Law
11	Peters	(West Ham Utd)	11	Lennox

Crowd: 99,063

England scorers: Charlton J, Hurst

Comments: Both teams scored twice in the last quarter of an hour, but the result flattered England. It was Bannockburn revisited, with goals from Denis Law, Bobby Lennox, and Jim McCalliog.

ENGLAND 2 Spain 0; at Wembley;
Wednesday 24th May 1967

	England			Spain
1	Bonetti	(Chelsea)	1	Iribar
2	Cohen	(Fulham)	2	Sanchis
3	Newton	(Blackburn)	3	Gallego
4	Mullery	(Tottenham)	4	Violeta
5	Labone	(Everton)	5	Reija
6	Moore*	(West Ham Utd)	6	Pirri
7	Ball	(Everton)	7	Glaria
8	Greaves	(Tottenham)	8	Garcia
9	Hurst	(West Ham Utd)	9	Amacio
10	Hunt	(Liverpool)	10	Grosso
11	Hollins	(Chelsea)	11	Gento

Crowd: 97,500

England scorers: Greaves, Hunt

Comments: Alf Ramsey made 6 changes from the Scotland humiliation and the home team responded with two goals in the last twenty minutes. John Hollins collected his only cap from this game.

Austria 0 ENGLAND 1; in Vienna;
Saturday 27th May 1967

1 Pichler	1 Bonetti	(Chelsea)
2 Wartusch	2 Newton	(Blackburn)
3 Glechner	3 Wilson	(Everton)
4 Sturmberger	4 Mullery	(Tottenham)
5 Fak	5 Labone	(Everton)
6 Eschlmuller	6 Moore*	(West Ham Utd)
7 Schmidt	7 Ball	(Everton)
8 Koglberger	8 Greaves	(Tottenham)
9 Wolny	9 Hurst	(West Ham Utd)
10 Siber	10 Hunt	(Liverpool)
11 Parits	11 Hunter	(Leeds United)

Crowd: 50,000

England scorer: Ball

Comments: Alan Ball scored the only goal halfway through the first half. Norman Hunter was yellow carded in this friendly. This fixture was the last England appearance for Jimmy Greaves.

Wales 0 ENGLAND 3; in Cardiff;
Saturday 21st October 1967 (European Championship)

1 Sprake	1 Banks	(Stoke City)
2 Rodrigues	2 Cohen	(Fulham)
3 Green	3 Newton	(Blackburn)
4 Hennessey	4 Mullery	(Tottenham)
5 England	5 Charlton J	(Leeds United)
6 Hole	6 Moore*	(West Ham Utd)
7 Rees	7 Ball	(Everton)
8 Durban	8 Hunt	(Liverpool)
9 Mahoney	9 Charlton R	(Man Utd)
10 Vernon	10 Hurst	(West Ham Utd)
11 Jones	11 Peters	(West Ham Utd)

Crowd: 44,960

England scorers: Peters, Charlton R, Ball (Pen)

Comments: Martin Peters gave the visitors the half-time lead, but the final two goals did not arrive until the last five minutes of this Home International and European Championship qualifier.

ENGLAND 2 Northern Ireland 0; at Wembley;
Wednesday 22nd November 1967 (European Championship)

1 Banks	(Stoke City)	1	Jennings
2 Cohen	(Fulham)	2	Parke
3 Wilson	(Everton)	3	Elder
4 Mullery	(Tottenham)	4	Stewart
5 Sadler	(Man Utd)	5	Neill
6 Moore*	(West Ham Utd)	6	Harvey
7 Thompson	(Liverpool)	7	Campbell
8 Hunt	(Liverpool)	8	Irvine
9 Charlton	(Man Utd)	9	Wilson
10 Hurst	(West Ham Utd)	10	Nicholson
11 Peters	(West Ham Utd)	11	Clements

Crowd: 85,000

England scorers: Hurst, Charlton

Comments: A goal in each half decided the outcome of this European Championship qualifier and Home International. David Sadler made his debut while George Cohen won his last cap.

ENGLAND 2 USSR 2; at Wembley;
Wednesday 6th December 1967

1 Banks	(Stoke City)	1	Pschenichnikov
2 Knowles	(Tottenham)	2	Anichkin
3 Wilson	(Everton)	3	Shesterneyov
4 Mullery	(Tottenham)	4	Khurtsilava
5 Sadler	(Man Utd)	5	Istomin
6 Moore*	(West Ham Utd)	6	Voronin
7 Ball	(Everton)	7	Chislenko
8 Hunt	(Liverpool)	8	Szabo
9 Charlton	(Man Utd)	9	Streltsov
10 Hurst	(West Ham Utd)	10	Banishevsky
11 Peters	(West Ham Utd)	11	Malofeyev

Crowd: 93,000

England scorers: Ball, Peters

Comments: Chislenko scored twice before half-time to convert a 1–0 deficit into a 2–1 lead. Martin Peters grabbed a second half equaliser on the debut of Cyril Knowles.

Scotland 1 ENGLAND 1; at Wembley;
Saturday 24th February 1968 (European Championship)

1	Simpson	1	Banks	(Stoke City)
2	Gemmell	2	Newton	(Blackburn)
3	McCreadie	3	Wilson	(Everton)
4	McNeill	4	Mullery	(Tottenham)
5	McKinnon	5	Labone	(Everton)
6	Greig	6	Moore*	(West Ham Utd)
7	Cooke	7	Ball	(Everton)
8	Bremner	8	Hurst	(West Ham Utd)
9	Hughes	9	Summerbee	(Man City)
10	Johnston	10	Charlton	(Man Utd)
11	Lennox	11	Peters	(West Ham Utd)

Crowd: 134,000

England scorer: Peters

Comments: Both goals came in the first half. England again failed to take 6 points from their 3 Home Internationals, but they had qualified for the knockout stages of the European Championship.

ENGLAND 1 Spain 0; at Wembley;
Wednesday 3rd April 1968 (European Championship)

1	Banks	(Stoke City)	1	Sadurni	
2	Knowles	(Tottenham)	2	Saez	
3	Wilson	(Everton)	3	Canos	
4	Mullery	(Tottenham)	4	Pirri	
5	Charlton J	(Leeds United)	5	Rodriguez	
6	Moore*	(West Ham Utd)	6	Zoco	
7	Ball	(Everton)	7	Polinario	
8	Hunt	(Liverpool)	8	Amancio	
9	Summerbee	(Man City)	9	Ansola	
10	Charlton R	(Man Utd)	10	Grosso	
11	Peters	(West Ham Utd)	11	Claramunt	

Crowd: 100,000

England scorer: Charlton R

Comments: Mike Summerbee made his home debut as Bobby Charlton scored inside the last ten minutes to give England a narrow first leg lead in this quarter-final encounter.

Spain 1 ENGLAND 2; in Madrid;
Wednesday 8th May 1968 (European Championship)

1	Sadurni	1	Bonetti	(Chelsea)
2	Saez	2	Newton	(Blackburn)
3	Rodriguez	3	Wilson	(Everton)
4	Canos	4	Mullery	(Tottenham)
5	Pirri	5	Labone	(Everton)
6	Zoco	6	Moore*	(West Ham Utd)
7	Climent	7	Ball	(Everton)
8	Amancio	8	Peters	(West Ham Utd)
9	Grosso	9	Charlton	(Man Utd)
10	Villaverde	10	Hunt	(Liverpool)
11	Gento	11	Hunter	(Leeds United)

Crowd: 120,000

England scorers: Peters, Hunter

Comments: After Amancio gave Spain the lead at the start of the second half, the visitors came from behind to reach the semi-finals which would be a one-off match in neutral Italy.

ENGLAND 3 Sweden 1; at Wembley;
Wednesday 22nd May 1968

1	Stepney	(Man Utd)	1	Larsson
2	Newton	(Blackburn)	2	Karlsson
3	Knowles	(Tottenham)	3	Kristensson
4	Mullery	(Tottenham)	4	Nordqvist
5	Labone	(Everton)	5	Grip
6	Moore*	(West Ham Utd)	6	Larsson
7	Bell	(Man City)	7	Eriksson
8	Peters	(West Ham Utd)	8	Ejderstedt
9	Charlton	(Man Utd) replaced by Hurst	9	Nordahl
10	Hunt	(Liverpool)	10	Persson
11	Hunter	(Leeds United)	11	Lindman

Crowd: 72,500

England scorers: Peters, Charlton, Hunt

Comments: England had wrapped this victory up with the first 2 goals just before half-time. Colin Bell and Alex Stepney collected first caps, a result of the successes of their 2 clubs that month.

West Germany 1 ENGLAND 0; in Hanover;
Saturday 1st June 1968

1 Wolter	1 Banks	(Stoke City)
2 Vogts	2 Newton	(Blackburn)
3 Lorenz	3 Knowles	(Tottenham)
4 Muller	4 Hunter	(Leeds United)
5 Fichtel	5 Labone	(Everton)
6 Weber	6 Moore*	(West Ham Utd)
7 Dorfel	7 Ball	(Everton)
8 Beckenbauer	8 Bell	(Man City)
9 Lohr	9 Summerbee	(Man City)
10 Overath	10 Hurst	(West Ham Utd)
11 Volkert	11 Thompson	(Liverpool)

Crowd: 79,124

Comments: Beckenbauer got a late winner as the Germans avenged their 1966 defeat. This was the last cap for Knowles. England fielded a Ball and a Bell, but it clearly didn't confuse too much!

ENGLAND 0 Yugoslavia 1; in Florence;
Wednesday 5th June 1968 (European Championship)

1 Banks	(Stoke City)	1 Pantelic
2 Newton	(Blackburn)	2 Fazlagic
3 Wilson	(Everton)	3 Damjanovic
4 Mullery	(Tottenham)	4 Pavlovic
5 Labone	(Everton)	5 Paunovic
6 Moore*	(West Ham Utd)	6 Holcer
7 Ball	(Everton)	7 Petkovic
8 Peters	(West Ham Utd)	8 Osim
9 Charlton	(Man Utd)	9 Musemic
10 Hunt	(Liverpool)	10 Trivic
11 Hunter	(Leeds United)	11 Dzajic

Crowd: 22,000

Comments: Alan Mullery became the first England player to be sent off when he received his red card 7 minutes from time. Shortly after, Dzajic scored and put Yugoslavia through to the final.

ENGLAND 2 USSR 0; in Rome;
Saturday 8th June 1968 (European Championship)

1	Banks	(Stoke City)		1	Pschenichnikov
2	Wright	(Everton)		2	Istomin
3	Wilson	(Everton)		3	Shesterneyov
4	Stiles	(Man Utd)		4	Kaplichny
5	Labone	(Everton)		5	Afonin
6	Moore*	(West Ham Utd)		6	Lenev
7	Hunter	(Leeds United)		7	Malofeyev
8	Hunt	(Liverpool)		8	Logofet
9	Charlton	(Man Utd)		9	Banishevsky
10	Hurst	(West Ham Utd)		10	Byshovets
11	Peters	(West Ham Utd)		11	Yevryuzhikhin

Crowd: 18,000

England scorers: Charlton, Hurst

Comments: A goal in each half gave England victory in this third place play-off. It was the debut for Tommy Wright and the final outing for his Everton team-mate and July 1966 hero Ray Wilson.

Romania 0 ENGLAND 0; in Bucharest;
Wednesday 6th November 1968

1	Gornea	1	Banks	(Stoke City)
2	Satmareanu	2	Wright	(Everton) replaced by McNab
3	Barbu	3	Newton	(Blackburn)
4	Dinu	4	Mullery	(Tottenham)
5	Mocanu	5	Labone	(Everton)
6	Gergely	6	Moore*	(West Ham Utd)
7	Petescu	7	Ball	(Everton)
8	Pircalab	8	Hunt	(Liverpool)
9	Dobrin	9	Charlton	(Man Utd)
10	Dumitrache	10	Hurst	(West Ham Utd)
11	Lucescu	11	Peters	(West Ham Utd)

Crowd: 60,000

Comments: Bob McNab came on after only ten minutes for the injured Wright to win his first cap. England and their hosts would become re-acquainted again the following January.

ENGLAND 1 Bulgaria 1; at Wembley; Wednesday 11th December 1968

1	West	(Everton)	1	Simeonov	
2	Newton	(Blackburn) replaced by Reaney	2	Peshev	
3	McNab	(Arsenal)	3	Dimitrov	
4	Mullery	(Tottenham)	4	Gaganelov	
5	Labone	(Everton)	5	Penev	
6	Moore*	(West Ham Utd)	6	Jechev	
7	Lee	(Man City)	7	Popov	
8	Bell	(Man City)	8	Bonev	
9	Charlton	(Man Utd)	9	Asparoukhov	
10	Hurst	(West Ham Utd)	10	Jakimov	
11	Peters	(West Ham Utd)	11	Dermendjiev	

Crowd: 80,000

England scorer: Hurst

Comments: Both goals were scored just before the interval. Francis Lee and Gordon West made their first starts for England while Paul Reaney won his first cap as a late substitute for Newton.

ENGLAND 1 Romania 1; at Wembley; Wednesday 15th January 1969

1	Banks	(Stoke City)	1	Gornea	
2	Wright	(Everton)	2	Satmareanu	
3	McNab	(Arsenal)	3	Boc	
4	Stiles	(Man Utd)	4	Dinu	
5	Charlton J	(Leeds United)	5	Deleanu	
6	Hunter	(Leeds United)	6	Anca	
7	Radford	(Arsenal)	7	Domide	
8	Hunt	(Liverpool)	8	Anweiller	
9	Charlton R*	(Man Utd)	9	Dembrovszki	
10	Hurst	(West Ham Utd)	10	Dumitrache	
11	Ball	(Everton)	11	Lucescu	

Crowd: 80,000

England scorer: Charlton J

Comments: Bobby Moore was absent for the first time since June 1966, so the other Bobby became captain. However, it was the other Charlton who scored! John Radford won his first cap.

ENGLAND 5 France 0; at Wembley;
Wednesday 12th March 1969

1	Banks	(Stoke City)		1	Carnus
2	Newton	(Blackburn)		2	Djorkaeff
3	Cooper	(Leeds United)		3	Bosquier
4	Mullery	(Tottenham)		4	Lemerre
5	Charlton	(Leeds United)		5	Rostagni
6	Moore*	(West Ham Utd)		6	Bonnel
7	Lee	(Man City)		7	Hernet
8	Bell	(Man City)		8	Simon
9	Hurst	(West Ham Utd)		9	Michel
10	Peters	(West Ham Utd)		10	Loubet
11	O'Grady	(Leeds United)		11	Bereta

Crowd: 85,000

England scorers: O'Grady, Hurst (3), Lee

Comments: A poor French team were well and truly despatched as Geoff Hurst netted his second Wembley hat-trick. Michael O'Grady opened the scoring and then never won another cap!

Northern Ireland 1 ENGLAND 3; in Belfast;
Saturday 3rd May 1969 (Home International)

1	Jennings		1	Banks	(Stoke City)
2	Craig		2	Newton	(Blackburn)
3	Harvey		3	McNab	(Arsenal)
4	Todd		4	Mullery	(Tottenham)
5	Neill		5	Labone	(Everton)
6	Nicholson		6	Moore*	(West Ham Utd)
7	McMordie		7	Ball	(Everton)
8	Jackson		8	Lee	(Man City)
9	Dougan		9	Charlton	(Man Utd)
10	Irvine		10	Hurst	(West Ham Utd)
11	Best		11	Peters	(West Ham Utd)

Crowd: 23,000

England scorers: Peters, Lee, Hurst (Pen)

Comments: Eric McMordie briefly put the hosts on level terms after they had trailed 1–0 at the interval, but two quick goals including Hurst's third penalty in two matches secured both points.

ENGLAND 2 Wales 1; at Wembley;
Wednesday 7th May 1969 (Home International)

1	West	(Everton)	1	Sprake	
2	Newton	(Blackburn)	2	Rodrigues	
3	Cooper	(Leeds United)	3	Thomas	
4	Moore*	(West Ham Utd)	4	Durban	
5	Charlton J	(Leeds United)	5	Powell	
6	Hunter	(Leeds United)	6	Burton	
7	Lee	(Man City)	7	Jones	
8	Bell	(Man City)	8	Davies R	
9	Astle	(West Brom)	9	Toshack	
10	Charlton R	(Man Utd)	10	Davies W	
11	Ball	(Everton)	11	Moore	

Crowd: 70,000

England scorers: Charlton R, Lee

Comments: Ron Davies gave the visitors the half-time lead before Franny Lee scored the winner which was his third goal in three consecutive matches. Jeff Astle won his first cap in this victory.

ENGLAND 4 Scotland 1; at Wembley;
Saturday 10th May 1969 (Home International)

1	Banks	(Stoke City)	1	Herriot	
2	Newton	(Blackburn)	2	McCreadie	
3	Cooper	(Leeds United)	3	Gemmell	
4	Mullery	(Tottenham)	4	Murdoch	
5	Labone	(Everton)	5	McNeill	
6	Moore*	(West Ham Utd)	6	Greig	
7	Lee	(Man City)	7	Henderson	
8	Ball	(Everton)	8	Bremner	
9	Charlton	(Man Utd)	9	Stein	
10	Hurst	(West Ham Utd)	10	Gilzean	
11	Peters	(West Ham Utd)	11	Gray	

Crowd: 89,902

England scorer: Peters (2), Hurst (2)

Comments: Although they conceded a goal in each match, England took six points in the Home International Championship for the first time since 1961. Peters and Hurst both scored in each half.

Mexico 0 ENGLAND 0; in Mexico City;
Sunday 1st June 1969

1	Castrejon	1 West	(Everton)
2	Alrjandrez	2 Newton	(Blackburn) replaced by Wright
3	Pena	3 Cooper	(Leeds United)
4	Nunez	4 Mullery	(Tottenham)
5	Perez	5 Labone	(Everton)
6	Gonzalez	6 Moore*	(West Ham Utd)
7	Munguia	7 Lee	(Man City)
8	Bustos	8 Ball	(Everton)
9	Borja	9 Charlton	(Man Utd)
10	Estrada	10 Hurst	(West Ham Utd)
11	Victorino	11 Peters	(West Ham Utd)

Crowd: 105,000

Comments: Gordon West kept a clean sheet as England acclimatised to Mexico and then never won another cap. When Wright replaced Newton, the visitors had 4 Everton players on the field.

Uruguay 1 ENGLAND 2; in Montevideo;
Sunday 8th June 1969

1	Maidana	1 Banks	(Stoke City)
2	Ancheta	2 Wright	(Everton)
3	Paz	3 Newton	(Blackburn)
4	Ubina	4 Mullery	(Tottenham)
5	Castillo	5 Labone	(Everton)
6	Mujica	6 Moore*	(West Ham Utd)
7	Cubilla	7 Lee	(Man City)
8	Cortes	8 Bell	(Man City)
9	Silva	9 Hurst	(West Ham Utd)
10	Matosas	10 Ball	(Everton)
11	Morales	11 Peters	(West Ham Utd)

Crowd: 54,161

England scorers: Lee, Hurst

Comments: The tourists conceded a very early lead to a Cubilla goal but soon Franny Lee equalised and then Geoff Hurst recorded the winner with ten minutes remaining in this friendly.

Brazil 2 ENGLAND 1; in Rio de Janeiro; Thursday 12th June 1969

1	Gilmar	1	Banks	(Stoke City)
2	Torres	2	Wright	(Everton)
3	Dias	3	Newton	(Blackburn)
4	Camargo	4	Mullery	(Tottenham)
5	Rildo	5	Labone	(Everton)
6	Clodoaldo	6	Moore*	(West Ham Utd)
7	Gerson	7	Ball	(Everton)
8	Jairzinho	8	Bell	(Man City)
9	Tostao	9	Charlton	(Man Utd)
10	Pele	10	Hurst	(West Ham Utd)
11	Edu	11	Peters	(West Ham Utd)

Crowd: 135,000

England scorer: Bell

Comments: Colin Bell gave the world champions an early lead. Gordon Banks then saved a penalty from Carlos Alberto, but Brazil scored two late goals to secure a win in front of a huge crowd.

Holland 0 ENGLAND 1; in Amsterdam; Wednesday 5th November 1969

1	Treijtel	1	Bonetti	(Chelsea)
2	Drost	2	Wright	(Everton)
3	Israel	3	Hughes	(Liverpool)
4	Eijkenbroek	4	Mullery	(Tottenham)
5	Krol	5	Charlton J	(Leeds United)
6	Rijnders	6	Moore*	(West Ham Utd)
7	Veenstra	7	Lee	(Man City) replaced by Thompson
8	Cruyff	8	Bell	(Man City)
9	Mulder	9	Charlton R	(Man Utd)
10	van Hanegem	10	Hurst	(West Ham Utd)
11	Rensenbrink	11	Peters	(West Ham Utd)

Crowd: 33,000

England scorer: Bell

Comments: Colin Bell grabbed a late winner against an emerging Dutch team that included a young Johan Cruyff. Meanwhile, a young Emlyn Hughes won his first cap in this friendly triumph.

ENGLAND 1 Portugal 0; at Wembley;
Wednesday 10th December 1969

1	Bonetti	(Chelsea)	1	Henrique
2	Reaney	(Leeds United)	2	Conceicao
3	Hughes	(Liverpool)	3	Cardoso
4	Mullery	(Tottenham)	4	Carlos
5	Charlton J	(Leeds United)	5	Murca
6	Moore*	(West Ham Utd)	6	da Conceicao
7	Lee	(Man City)	7	Guerreiro
8	Bell	(Man City) replaced by Peters	8	Graca
9	Astle	(West Brom)	9	Antonio
10	Charlton R	(Man Utd)	10	Simoes
11	Ball	(Everton)	11	Joao

Crowd: 100,000

England scorer: Charlton J

Comments: Portugal still had no answer for England as big Jack Charlton scored his sixth and final international goal and Peter Bonetti kept his fifth clean sheet in his sixth appearance in goal.

ENGLAND 0 Holland 0; at Wembley;
Wednesday 14th January 1970

1	Banks	(Stoke City)	1	van Beveren
2	Newton	(Everton)	2	Drost
3	Cooper	(Leeds United)	3	Israel
4	Peters	(West Ham Utd)	4	Eijkenbroek
5	Charlton J	(Leeds United)	5	Krol
6	Hunter	(Leeds United)	6	Rijnders
7	Lee	(Man City) replaced by Mullery	7	Jansen
8	Bell	(Man City)	8	van Dijk
9	Jones	(Leeds United) replaced by Hurst	9	Cruyff
10	Charlton R*	(Man Utd)	10	van Hanegem
11	Storey-Moore	(Notts Forest)	11	Kiezer

Crowd: 75,000.

Comments: Ian Storey-Moore won his only cap whilst Mick Jones made his last appearance in this goal-less draw. Jones was one of four Leeds United players in the starting line-up.

Belgium 1 ENGLAND 3; in Brussels;
Wednesday 25th February 1970

1 Trappeniers	1 Banks	(Stoke City)
2 Heylens	2 Wright	(Everton)
3 Dewalque	3 Cooper	(Leeds United)
4 Jeck	4 Moore*	(West Ham Utd)
5 Thissen	5 Labone	(Everton)
6 van Moer	6 Hughes	(Liverpool)
7 Dockx	7 Lee	(Man City)
8 Polleunis	8 Ball	(Everton)
9 Semmeling	9 Osgood	(Chelsea)
10 Devrindt	10 Hurst	(West Ham Utd)
11 van Himst	11 Peters	(West Ham Utd)

Crowd: 20,594

England scorers: Ball (2), Hurst

Comments: Alan Ball scored the first and last goals of this pre-World Cup friendly as England returned to winning ways. Chelsea legend Peter Osgood made his debut in this away win.

Wales 1 ENGLAND 1; in Cardiff;
Saturday 18th April 1970 (Home International)

1 Millington	1 Banks	(Stoke City)
2 Rodrigues	2 Wright	(Everton)
3 Thomas	3 Hughes	(Liverpool)
4 Hennessey	4 Mullery	(Tottenham)
5 England	5 Labone	(Everton)
6 Powell	6 Moore*	(West Ham Utd)
7 Kyzywicki	7 Lee	(Man City)
8 Durban	8 Ball	(Everton)
9 Davies	9 Charlton	(Man Utd)
10 Moore	10 Hurst	(West Ham Utd)
11 Rees	11 Peters	(West Ham Utd)

Crowd: 50,000

England scorer: Lee

Comments: Richard Kyzywicki opened the scoring just before half-time and England were grateful for a Franny Lee equaliser inside the last twenty minutes for a share of the points.

ENGLAND 3 Northern Ireland 1; at Wembley;
Tuesday 21st April 1970 (Home International)

1 Banks	(Stoke City)	1	Jennings
2 Newton	(Everton) replaced by Bell	2	Craig
3 Hughes	(Liverpool)	3	Clements
4 Mullery	(Tottenham)	4	O'Kane
5 Moore	(West Ham Utd)	5	Neill
6 Stiles	(Man Utd)	6	Nicholson
7 Coates	(Burnley)	7	McMordie
8 Kidd	(Man Utd)	8	Best
9 Charlton*	(Man Utd)	9	Dougan
10 Hurst	(West Ham Utd)	10	O'Doherty
11 Peters	(Tottenham)	11	Lutton

Crowd: 100,000

England scorers: Peters, Hurst, Charlton

Comments: Peters gave the hosts an early lead but a certain George Best equalised shortly after the break. However the last say went to Bobby Charlton who was winning his 100th cap.

Scotland 0 ENGLAND 0; in Glasgow;
Saturday 25th April 1970 (Home International)

1 Cruickshank	1	Banks	(Stoke City)	
2 Gemmell	2	Newton	(Everton)	
3 Dickson	3	Hughes	(Liverpool)	
4 Greig	4	Stiles	(Man Utd)	
5 McKinnon	5	Labone	(Everton)	
6 Moncur	6	Moore*	(West Ham Utd)	
7 Johnstone	7	Thompson	(Liverpool) replaced by Mullery	
8 Hay	8	Ball	(Everton)	
9 Stein	9	Astle	(West Brom)	
10 O'Hare	10	Hurst	(West Ham Utd)	
11 Carr	11	Peters	(Tottenham)	

Crowd: 137,438

Comments: Another huge Hampden Park crowd saw Gordon Banks achieve England's first shut-out against the Scots since 1959. This was also the last cap for Stiles and Thompson.

Colombia 0 ENGLAND 4; in Bogota;
Wednesday 20th May 1970

1	Quintana	1	Banks	(Stoke City)
2	Segovia	2	Newton	(Everton)
3	Segrera	3	Cooper	(Leeds United)
4	Lopez	4	Mullery	(Tottenham)
5	Hernandez	5	Labone	(Everton)
6	Canon	6	Moore*	(West Ham Utd)
7	Lopez	7	Lee	(Man City)
8	Garcia	8	Ball	(Everton)
9	Carlos Paz	9	Charlton	(Man Utd)
10	Brand	10	Hurst	(West Ham Utd)
11	Gallego	11	Peters	(Tottenham)

Crowd: 36,000

England scorers: Peters (2), Charlton, Ball

Comments: All 4 goals were recorded in the first half as the world champions warmed up for their defence of the Jules Rimet Trophy. This was Bobby Charlton's 49th and final England goal.

Ecuador 0 ENGLAND 2; in Quito;
Sunday 24th May 1970

1	Meija	1	Banks	(Stoke City)
2	Uteras	2	Newton	(Everton)
3	Campoverde	3	Cooper	(Leeds United)
4	Portilla	4	Mullery	(Tottenham)
5	Valencia	5	Labone	(Everton)
6	Bolanos	6	Moore*	(West Ham Utd)
7	Cardenas	7	Lee	(Man City) replaced by Kidd
8	Munoz	8	Ball	(Everton)
9	Penaherrera	9	Charlton	(Man Utd) replaced by Sadler
10	Carrera	10	Hurst	(West Ham Utd)
11	Larrea	11	Peters	(Tottenham)

Crowd: 29,706

England scorers: Lee, Kidd

Comments: Franny Lee scored inside five minutes and then in the second-half his replacement Brian Kidd scored within five minutes of coming on. Both substitutes were 'Red Devils'.

ENGLAND 1 Romania 0; in Guadalajara;
Tuesday 2nd June 1970 (World Cup finals)

1	Banks	(Stoke City)	1	Adamache	
2	Newton	(Everton) replaced by Wright	2	Satmareanu	
3	Cooper	(Leeds United)	3	Lupescu	
4	Mullery	(Tottenham)	4	Dinu	
5	Labone	(Everton)	5	Mocanu	
6	Moore*	(West Ham Utd)	6	Dumitru	
7	Lee	(Man City) replaced by Osgood	7	Nunweiller	
8	Ball	(Everton)	8	Dembrovszki	
9	Charlton	(Man Utd)	9	Tataru	
10	Hurst	(West Ham Utd)	10	Dumitrache	
11	Peters	(Tottenham)	11	Lucescu	

Crowd: 50,560

England scorer: Hurst

Comments: Geoff Hurst scored halfway through the second half as England began the World Cup finals with their fourth successive clean sheet.

ENGLAND 0 Brazil 1; in Guadalajara;
Sunday 7th June 1970 (World Cup finals)

1	Banks	(Stoke City)	1	Felix	
2	Wright	(Everton)	2	Torres	
3	Cooper	(Leeds United)	3	Brito	
4	Mullery	(Tottenham)	4	Piazza	
5	Labone	(Everton)	5	Everaldo	
6	Moore*	(West Ham Utd)	6	Clodoaldo	
7	Lee	(Man City) replaced by Bell	7	Cesar Caju	
8	Ball	(Everton)	8	Jairzinho	
9	Charlton	(Man Utd) replaced by Astle	9	Tostao	
10	Hurst	(West Ham Utd)	10	Pele	
11	Peters	(Tottenham)	11	Rivellino	

Crowd: 66,843

Comments: This was a clash between the teams that had won the last 3 world cups. Jairzinho scored just before the hour mark, but the game is remembered for 'that Banks save' from Pele.

ENGLAND 1 Czechoslovakia 0; in Guadalajara; Thursday 11th June 1970 (World Cup finals)

1 Banks	(Stoke City)	1 Viktor
2 Newton	(Everton)	2 Dobias
3 Cooper	(Leeds United)	3 Migas
4 Mullery	(Tottenham)	4 Hrivnak
5 Charlton J	(Leeds United)	5 Hagara
6 Moore*	(West Ham Utd)	6 Pollak
7 Bell	(Man City)	7 Kuna
8 Charlton R	(Man Utd) replaced by Ball	8 Vesely
9 Astle	(West Brom)	9 Petras
10 Clarke	(Leeds United) replaced by Osgood	10 Adamec
11 Peters	(Tottenham)	11 Jokl

Crowd: 49,292

England scorer: Clarke (Pen)

Comments: England squeezed into the quarter-finals when debutant Allan Clarke slotted home a penalty at the start of the second half. This was the last cap for Jeff Astle and Jack Charlton.

ENGLAND 2 West Germany 3 [After extra time]; in Leon; Sunday 14th June 1970 (World Cup finals)

1 Bonetti	(Chelsea)	1 Maier
2 Newton	(Everton)	2 Schnellinger
3 Cooper	(Leeds United)	3 Vogts
4 Mullery	(Tottenham)	4 Fichtel
5 Labone	(Everton)	5 Hottges
6 Moore*	(West Ham Utd)	6 Beckenbauer
7 Lee	(Man City)	7 Overath
8 Ball	(Everton)	8 Seeler
9 Charlton	(Man Utd) replaced by Bell	9 Libuda
10 Hurst	(West Ham Utd)	10 Muller
11 Peters	(Tottenham) replaced by Hunter	11 Lohr

Crowd: 32,000

England scorers: Mullery, Peters

Comments: Peters put England 2-0 ahead at the start of the second half, but then the ill-fated comeback took place. Bonetti, Charlton, Labone, and Newton never played for England again.

ENGLAND 3 East Germany 1; at Wembley;
Wednesday 25th November 1970

1 Shilton	(Leicester City)	1 Croy
2 Hughes	(Liverpool)	2 Rock
3 Cooper	(Leeds United)	3 Kurbjuweit
4 Mullery	(Tottenham)	4 Sammer
5 Sadler	(Man Utd)	5 Strempel
6 Moore*	(West Ham Utd)	6 Ganzera
7 Lee	(Man City)	7 Irmscher
8 Ball	(Everton)	8 Stein
9 Hurst	(West Ham Utd)	9 Kreische
10 Clarke	(Leeds United)	10 Ducke
11 Peters	(Tottenham)	11 Vogel

Crowd: 93,000

England scorers: Lee, Peters, Clarke

Comments: England led 2-0 and although Vogel pulled a goal back before half-time, the home team were able to win this time against German opposition! Peter Shilton made his debut.

Malta 0 ENGLAND 1; in Gzira;
Wednesday 3rd February 1971 (European Championship)

1 Mizzi	1 Banks	(Stoke City)
2 Grima	2 Reaney	(Leeds United)
3 Mallia	3 Hughes	(Liverpool)
4 Camilleri	4 Mullery*	(Tottenham)
5 Micallef	5 McFarland	(Derby County)
6 Darmanin	6 Hunter	(Leeds United)
7 Cocks	7 Ball	(Everton)
8 Vassallo	8 Chivers	(Tottenham)
9 Cini	9 Royle	(Everton)
10 Theobald	10 Harvey	(Everton)
11 Arpa	11 Peters	(Tottenham)

Crowd: 41,534

England scorer: Peters

Comments: Martin Peters was only one of four survivors from the previous match and he duly scored. This was the first cap for Chivers, McFarland, and Royle, and the only cap for Colin Harvey.

ENGLAND 3 Greece 0; at Wembley;
Wednesday 21st April 1971 (European Championship)

1	Banks	(Stoke City)	1	Christidis
2	Storey	(Arsenal)	2	Kaitatzis
3	Hughes	(Liverpool)	3	Spyridon
4	Mullery	(Tottenham)	4	Toskas
5	McFarland	(Derby County)	5	Kambas
6	Moore*	(West Ham Utd)	6	Stathopoulos
7	Lee	(Man City)	7	Synetopoulos
8	Ball	(Everton) replaced by Coates	8	Koudas
9	Chivers	(Tottenham)	9	Dedes
10	Hurst	(West Ham Utd)	10	Papaioannou
11	Peters	(Tottenham)	11	Kritkopoulos

Crowd: 55,123

England scorers: Chivers, Hurst, Lee

Comments: Martin Chivers gave the home team the interval lead which was then extended by Lee and Hurst after the break. Peter Storey won his first cap, replacing Paul Reaney at full-back.

ENGLAND 5 Malta 0; at Wembley;
Wednesday 12th May 1971 (European Championship)

1	Banks	(Stoke City)	1	Borg-Bonaci
2	Lawler	(Liverpool)	2	Pace
3	Cooper	(Leeds United)	3	Grima
4	Moore*	(West Ham Utd)	4	Camilleri
5	McFarland	(Derby County)	5	Darmanin
6	Hughes	(Liverpool)	6	Delia
7	Lee	(Man City)	7	Cocks
8	Coates	(Tottenham)	8	Vassallo
9	Chivers	(Tottenham)	9	Bonett
10	Clarke	(Leeds United)	10	Theobald
11	Peters	(Tottenham) replaced by Ball	11	Arpa

Crowd: 41,534

England scorers: Chivers (2), Lee, Clarke (Pen), Lawler

Comments: Martin Chivers scored at the beginning of each half while Chris Lawler rounded off the goals rout on his debut, in this European Championship qualifying group match.

Northern Ireland 0 ENGLAND 1; in Belfast;
Saturday 15th May 1971 (Home International)

1 Jennings	1 Banks	(Stoke City)
2 Rice	2 Madeley	(Leeds United)
3 Nelson	3 Cooper	(Leeds United)
4 O'Kane	4 Storey	(Arsenal)
5 Hunter	5 McFarland	(Derby County)
6 Nicholson	6 Moore*	(West Ham Utd)
7 Hamilton	7 Lee	(Man City)
8 McMordie	8 Ball	(Everton)
9 Dougan	9 Chivers	(Tottenham)
10 Clements	10 Clarke	(Leeds United)
11 Best	11 Peters	(Tottenham)

Crowd: 33,000

England scorer: Clarke

Comments: Allan Clarke grabbed a late winner on the debut of his club team-mate Paul Madeley. George Best actually headed the ball out of Banks's hands and scored, but the goal was ruled out.

ENGLAND 0 Wales 0; at Wembley;
Wednesday 19th May 1971 (Home International)

1 Shilton	(Leicester City)	1 Sprake
2 Lawler	(Liverpool)	2 Rodrigues
3 Cooper	(Leeds United)	3 Thomas
4 Smith	(Liverpool)	4 James
5 Lloyd	(Notts Forest)	5 Roberts
6 Hughes	(Liverpool)	6 Yorath
7 Lee	(Man City)	7 Phillips
8 Brown	(West Brom) replaced by Clarke	8 Durban
9 Hurst	(West Ham Utd)	9 Davies
10 Coates	(Tottenham)	10 Toshack
11 Peters*	(Tottenham)	11 Reece

Crowd: 70,000

Comments: Larry Lloyd made his debut while Tony Brown and Tommy Smith won their only caps. England had now kept five successive clean sheets. Even Gary Sprake achieved a shut-out too.

ENGLAND 3 Scotland 1; at Wembley;
Saturday 22nd May 1971 (Home International)

1 Banks	(Stoke City)	1 Clark
2 Lawler	(Liverpool)	2 Greig
3 Cooper	(Leeds United)	3 Brogan
4 Storey	(Arsenal)	4 Bremner
5 McFarland	(Derby County)	5 McLintock
6 Moore*	(West Ham Utd)	6 Moncur
7 Lee	(Man City) replaced by Clarke	7 Johnstone
8 Ball	(Everton)	8 Robb
9 Chivers	(Tottenham)	9 Curran
10 Hurst	(West Ham Utd)	10 Green
11 Peters	(Tottenham)	11 Cormack

Crowd: 91,469

England scorers: Chivers (2), Peters

Comments: Although Hugh Curran quickly cancelled out Chivers's first goal, England were 3–1 ahead by half-time. The home team had earned themselves another British Championship success.

Switzerland 2 ENGLAND 3; in Basle;
Wednesday 13th October 1971 (European Championship)

1 Kunz	1 Banks	(Stoke City)
2 Chapuisat	2 Lawler	(Liverpool)
3 Ramseier	3 Cooper	(Leeds United)
4 Weibel	4 Mullery	(Tottenham)
5 Stierli	5 McFarland	(Derby County)
6 Odermatt	6 Moore*	(West Ham Utd)
7 Kuhn	7 Lee	(Man City)
8 Blattler	8 Madeley	(Leeds United)
9 Balmer	9 Chivers	(Tottenham)
10 Kunzli	10 Hurst	(West Ham Utd) replaced by Radford
11 Jeandupeux	11 Peters	(Tottenham)

Crowd: 47,877

England scorers: Hurst, Chivers, Weibel (OG)

Comments: Hurst scored inside the first minute but England were held 2–2 at half-time. It took a late own goal to decide the match. Lawler, Mullery, and Radford all made their last appearances.

ENGLAND 1 Switzerland 1; at Wembley;
Tuesday 9th November 1971 (European Championship)

1	Shilton	(Leicester City)	1	Prosperi
2	Madeley	(Leeds United)	2	Ramseier
3	Cooper	(Leeds United)	3	Chapuisat
4	Storey	(Arsenal)	4	Perroud
5	Lloyd	(Notts Forest)	5	Stierli
6	Moore*	(West Ham Utd)	6	Odermatt
7	Summerbee	(Man City) replaced by Marsh	7	Blattler
8	Ball	(Everton)	8	Kuhn
9	Hurst	(West Ham Utd)	9	Balmer
10	Lee	(Man City) replaced by Chivers	10	Kunzli
11	Hughes	(Liverpool)	11	Jeandupeux

Crowd: 90,423

England scorer: Summerbee

Comments: Both goals came in the first half, with Mike Summerbee giving the hosts an early lead. Rodney Marsh of Queen's Park Rangers came on as a late substitute to win his first England cap.

Greece 0 ENGLAND 2; in Athens;
Tuesday 30th November 1971 (European Championship)

1	Christidis	1	Banks	(Stoke City)
2	Pallas	2	Madeley	(Leeds United)
3	Kapsis	3	Hughes	(Liverpool)
4	Aggelis	4	Bell	(Man City)
5	Eleftherakis	5	McFarland	(Derby County)
6	Domazos	6	Moore*	(West Ham Utd)
7	Nikolaidis	7	Lee	(Man City)
8	Koudas	8	Ball	(Everton)
9	Antoniadis	9	Chivers	(Tottenham)
10	Papaioannou	10	Hurst	(West Ham Utd)
11	Dedes	11	Peters	(Tottenham)

Crowd: 34,014

England scorers: Hurst, Chivers

Comments: Both goals came after the interval. Hurst opened the scoring with his 24th and final England goal and Chivers scored in the last minute against a team managed by Mr. Billy Bingham.

ENGLAND 1 West Germany 3; at Wembley;
Saturday 29th April 1972 (European Championship)

1	Banks	(Stoke City)	1	Maier
2	Madeley	(Leeds United)	2	Hottges
3	Hughes	(Liverpool)	3	Breitner
4	Bell	(Man City)	4	Schwarzenbeck
5	Moore*	(West Ham Utd)	5	Beckenbauer
6	Hunter	(Leeds United)	6	Wimmer
7	Lee	(Man City)	7	Grabowski
8	Ball	(Everton)	8	Hoeness
9	Chivers	(Tottenham)	9	Muller
10	Hurst	(West Ham Utd) replaced by Marsh	10	Netzer
11	Peters	(Tottenham)	11	Held

Crowd: 100,000

England scorer: Lee

Comments: Franny Lee cancelled out the Germans' interval lead but never played for England again. This was also the last outing for Hurst as the away team grabbed 2 late goals for a 1st leg win.

West Germany 0 ENGLAND 0; in Berlin;
Saturday 13th May 1972 (European Championship)

1	Maier	1	Banks	(Stoke City)
2	Hottges	2	Madeley	(Leeds United)
3	Breitner	3	Hughes	(Liverpool)
4	Schwarzenbeck	4	Storey	(Arsenal)
5	Beckenbauer	5	McFarland	(Derby County)
6	Wimmer	6	Moore*	(West Ham Utd)
7	Hoeness	7	Ball	(Arsenal)
8	Flore	8	Bell	(Man City)
9	Muller	9	Chivers	(Tottenham)
10	Netzer	10	Marsh	(Man City) replaced by Summerbee
11	Held	11	Hunter	(Leeds United) replaced by Peters

Crowd: 76,200.

Comments: A failure to score ensured that England were again evicted at the quarter-finals stage of a major tournament by the West Germans as they were defeated 3–1 on aggregate.

Wales 0 ENGLAND 3; in Cardiff;
Saturday 20th May 1972 (Home International)

1 Sprake	1 Banks	(Stoke City)
2 Rodrigues	2 Madeley	(Leeds United)
3 Thomas	3 Hughes	(Liverpool)
4 Hennessey	4 Storey	(Arsenal)
5 England	5 McFarland	(Derby County)
6 Roberts	6 Moore*	(West Ham Utd)
7 Yorath	7 Summerbee	(Man City)
8 Davies	8 Bell	(Man City)
9 Davies	9 MacDonald	(Newcastle Utd)
10 Toshack	10 Marsh	(Man City)
11 Durban	11 Hunter	(Leeds United)

Crowd: 34,000

England scorers: Hughes, Marsh, Bell

Comments: Emlyn Hughes scored his only England goal to secure a 1–0 half-time lead. Rodney Marsh also scored his only England goal while Malcolm MacDonald made his debut appearance.

ENGLAND 0 Northern Ireland 1; at Wembley;
Tuesday 23rd May 1972 (Home International)

1 Shilton	(Leicester City)	1 Jennings
2 Todd	(Derby County)	2 Rice
3 Hughes	(Liverpool)	3 Nelson
4 Storey	(Arsenal)	4 O'Kane
5 Lloyd	(Notts Forest)	5 Hamilton
6 Hunter	(Leeds United)	6 Nicholson
7 Summerbee	(Man City)	7 McMordie
8 Bell*	(Man City)	8 Hunter
9 MacDonald	(Newcastle Utd) replaced by Chivers	9 Dougan
10 Marsh	(Man City)	10 Clements
11 Currie	(Sheffield United) replaced by Peters	11 Neill

Crowd: 64,000

Comments: Even in the absence of the increasingly wayward George Best, Northern Ireland still managed to achieve their first Wembley win since 1957 thanks to a first-half goal from Terry Neill.

Scotland 0 ENGLAND 1; in Glasgow;
Saturday 27th May 1972 (Home International)

1 Clark	1 Banks	(Stoke City)
2 Brownlie	2 Madeley	(Leeds United)
3 Donachie	3 Hughes	(Liverpool)
4 Bremner	4 Storey	(Arsenal)
5 McNeill	5 McFarland	(Derby County)
6 Moncur	6 Moore*	(West Ham Utd)
7 Lorimer	7 Ball	(Arsenal)
8 Hartford	8 Bell	(Man City)
9 Macari	9 Chivers	(Tottenham)
10 Law	10 Marsh	(Man City) replaced by MacDonald
11 Gemmill	11 Hunter	(Leeds United)

Crowd: 119,325

England scorer: Ball

Comments: Alan Ball scored the only goal in the first half to take the heat off Sir Alf Ramsey after 2 recent home defeats. Another July 1966 hero, Gordon Banks, made his last appearance in goal.

ENGLAND 1 Yugoslavia 1; at Wembley;
Wednesday 11th October 1972

1 Shilton	(Leicester City)	1 Maric	
2 Lampard	(West Ham Utd)	2 Krivokuca	
3 Mills	(Ipswich Town)	3 Stepanovic	
4 Storey	(Arsenal)	4 Pavlovic	
5 Blockley	(Arsenal)	5 Katalinski	
6 Moore*	(West Ham Utd)	6 Paunovic	
7 Royle	(Everton)	7 Petkovic	
8 Bell	(Man City)	8 Vladic	
9 Channon	(Southampton)	9 Bajevic	
10 Marsh	(Man City)	10 Acimovic	
11 Ball	(Arsenal)	11 Dzajic	

Crowd: 50,000

England scorer: Royle

Comments: Joe Royle scored just before half-time while the away team equalised soon after the break. First caps were awarded to Jeff Blockley, Mick Channon, Frank Lampard, and Mick Mills.

Wales 0 ENGLAND 1; in Cardiff;
Wednesday 15th November 1972 (World Cup qualifier)

1	Sprake	1	Clemence	(Liverpool)
2	Rodrigues	2	Storey	(Arsenal)
3	Thomas	3	Hughes	(Liverpool)
4	Hennessey	4	Hunter	(Leeds United)
5	England	5	McFarland	(Derby County)
6	Hockey	6	Moore*	(West Ham Utd)
7	Phillips	7	Keegan	(Liverpool)
8	Mahoney	8	Chivers	(Tottenham)
9	Davies	9	Marsh	(Man City)
10	Toshack	10	Bell	(Man City)
11	James	11	Ball	(Arsenal)

Crowd: 36,000

England scorer: Bell

Comments: Colin Bell scored just before the interval as England got their World Cup qualifying campaign off to a good start. Liverpool's Ray Clemence and Kevin Keegan made their debuts.

ENGLAND 1 Wales 1; at Wembley;
Sunday 21st January 1973 (World Cup qualifier)

1	Clemence	(Liverpool)	1	Sprake
2	Storey	(Arsenal)	2	Rodrigues
3	Hughes	(Liverpool)	3	Thomas
4	Hunter	(Leeds United)	4	Hockey
5	McFarland	(Derby County)	5	England
6	Moore*	(West Ham Utd)	6	Roberts
7	Keegan	(Liverpool)	7	Evans
8	Bell	(Man City)	8	Mahoney
9	Chivers	(Tottenham)	9	Toshack
10	Marsh	(Man City)	10	Yorath
11	Ball	(Arsenal)	11	James

Crowd: 62,000

England scorer: Hunter

Comments: John Toshack gave Wales the lead midway through the first half, but Hunter equalised before the break. England had dropped a precious point and Marsh never won another cap.

Scotland 0 ENGLAND 5; in Glasgow; Wednesday 14th February 1973

1	Clark	1	Shilton	(Leicester City)
2	Forsyth	2	Storey	(Arsenal)
3	Donachie	3	Hughes	(Liverpool)
4	Bremner	4	Bell	(Man City)
5	Colquhoun	5	Madeley	(Leeds United)
6	Buchan	6	Moore*	(West Ham Utd)
7	Lorimer	7	Ball	(Arsenal)
8	Dalglish	8	Channon	(Southampton)
9	Macari	9	Chivers	(Tottenham)
10	Graham	10	Clarke	(Leeds United)
11	Morgan	11	Peters	(Tottenham)

Crowd: 48,470

England scorers: Lorimer (OG), Clarke (2), Channon, Chivers

Comments: England marked the centenary of the Scottish FA with 3 goals in the first 15 minutes and two more near the end. Bobby Moore also collected his one hundredth cap after this 'friendly'.

Northern Ireland 1 ENGLAND 2; at Goodison Park; Saturday 12th May 1973 (Home International)

1	Jennings	1	Shilton	(Leicester City)
2	Rice	2	Storey	(Arsenal)
3	Craig	3	Nish	(Derby County)
4	Neill	4	Bell	(Man City)
5	Hunter	5	McFarland	(Derby County)
6	Clements	6	Moore*	(West Ham Utd)
7	Hamilton	7	Ball	(Arsenal)
8	Jackson	8	Channon	(Southampton)
9	Morgan	9	Chivers	(Tottenham)
10	O'Neill	10	Richards	(Wolves)
11	Anderson	11	Peters	(Tottenham)

Crowd: 29,865

England scorer: Chivers (2)

Comments: Northern Ireland were obliged to play this 'home fixture' at Everton due to troubles in Ulster. Martin Chivers inflicted more trouble, giving England an early lead and then a late winner.

ENGLAND 3 Wales 0; at Wembley;
Tuesday 15th May 1973 (Home International)

1 Shilton	(Leicester City)	1 Phillips
2 Storey	(Arsenal)	2 Rodrigues
3 Hughes	(Liverpool)	3 Thomas
4 Bell	(Man City)	4 Hockey
5 McFarland	(Derby County)	5 England
6 Moore*	(West Ham Utd)	6 Roberts
7 Ball	(Arsenal)	7 James
8 Channon	(Southampton)	8 Mahoney
9 Chivers	(Tottenham)	9 Toshack
10 Clarke	(Leeds United)	10 Page
11 Peters	(Tottenham)	11 Evans

Crowd: 38,000

England scorers: Chivers, Channon, Peters

Comments: The home team collected both points from this Home International clash courtesy of first-half goals from Chivers and then Channon followed by a second-half effort from Peters.

ENGLAND 1 Scotland 0; at Wembley;
Saturday 19th May 1973 (Home International)

1 Shilton	(Leicester City)	1 Hunter
2 Storey	(Arsenal)	2 Jardine
3 Hughes	(Liverpool)	3 McGrain
4 Bell	(Man City)	4 Bremner
5 McFarland	(Derby County)	5 Holton
6 Moore*	(West Ham Utd)	6 Johnstone
7 Ball	(Arsenal)	7 Morgan
8 Channon	(Southampton)	8 Macari
9 Chivers	(Tottenham)	9 Dalglish
10 Clarke	(Leeds United)	10 Hay
11 Peters	(Tottenham)	11 Lorimer

Crowd: 95,950

England scorer: Peters

Comments: England earned all 6 points in the Home International Championship due to a second-half goal from Peters. Scotland would have the last laugh when they qualified for the World Cup.

Czechoslovakia 1 ENGLAND 1; in Prague; Sunday 27th May 1973

1	Viktor	1	Shilton	(Leicester City)
2	Pivarnik	2	Madeley	(Leeds United)
3	Zlocha	3	Storey	(Arsenal)
4	Samek	4	Bell	(Man City)
5	Hagara	5	McFarland	(Derby County)
6	Bicovsky	6	Moore*	(West Ham Utd)
7	Kuna	7	Ball	(Arsenal)
8	Novak	8	Channon	(Southampton)
9	Vesely	9	Chivers	(Tottenham)
10	Nehoda	10	Clarke	(Leeds United)
11	Stratlil	11	Peters	(Tottenham)

Crowd: 25,000

England scorer: Clarke

Comments: Allan Clarke rescued a draw for the away team with a very late equaliser after Novak had scored first. England were warming up for their crucial World Cup engagement in Poland.

Poland 2 ENGLAND 0; in Chorzow; Wednesday 6th June 1973 (World Cup qualifier)

1	Tomaszewski	1	Shilton	(Leicester City)
2	Rzesny	2	Madeley	(Leeds United)
3	Bulzacki	3	Hughes	(Liverpool)
4	Gorgon	4	Storey	(Arsenal)
5	Musial	5	McFarland	(Derby County)
6	Kraska	6	Moore*	(West Ham Utd)
7	Cmikiewicz	7	Ball	(Arsenal)
8	Deyna	8	Bell	(Man City)
9	Banas	9	Chivers	(Tottenham)
10	Lubanski	10	Clarke	(Leeds United)
11	Gadocha	11	Peters	(Tottenham)

Crowd: 105,000

Comments: Alan Ball was sent off fifteen minutes from the end for fighting, by which time the visitors were already two goals in arrears. England's World Cup hopes were now left on a knife edge.

USSR 1 ENGLAND 2; in Moscow;
Sunday 10th June 1973

1 Rudakov	1 Shilton	(Leicester City)
2 Olshenski	2 Madeley	(Leeds United)
3 Khurtzilava	3 Hughes	(Liverpool)
4 Lovchev	4 Storey	(Arsenal)
5 Kaplichni	5 McFarland	(Derby County)
6 Kuznetsov	6 Moore*	(West Ham Utd)
7 Muntian	7 Currie	(Sheffield United)
8 Papaev	8 Channon	(Southampton) replaced by Summerbee
9 Andreasyan	9 Chivers	(Tottenham)
10 Onischenko	10 Clarke	(Leeds United) replaced by MacDonald
11 Blokhin	11 Peters	(Tottenham) replaced by Hunter

Crowd: 75,000

England scorers: Chivers, Khurtzilava (OG)

Comments: Morale was restored after Chivers gave England an early lead, which was doubled in the second half, thanks to an own goal. Mike Summerbee won his last cap in this friendly triumph.

Italy 2 ENGLAND 0; in Turin;
Thursday 14th June 1973

1 Zoff	1 Shilton	(Leicester City)
2 Sabadini	2 Madeley	(Leeds United)
3 Facchetti	3 Hughes	(Liverpool)
4 Benetti	4 Storey	(Arsenal)
5 Morini	5 McFarland	(Derby County)
6 Burgnich	6 Moore*	(West Ham Utd)
7 Mazzola	7 Currie	(Sheffield United)
8 Capello	8 Channon	(Southampton)
9 Anastasi	9 Chivers	(Tottenham)
10 Rivera	10 Clarke	(Leeds United)
11 Pulici	11 Peters	(Tottenham)

Crowd: 44,941

Comments: A certain Fabio Capello added a second half goal to Italy's 1-0 interval lead as Italy marked the 75th anniversary of their football federation. This was Peter Storey's last England match.

ENGLAND 7 Austria 0; at Wembley;
Wednesday 26th September 1973

1 Shilton	(Leicester City)	1 Koncilia
2 Madeley	(Leeds United)	2 Sara
3 Hughes	(Liverpool)	3 Schmidradner
4 Bell	(Man City)	4 Krieger
5 McFarland	(Derby County)	5 Eigenstiller
6 Hunter	(Leeds United)	6 Hattenburger
7 Currie	(Sheffield United)	7 Starek
8 Channon	(Southampton)	8 Ettmayer
9 Chivers	(Tottenham)	9 Kreuz
10 Clarke	(Leeds United)	10 Krankl
11 Peters*	(Tottenham)	11 Jara

Crowd: 48,000

England scorers: Channon (2), Clarke (2), Chivers, Currie, Bell

Comments: Austria were hardly pushovers, so this goals rampage was a big boost ahead of the decisive World Cup qualifier. England ought to have saved 1 of these goals for the Poland match!

ENGLAND 1 Poland 1; at Wembley;
Wednesday 17th October 1973 (World Cup qualifier)

1 Shilton	(Leicester City)	1 Tomaszewski
2 Madeley	(Leeds United)	2 Szymanowski
3 Hughes	(Liverpool)	3 Gorgon
4 Bell	(Man City)	4 Musial
5 McFarland	(Derby County)	5 Bulzacki
6 Hunter	(Leeds United)	6 Kasperczak
7 Currie	(Sheffield United)	7 Lato
8 Channon	(Southampton)	8 Cmikiewicz
9 Chivers	(Tottenham) replaced by Hector	9 Deyna
10 Clarke	(Leeds United)	10 Domarski
11 Peters*	(Tottenham)	11 Gadocha

Crowd: 100,000

England scorer: Clarke (Pen)

Comments: Tomaszewski, dubbed a "clown" by Brian Clough defied England, and the home team were thus denied a place at the World Cup finals. Kevin Hector of Derby County made his debut.

ENGLAND 0 Italy 1; at Wembley;
Wednesday 14th November 1973

1	Shilton	(Leicester City)	1	Zoff
2	Madeley	(Leeds United)	2	Sabadini
3	Hughes	(Liverpool)	3	Facchetti
4	Bell	(Man City)	4	Benetti
5	McFarland	(Derby County)	5	Belugi
6	Moore*	(West Ham Utd)	6	Burgnich
7	Currie	(Sheffield United)	7	Causio
8	Channon	(Southampton)	8	Capello
9	Osgood	(Chelsea)	9	Chinaglia
10	Clarke	(Leeds United) replaced by Hector	10	Rivera
11	Peters	(Tottenham)	11	Riva

Crowd: 88,000

Comments: Capello again scored the only goal, in the dying minutes, as Dino Zoff kept another clean sheet versus England. Kevin Hector, Bobby Moore, and Peter Osgood never played again.

Portugal 0 ENGLAND 0; in Lisbon;
Wednesday 3rd April 1974

1	Damas	1	Parkes	(QPR)
2	Rebelo	2	Nish	(Derby County)
3	Coelho	3	Pejic	(Stoke City)
4	Mendes	4	Dobson	(Burnley)
5	Correia	5	Watson	(Sunderland)
6	Machado	6	Todd	(Derby County)
7	Arnaldo	7	Bowles	(QPR)
8	Oliveira	8	Channon	(Southampton)
9	Jordao	9	MacDonald	(Newcastle Utd) replaced by Ball
10	Baptista	10	Brooking	(West Ham Utd)
11	Joao	11	Peters*	(Tottenham)

Crowd: 20,000

Comments: England were clearly in transition as first caps were handed to Dobson, Pejic, Todd, Watson, and the QPR duo of Bowles and Parkes. This was Sir Alf Ramsey's last match as the boss.

Wales 0 ENGLAND 2; in Cardiff;
Saturday 11th May 1974 (Home International)

1	Phillips	1	Shilton	(Leicester City)
2	Roberts	2	Nish	(Derby County)
3	Thomas	3	Pejic	(Stoke City)
4	Mahoney	4	Hughes*	(Liverpool)
5	Roberts	5	McFarland	(Derby County)
6	Roberts	6	Todd	(Derby County)
7	Reece	7	Keegan	(Liverpool)
8	Villars	8	Bell	(Man City)
9	Davies	9	Channon	(Southampton)
10	Yorath	10	Weller	(Leicester City)
11	James	11	Bowles	(QPR)

Crowd: 25,734

England scorers: Bowles, Keegan

Comments: Joe Mercer took charge of England for the duration of the summer fixtures, and Keith Weller made his debut. Stan Bowles and then Kevin Keegan scored either side of half-time.

ENGLAND 1 Northern Ireland 0; at Wembley;
Wednesday 15th May 1974 (Home International)

1	Shilton	(Leicester City)	1	Jennings
2	Nish	(Derby County)	2	Rice
3	Pejic	(Stoke City)	3	Nelson
4	Hughes*	(Liverpool)	4	O'Kane
5	McFarland	(Derby County) replaced by Hunter	5	Hunter
6	Todd	(Derby County)	6	Clements
7	Keegan	(Liverpool)	7	Hamilton
8	Weller	(Leicester City)	8	Cassidy
9	Channon	(Southampton)	9	Morgan
10	Bell	(Manchester City)	10	McIlroy
11	Bowles	(QPR) replaced by Worthington	11	McGrath

Crowd: 45,500

England scorer: Weller

Comments: This was a proud match for Leicester City. Keith Weller scored a late goal, Peter Shilton kept a clean sheet, and Frank Worthington became the third Leicester player on the pitch.

Scotland 2 ENGLAND 0; in Glasgow;
Saturday 18th May 1974 (Home International)

1	Harvey	1 Shilton	(Leicester City)
2	Jardine	2 Nish	(Derby County)
3	McGrain	3 Pejic	(Stoke City)
4	Bremner	4 Hughes*	(Liverpool)
5	Holton	5 Hunter	(Leeds United) replaced by Watson
6	Blackley	6 Todd	(Derby County)
7	Johnstone	7 Channon	(Southampton)
8	Lorimer	8 Bell	(Man City)
9	Jordan	9 Worthington	(Leicester City) replaced byMcDonald
10	Dalglish	10 Weller	(Leicester City)
11	Hay	11 Peters	(Tottenham)

Crowd: 94,487

Comments: Joe Jordan gave the Scots an early lead which was doubled on the half hour mark by a ColinTodd own goal. Nish, Pejic, and the great Martin Peters never played for England again.

ENGLAND 2 Argentina 2; at Wembley;
Wednesday 22nd May 1974

1	Shilton	(Leicester City)	1	Carnevali
2	Hughes*	(Liverpool)	2	Glaria
3	Lindsay	(Liverpool)	3	Perfumo
4	Todd	(Derby County)	4	Bargas
5	Watson	(Sunderland)	5	Sa
6	Bell	(Man City)	6	Telch
7	Keegan	(Liverpool)	7	Balbuena
8	Channon	(Southampton)	8	Brindisi
9	Worthington	(Leicester City)	9	Kempes
10	Weller	(Leicester City)	10	Squeo
11	Brooking	(West Ham Utd)	11	Ayala

Crowd: 68,000

England scorers: Channon, Worthington

Comments: Channon scored on half-time and then Worthington made it 2-0 but the great Mario Kempes then scored twice. Alec Lindsay made his debut while Keith Weller won his last cap.

East Germany 1 ENGLAND 1; in Leipzig; Wednesday 29th May 1974

1 Croy	1 Clemence	(Liverpool)
2 Bransch	2 Hughes*	(Liverpool)
3 Fritsche	3 Lindsay	(Liverpool)
4 Weise	4 Todd	(Derby County)
5 Waetzlich	5 Watson	(Sunderland)
6 Irmscher	6 Dobson	(Burnley)
7 Sparwasser	7 Keegan	(Liverpool)
8 Pommerencke	8 Channon	(Southampton)
9 Lowe	9 Worthington	(Leicester City)
10 Streich	10 Bell	(Man City)
11 Vogel	11 Brooking	(West Ham Utd)

Crowd: 100,000

England scorer: Channon

Comments: Micky Channon scored the equaliser as poor England gave East Germany some pre-World Cup practice. Four players from the emerging giant of Liverpool were in the starting line-up.

Bulgaria 0 ENGLAND 1; in Sofia; Saturday 1st June 1974

1 Goranov	1 Clemence	(Liverpool)
2 Zafirov	2 Hughes*	(Liverpool)
3 Velichkov	3 Todd	(Derby County)
4 Kolev	4 Watson	(Sunderland)
5 Penev	5 Lindsay	(Liverpool)
6 Jechev	6 Dobson	(Burnley)
7 Voinov	7 Brooking	(West Ham Utd)
8 Bonev	8 Bell	(Man City)
9 Michailov	9 Keegan	(Liverpool)
10 Borisov	10 Channon	(Southampton)
11 Denev	11 Worthington	(Leicester City)

Crowd: 60,000

England scorer: Worthington

Comments: Frank Worthington scored the second of his two England goals just before half-time as England again helped another country to prepare for the World Cup finals in West Germany.

Yugoslavia 2 ENGLAND 2; in Belgrade;
Wednesday 5th June 1974

1	Maric	1 Clemence	(Liverpool)
2	Buljan	2 Hughes*	(Liverpool)
3	Krivokuca	3 Lindsay	(Liverpool)
4	Muznic	4 Todd	(Derby County)
5	Katalinski	5 Watson	(Sunderland)
6	Bogicevic	6 Dobson	(Burnley)
7	Petkovic	7 Keegan	(Liverpool)
8	Oblak	8 Channon	(Southampton)
9	Surjak	9 Worthington	(Leicester City) replaced by McDonald
10	Acimovic	10 Bell	(Man City)
11	Dzajic	11 Brooking	(West Ham Utd)

Crowd: 90,000

England scorers: Channon, Keegan

Comments: Channon gave England an early lead and then Keegan scored a late equaliser against a team that was in Scotland's group in the forthcoming World Cup. This was Mercer's last game.

ENGLAND 3 Czechoslovakia 0; at Wembley;
Wednesday 30th October 1974 (European Championship)

1 Clemence	(Liverpool)	1	Viktor
2 Madeley	(Leeds United)	2	Pivarnik
3 Hughes*	(Liverpool)	3	Ondrus
4 Dobson	(Everton) replaced by Brooking	4	Capkovic
5 Watson	(Sunderland)	5	Varadin
6 Hunter	(Leeds United)	6	Gajdusek
7 Bell	(Man City)	7	Bicovsky
8 Francis	(QPR)	8	Pekarik
9 Worthington	(Leicester City) replaced by Thomas	9	Svehlik
10 Channon	(Southampton)	10	Masny
11 Keegan	(Liverpool)	11	Stratlil

Crowd: 83,858

England scorers: Channon, Bell (2)

Comments: Channon and Bell left it late to give new boss Don Revie a winning start. Queen's Park Rangers supplied 2 new players: Gerry Francis and David Thomas. This was Hunter's last cap.

ENGLAND 0 Portugal 0; at Wembley;
Wednesday 20th November 1974 (European Championship)

1	Clemence	(Liverpool)		1	Damas
2	Madeley	(Leeds United)		2	Correia
3	Watson	(Sunderland)		3	Coehlo
4	Hughes*	(Liverpool)		4	Alhinho
5	Cooper	(Leeds United) replaced by Todd		5	Osvaldinho
6	Brooking	(West Ham Utd)		6	Teixeira
7	Francis	(QPR)		7	Alves
8	Bell	(Man City)		8	Martins
9	Thomas	(QPR)		9	Nene
10	Channon	(Southampton)		10	Machado
11	Clarke	(Leeds United) replaced by Worthington	11	Chico

Crowd: 84,461

Comments: Ray Clemence and his defence achieved their third shut-out in 4 matches as these two teams drew 0-0 for the second time in 1974. This was the last match for Cooper and Worthington.

ENGLAND 2 West Germany 0; at Wembley;
Wednesday 12th March 1975

1	Clemence	(Liverpool)		1	Maier
2	Whitworth	(Leicester City)		2	Vogts
3	Gillard	(QPR)		3	Beckenbauer
4	Bell	(Man City)		4	Korbel
5	Watson	(Sunderland)		5	Bonhof
6	Todd	(Derby County)		6	Cullmann
7	Ball*	(Arsenal)		7	Flore
8	MacDonald	(Newcastle Utd)		8	Wimmer
9	Channon	(Southampton)		9	Ritschel
10	Hudson	(Stoke City)		10	Kostedde
11	Keegan	(Liverpool)		11	Holzenbein

Crowd: 100,000

England scorers: Bell, MacDonald

Comments: Having failed to qualify for last year's World Cup finals, England then proceeded to beat the eventual winners. Ian Gillard, Alan Hudson, and Steve Whitworth all won their first caps.

ENGLAND 5 Cyprus 0; at Wembley;
Wednesday 16th April 1975 (European Championship)

1	Shilton	(Stoke City)	1	Alkiviades	
2	Madeley	(Leeds United)	2	Kovis	
3	Watson	(Sunderland)	3	Kizas	
4	Todd	(Derby County)	4	Pantziaras	
5	Beattie	(Ipswich Town)	5	Koureas	
6	Bell	(Man City)	6	Savva	
7	Ball*	(Arsenal)	7	Theodorou	
8	Hudson	(Stoke City)	8	Stefanis	
9	Channon	(Southampton) replaced by Thomas	9	Markou	
10	MacDonald	(Newcastle Utd)	10	Charalambous	
11	Keegan	(Liverpool)	11	Stylianou	

Crowd: 68,245

England scorer: MacDonald (5)

Comments: Having failed to score in his first 7 caps, 'Supermac' MacDonald netted 6 times in 2 games and then didn't score in his final 5 outings. He was the first Magpie to score since the 1950s.

Cyprus 0 ENGLAND 1; in Limassol;
Sunday 11th May 1975 (European Championship)

1	Constantinou	1	Clemence	(Liverpool)	
2	Kovis	2	Whitworth	(Leicester City)	
3	Kizas	3	Beattie	(Ipswich Town) replaced by Hughes	
4	Stylianou	4	Watson	(Sunderland)	
5	Pantziaras	5	Todd	(Derby County)	
6	Stefanis	6	Bell	(Man City)	
7	Constantinou	7	Thomas	(QPR)	
8	Miamiliotis	8	Ball*	(Arsenal)	
9	Savva	9	Channon	(Southampton)	
10	Charalambous	10	MacDonald	(Newcastle Utd)	
11	Kalogiros	11	Keegan	(Liverpool) replaced by Tueart	

Crowd: 68,245

England scorer: Keegan

Comments: Kevin Keegan gave the away team an early lead, but an expected goals avalanche against the 'no-hopers' of Cyprus did not materialise. Dennis Tueart came on to win his first cap.

Northern Ireland o ENGLAND o; in Belfast;
Saturday 17th May 1975 (Home International)

1	Jennings	1	Clemence	(Liverpool)
2	Rice	2	Whitworth	(Leicester City)
3	O'Kane	3	Hughes	(Liverpool)
4	Nicholl	4	Bell	(Man City)
5	Hunter	5	Watson	(Sunderland)
6	Clements	6	Todd	(Derby County)
7	Hamilton	7	Ball*	(Arsenal)
8	O'Neill	8	Viljoen	(Ipswich Town)
9	Spence	9	McDonald	(Newcastle Utd) replaced by Channon
10	McIlroy	10	Keegan	(Liverpool)
11	Jackson	11	Tueart	(Man City)

Crowd: 36,500

Comments: This was Ray Clemence's sixth clean sheet in seven internationals and England's sixth successive shut-out. Even the great Pat Jennings managed a rare clean sheet against England.

ENGLAND 2 Wales 2; at Wembley;
Wednesday 21st May 1975 (Home International)

1	Clemence	(Liverpool)	1	Davies
2	Whitworth	(Leicester City)	2	Page
3	Gillard	(QPR)	3	Thomas
4	Francis	(QPR)	4	Mahoney
5	Watson	(Sunderland)	5	Roberts
6	Todd	(Derby County)	6	Phillips
7	Ball*	(Arsenal)	7	Griffiths
8	Channon	(Southampton) replaced by Little	8	Flynn
9	Johnson	(Ipswich Town)	9	Smallman
10	Viljoen	(Ipswich Town)	10	Toshack
11	Thomas	(QPR)	11	James

Crowd: 53,000

England scorer: Johnson (2)

Comments: Debutant David Johnson scored the first and last goals of this game. Wales held a 2–1 lead in the second half. This was the last cap for Viljoen and the only cap for Aston Villa's Brian Little.

ENGLAND 5 Scotland 1; at Wembley;
Saturday 24th May 1975 (Home International)

1 Clemence	(Liverpool)	1 Kennedy	
2 Whitworth	(Leicester City)	2 Jardine	
3 Beattie	(Ipswich Town)	3 McGrain	
4 Bell	(Man City)	4 Munro	
5 Watson	(Sunderland)	5 McQueen	
6 Todd	(Derby County)	6 Rioch	
7 Ball*	(Arsenal)	7 Dalglish	
8 Channon	(Southampton)	8 Conn	
9 Johnson	(Ipswich Town)	9 Parlane	
10 Francis	(QPR)	10 MacDougall	
11 Keegan	(Liverpool) replaced by Thomas	11 Duncan	

Crowd: 98,241

England scorers: Francis (2), Beattie, Bell, Johnson

Comments: By the time that Rioch converted a penalty just before half-time, England were already 3–0 ahead. This was the last cap for Alan Ball. What a way to go out for the World Cup hero.

Switzerland 1 ENGLAND 2; in Basle;
Wednesday 3rd September 1975

1 Burgener	1 Clemence	(Liverpool)	
2 Stohler	2 Whitworth	(Leicester City)	
3 Trinchero	3 Todd	(Derby County)	
4 Guyot	4 Watson	(Man City)	
5 Fischbach	5 Beattie	(Ipswich Town)	
6 Schild	6 Bell	(Man City)	
7 Hasler	7 Currie	(Sheffield United)	
8 Botteron	8 Francis*	(QPR)	
9 Pfister	9 Channon	(Southampton)	
10 Muller	10 Johnson	(Ipswich Town) replaced by MacDonald	
11 Jeandupeux	11 Keegan	(Liverpool)	

Crowd: 25,000

England scorers: Keegan, Channon

Comments: Kevin Keegan scored in the first ten minutes and then missed a penalty shortly afterwards, before Micky Channon doubled the lead. All the goals in this friendly came in the first half.

Czechoslovakia 2 ENGLAND 1; in Bratislava;
Thursday 30th October 1975 (European Championship)

1 Viktor	1 Clemence	(Liverpool)
2 Pivarnik	2 Madeley	(Leeds United)
3 Ondrus	3 Gillard	(QPR)
4 Jurkemik	4 Francis*	(QPR)
5 Gogh	5 McFarland	(Derby County) replaced by Watson
6 Pollak	6 Todd	(Derby County)
7 Bicovsky	7 Keegan	(Liverpool)
8 Knapp	8 Channon	(Southampton) replaced by Thomas
9 Masny	9 MacDonald	(Newcastle Utd)
10 Gallis	10 Clarke	(Leeds United)
11 Nehoda	11 Bell	(Man City)

Crowd: 45,000

England scorer: Channon

Comments: Another goal from Channon had given the visitors the lead. However the Czechs bounced back to win the match and also the competition. This was the last cap for Bell and Gillard.

Portugal 1 ENGLAND 1; in Lisbon;
Wednesday 19th November 1975 (European Championship)

1 Damas	1 Clemence	(Liverpool)
2 Rebelo	2 Whitworth	(Leicester City)
3 Rodrigues	3 Beattie	(Ipswich Town)
4 Freitas	4 Francis*	(QPR)
5 Correia	5 Watson	(Man City)
6 Machado	6 Todd	(Derby County)
7 Alves	7 Keegan	(Liverpool)
8 Oliveira	8 Channon	(Southampton)
9 Nene	9 MacDonald	(Newcastle Utd) replaced by Clarke
10 Batista	10 Brooking	(West Ham Utd)
11 Monhos	11 Madeley	(Leeds United) replaced by Thomas

Crowd: 60,000

England scorer: Channon

Comments: The popular Mick Channon pulled England level before half-time, but the away team had to settle for a point. Clarke, MacDonald, Thomas, and Whitworth all collected their final caps.

Wales 1 ENGLAND 2; in Wrexham;
Wednesday 24th March 1976

1	Lloyd	1	Clemence	(Liverpool)
2	Page	2	Cherry	(Leeds United) replaced by Clement
3	Jones	3	Mills	(Ipswich Town)
4	Yorath	4	Neal	(Liverpool)
5	Evans	5	Thompson	(Liverpool)
6	Phillips	6	Doyle	(Man City)
7	Harris	7	Keegan*	(Liverpool)
8	Flynn	8	Channon	(Southampton) replaced by Taylor
9	Curtis	9	Boyer	(Norwich City)
10	Roberts	10	Brooking	(West Ham Utd)
11	Griffiths	11	Kennedy	(Liverpool)

Crowd: 20,927

England scorers: Kennedy, Taylor

Comments: Debutant Ray Kennedy gave England the lead. Peter Taylor of Crystal Palace then came off the bench to seal the win in his first match. Phil Boyer won his only cap in this friendly.

Wales 0 ENGLAND 1; in Cardiff;
Saturday 8th May 1976 (Home International)

1	Davies	1	Clemence	(Liverpool)
2	Page	2	Clement	(QPR)
3	Thomas	3	Mills	(Ipswich Town)
4	Mahoney	4	Towers	(Sunderland)
5	Evans	5	Greenhoff	(Man Utd)
6	Phillips	6	Thompson	(Liverpool)
7	Yorath	7	Keegan	(Liverpool)
8	Flynn	8	Francis*	(QPR)
9	Curtis	9	Pearson	(Man Utd)
10	Toshack	10	Kennedy	(Liverpool)
11	James	11	Taylor	(Crystal Palace)

Crowd: 24,592

England scorer: Taylor

Comments: Peter Taylor's second goal in his second match decided this Home International. Brian Greenhoff, Stuart Pearson, and Tony Towers all won their first caps in this narrow win.

ENGLAND 4 Northern Ireland 0; at Wembley; Tuesday 11th May 1976 (Home International)

1	Clemence	(Liverpool)	1	Jennings
2	Todd	(Derby County)	2	Rice
3	Mills	(Ipswich Town)	3	Nelson
4	Thompson	(Liverpool)	4	Clements
5	Greenhoff	(Man Utd)	5	Hunter
6	Kennedy	(Liverpool)	6	Nicholl
7	Keegan	(Liverpool) replaced by Royle	7	Hamilton
8	Francis*	(QPR)	8	Cassidy
9	Pearson	(Man Utd)	9	McCreery
10	Channon	(Southampton)	10	Spence
11	Taylor	(Crystal Palace) replaced by Towers	11	McIlroy

Crowd: 48,000

England scorers: Francis, Channon (2), Pearson

Comments: The new look England team scored two goals in each half to record a comfortable win. Four Liverpool players were in the starting line-up, although none of them scored a goal.

Scotland 2 ENGLAND 1; in Glasgow; Saturday 15th May 1976 (Home International)

1	Rough	1	Clemence	(Liverpool)
2	McGrain	2	Todd	(Derby County)
3	Donachie	3	Mills	(Ipswich Town)
4	Forsyth	4	Thompson	(Liverpool)
5	Jackson	5	McFarland	(Derby County) replaced by Doyle
6	Rioch	6	Kennedy	(Liverpool)
7	Dalglish	7	Keegan	(Liverpool)
8	Masson	8	Francis*	(QPR)
9	Jordan	9	Pearson	(Man Utd) replaced by Cherry
10	Gemmill	10	Channon	(Southampton)
11	Gray	11	Taylor	(Crystal Palace)

Crowd: 85,167

England scorer: Channon

Comments: Although Micky Channon gave the visitors an early lead, Don Masson soon equalised. Then, early in the second half, Kenny Dalglish scored the winner against the 'auld enemy'.

ENGLAND 0 Brazil 1; in Los Angeles;
Sunday 23rd May 1976

1 Clemence	(Liverpool)	1 Leao
2 Todd	(Derby County)	2 Orlando
3 Doyle	(Man City)	3 Miguel
4 Thompson	(Liverpool)	4 Beto Fuscao
5 Mills	(Ipswich Town)	5 Antonio
6 Francis*	(QPR)	6 Falcao
7 Cherry	(Leeds United)	7 Rivellino
8 Brooking	(West Ham Utd)	8 Gil
9 Keegan	(Liverpool)	9 Zico
10 Pearson	(Man Utd)	10 Neca
11 Channon	(Southampton)	11 Lula

Crowd: 32,900

Comments: England conceded a very late goal to the substitute Roberto Dinamite! This match formed part of the United States Bicentennial Tournament.

ENGLAND 3 Italy 2; in New York;
Friday 28th May 1976

1 Rimmer	(Aston Villa) replaced by Corrigan	1 Zoff
2 Clement	(QPR)	2 Roggi
3 Neal	(Liverpool) replaced by Mills	3 Rocca
4 Thompson	(Liverpool)	4 Benetti
5 Doyle	(Man City)	5 Bellugi
6 Towers	(Sunderland)	6 Facchetti
7 Wilkins	(Chelsea)	7 Causio
8 Channon*	(Southampton)	8 Capello
9 Royle	(Man City)	9 Graziani
10 Brooking	(West Ham Utd)	10 Antognoni
11 Hill	(Man Utd)	11 Pulici

Crowd: 40,650

England scorers: Channon (2), Thompson

Comments: Graziani scored in quick succession to give Italy a 2–0 half-time lead. However, captain for the day, Mike Channon, sealed a remarkable win. Jimmy Rimmer won his only England cap.

Finland 1 ENGLAND 4; in Helsinki;
Sunday 13th June 1976 (World Cup qualifier)

1	Enckleman	1	Clemence	(Liverpool)
2	Vihtila	2	Todd	(Derby County)
3	Makynen	3	Mills	(Ipswich Town)
4	Tolsa	4	Thompson	(Liverpool)
5	Ranta	5	Madeley	(Leeds United)
6	Jantunen	6	Cherry	(Leeds United)
7	Suomalainen	7	Keegan	(Liverpool)
8	Heiskanen	8	Channon	(Southampton)
9	Heiskanen	9	Pearson	(Man Utd)
10	Rissanen	10	Brooking	(West Ham Utd)
11	Paatelainen	11	Francis*	(QPR)

Crowd: 24,000

England scorers: Pearson, Keegan (2), Channon

Comments: The Finns briefly cancelled out Stuart Pearson's early goal, but Don Revie's team eventually strolled to victory in this World Cup qualifier. This was the last match for Gerry Francis.

ENGLAND 1 Republic of Ireland 1; at Wembley;
Wednesday 8th September 1976

1	Clemence	(Liverpool)	1	Kearns
2	Todd	(Derby County)	2	Mulligan
3	Madeley	(Leeds United)	3	Holmes
4	Cherry	(Leeds United)	4	Martin
5	McFarland	(Derby County)	5	O'Leary
6	Greenhoff	(Man Utd)	6	Brady
7	Keegan*	(Liverpool)	7	Daly
8	Wilkins	(Chelsea)	8	Conroy
9	Pearson	(Man Utd)	9	Heighway
10	Brooking	(West Ham Utd)	10	Giles
11	George	(Derby County) replaced by Hill	11	Givens

Crowd: 51,000

England scorer: Pearson

Comments: Stuart Pearson put the hosts in front on the stroke of half-time, but Gerry Daly equalised with a penalty. This was the only (brief) international appearance for Charlie George.

ENGLAND 2 Finland 1; at Wembley;
Wednesday 13th October 1976 (World Cup qualifier)

1 Clemence	(Liverpool)	1 Enckleman
2 Todd	(Derby County)	2 Heikkinen
3 Beattie	(Ipswich Town)	3 Vihtila
4 Thompson	(Liverpool)	4 Makynen
5 Greenhoff	(Man Utd)	5 Ranta
6 Wilkins	(Chelsea)	6 Jantunen
7 Keegan*	(Liverpool)	7 Suomalainen
8 Channon	(Southampton)	8 Toivola
9 Royle	(Man City)	9 Nieminen
10 Brooking	(West Ham Utd) replaced by Hill	10 Heiskanen
11 Tueart	(Man City) replaced by Mills	11 Paatelainen

Crowd: 92,000

England scorers: Tueart, Royle

Comments: Dennis Tueart scored a very early goal, but early in the second half his fellow Manchester City colleague Joe Royle was required to restore the lead. This was a far from emphatic win.

Italy 2 ENGLAND 0; in Rome;
Wednesday 17th November 1976 (World Cup qualifier)

1 Zoff	1 Clemence	(Liverpool)
2 Cuccureddu	2 Clement	(QPR) replaced by Beattie
3 Facchetti	3 Mills	(Ipswich Town)
4 Gentile	4 Greenhoff	(Man Utd)
5 Tardelli	5 McFarland	(Derby County)
6 Causio	6 Hughes	(Liverpool)
7 Benetti	7 Keegan*	(Liverpool)
8 Antognoni	8 Channon	(Southampton)
9 Capello	9 Bowles	(QPR)
10 Graziani	10 Cherry	(Leeds United)
11 Bettega	11 Brooking	(West Ham Utd)

Crowd: 70,718

Comments: Goals from Antognoni and Bettega towards the end of each half put England's World Cup hopes in serious jeopardy. This was the last international appearance for Roy McFarland.

ENGLAND 0 Holland 2; at Wembley;
Wednesday 9th February 1977

1 Clemence	(Liverpool)	1 Schrijvers
2 Clement	(QPR)	2 Suurbier
3 Beattie	(Ipswich Town)	3 Krol
4 Doyle	(Man City)	4 Rijsbergen
5 Watson	(Man City)	5 Hovenkamp
6 Madeley	(Leeds United) replaced by Pearson	6 van der Kerkhof
7 Keegan*	(Liverpool)	7 Peters
8 Greenhoff	(Man Utd) replaced by Todd	8 Neeskens
9 Francis	(Birmingham City)	9 Rep
10 Bowles	(QPR)	10 Cruyff
11 Brooking	(West Ham Utd)	11 Resenbrink

Crowd: 90,260

Comments: Jan Peters scored twice before half-time to win this friendly. This latest setback was the last outing for Bowles, Clement, Doyle, and Madeley, as well as the debut for Trevor Francis.

ENGLAND 5 Luxembourg 0; at Wembley;
Wednesday 30th March 1977 (World Cup qualifier)

1 Clemence	(Liverpool)	1 Zender
2 Gidman	(Aston Villa)	2 Fandel
3 Cherry	(Leeds United)	3 Margue
4 Kennedy	(Liverpool)	4 Mond
5 Watson	(Man City)	5 Pilot
6 Hughes	(Liverpool)	6 Zuang
7 Keegan*	(Liverpool)	7 Dresch
8 Channon	(Southampton)	8 Domenico
9 Royle	(Man City) replaced by Mariner	9 Braun
10 Francis	(Birmingham City)	10 Philipp
11 Hill	(Man Utd)	11 Dussier

Crowd: 81,718

England scorers: Keegan, Francis, Kennedy, Channon (2)

Comments: Although Keegan scored an early goal, England only led 1–0 at half-time. This was the last cap for Joe Royle, the only cap for John Gidman, and the debut for Ipswich's Paul Mariner.

Northern Ireland 1 ENGLAND 2; in Belfast; Saturday 28th May 1977 (Home International)

1 Jennings	1 Shilton	(Stoke City)
2 Nicholl	2 Cherry	(Leeds United)
3 Rice	3 Mills	(Ipswich Town)
4 Jackson	4 Greenhoff	(Man Utd)
5 Hunter	5 Watson	(Man City)
6 Hamilton	6 Todd	(Derby County)
7 McGrath	7 Wilkins	(Chelsea) replaced by Talbot
8 McIlroy	8 Channon*	(Southampton)
9 Armstrong	9 Mariner	(Ipswich Town)
10 McCreery	10 Brooking	(West Ham Utd)
11 Anderson	11 Tueart	(Man City)

Crowd: 35,000

England scorers: Channon, Tueart

Comments: Chris McGrath gave the home team a very early lead, but Dennis Tueart was the heartbreaker, scoring the winner in the last five minutes. This was the last England game for Colin Todd.

ENGLAND 0 Wales 1; at Wembley; Tuesday 31st May 1977 (Home International)

1 Shilton	(Stoke City)	1 Davies
2 Neal	(Liverpool)	2 Thomas
3 Mills	(Ipswich Town)	3 Jones
4 Greenhoff	(Man Utd)	4 Mahoney
5 Watson	(Man City)	5 Evans
6 Hughes	(Liverpool)	6 Phillips
7 Keegan*	(Liverpool)	7 Sayer
8 Channon	(Southampton)	8 Flynn
9 Pearson	(Man Utd)	9 Yorath
10 Brooking	(West Ham Utd) replaced by Tueart	10 Deacy
11 Kennedy	(Liverpool)	11 James

Crowd: 48,000

Comments: Leighton James converted a penalty just before half-time as England slipped to their third defeat in their last five matches. Worse was soon to follow for Don Revie and his team.

ENGLAND 1 Scotland 2; at Wembley;
Saturday 4th June 1977 (Home International)

1	Clemence	(Liverpool)		1	Rough
2	Neal	(Liverpool)		2	McGrain
3	Mills	(Ipswich Town)		3	Donachie
4	Greenhoff	(Man Utd) replaced by Cherry		4	Forsyth
5	Watson	(Man City)		5	McQueen
6	Hughes*	(Liverpool)		6	Rioch
7	Francis	(Birmingham City)		7	Masson
8	Channon	(Southampton)		8	Dalglish
9	Pearson	(Man Utd)		9	Jordan
10	Talbot	(Ipswich Town)		10	Hartford
11	Kennedy	(Liverpool) replaced by Tueart		11	Johnston

Crowd: 98,103

England scorer: Channon (Pen)

Comments: Gordon McQueen gave the visitors the lead just before the break, which Kenny Dalglish extended just short of the hour mark. The Scots celebrated with a notorious pitch invasion.

Brazil 0 ENGLAND 0; in Rio de Janeiro;
Wednesday 8th June 1977

1	Leao		1	Clemence	(Liverpool)
2	Ze Maria		2	Neal	(Liverpool)
3	Amaral		3	Cherry	(Leeds United)
4	Edinho		4	Greenhoff	(Man Utd)
5	Neto		5	Watson	(Man City)
6	Cerezo		6	Hughes*	(Liverpool)
7	Zico		7	Keegan	(SV Hamburg)
8	Rivellino		8	Francis	(Birmingham City)
9	Gil		9	Pearson	(Man Utd) replaced by Channon
10	Dinamite		10	Wilkins	(Chelsea) replaced by Kennedy
11	Cesar Caju		11	Talbot	(Ipswich Town)

Crowd: 77,000

Comments: Toothless England failed to score for the fourth time in seven matches. Don Revie was absent, choosing instead to watch Italy beat Finland 3–0 in a crucial World Cup qualifier.

Argentina 1 ENGLAND 1; in Buenos Aires;
Sunday 12th June 1977

1 Baley	1 Clemence	(Liverpool)
2 Killer	2 Neal	(Liverpool)
3 Passarella	3 Cherry	(Leeds United)
4 Pernia	4 Greenhoff	(Man Utd) replaced by Kennedy
5 Tarantini	5 Watson	(Man City)
6 Ardiles	6 Hughes*	(Liverpool)
7 Bochini	7 Keegan	(SV Hamburg)
8 Gallego	8 Channon	(Southampton)
9 Bertoni	9 Pearson	(Man Utd)
10 Luque	10 Wilkins	(Chelsea)
11 Ortiz	11 Talbot	(Ipswich Town)

Crowd: 60,000

England scorer: Pearson

Comments: Both goals came in the first quarter of an hour, but they were overshadowed by the sendings off of Cherry and Bertoni. In a year from now Argentina would be world champions!

Uruguay 0 ENGLAND 0; in Montevideo;
Wednesday 15th June 1977

1 Clavijo	1 Clemence	(Liverpool)
2 Rivadavia	2 Neal	(Liverpool)
3 Salomon	3 Cherry	(Leeds United)
4 Santos	4 Greenhoff	(Man Utd) replaced by Kennedy
5 Pereira	5 Watson	(Man City)
6 Javier	6 Hughes*	(Liverpool)
7 Rodriguez	7 Keegan	(SV Hamburg)
8 Carrasco	8 Channon	(Southampton)
9 Santelli	9 Pearson	(Man Utd)
10 Maneiro	10 Wilkins	(Chelsea)
11 Olivera	11 Talbot	(Ipswich Town)

Crowd: 25,000

Comments: A third successive away draw against South American opposition was quite commendable, but with only 3 wins from 11 matches, Don Revie was relieved of his duties after this.

ENGLAND 0 Switzerland 0; at Wembley;
Wednesday 7th September 1977

1	Clemence	(Liverpool)	1	Burgener
2	Neal	(Liverpool)	2	Chapuisat
3	Cherry	(Leeds United)	3	Trinchero
4	McDermott	(Liverpool)	4	Bizzini
5	Watson	(Man City)	5	Fischbach
6	Hughes*	(Liverpool)	6	Barberis
7	Keegan	(SV Hamburg)	7	Hasler
8	Channon	(Southampton) replaced by Hill	8	Botteron
9	Francis	(Birmingham City)	9	Elsener
10	Kennedy	(Liverpool)	10	Kuttel
11	Callaghan	(Liverpool) replaced by Wilkins	11	Demarmels

Crowd: 42,000

Comments: Not even the presence of the new manager Ron Greenwood could inspire England as they now recorded six matches without a win. Terry McDermott made his debut in this friendly.

Luxembourg 0 ENGLAND 2; in Luxembourg City;
Wednesday 12th October 1977 (World Cup qualifier)

1	Moes	1	Clemence	(Liverpool)
2	Barthel	2	Cherry	(Leeds United)
3	Fandel	3	Watson	(Man City) replaced by Beattie
4	Mond	4	Hughes*	(Liverpool)
5	Rohmann	5	Kennedy	(Liverpool)
6	Philipp	6	Callaghan	(Liverpool)
7	Michaux	7	McDermott	(Liverpool) replaced by Whymark
8	Zuang	8	Wilkins	(Chelsea)
9	Dussier	9	Francis	(Birmingham City)
10	Braun	10	Mariner	(Ipswich Town)
11	Monacelli	11	Hill	(Man Utd)

Crowd: 10,621

England scorers: Kennedy, Mariner

Comments: It took a last minute effort from Paul Mariner to seal the victory as England made hard work of this match. Ipswich Town's Trevor Whymark won his only cap as a substitute here.

ENGLAND 2 Italy 0; at Wembley;
Wednesday 16th November 1977 (World Cup qualifier)

1	Clemence	(Liverpool)		1	Zoff
2	Neal	(Liverpool)		2	Tardelli
3	Cherry	(Leeds United)		3	Mozzini
4	Wilkins	(Chelsea)		4	Facchetti
5	Watson	(Man City)		5	Gentile
6	Hughes*	(Liverpool)		6	Zaccarelli
7	Keegan	(SV Hamburg) replaced by Francis		7	Benetti
8	Coppell	(Man Utd)		8	Antognoni
9	Latchford	(Everton) replaced by Pearson		9	Causio
10	Brooking	(West Ham Utd)		10	Graziani
11	Barnes	(Man City)		11	Bettega

Crowd: 92,500

England scorers: Keegan, Brooking

Comments: This was a bitter-sweet triumph, because England finished agonisingly behind Italy on goal difference and thus failed to qualify for the World Cup finals, despite this impressive win.

West Germany 2 ENGLAND 1; in Munich;
Wednesday 22nd February 1978

1	Maier	1	Clemence	(Liverpool)
2	Vogts	2	Neal	(Liverpool)
3	Zimmermann	3	Mills	(Ipswich Town)
4	Bonhof	4	Wilkins	(Chelsea)
5	Schwarzenbeck	5	Watson	(Man City)
6	Russmann	6	Hughes*	(Liverpool)
7	Abramczik	7	Keegan	(SV Hamburg) replaced by Francis
8	Flore	8	Coppell	(Man Utd)
9	Holzenbein	9	Pearson	(Man Utd)
10	Neumann	10	Brooking	(West Ham Utd)
11	Rummenigge	11	Barnes	(Man City)

Crowd: 77,850

England scorer: Pearson

Comments: Here was another West German comeback. Pearson gave the visitors the lead just before the break, only for Bonhof to score the winner for the world champions in the last 5 minutes.

ENGLAND 1 Brazil 1; at Wembley;
Wednesday 19th April 1978

1	Corrigan	(Man City)		1	Leao
2	Mills	(Ipswich Town)		2	Ze Maria
3	Cherry	(Leeds United)		3	Abel
4	Greenhoff	(Man Utd)		4	Amaral
5	Watson	(Man City)		5	Edinho
6	Currie	(Leeds United)		6	Cerezo
7	Keegan*	(SV Hamburg)		7	Rivelino
8	Coppell	(Man Utd)		8	Gil
9	Latchford	(Everton)		9	Zico
10	Francis	(Birmingham City)		10	Nunes
11	Barnes	(Man City)		11	Dirceu

Crowd: 92,500

England scorer: Keegan

Comments: Both goals were scored in the first-half as poor old England yet again were sportingly providing an opposing team with match practice ahead of the World Cup finals in Argentina.

Wales 1 ENGLAND 3; in Cardiff;
Saturday 13th May 1978 (Home International)

1	Davies	1	Shilton	(Notts Forest)
2	Page	2	Mills*	(Ipswich Town)
3	Jones	3	Cherry	(Leeds United) replaced by Currie
4	Phillips	4	Greenhoff	(Man Utd)
5	Jones	5	Watson	(Man City)
6	Yorath	6	Wilkins	(Chelsea)
7	Harris	7	Coppell	(Man Utd)
8	Flynn	8	Francis	(Birmingham City)
9	Curtis	9	Latchford	(Everton) replaced by Mariner
10	Dwyer	10	Brooking	(West Ham Utd)
11	Thomas	11	Barnes	(Man City)

Crowd: 17,698

England scorers: Latchford, Currie, Barnes

Comments: Bob Latchford gave England an early lead, but when Phil Dwyer equalised just after the hour mark, it needed two late goals from Tony Currie and Peter Barnes to secure victory.

ENGLAND 1 Northern Ireland 0; at Wembley; Tuesday 16th May 1978 (Home International)

1	Clemence	(Liverpool)	1	Platt
2	Neal	(Liverpool)	2	Hamilton
3	Mills	(Ipswich Town)	3	Scott
4	Wilkins	(Chelsea)	4	Nicholl
5	Watson	(Man City)	5	Nicholl
6	Hughes*	(Liverpool)	6	McIlroy
7	Currie	(Leeds United)	7	McCreery
8	Coppell	(Man Utd)	8	O'Neill
9	Pearson	(Man Utd)	9	Anderson
10	Woodcock	(Notts Forest)	10	Armstrong
11	Greenhoff	(Man Utd)	11	McGrath

Crowd: 55,000

England scorer: Neal

Comments: Phil Neal scored the only goal on the stroke of half-time against Danny Blanchflower's team. Tony Woodcock won his first cap while Stuart Pearson was playing in his last match.

Scotland 0 ENGLAND 1; in Glasgow; Saturday 20th May 1978 (Home International)

1	Rough	1	Clemence	(Liverpool)	
2	Kennedy	2	Neal	(Liverpool)	
3	Donachie	3	Mills	(Ipswich Town)	
4	Forsyth	4	Currie	(Leeds United)	
5	Burns	5	Watson	(Man City)	
6	Rioch	6	Hughes*	(Liverpool) replaced by Greenhoff	
7	Masson	7	Wilkins	(Chelsea)	
8	Hartford	8	Coppell	(Man Utd)	
9	Jordan	9	Mariner	(Ipswich Town) replaced by Brooking	
10	Dalglish	10	Francis	(Birmingham City)	
11	Johnston	11	Barnes	(Man City)	

Crowd: 88,319

England scorer: Coppell

Comments: Ally MacLeod's team may have been going to the World Cup finals, but a late Steve Coppell goal earned England the Home International Championship, with maximum points.

ENGLAND 4 Hungary 1; at Wembley;
Wednesday 24th May 1978

1	Shilton	(Notts Forest)	1	Gujdar
2	Neal	(Liverpool)	2	Torok
3	Mills	(Ipswich Town)	3	Kocsis
4	Wilkins	(Chelsea)	4	Kereki
5	Watson	(Man City) replaced by Greenhoff	5	Toth
6	Hughes*	(Liverpool)	6	Nyalisi
7	Keegan	(SV Hamburg)	7	Pinter
8	Coppell	(Man Utd)	8	Zombori
9	Francis	(Birmingham City)	9	Fazekas
10	Brooking	(West Ham Utd) replaced by Currie	10	Torocsik
11	Barnes	(Man City)	11	Nagy

Crowd: 75,000

England scorers: Barnes, Neal (Pen), Francis, Currie

Comments: The home team netted three times in the first half as they eased to their fourth successive win. What a pity that they were not eligible to carry this form into the World Cup finals.

Denmark 3 ENGLAND 4; in Copenhagen;
Wednesday 20th September 1978 (European Championship)

1	Jensen	1	Clemence	(Liverpool)
2	Nielsen	2	Neal	(Liverpool)
3	Jensen	3	Mills	(Ipswich Town)
4	Rontved	4	Wilkins	(Chelsea)
5	Lerby	5	Watson	(Man City)
6	Arnesen	6	Hughes*	(Liverpool)
7	Lund	7	Keegan	(SV Hamburg)
8	Nielsen	8	Coppell	(Man Utd)
9	Simonsen	9	Latchford	(Everton)
10	Nielsen	10	Brooking	(West Ham Utd)
11	Kristensen	11	Barnes	(Man City)

Crowd: 47,600

England scorers: Keegan (2), Latchford, Neal

Comments: Kevin Keegan gave the away team a 2–0 lead, but Denmark soon brought the teams level at half-time. It took another goal from Phil Neal in the last 10 minutes to make sure of 2 points.

Republic of Ireland 1 ENGLAND 1; in Dublin; Wednesday 25th October 1978 (European Championship)

1 Kearns	1 Clemence	(Liverpool)
2 Mulligan	2 Neal	(Liverpool)
3 Holmes	3 Mills	(Ipswich Town)
4 Lawrenson	4 Wilkins	(Chelsea)
5 O'Leary	5 Watson	(Man City) replaced by Thompson
6 Daly	6 Hughes*	(Liverpool)
7 Grealish	7 Keegan	(SV Hamburg)
8 Brady	8 Coppell	(Man Utd)
9 Ryan	9 Latchford	(Everton)
10 Givens	10 Brooking	(West Ham Utd)
11 McGee	11 Barnes	(Man City) replaced by Woodcock

Crowd: 55,000

England scorer: Latchford

Comments: Bob Latchford put the visitors into the lead inside the first ten minutes, but Gerry Daly soon equalised to share the points in this group qualifier at Lansdowne Road.

ENGLAND 1 Czechoslovakia 0; at Wembley; Wednesday 29th November 1978

1 Shilton	(Notts Forest)	1 Michalik
2 Anderson	(Notts Forest)	2 Barmos
3 Cherry	(Leeds United)	3 Vojacek
4 Thompson	(Liverpool)	4 Jurkemik
5 Watson	(Man City)	5 Gogh
6 Wilkins	(Chelsea)	6 Kozak
7 Keegan*	(SV Hamburg)	7 Jarusek
8 Coppell	(Man Utd)	8 Stambachr
9 Woodcock	(Notts Forest) replaced by Latchford	9 Masny
10 Currie	(Leeds United)	10 Nehoda
11 Barnes	(Man City)	11 Gajusek

Crowd: 92,000

England scorer: Coppell

Comments: Steve Coppell scored the only goal in the second half as England extended their unbeaten run to eight matches. Yet another Brian Clough prodigy, Viv Anderson, made his debut.

ENGLAND 4 Northern Ireland 0; at Wembley; Wednesday 7th February 1979 (European Championship)

1	Clemence	(Liverpool)	1	Jennings
2	Neal	(Liverpool)	2	Rice
3	Mills	(Ipswich Town)	3	Nelson
4	Currie	(Leeds United)	4	Nicholl
5	Watson	(Man City)	5	Nicholl
6	Hughes*	(Liverpool)	6	McCreery
7	Keegan	(SV Hamburg)	7	O'Neill
8	Coppell	(Man Utd)	8	McIlroy
9	Latchford	(Everton)	9	Armstrong
10	Brooking	(West Ham Utd)	10	Caskey
11	Barnes	(Man City)	11	Cochrane

Crowd: 92,000

England scorers: Keegan, Latchford (2), Watson

Comments: This was a comfortable win for the home team, although they only led 1–0 at half-time. Early in the second half Bob Latchford scored his final two England goals in this group qualifier.

Northern Ireland 0 ENGLAND 2; in Belfast; Saturday 19th May 1979 (Home International)

1	Jennings	1	Clemence	(Liverpool)
2	Rice	2	Neal	(Liverpool)
3	Nelson	3	Mills*	(Ipswich Town)
4	Nicholl	4	Thompson	(Liverpool)
5	Nicholl	5	Watson	(Man City)
6	Moreland	6	Currie	(Leeds United)
7	Hamilton	7	Coppell	(Man Utd)
8	McIlroy	8	Wilkins	(Chelsea)
9	Armstrong	9	Latchford	(Everton)
10	Caskey	10	McDermott	(Liverpool)
11	Cochrane	11	Barnes	(Man City)

Crowd: 35,000

England scorers: Watson, Coppell

Comments: Two early goals were enough to put this match to bed. Big Dave Watson netted his second goal in consecutive matches, both scored against Pat Jennings of Northern Ireland.

ENGLAND 0 Wales 0; at Wembley;
Wednesday 23rd May 1979 (Home International)

1	Corrigan	(Man City)	1	Davies
2	Cherry	(Leeds United)	2	Stevenson
3	Sansom	(Crystal Palace)	3	Jones
4	Wilkins	(Chelsea) replaced by Brooking	4	Phillips
5	Watson	(Man City)	5	Yorath
6	Hughes*	(Liverpool)	6	Mahoney
7	Keegan	(SV Hamburg) replaced by Coppell	7	James
8	Currie	(Leeds United)	8	Flynn
9	Latchford	(Everton)	9	Dwyer
10	McDermott	(Liverpool)	10	Toshack
11	Cunningham	(West Brom)	11	Curtis

Crowd: 70,220

Comments: This was the third consecutive visit to Wembley where the Welsh escaped with at least one Home International point. Laurie Cunningham and Kenny Sansom made their debuts.

ENGLAND 3 Scotland 1; at Wembley;
Saturday 26th May 1979 (Home International)

1	Clemence	(Liverpool)	1	Wood
2	Neal	(Liverpool)	2	Burley
3	Mills*	(Ipswich Town)	3	Gray
4	Thompson	(Liverpool)	4	Wark
5	Watson	(Man City)	5	McQueen
6	Wilkins	(Chelsea)	6	Hegarty
7	Keegan	(SV Hamburg)	7	Dalglish
8	Coppell	(Man Utd)	8	Hartford
9	Latchford	(Everton)	9	Jordan
10	Brooking	(West Ham Utd)	10	Souness
11	Barnes	(Man City)	11	Graham

Crowd: 100,000

England scorers: Barnes, Coppell, Keegan

Comments: John Wark gave the Scots the lead but Peter Barnes equalised on the stroke of half-time. Two further goals secured the triumph and extended the unbeaten sequence to 12 matches.

Bulgaria 0 ENGLAND 3; in Sofia;
Wednesday 6th June 1979 (European Championship)

1 Filipov	1 Clemence	(Liverpool)
2 Grincharov	2 Neal	(Liverpool)
3 Ivkov	3 Mills*	(Ipswich Town)
4 Iliev	4 Thompson	(Liverpool)
5 Vasilev	5 Watson	(Werder Bremen)
6 Zdravkov	6 Wilkins	(Chelsea)
7 Borisov	7 Keegan	(SV Hamburg)
8 Panov	8 Coppell	(Man Utd)
9 Voinov	9 Latchford	(Everton) replaced by Francis
10 Jelyazkov	10 Brooking	(West Ham Utd)
11 Tzvetkov	11 Barnes	(Man City) replaced by Woodcock

Crowd: 47,500

England scorers: Keegan, Watson, Barnes

Comments: Dave Watson and Peter Barnes both scored soon after half-time to wrap up both points as England continued to make impressive progress towards the European Championship finals.

Sweden 0 ENGLAND 0; in Stockholm;
Sunday 10th June 1979

1 Moller	1 Shilton	(Notts Forest)
2 Arvidson	2 Anderson	(Notts Forest)
3 Ahman	3 Cherry	(Leeds United)
4 Erlandsson	4 McDermott	(Liverpool) replaced by Wilkins
5 Borg	5 Watson	(Werder Bremen) replaced by Thompson
6 Nordgren	6 Hughes*	(Liverpool)
7 Torstensson	7 Keegan	(SV Hamburg)
8 Linderoth	8 Francis	(Notts Forest)
9 Gronhagen	9 Woodcock	(Notts Forest)
10 Cervin	10 Currie	(Leeds United) replaced by Brooking
11 Johansson	11 Cunningham	(West Brom)

Crowd: 35,691

Comments: England's new superpower, Nottingham Forest, supplied 4 members of the line-up as England achieved their 13th shut-out in the last 21 matches. This was Tony Currie's last match.

Austria 4 ENGLAND 3; in Vienna;
Wednesday 13th June 1979

1 Koncilia	1 Shilton	(Notts Forest) replaced by Clemence
2 Sara	2 Neal	(Liverpool)
3 Obermayer	3 Mills	(Ipswich Town)
4 Pezzey	4 Thompson	(Liverpool)
5 Baumeister	5 Watson	(Werder Bremen)
6 Hattenburger	6 Wilkins	(Chelsea)
7 Kreuz	7 Keegan*	(SV Hamburg)
8 Jara	8 Coppell	(Man Utd)
9 Welzl	9 Latchford	(Everton) replaced by Francis
10 Prohaska	10 Brooking	(West Ham Utd)
11 Jurtin	11 Barnes	(Man City) replaced by Cunningham

Crowd: 30,000

England scorers: Keegan, Coppell, Wilkins

Comments: England were 3–1 behind at the interval before they pulled level halfway through the second half, but Austria inched ahead again. This was Bob Latchford's last international match.

ENGLAND 1 Denmark 0; at Wembley;
Wednesday 12th September 1979 (European Championship)

1 Clemence	(Liverpool)	1 Jensen	
2 Neal	(Liverpool)	2 Elkjaer	
3 Mills	(Ipswich Town)	3 Jensen	
4 Thompson	(Liverpool)	4 Nielsen	
5 Watson	(Werder Bremen)	5 Simonsen	
6 Wilkins	(Man Utd)	6 Arnesen	
7 Coppell	(Man Utd)	7 Lerby	
8 McDermott	(Liverpool)	8 Ziegler	
9 Keegan*	(SV Hamburg)	9 Busk	
10 Brooking	(West Ham Utd)	10 Hojgaard	
11 Barnes	(West Brom)	11 Olsen	

Crowd: 85,000

England scorer: Keegan

Comments: The home team completed the double over Denmark thanks to the captain who scored after a quarter of an hour. England were well en route to the finals in Italy next year.

Northern Ireland 1 ENGLAND 5; in Belfast; Wednesday 17th October 1979 (European Championship)

1	Jennings	1	Shilton	(Notts Forest)
2	Rice	2	Neal	(Liverpool)
3	Nelson	3	Mills*	(Ipswich Town)
4	Nicholl	4	Thompson	(Liverpool)
5	Hunter	5	Watson	(Southampton)
6	McCreery	6	Wilkins	(Man Utd)
7	McIlroy	7	Keegan	(SV Hamburg)
8	Cassidy	8	Coppell	(Man Utd)
9	Armstrong	9	Francis	(Notts Forest)
10	Finney	10	Brooking	(West Ham Utd) replaced by McDermott
11	Moreland	11	Woodcock	(Notts Forest)

Crowd: 25,000

England scorers: Francis (2), Woodcock (2), Nicholl (OG)

Comments: A Vic Moreland penalty at the start of the second half reduced the arrears to 2-1 but the home team were put to the sword by a pair of goals from a pair of Nottingham Forest players.

ENGLAND 2 Bulgaria 0; at Wembley; Thursday 22nd November 1979 (European Championship)

1	Clemence	(Liverpool)	1	Hristov
2	Anderson	(Notts Forest)	2	Karakolev
3	Sansom	(Crystal Palace)	3	Iliev
4	Thompson*	(Liverpool)	4	Dimitrov
5	Watson	(Werder Bremen)	5	Barzov
6	Wilkins	(Man Utd)	6	Markov
7	Reeves	(Norwich City)	7	Velitschkov
8	Hoddle	(Tottenham)	8	Dimitrov
9	Francis	(Notts Forest)	9	Jelyazkov
10	Kennedy	(Liverpool)	10	Tzvetkov
11	Woodcock	(Cologne)	11	Bonev

Crowd: 71,491

England scorers: Watson, Hoddle

Comments: Central defender Dave Watson scored his fourth international goal of the year, while debutant Glenn Hoddle doubled the lead in the second half. Kevin Reeves also won his first cap.

ENGLAND 2 Republic of Ireland 0; at Wembley; Wednesday 6th February 1980 (European Championship)

1	Clemence	(Liverpool)		1	Peyton
2	Cherry	(Leeds United)		2	Hughton
3	Sansom	(Crystal Palace)		3	Grimes
4	Thompson	(Liverpool)		4	Lawrenson
5	Watson	(Southampton)		5	O'Leary
6	Robson	(West Brom)		6	Brady
7	Keegan*	(SV Hamburg)		7	Daly
8	McDermott	(Liverpool)		8	Grealish
9	Johnson	(Liverpool) replaced by Coppell		9	Heighway
10	Woodcock	(Cologne)		10	Stapleton
11	Cunningham	(Real Madrid)		11	O'Brien

Crowd: 90,299

England scorer: Keegan (2)

Comments: The great Kevin Keegan scored in each half as England rounded off their successful qualifying campaign with a win. Another 'great', Bryan Robson, began his England journey here.

Spain 0 ENGLAND 2; in Barcelona; Wednesday 26th March 1980

1	Arconada		1	Shilton	(Notts Forest)
2	Urquiaga		2	Neal	(Liverpool) replaced by Hughes
3	Migueli		3	Mills	(Ipswich Town)
4	Alesanco		4	Thompson	(Liverpool)
5	Gordillo		5	Watson	(Southampton)
6	Uria		6	Wilkins	(Man Utd)
7	Saura		7	Keegan*	(SV Hamburg)
8	Guisasola		8	Coppell	(Man Utd)
9	Juanito		9	Francis	(Notts Forest) replaced by Cunningham
10	Satrusegui		10	Kennedy	(Liverpool)
11	Dani		11	Woodcock	(Cologne)

Crowd: 50,000

England scorers: Woodcock, Francis

Comments: A goal in each half provided the away team with a morale-booster ahead of the forthcoming European Championship finals. It was a happy fiftieth cap for the captain, Kevin Keegan.

ENGLAND 3 Argentina 1; at Wembley;
Tuesday 13th May 1980

1	Clemence	(Liverpool)		1	Fillol
2	Neal	(Liverpool) replaced by Cherry		2	van Tuyne
3	Sansom	(Crystal Palace)		3	Tarantini
4	Thompson	(Liverpool)		4	Olguin
5	Watson	(Southampton)		5	Gallego
6	Wilkins	(Man Utd)		6	Passarella
7	Keegan*	(SV Hamburg)		7	Santamaria
8	Coppell	(Man Utd)		8	Barbas
9	Johnson	(Liverpool) replaced by Birtles		9	Luque
10	Woodcock	(Cologne)		10	Maradona
11	Kennedy	(Liverpool) replaced by Brooking		11	Valencia

Crowd: 92,000

England scorers: Johnson (2), Keegan

Comments: England began this match with 5 Liverpool players and one of them, David Johnson, gave the hosts a 2–0 lead against the world champions. Garry Birtles made his debut in this win.

Wales 4 ENGLAND 1; in Wrexham;
Saturday 17th May 1980 (Home International)

1	Davies	1	Clemence	(Liverpool)
2	Nicholas	2	Neal	(Liverpool) replaced by Sansom
3	Jones	3	Cherry	(Leeds United)
4	Yorath	4	Thompson*	(Liverpool)
5	Jones	5	Lloyd	(Liverpool) replaced by Wilkins
6	Price	6	Kennedy	(Liverpool)
7	Giles	7	Coppell	(Man Utd)
8	Flynn	8	Hoddle	(Tottenham)
9	Walsh	9	Mariner	(Ipswich Town)
10	Thomas	10	Brooking	(West Ham Utd)
11	James	11	Barnes	(West Brom)

Crowd: 24,358

England scorer: Mariner

Comments: High-flying England were cut down to size by a rampant Wales who recovered from a 1–0 deficit to lead 2–1 at half-time. Phil Thompson put through his own net in this humiliation.

**ENGLAND 1 Northern Ireland 1; at Wembley;
Tuesday 20th May 1980 (Home International)**

1 Corrigan	(Man City)	1	Platt
2 Cherry	(Leeds United)	2	Nicholl
3 Sansom	(Crystal Palace)	3	Donaghy
4 Brooking	(West Ham Utd)	4	McIlroy
5 Watson	(Southampton)	5	Nicholl
6 Hughes*	(Wolves)	6	O'Neill
7 McDermott	(Liverpool)	7	Brotherston
8 Wilkins	(Man Utd)	8	Cassidy
9 Johnson	(Liverpool)	9	Finney
10 Reeves	(Man City) replaced by Mariner	10	Armstrong
11 Devonshire	(West Ham Utd)	11	Hamilton

Crowd: 33,676

England scorer: Johnson

Comments: Johnson gave England the lead with less than ten minutes to go, but substitute Terry Cochrane soon equalised for a share of the points. Alan Devonshire made his debut in this draw.

**Scotland 0 ENGLAND 2; in Glasgow;
Saturday 24th May 1980 (Home International)**

1 Rough	1 Clemence	(Liverpool)	
2 McGrain	2 Cherry	(Leeds United)	
3 Munro	3 Sansom	(Crystal Palace)	
4 Miller	4 Thompson*	(Liverpool)	
5 Hegarty	5 Watson	(Southampton)	
6 McLeish	6 Wilkins	(Man Utd)	
7 Strachan	7 Coppell	(Man Utd)	
8 Dalglish	8 McDermott	(Liverpool)	
9 Jordan	9 Johnson	(Liverpool)	
10 Gemmill	10 Mariner	(Ipswich Town) replaced by Hughes	
11 Aitken	11 Brooking	(West Ham Utd)	

Crowd: 85,500

England scorers: Brooking, Coppell

Comments: The away team ended a poor Home International Championship campaign on a high with a goal in each half. This was the last international outing for 'Crazy Horse' Emlyn Hughes.

Australia 1 ENGLAND 2; in Sydney;
Saturday 31st May 1980

1 Woodhouse	1 Corrigan	(Man City)
2 Perry	2 Cherry*	(Leeds United)
3 Muir	3 Lampard	(West Ham Utd)
4 Prskalo	4 Talbot	(Arsenal)
5 Tansey	5 Osman	(Ipswich Town)
6 Henderson	6 Butcher	(Ipswich Town)
7 Yzendoorn	7 Robson	(West Brom) replaced by Greenhoff
8 Rooney	8 Sunderland	(Arsenal) replaced by Ward
9 Jankovic	9 Mariner	(Ipswich Town)
10 Cole	10 Hoddle	(Tottenham)
11 Boden	11 Armstrong	(Southampton) replaced by Devonshire

Crowd: 45,000

England scorers: Hoddle, Mariner

Comments: In this full international, Armstrong, Butcher, and Osman made their debut, Sunderland and Ward collected their only cap, and Greenhoff, Lampard, and Talbot earned their final caps!

ENGLAND 1 Belgium 1; in Turin;
Thursday 12th June 1980 (European Championship)

1 Clemence	(Liverpool)	1 Pfaff
2 Neal	(Liverpool)	2 Gerets
3 Sansom	(Crystal Palace)	3 Millecamps
4 Thompson	(Liverpool)	4 Meeuws
5 Watson	(Werder Bremen)	5 Renquin
6 Wilkins	(Man Utd)	6 van Moer
7 Keegan*	(SV Hamburg)	7 Vandereycken
8 Coppell	(Man Utd) replaced by McDermott	8 Cools
9 Johnson	(Liverpool) replaced by Kennedy	9 van der Elst
10 Woodcock	(Cologne)	10 Vandenbergh
11 Brooking	(West Ham Utd)	11 Ceulemans

Crowd: 15,186

England scorer: Wilkins

Comments: Ray Wilkins gave England the lead but Jan Ceulemans quickly equalised as England had to settle for a point. David Johnson was substituted and he never played for England again.

Italy 1 ENGLAND 0; in Turin;
Sunday 15th June 1980 (European Championship)

1	Zoff		1	Shilton	(Notts Forest)
2	Gentile		2	Neal	(Liverpool)
3	Oriali		3	Sansom	(Crystal Palace)
4	Benetti		4	Thompson	(Liverpool)
5	Collovati		5	Watson	(Werder Bremen)
6	Scirea		6	Wilkins	(Man Utd)
7	Causio		7	Keegan*	(SV Hamburg)
8	Tardelli		8	Coppell	(Man Utd)
9	Graziani		9	Birtles	(Notts Forest) replaced by Mariner
10	Antognoni		10	Kennedy	(Liverpool)
11	Bettega		11	Woodcock	(Cologne)

Crowd: 59,649

Comments: Marco Tardelli scored a late goal for the hosts, and then England were frustrated by time-wasting, not to mention crowd trouble too. This was Ray Kennedy's last England appearance.

ENGLAND 2 Spain 1; in Naples;
Wednesday 18th June 1980 (European Championship)

1	Clemence	(Liverpool)	1	Arconada
2	Anderson	(Notts Forest)	2	Cundi
3	Mills	(Ipswich Town) replaced by Cherry	3	Gordillo
4	Thompson	(Liverpool)	4	Olmo
5	Watson	(Southampton)	5	Alesanco
6	Wilkins	(Man Utd)	6	Juanito
7	McDermott	(Liverpool)	7	Uria
8	Hoddle	(Tottenham) replaced by Mariner	8	Saura
9	Keegan*	(SV Hamburg)	9	Santillana
10	Woodcock	(Cologne)	10	Zamora
11	Brooking	(West Ham Utd)	11	Cardenosa

Crowd: 14,000

England scorers: Brooking, Woodcock

Comments: Brooking gave England the interval lead. Then substitute Dani scored a penalty and missed another, before Woodcock restored the lead. This didn't prevent their exit from the finals.

ENGLAND 4 Norway 0; at Wembley;
Wednesday 10th September 1980 (World Cup qualifier)

1	Shilton	(Notts Forest)	1	Jacobsen
2	Anderson	(Notts Forest)	2	Berntsen
3	Sansom	(Arsenal)	3	Kordahl
4	Thompson*	(Liverpool)	4	Jan Aas
5	Butcher	(Ipswich Town)	5	Grondalen
6	Robson	(West Brom)	6	Albertsen
7	Gates	(Ipswich Town)	7	Hareide
8	McDermott	(Liverpool)	8	Dokken
9	Mariner	(Ipswich Town)	9	Okland
10	Woodcock	(Cologne)	10	Jacobsen
11	Rix	(Arsenal)	11	Erlandsen

Crowd: 48,200

England scorers: McDermott (2), Woodcock, Mariner

Comments: Terry McDermott hadn't scored in his first 12 matches and then 2 goals came at once. The floodgates didn't open until after the break with 3 goals, as Gates and Rix made their debut.

Romania 2 ENGLAND 1; in Bucharest;
Wednesday 15th October 1980 (World Cup qualifier)

1	Iordache	1	Clemence	(Liverpool)	
2	Negrila	2	Neal	(Liverpool)	
3	Stefanescu	3	Sansom	(Crystal Palace)	
4	Sames	4	Thompson*	(Liverpool)	
5	Munteanu	5	Watson	(Southampton)	
6	Ticleanu	6	Robson	(West Brom)	
7	Beldeanu	7	Rix	(Arsenal)	
8	Iordanescu	8	McDermott	(Liverpool)	
9	Crisan	9	Birtles	(Notts Forest) replaced by Cunningham	
10	Camataru	10	Woodcock	(Cologne)	
11	Raducanu	11	Gates	(Ipswich Town) replaced by Coppell	

Crowd: 80,000

England scorer: Woodcock

Comments: Woodcock equalised after half-time. Then the hosts scored a penalty as England succumbed to another east European team. This was the last cap for Birtles, Gates, and Cunningham.

ENGLAND 2 Switzerland 1; at Wembley;
Wednesday 19th November 1980 (World Cup qualifier)

1 Shilton	(Notts Forest)	1 Burgener
2 Neal	(Liverpool)	2 Geiger
3 Sansom	(Arsenal)	3 Hermann
4 Robson	(West Brom)	4 Ludi
5 Martin	(West Ham Utd)	5 Wehrli
6 Mills*	(Ipswich Town)	6 Pfister
7 Coppell	(Man Utd)	7 Barberis
8 McDermott	(Liverpool)	8 Botteron
9 Mariner	(Ipswich Town)	9 Tanner
10 Brooking	(West Ham Utd) replaced by Rix	10 Schonenberger
11 Woodcock	(Cologne)	11 Elsener

Crowd: 70,000

England scorers: Tanner (OG), Mariner

Comments: Ron Greenwood's team were 2–0 ahead at the interval and held on for both qualifying points after the Swiss had grabbed a late consolation. This was the debut for big Alvin Martin.

ENGLAND 1 Spain 2; at Wembley;
Wednesday 25th March 1981

1 Clemence	(Liverpool)	1 Arconada
2 Neal	(Liverpool)	2 Camacho
3 Sansom	(Arsenal)	3 Gordillo
4 Robson	(West Brom)	4 Joaquin
5 Watson	(Southampton)	5 Tendillo
6 Osman	(Ipswich Town)	6 Maceda
7 Keegan*	(Southampton)	7 Marcos
8 Francis	(Notts Forest) replaced by Barnes	8 Victor
9 Mariner	(Ipswich Town)	9 Juanito
10 Brooking	(West Ham Utd) replaced by Wilkins	10 Satrusegui
11 Hoddle	(Tottenham)	11 Zamora

Crowd: 71,840

England scorer: Hoddle

Comments: The scorers of both Spanish goals were called Jesus, and England themselves could have done with some divine inspiration as they slumped to a defeat in this friendly encounter.

ENGLAND 0 Romania 0; at Wembley;
Wednesday 29th April 1981 (World Cup qualifier)

1 Shilton	(Notts Forest)		1 Iordache
2 Anderson	(Notts Forest)		2 Negrila
3 Sansom	(Arsenal)		3 Munteanu
4 Robson	(West Brom)		4 Sames
5 Watson*	(Southampton)		5 Stefanescu
6 Osman	(Ipswich Town)		6 Beldeanu
7 Wilkins	(Man Utd)		7 Crisan
8 Brooking	(West Ham Utd) replaced by McDermott	8	Iordanescu
9 Coppell	(Man Utd)		9 Camataru
10 Francis	(Notts Forest)		10 Stoica
11 Woodcock	(Cologne)		11 Balaci

Crowd: 62,500

Comments: Although Shilton and his defence kept a clean sheet, England did their World Cup hopes no favours by drawing at home to a team that they had already lost to the previous year.

ENGLAND 0 Brazil 1; at Wembley;
Tuesday 12th May 1981

1 Clemence*	(Liverpool)		1 Peres
2 Neal	(Liverpool)		2 Edevaldo
3 Sansom	(Arsenal)		3 Oscar
4 Robson	(West Brom)		4 Luizinho
5 Watson	(Southampton)		5 Junior
6 Wilkins	(Man Utd)		6 Cerezo
7 Coppell	(Man Utd)		7 Socrates
8 McDermott	(Liverpool)		8 Zico
9 Withe	(Aston Villa)		9 Isidoro
10 Rix	(Arsenal)		10 Reinaldo
11 Barnes	(West Brom)		11 Eder

Crowd: 75,000

Comments: The great Zico scored the only goal inside the first fifteen minutes as England failed to win at home for the third consecutive match. Peter Withe made his debut in this latest setback.

ENGLAND 0 Wales 0; at Wembley;
Wednesday 20th May 1981 (Home International)

1 Corrigan	(Man City)	1 Davies
2 Anderson	(Notts Forest)	2 Jones
3 Sansom	(Crystal Palace)	3 Ratcliffe
4 Robson	(West Brom)	4 Nicholas
5 Watson*	(Southampton)	5 Phillips
6 Wilkins	(Man Utd)	6 Price
7 Coppell	(Man Utd)	7 Harris
8 Hoddle	(Tottenham)	8 Flynn
9 Withe	(Aston Villa) replaced by Woodcock	9 Walsh
10 Rix	(Arsenal)	10 Thomas
11 Barnes	(West Brom)	11 James

Crowd: 34,280

Comments: A very poor turnout at Wembley were treated to another tooth-less display as Wales escaped with a point as England's poor run of form continued to deteriorate.

ENGLAND 0 Scotland 1; at Wembley;
Saturday 23rd May 1981 (Home International)

1 Corrigan	(Man City)	1 Rough
2 Anderson	(Notts Forest)	2 McGrain
3 Sansom	(Crystal Palace)	3 Gray
4 Wilkins	(Man Utd)	4 Stewart
5 Watson*	(Southampton) replaced by Martin	5 McLeish
6 Robson	(West Brom)	6 Miller
7 Coppell	(Man Utd)	7 Provan
8 Hoddle	(Tottenham)	8 Archibald
9 Withe	(Aston Villa)	9 Jordan
10 Rix	(Arsenal)	10 Hartford
11 Woodcock	(Cologne) replaced by Francis	11 Robertson

Crowd: 90,000

Comments: England's appalling home form plumbed new depths as they failed to score for the fourth successive match. John Robertson converted a second-half penalty for the victorious Scots.

Switzerland 2 ENGLAND 1; in Basle;
Saturday 30th May 1981 (World Cup qualifier)

1 Burgener	1 Clemence	(Liverpool)
2 Zappa	2 Mills	(Ipswich Town)
3 Hermann	3 Sansom	(Crystal Palace)
4 Egli	4 Wilkins	(Man Utd)
5 Ludi	5 Watson	(Southampton) replaced by Barnes
6 Wehrli	6 Osman	(Ipswich Town)
7 Botteron	7 Keegan*	(Southampton)
8 Barberis	8 Robson	(West Brom)
9 Scheiwiler	9 Coppell	(Man Utd)
10 Elsener	10 Mariner	(Ipswich Town)
11 Sulser	11 Francis	(Notts Forest) replaced by McDermott

Crowd: 40,000

England scorer: McDermott

Comments: Clueless England were 2 goals behind at half-time as their pitiful form seriously threatened their hopes of qualifying for the World Cup finals. Crowd trouble also reared its ugly head.

Hungary 1 ENGLAND 3; in Budapest;
Saturday 6th June 1981 (World Cup qualifier)

1 Katzirz	1 Clemence	(Liverpool)
2 Martos	2 Neal	(Liverpool)
3 Balint	3 Mills	(Ipswich Town)
4 Varga	4 Thompson	(Liverpool)
5 Muller	5 Watson	(Southampton)
6 Garaba	6 Robson	(West Brom)
7 Fazekas	7 Keegan*	(Southampton)
8 Nyalisi	8 McDermott	(Liverpool)
9 Kiss	9 Mariner	(Ipswich Town)
10 Mucha	10 Brooking	(West Ham Utd) replaced by Wilkins
11 Torocsik	11 Coppell	(Man Utd)

Crowd: 65,000

England scorers: Brooking (2), Keegan (Pen)

Comments: Trevor Brooking twice gave the visitors the lead as England reminded themselves that they could play football. This triumph rekindled hopes of qualifying for the World Cup finals.

Norway 2 ENGLAND 1; in Oslo;
Wednesday 9th September 1981 (World Cup qualifier)

1 Antonsen	1 Clemence	(Liverpool)
2 Berntsen	2 Neal	(Liverpool)
3 Hareide	3 Mills	(Ipswich Town)
4 Jan Aas	4 Thompson	(Liverpool)
5 Grondalen	5 Osman	(Ipswich Town)
6 Albertsen	6 Robson	(West Brom)
7 Giske	7 Keegan*	(Southampton)
8 Thoresen	8 Francis	(Notts Forest)
9 Okland	9 Mariner	(Ipswich Town) replaced by Withe
10 Jacobsen	10 Hoddle	(Tottenham) replaced by Barnes
11 Lund	11 McDermott	(Liverpool)

Crowd: 28,500

England scorer: Robson

Comments: Although Robson gave the away team an early lead, the Norwegians had gone ahead by half-time. This latest humiliation was ecstatically greeted by one Norwegian commentator!

ENGLAND 1 Hungary 0; at Wembley;
Wednesday 18th November 1981 (World Cup qualifier)

1 Shilton	(Notts Forest)	1 Meszaros
2 Neal	(Liverpool)	2 Martos
3 Mills	(Ipswich Town)	3 Balint
4 Thompson	(Liverpool)	4 Toth
5 Martin	(West Ham Utd)	5 Muller
6 Robson	(West Brom)	6 Garaba
7 Keegan*	(Southampton)	7 Fazekas
8 Coppell	(Man Utd) replaced by Morley	8 Csapo
9 Mariner	(Ipswich Town)	9 Torocsik
10 Brooking	(West Ham Utd)	10 Kiss
11 McDermott	(Liverpool)	11 Sallai

Crowd: 92,000

England scorer: Mariner

Comments: Paul Mariner's early goal steadied the nerves as England squeezed into the World Cup finals in Spain. Tony Morley won his first cap in this crucial qualifier.

ENGLAND 4 Northern Ireland 0; at Wembley;
Tuesday 23rd February 1982 (Home International)

1	Clemence	(Tottenham)	1	Jennings	
2	Anderson	(Notts Forest)	2	Nicholl	
3	Sansom	(Arsenal)	3	Nelson	
4	Wilkins	(Man Utd)	4	Donaghy	
5	Watson	(Stoke City)	5	Nicholl	
6	Foster	(Brighton And Hove Albion)	6	O'Neill	
7	Keegan*	(Southampton)	7	Brotherston	
8	Robson	(Man Utd)	8	O'Neill	
9	Francis	(Man City) replaced by Regis	9	Armstrong	
10	Hoddle	(Tottenham)	10	McIlroy	
11	Morley	(Aston Villa) replaced by Woodcock	11	Hamilton	

Crowd: 54,900

England scorers: Robson, Keegan, Wilkins, Hoddle

Comments: Bryan Robson scored in the first minute, but it took two very late goals to seal Northern Ireland's fate. Steve Foster and West Brom's Cyrille Regis both won their first caps.

Wales 0 ENGLAND 1; in Cardiff;
Tuesday 27th April 1982 (Home International)

1	Davies	1	Corrigan	(Man City)
2	Marustik	2	Neal	(Liverpool)
3	Jones	3	Sansom	(Arsenal)
4	Nicholas	4	Thompson*	(Liverpool)
5	Stevenson	5	Butcher	(Ipswich Town)
6	Ratcliffe	6	Robson	(Man Utd)
7	James	7	Wilkins	(Man Utd)
8	Flynn	8	Francis	(Man City) replaced by Regis
9	Rush	9	Withe	(Aston Villa)
10	Curtis	10	Hoddle	(Tottenham) replaced by McDermott
11	Thomas	11	Morley	(Aston Villa)

Crowd: 25,000

England scorer: Francis

Comments: Just before being substituted, Trevor Francis signed off with a goal fifteen minutes from time as England achieved their third consecutive clean sheet.

ENGLAND 2 Holland 0; at Wembley;
Tuesday 25th May 1982

1 Shilton*	(Notts Forest)	1 van Breukelen
2 Neal	(Liverpool)	2 Ophof
3 Sansom	(Arsenal)	3 Metgod
4 Thompson	(Liverpool)	4 van der Korput
5 Foster	(Brighton And Hove Albion)	5 Boeve
6 Robson	(Man Utd)	6 Peters
7 Wilkins	(Man Utd)	7 Krol
8 Devonshire	(West Ham Utd) replaced by Rix	8 Muhren
9 Mariner	(Ipswich Town) replaced by Barnes	9 la Ling
10 McDermott	(Liverpool)	10 Kieft
11 Woodcock	(Cologne)	11 Tahamata

Crowd: 69,000

England scorers: Woodcock, Mariner

Comments: Two goals shortly after half-time provided England with another morale-boosting win, ahead of the World Cup finals in Spain. Peter Barnes made his last appearance in this triumph.

Scotland 0 ENGLAND 1; in Glasgow;
Saturday 29th May 1982 (Home International)

1 Rough	1 Shilton	(Notts Forest)
2 Burley	2 Mills	(Ipswich Town)
3 McGrain	3 Sansom	(Arsenal)
4 Hansen	4 Thompson	(Liverpool)
5 Evans	5 Butcher	(Ipswich Town)
6 Narey	6 Robson	(Man Utd)
7 Souness	7 Keegan*	(Southampton) replaced by McDermott
8 Dalglish	8 Coppell	(Man Utd)
9 Jordan	9 Mariner	(Ipswich Town) replaced by Francis
10 Hartford	10 Brooking	(West Ham Utd)
11 Brazil	11 Wilkins	(Man Utd)

Crowd: 80,529

England scorer: Mariner

Comments: An early goal from Paul Mariner yielded maximum points and triumph in the Home International Championship for the visitors as both teams prepared for the World Cup tournament.

Iceland 1 ENGLAND 1; in Reykjavik;
Wednesday 2nd June 1982

1	Baldursson	1	Corrigan	(Man City)
2	Oskarsson	2	Anderson	(Notts Forest)
3	Jonsson	3	Neal*	(Liverpool)
4	Geirsson	4	Watson	(Stoke City)
5	Haraldsson	5	Osman	(Ipswich Town)
6	Thordarson	6	McDermott	(Liverpool)
7	Gudlaugsson	7	Hoddle	(Tottenham)
8	Edvaldsson	8	Devonshire	(West Ham Utd) replaced by Perryman
9	Gudjohnsen	9	Withe	(Aston Villa)
10	Gudmundsson	10	Regis	(West Brom) replaced by Goddard
11	Thordarson	11	Morley	(Aston Villa)

Crowd: 10,814

England scorer: Goddard

Comments: Paul Goddard came off the bench on his debut and promptly scored. This was the only cap for him and Steve Perryman, and the last appearance for Corrigan, McDermott, and Watson.

Finland 1 ENGLAND 4; in Helsinki;
Thursday 3rd June 1982

1	Alaja	1	Clemence	(Tottenham)
2	Lahtinen	2	Mills	(Ipswich Town)
3	Ikalainen	3	Sansom	(Arsenal)
4	Granskog	4	Thompson	(Liverpool)
5	Pekonen	5	Martin	(West Ham Utd)
6	Turunen	6	Robson	(Man Utd) replaced by Rix
7	Haaskivi	7	Keegan*	(Southampton)
8	Ruatianen	8	Coppell	(Man Utd) replaced by Francis
9	Himanka	9	Mariner	(Ipswich Town)
10	Ismail	10	Brooking	(West Ham Utd) replaced by Woodcock
11	Neiminen	11	Wilkins	(Man Utd)

Crowd: 21,521

England scorers: Mariner (2), Robson (2)

Comments: Mariner and Robson scored in each half as the away team's last World Cup rehearsal went according to plan. This was however the last time that Keegan started an England match.

ENGLAND 3 France 1; in Bilbao;
Wednesday 16th June 1982 (World Cup finals)

1 Shilton	(Notts Forest)	1	Ettori
2 Mills*	(Ipswich Town)	2	Battiston
3 Sansom	(Arsenal) replaced by Neal	3	Bossis
4 Thompson	(Liverpool)	4	Tresor
5 Butcher	(Ipswich Town)	5	Lopez
6 Robson	(Man Utd)	6	Larios
7 Coppell	(Man Utd)	7	Girard
8 Francis	(Man City)	8	Giresse
9 Mariner	(Ipswich Town)	9	Rocheteau
10 Rix	(Arsenal)	10	Platini
11 Wilkins	(Man Utd)	11	Soler

Crowd: 44,172

England scorers: Robson (2), Mariner

Comments: The great Bryan Robson opened the scoring in the first thirty seconds and then restored England's lead in the second half. Paul Mariner then completed this fine win with a late goal.

ENGLAND 2 Czechoslovakia 0; in Bilbao;
Sunday 20th June 1982 (World Cup finals)

1 Shilton	(Notts Forest)	1	Seman
2 Mills*	(Ipswich Town)	2	Barmos
3 Sansom	(Arsenal)	3	Radimec
4 Thompson	(Liverpool)	4	Vojacek
5 Butcher	(Ipswich Town)	5	Vojacek
6 Robson	(Man Utd) replaced by Hoddle	6	Chaloupka
7 Coppell	(Man Utd)	7	Berger
8 Francis	(Man City)	8	Jurkemik
9 Mariner	(Ipswich Town)	9	Janecka
10 Rix	(Arsenal)	10	Nehoda
11 Wilkins	(Man Utd)	11	Visek

Crowd: 41,123

England scorers: Francis, Barmos (OG)

Comments: Two goals in quick succession in the second half broke the Czechs' resistance as an impressive England seized 2 more points. The Czechs were managed by a certain Dr Jozef Venglos.

ENGLAND 1 Kuwait 0; in Bilbao;
Friday 25th June 1982 (World Cup finals)

1 Shilton	(Notts Forest)	1 Al-Tarabulsi
2 Neal	(Liverpool)	2 Saeed
3 Mills*	(Ipswich Town)	3 Ma'Yoof
4 Thompson	(Liverpool)	4 Mubarak
5 Foster	(Brighton And Hove Albion)	5 Al-Mubarak
6 Hoddle	(Tottenham)	6 Al-Boloushi
7 Coppell	(Man Utd)	7 Al-Houti
8 Francis	(Man City)	8 Marzouq
9 Mariner	(Ipswich Town)	9 Al-Anbari
10 Rix	(Arsenal)	10 Al-Suwaayed
11 Wilkins	(Man Utd)	11 Al-Dakhil

Crowd: 39,700

England scorer: Francis

Comments: A goal from Trevor Francis just before the half hour enabled England to finish the first group phase with maximum points. Steve Foster made his last appearance in this victory.

ENGLAND 0 West Germany 0; in Madrid;
Tuesday 29th June 1982 (World Cup finals)

1 Shilton	(Notts Forest)	1 Schumacher
2 Mills*	(Ipswich Town)	2 Kaltz
3 Sansom	(Arsenal)	3 Forster
4 Thompson	(Liverpool)	4 Stielike
5 Butcher	(Ipswich Town)	5 Briegel
6 Robson	(Man Utd)	6 Dremmler
7 Coppell	(Man Utd)	7 Forster
8 Francis	(Man City) replaced by Woodcock	8 Breitner
9 Mariner	(Ipswich Town)	9 Muller
10 Rix	(Arsenal)	10 Reinders
11 Wilkins	(Man Utd)	11 Rummenigge

Crowd: 90,089

Comments: It wouldn't be the World Cup without a titanic struggle against the West Germans. This time it finished honours even, but it was the Deutschlanders who would go on to the final.

Spain 0 ENGLAND 0; in Madrid;
Monday 5th July 1982 (World Cup finals)

1	Arconada	1	Shilton	(Notts Forest)
2	Urquiaga	2	Mills*	(Ipswich Town)
3	Tendillo	3	Sansom	(Arsenal)
4	Alesanco	4	Thompson	(Liverpool)
5	Gordillo	5	Butcher	(Ipswich Town)
6	Saura	6	Robson	(Man Utd)
7	Alonso	7	Rix	(Arsenal) replaced by Brooking
8	Zamora	8	Francis	(Man City)
9	Camacho	9	Mariner	(Ipswich Town)
10	Satrusegui	10	Woodcock	(Arsenal) replaced by Keegan
11	Santillana	11	Wilkins	(Man Utd)

Crowd: 75,000

Comments: A semi-fit Keegan was summoned from the bench to work a miracle but England could not find the 2 goals they needed to reach the semi-finals. This was Ron Greenwood's last match.

Denmark 2 ENGLAND 2; in Copenhagen;
Wednesday 22nd September 1982 (European Championship)

1	Rasmussen	1	Shilton	(Southampton)
2	Bastrup	2	Neal	(Liverpool)
3	Elkjaer	3	Sansom	(Arsenal)
4	Bertlesen	4	Wilkins*	(Man Utd)
5	Hansen	5	Osman	(Ipswich Town)
6	Lerby	6	Butcher	(Ipswich Town)
7	Olsen	7	Morley	(Aston Villa) replaced by Hill
8	Rasmussen	8	Robson	(Man Utd)
9	Busk	9	Mariner	(Ipswich Town)
10	Nielsen	10	Francis	(Sampdoria)
11	Rontved	11	Rix	(Arsenal)

Crowd: 44,300

England scorer: Francis (2)

Comments: Jesper Olsen snatched a crucial last-gasp equaliser as the first match of the Bobby Robson era ended with a commendable draw. Luton Town's Ricky Hill won his first England cap.

ENGLAND 1 West Germany 2; at Wembley;
Wednesday 13th October 1982

1	Shilton	(Southampton)		1	Schumacher
2	Mabbutt	(Tottenham)		2	Kaltz
3	Sansom	(Arsenal)		3	Strack
4	Thompson	(Liverpool)		4	Forster
5	Butcher	(Ipswich Town)		5	Forster
6	Wilkins*	(Man Utd)		6	Dremmler
7	Hill	(Luton Town)		7	Briegel
8	Regis	(West Brom) replaced by Blissett		8	Matthaus
9	Mariner	(Ipswich Town) replaced by Woodcock		9	Rummenigge
10	Armstrong	(Southampton) replaced by Rix		10	Meier
11	Devonshire	(West Ham Utd)		11	Allofs

Crowd: 68,000

England scorer: Woodcock

Comments: The great Karl-Heinz Rummenigge gave the visitors a 2–goal lead late in the game before Woodcock reduced the deficit. Gary Mabbutt and Watford's Luther Blissett made their debut.

Greece 0 ENGLAND 3; in Thessaloniki;
Wednesday 17th November 1982 (European Championship)

1	Sarganis		1	Shilton	(Southampton)
2	Gounaris		2	Neal	(Liverpool)
3	Iosifidis		3	Sansom	(Arsenal)
4	Kapsis		4	Thompson	(Liverpool)
5	Firos		5	Martin	(West Ham Utd)
6	Michos		6	Robson*	(Man Utd)
7	Livathinos		7	Lee	(Liverpool)
8	Ardizoglou		8	Mabbutt	(Tottenham)
9	Mitropoulos		9	Mariner	(Ipswich Town)
10	Anastopoulos		10	Woodcock	(Arsenal)
11	Mavros		11	Morley	(Aston Villa)

Crowd: 41,554

England scorers: Woodcock (2), Lee

Comments: Tony Woodcock scored in the first minute and Sammy Lee completed the scoring in the second half, on his debut. This was the last appearance for Tony Morley and Phil Thompson.

ENGLAND 9 Luxembourg 0; at Wembley;
Wednesday 15th December 1982 (European Championship)

1 Clemence	(Tottenham)	1 Moes
2 Neal	(Liverpool)	2 Girres
3 Sansom	(Arsenal)	3 Meunier
4 Robson*	(Man Utd)	4 Rohmann
5 Martin	(West Ham Utd)	5 Clemens
6 Butcher	(Ipswich Town)	6 Bossi
7 Coppell	(Man Utd) replaced by Chamberlain	7 Hellers
8 Lee	(Liverpool)	8 Weis
9 Woodcock	(Arsenal)	9 Dresch
10 Blissett	(Watford)	10 Reiter
11 Mabbutt	(Tottenham) replaced by Hoddle	11 di Domenico

Crowd: 33,980

England scorers: Bossi (OG), Coppell, Woodcock, Blissett (3), Chamberlain, Hoddle, Neal

Comments: Stoke City's Mark Chamberlain came off the bench and scored on his debut. Hoddle also came on as a substitute and scored. However, the show was stolen by Blissett's hat-trick.

ENGLAND 2 Wales 1; at Wembley;
Wednesday 23rd February 1983 (Home International)

1 Shilton*	(Southampton)	1 Southall
2 Neal	(Liverpool)	2 Jones
3 Statham	(West Brom)	3 Ratcliffe
4 Lee	(Liverpool)	4 Mahoney
5 Martin	(West Ham Utd)	5 Price
6 Butcher	(Ipswich Town)	6 Jackett
7 Mabbutt	(Tottenham)	7 James
8 Blissett	(Watford)	8 Flynn
9 Mariner	(Ipswich Town)	9 Rush
10 Cowans	(Aston Villa)	10 Davies
11 Devonshire	(West Ham Utd)	11 Thomas

Crowd: 24,000

England scorers: Butcher, Neal (Pen)

Comments: Ian Rush gave Wales an early lead, but his Liverpool colleague Phil Neal settled the issue with a late penalty. Gordon Cowans and Derek Statham made their debut in this narrow win.

ENGLAND 0 Greece 0; at Wembley;
Wednesday 30th March 1983 (European Championship)

1 Shilton*	(Southampton)	1	Sarganis
2 Neal	(Liverpool)	2	Gounaris
3 Sansom	(Arsenal)	3	Karoulias
4 Lee	(Liverpool)	4	Galitsios
5 Martin	(West Ham Utd)	5	Michos
6 Butcher	(Ipswich Town)	6	Xanthopoulos
7 Coppell	(Man Utd)	7	Mitropoulos
8 Mabbutt	(Tottenham)	8	Kouis
9 Francis	(Sampdoria)	9	Kousoulakis
10 Woodcock	(Arsenal) replaced by Blissett	10	Anastopoulos
11 Devonshire	(West Ham Utd) replaced by Rix	11	Kostikos

Crowd: 48,500

Comments: This stalemate undermined England's chances of reaching the European Championship finals in France next year, and it also ended the international career of Steve Coppell.

ENGLAND 2 Hungary 0; at Wembley;
Wednesday 27th April 1983 (European Championship)

1 Shilton*	(Southampton)	1	Katzirz
2 Neal	(Liverpool)	2	Martos
3 Sansom	(Arsenal)	3	Kocsis
4 Lee	(Liverpool)	4	Garaba
5 Martin	(West Ham Utd)	5	Toth
6 Butcher	(Ipswich Town)	6	Hannich
7 Mabbutt	(Tottenham)	7	Nyalisi
8 Francis	(Sampdoria)	8	Kardos
9 Withe	(Aston Villa)	9	Varga
10 Blissett	(Watford)	10	Kiss
11 Cowans	(Aston Villa)	11	Hajszan

Crowd: 55,000

England scorers: Francis, Withe

Comments: Peter Withe finally scored for the home team, at the seventh time of asking, as he added to the 1-0 interval lead. England had collected their fourth clean sheet in their last five matches.

Northern Ireland 0 ENGLAND 0; in Belfast; Saturday 28th May 1983 (Home International)

1	Jennings	1	Shilton*	(Southampton)
2	Nicholl	2	Neal	(Liverpool)
3	Donaghy	3	Sansom	(Arsenal)
4	Nicholl	4	Hoddle	(Tottenham)
5	McClelland	5	Roberts	(Tottenham)
6	McIlroy	6	Butcher	(Ipswich Town)
7	Mullen	7	Mabbutt	(Tottenham)
8	Armstrong	8	Francis	(Sampdoria)
9	Hamilton	9	Withe	(Aston Villa)
10	Stewart	10	Blissett	(Watford) replaced by Barnes
11	O'Neill	11	Cowans	(Aston Villa)

Crowd: 22,000

Comments: John Barnes won his first cap when he replaced his club team-mate Luther Blissett, but even he could not break the deadlock. Graham Roberts also made his debut in this match.

ENGLAND 2 Scotland 0; at Wembley; Wednesday 1st June 1983 (Home International)

1	Shilton	(Southampton)	1	Leighton
2	Neal	(Liverpool)	2	Gough
3	Sansom	(Arsenal)	3	Gray
4	Lee	(Liverpool)	4	Narey
5	Roberts	(Tottenham)	5	McLeish
6	Butcher	(Ipswich Town)	6	Miller
7	Robson*	(Man Utd) replaced by Mabbutt	7	Strachan
8	Francis	(Sampdoria)	8	Souness
9	Withe	(Aston Villa) replaced by Blissett	9	Gray
10	Hoddle	(Tottenham)	10	Nicholas
11	Cowans	(Aston Villa)	11	Bannon

Crowd: 84,000

England scorers: Robson, Cowans

Comments: The returning captain Bryan Robson scored an early goal and then had to be substituted soon after. Gordon Cowans added a second shortly after the interval for a comfortable win.

Australia o ENGLAND o; in Sydney;
Sunday 12th June 1983

1 Greedy	1 Shilton*	(Southampton)
2 Davidson	2 Thomas	(Coventry City)
3 Yankos	3 Statham	(West Brom) replaced by Barnes
4 Ratcliffe	4 Williams	(Southampton)
5 O'Connor	5 Osman	(Ipswich Town)
6 Jennings	6 Butcher	(Ipswich Town)
7 Watson	7 Barham	(Norwich City)
8 Cant	8 Gregory	(QPR)
9 Katholos	9 Blissett	(Watford) replaced by Walsh
10 Kosmina	10 Francis	(Sampdoria)
11 O'Connor	11 Cowans	(Aston Villa)

Crowd: 28,000

Comments: It wasn't exactly the Ashes as both teams battled at Sydney Cricket Ground. First caps were awarded to Mark Barham, John Gregory, Danny Thomas, Paul Walsh, and Steve Williams.

Australia o ENGLAND 1; in Brisbane;
Wednesday 15th June 1983

1 Greedy	1 Shilton*	(Southampton)
2 Davidson	2 Neal	(Liverpool)
3 Yankos	3 Statham	(West Brom) replaced by Williams
4 Ratcliffe	4 Barham	(Norwich City)
5 O'Connor	5 Osman	(Ipswich Town)
6 Jennings	6 Butcher	(Ipswich Town)
7 Watson	7 Gregory	(QPR)
8 Katholos	8 Francis	(Sampdoria)
9 Cant	9 Walsh	(Luton Town)
10 Kosmina	10 Cowans	(Aston Villa)
11 O'Connor	11 Barnes	(Watford)

Crowd: 16,000

England scorer: Walsh

Comments: Paul Walsh scored just short of the hour mark to clinch this friendly win. This match concluded the short international careers of Mark Barham and Derek Statham.

Australia 1 ENGLAND 1; in Melbourne;
Sunday 19th June 1983

1 Greedy	1 Shilton*	(Southampton) replaced by Spink
2 Davidson	2 Neal	(Liverpool) replaced by Thomas
3 Yankos	3 Pickering	(Sunderland)
4 Ratcliffe	4 Lee	(Liverpool)
5 O'Connor	5 Osman	(Ipswich Town)
6 Jennings	6 Butcher	(Ipswich Town)
7 Watson	7 Gregory	(QPR)
8 Cant	8 Francis	(Sampdoria)
9 Murphy	9 Walsh	(Luton Town) replaced by Blissett
10 Kosmina	10 Cowans	(Aston Villa)
11 O'Connor	11 Barnes	(Watford)

Crowd: 20,000

England scorer: Francis

Comments: It took an own goal from Phil Neal to end Peter Shilton's run of six matches without conceding a goal. Nick Pickering and Nigel Spink won their only caps in this drawn encounter.

ENGLAND 0 Denmark 1; at Wembley;
Wednesday 21st September 1983 (European Championship)

1 Shilton*	(Southampton)	1	Kjaer
2 Neal	(Liverpool)	2	Simonsen
3 Sansom	(Arsenal)	3	Berggreen
4 Lee	(Liverpool) replaced by Blissett	4	Bertlesen
5 Osman	(Ipswich Town)	5	Laudrup
6 Butcher	(Ipswich Town)	6	Lerby
7 Wilkins	(Man Utd)	7	Olsen
8 Gregory	(QPR)	8	Rasmussen
9 Mariner	(Ipswich Town)	9	Busk
10 Francis	(Sampdoria)	10	Nielsen
11 Barnes	(Watford) replaced by Chamberlain	11	Olsen

Crowd: 82,500

Comments: Former European Player Of The Year Allan Simonsen converted a penalty just before half time which effectively ended England's chances of reaching the tournament finals in 1984.

Hungary 0 ENGLAND 3; in Budapest;
Wednesday 12th October 1983 (European Championship)

1	Kovacs	1	Shilton	(Southampton)
2	Csonka	2	Gregory	(QPR)
3	Kardos	3	Sansom	(Arsenal)
4	Garaba	4	Lee	(Liverpool)
5	Varga	5	Martin	(West Ham Utd)
6	Hannich	6	Butcher	(Ipswich Town)
7	Csongradi	7	Robson*	(Man Utd)
8	Nyalisi	8	Hoddle	(Tottenham)
9	Burcsa	9	Mariner	(Ipswich Town)
10	Dajca	10	Blissett	(Accrington Stanley) replaced by Withe
11	Hajszan	11	Mabbutt	(Tottenham)

Crowd: 25,000

England scorers: Hoddle, Lee, Mariner

Comments: All three goals arrived in the first half as England successfully despatched hapless Hungary for a fourth time in three years in a qualifying group match.

Luxembourg 0 ENGLAND 4; in Luxembourg City;
Wednesday 16th November 1983 (European Championship)

1	Defrang	1	Clemence	(Tottenham)
2	Michaux	2	Duxbury	(Man Utd)
3	Bossi	3	Sansom	(Arsenal)
4	Dresch	4	Lee	(Liverpool)
5	Meunier	5	Martin	(West Ham Utd)
6	Langers	6	Butcher	(Ipswich Town)
7	Wagner	7	Robson*	(Man Utd)
8	Hellers	8	Hoddle	(Tottenham)
9	Barboni	9	Mariner	(Ipswich Town)
10	Reiter	10	Woodcock	(Arsenal) replaced by Barnes
11	Malget	11	Devonshire	(West Ham Utd)

Crowd: 5,400

England scorers: Robson (2), Mariner, Butcher

Comments: Two goals in each half settled this 'formality' of a fixture. Mike Duxbury won his first cap, while Ray Clemence and Alan Devonshire played their last England match.

France 2 ENGLAND 0; in Paris;
Wednesday 29th February 1984

1	Bats	1 Shilton	(Southampton)
2	Battiston	2 Duxbury	(Man Utd)
3	Le Roux	3 Sansom	(Arsenal)
4	Bossis	4 Lee	(Liverpool) replaced by Barnes
5	Amoros	5 Roberts	(Tottenham)
6	Giresse	6 Butcher	(Ipswich Town)
7	Tigana	7 Robson*	(Man Utd)
8	Fernandez	8 Stein	(Luton Town) replaced by Woodcock
9	Platini	9 Walsh	(Luton Town)
10	Toure	10 Hoddle	(Tottenham)
11	Bellone	11 Williams	(Southampton)

Crowd: 43,000

Comments: French superstar Michel Platini scored the match's two goals in the second half as France prepared to host the European Championships. Brian Stein won his only cap in this defeat.

ENGLAND 1 Northern Ireland 0; at Wembley;
Wednesday 4th April 1984 (Home International)

1	Shilton	(Southampton)	1	Platt
2	Anderson	(Notts Forest)	2	Nicholl
3	Kennedy	(Liverpool)	3	McClelland
4	Lee	(Liverpool)	4	McElhinney
5	Roberts	(Tottenham)	5	Donaghy
6	Butcher	(Ipswich Town)	6	Armstrong
7	Robson*	(Man Utd)	7	O'Neill
8	Wilkins	(Man Utd)	8	Hamilton
9	Woodcock	(Arsenal)	9	Whiteside
10	Francis	(Sampdoria)	10	McIlroy
11	Rix	(Arsenal)	11	Stewart

Crowd: 24,000

England scorer: Woodcock

Comments: Woodcock scored the winner just after the break. Alan Kennedy made his debut in what was the last Home International between the 2 countries before England pulled the plug out.

Wales 1 ENGLAND 0; in Wrexham;
Wednesday 2nd May 1984 (Home International)

1 Southall	1 Shilton	(Southampton)
2 Phillips	2 Duxbury	(Man Utd)
3 Jones	3 Kennedy	(Liverpool)
4 James	4 Lee	(Liverpool)
5 Hopkins	5 Martin	(West Ham Utd) replaced by Fenwick
6 Ratcliffe	6 Wright	(Southampton)
7 Davies	7 Wilkins*	(Man Utd)
8 Davies	8 Gregory	(QPR)
9 Rush	9 Walsh	(Luton Town)
10 Hughes	10 Woodcock	(Arsenal)
11 Thomas	11 Armstrong	(Southampton) replaced by Blissett

Crowd: 14,250

Comments: The England careers of Terry Fenwick and Mark Wright made the worst possible start as Mark Hughes helped inflict another Wrexham reverse in their final Home International fixture.

Scotland 1 ENGLAND 1; in Glasgow;
Saturday 26th May 1984 (Home International)

1 Leighton	1 Shilton	(Southampton)
2 Gough	2 Duxbury	(Man Utd)
3 Albiston	3 Sansom	(Arsenal)
4 Wark	4 Wilkins	(Man Utd)
5 McLeish	5 Roberts	(Tottenham)
6 Miller	6 Fenwick	(QPR)
7 Strachan	7 Chamberlain	(Stoke City) replaced by Hunt
8 Archibald	8 Robson*	(Man Utd)
9 McGhee	9 Woodcock	(Arsenal) replaced by Lineker
10 Bett	10 Blissett	(Accrington Stanley)
11 Cooper	11 Barnes	(Watford)

Crowd: 73,064

England scorer: Woodcock

Comments: Both goals came in the first half as England ended their mediocre final Home Internationals campaign with a decent draw. Gary Lineker and West Brom's Steve Hunt made their debuts.

ENGLAND 0 USSR 2; at Wembley;
Saturday 2nd June 1984

1	Shilton	(Southampton)		1	Daseyev
2	Duxbury	(Man Utd)		2	Sulakvelidze
3	Sansom	(Arsenal)		3	Chivadze
4	Wilkins	(AC Milan)		4	Baltacha
5	Roberts	(Tottenham)		5	Demianenko
6	Fenwick	(QPR)		6	Aleinikov
7	Chamberlain	(Stoke City)		7	Litovchenko
8	Robson*	(Man Utd)		8	Oganesian
9	Francis	(Sampdoria) replaced by Hateley		9	Zygmantovich
10	Blissett	(Accrington Stanley)		10	Rodionov
11	Barnes	(Watford) replaced by Hunt		11	Blokhin

Crowd: 38,125

Comments: The home team were sunk by two second half goals from a highly-rated Russian outfit. Mark Hateley made his debut while Blissett, Hunt, and Roberts collected their final caps.

Brazil 0 ENGLAND 2; in Rio de Janeiro;
Sunday 10th June 1984

1	Costa		1	Shilton	(Southampton)
2	Leandro		2	Duxbury	(Man Utd)
3	Mozer		3	Sansom	(Arsenal)
4	Gomes		4	Wilkins	(AC Milan)
5	Junior		5	Watson	(Norwich City)
6	Pires		6	Fenwick	(QPR)
7	Zenon		7	Robson*	(Man Utd)
8	Assis		8	Chamberlain	(Stoke City)
9	Gaucho		9	Hateley	(Portsmouth)
10	Dinamite		10	Woodcock	(Arsenal) replaced by Allen
11	Tato		11	Barnes	(Watford)

Crowd: 73,064

England scorers: Barnes, Hateley

Comments: Just before half-time John Barnes danced through the Brazilian defence to score a goal which built a reputation that he found hard to live up to. Clive Allen also won his first cap.

Uruguay 2 ENGLAND 0; in Montevideo; Wednesday 13th June 1984

1 Rodriguez	1 Shilton	(Southampton)
2 Gutierrez	2 Duxbury	(Man Utd)
3 Acevedo	3 Sansom	(Arsenal)
4 Montelongo	4 Wilkins	(AC Milan)
5 Bossio	5 Watson	(Norwich City)
6 Martinez	6 Fenwick	(QPR)
7 Aguilera	7 Robson*	(Man Utd)
8 Perdomo	8 Chamberlain	(Stoke City)
9 Cabrera	9 Hateley	(Portsmouth)
10 Carrasco	10 Allen	(Tottenham) replaced by Woodcock
11 Acosta	11 Barnes	(Watford)

Crowd: 34,500

Comments: England did themselves no favours by conceding a penalty in the first ten minutes. It was so typical of Bobby Robson's team to win away to Brazil and then lose to Uruguay.

Chile 0 ENGLAND 0; in Santiago; Sunday 17th June 1984

1 Rojas	1 Shilton	(Southampton)
2 Tabilo	2 Duxbury	(Man Utd)
3 Gomez	3 Sansom	(Arsenal)
4 Hormaabal	4 Wilkins	(AC Milan)
5 Araya	5 Watson	(Norwich City)
6 Hisis	6 Fenwick	(QPR)
7 Toro	7 Robson*	(Man Utd)
8 Soto	8 Chamberlain	(Stoke City) replaced by Lee
9 Veneas	9 Hateley	(Portsmouth)
10 Arvena	10 Allen	(Tottenham)
11 Covarrubias	11 Barnes	(Watford)

Crowd: 10,000

Comments: Peter Shilton and his defence secured their second shut-out of their South American tour in front of a tiny crowd. Substitute Sammy Lee had his final England outing in this draw.

ENGLAND 1 East Germany 0; at Wembley;
Wednesday 19th September 1984

1 Shilton	(Southampton)	1 Muller
2 Duxbury	(Man Utd)	2 Dorner
3 Sansom	(Arsenal)	3 Kreer
4 Williams	(Southampton)	4 Stahmann
5 Wright	(Southampton)	5 Zotzsche
6 Butcher	(Ipswich Town)	6 Liebers
7 Robson*	(Man Utd)	7 Troppa
8 Wilkins	(AC Milan)	8 Ernst
9 Mariner	(Arsenal) replaced by Hateley	9 Steinbach
10 Woodcock	(Arsenal) replaced by Francis	10 Streich
11 Barnes	(Watford)	11 Minge

Crowd: 23,951

England scorer: Robson

Comments: It took a late goal from the England captain to decide this friendly between the Cold War foes. A pitifully small crowd greeted the occasion.

ENGLAND 5 Finland 0; at Wembley;
Wednesday 17th October 1984 (World Cup qualifier)

1 Shilton	(Southampton)	1 Huttunen
2 Duxbury	(Man Utd) replaced by Stevens	2 Pekonen
3 Sansom	(Arsenal)	3 Kymalainen
4 Williams	(Southampton)	4 Lahtinen
5 Wright	(Southampton)	5 Petaja
6 Butcher	(Ipswich Town)	6 Haaskivi
7 Robson*	(Man Utd) replaced by Chamberlain	7 Houtsonen
8 Wilkins	(AC Milan)	8 Ukkonen
9 Hateley	(AC Milan)	9 Ikalainen
10 Woodcock	(Arsenal)	10 Rautiainen
11 Barnes	(Watford)	11 Valvee

Crowd: 47,234

England scorers: Hateley (2), Woodcock, Robson, Sansom

Comments: Kenny Sansom scored his only England goal to round off this rout as England opened their World Cup qualifying campaign. Tottenham's Gary Stevens collected his first cap.

Turkey 0 ENGLAND 8; in Istanbul;
Wednesday 14th November 1984 (World Cup qualifier)

1	Duran	1	Shilton	(Southampton)
2	Kartal	2	Anderson	(Notts Forest)
3	Altintas	3	Sansom	(Arsenal)
4	Serdal	4	Williams	(Southampton) replaced by Stevens
5	Pamirodlu	5	Wright	(Southampton)
6	Cetiner	6	Butcher	(Ipswich Town)
7	Yetkiner	7	Robson*	(Man Utd)
8	Dilmen	8	Wilkins	(AC Milan)
9	Kelodlu	9	Withe	(Aston Villa)
10	Teufecki	10	Woodcock	(Arsenal) replaced by Francis
11	Keser	11	Barnes	(Watford)

Crowd: 26,494

England scorers: Robson (3), Woodcock (2), Barnes (2), Anderson

Comments: Rampaging England had registered 7 goals with still half an hour left of this World Cup qualifier. They had now scored 13 times in two matches and kept four successive clean sheets.

Northern Ireland 0 ENGLAND 1; in Belfast;
Wednesday 27th February 1985 (World Cup qualifier)

1	Jennings	1	Shilton	(Southampton)
2	Nicholl	2	Anderson	(Notts Forest)
3	McClelland	3	Sansom	(Arsenal)
4	O'Neill	4	Steven	(Everton)
5	Donaghy	5	Martin	(West Ham Utd)
6	McIlroy	6	Butcher	(Ipswich Town)
7	Ramsey	7	Stevens	(Tottenham)
8	Armstrong	8	Wilkins*	(AC Milan)
9	Stewart	9	Hateley	(AC Milan)
10	Quinn	10	Woodcock	(Arsenal) replaced by Francis
11	Whiteside	11	Barnes	(Watford)

Crowd: 28,000

England scorer: Hateley

Comments: Big Mark Hateley scored with just over 10 minutes remaining to hand the visitors both points in this group qualifier. Trevor Steven made his international debut in this narrow win.

ENGLAND 2 Republic of Ireland 1; at Wembley; Tuesday 26th March 1985

1 Bailey	(Man Utd)	1	Bonner
2 Anderson	(Notts Forest)	2	Hughton
3 Sansom	(Arsenal)	3	Lawrenson
4 Steven	(Everton)	4	McCarthy
5 Wright	(Southampton)	5	Beglin
6 Butcher	(Ipswich Town)	6	Whelan
7 Robson*	(Man Utd) replaced by Hoddle	7	Waddock
8 Wilkins	(AC Milan)	8	Brady
9 Hateley	(AC Milan) replaced by Davenport	9	McGrath
10 Lineker	(Leicester City)	10	O'Keeffe
11 Waddle	(Newcastle Utd)	11	Stapleton

Crowd: 34,793

England scorers: Steven, Lineker

Comments: Lineker sealed the victory in his first start before Liam Brady scored a late consolation. Peter Davenport won his only cap while Gary Bailey and Chris Waddle also made their debut.

Romania 0 ENGLAND 0; in Bucharest; Wednesday 1st May 1985 (World Cup qualifier)

1 Lung	1 Shilton	(Southampton)	
2 Negrila	2 Anderson	(Notts Forest)	
3 Iorgulescu	3 Sansom	(Arsenal)	
4 Stefanescu	4 Steven	(Everton)	
5 Ungureanu	5 Wright	(Southampton)	
6 Rednic	6 Butcher	(Ipswich Town)	
7 Klein	7 Robson*	(Man Utd)	
8 Boloni	8 Wilkins	(AC Milan)	
9 Hagi	9 Mariner	(Arsenal) replaced by Lineker	
10 Coras	10 Francis	(Sampdoria)	
11 Camataru	11 Barnes	(Watford) replaced by Waddle	

Crowd: 70,000

Comments: England lost on their last World Cup trip to Romania, so this stalemate was an improvement. Nevertheless, the substituted Paul Mariner played for England for the last time.

Finland 1 ENGLAND 1; in Helsinki;
Wednesday 22nd May 1985 (World Cup qualifier)

1	Huttunen	1 Shilton	(Southampton)
2	Lahtinen	2 Anderson	(Notts Forest)
3	Kymalainen	3 Sansom	(Arsenal)
4	Ikalainen	4 Steven	(Everton) replaced by Waddle
5	Nieminen	5 Fenwick	(QPR)
6	Turunen	6 Butcher	(Ipswich Town)
7	Houtsonen	7 Robson*	(Man Utd)
8	Ukkonen	8 Wilkins	(AC Milan)
9	Lipponen	9 Hateley	(AC Milan)
10	Rautiainen	10 Francis	(Sampdoria)
11	Rantanen	11 Barnes	(Watford)

Crowd: 30,000

England scorer: Hateley

Comments: England had to settle for another away point thanks to Hateley's second-half equaliser in this qualifier. The scorer was one of three players from an Italian club in the starting eleven.

Scotland 1 ENGLAND 0; in Glasgow;
Saturday 25th May 1985 (the Rous Cup)

1	Leighton	1 Shilton	(Southampton)
2	Gough	2 Anderson	(Notts Forest)
3	Malpas	3 Sansom	(Arsenal)
4	Aitken	4 Hoddle	(Tottenham) replaced by Lineker
5	McLeish	5 Fenwick	(QPR)
6	Miller	6 Butcher	(Ipswich Town)
7	Strachan	7 Robson*	(Man Utd)
8	Souness	8 Wilkins	(AC Milan)
9	Archibald	9 Hateley	(AC Milan)
10	Bett	10 Francis	(Sampdoria)
11	Speedie	11 Barnes	(Watford) replaced by Waddle

Crowd: 66,489

Comments: The goals had now dried up for the visitors as Richard Gough scored the winner halfway through the second half. Tragically, Jock Stein, the Scotland manager, died later in the year of a heart attack.

ENGLAND 1 Italy 2; in Mexico City;
Thursday 6th June 1985

1	Shilton	(Southampton)		1	Galli
2	Stevens	(Everton)		2	Bergomi
3	Sansom	(Arsenal)		3	Vierchowod
4	Steven	(Everton) replaced by Hoddle		4	Baresi
5	Wright	(Southampton)		5	Collovati
6	Butcher	(Ipswich Town)		6	Tricella
7	Robson*	(Man Utd)		7	Conti
8	Wilkins	(AC Milan)		8	Bagni
9	Hateley	(AC Milan)		9	Galderisi
10	Francis	(Sampdoria) replaced by Lineker		10	di Gennaro
11	Waddle	(Newcastle Utd) replaced by Barnes		11	Altobelli

Crowd: 7,000

England scorer: Hateley

Comments: Another Gary Stevens was making his debut in front of a lamentably low crowd. Hateley scored an equaliser only for Altobelli to convert a penalty in the dying seconds of this fixture.

Mexico 1 ENGLAND 0; in Mexico City;
Sunday 9th June 1985

1	Larios		1	Bailey	(Man Utd)
2	Trejo		2	Anderson	(Notts Forest)
3	Barbosa		3	Sansom	(Arsenal)
4	Quirarte		4	Hoddle	(Tottenham) replaced by Dixon
5	Amador		5	Fenwick	(QPR)
6	Munoz		6	Watson	(Norwich City)
7	Espana		7	Robson*	(Man Utd)
8	Negrete		8	Wilkins	(AC Milan) replaced by Reid
9	Boy		9	Hateley	(AC Milan)
10	Aguirre		10	Francis	(Sampdoria)
11	Flores		11	Barnes	(Watford) replaced by Waddle

Crowd: 15,000

Comments: Kerry Dixon and Peter Reid came on in the second half to win their first caps but they could not stop England slumping to defeat in this summer tournament match against the hosts.

ENGLAND 3 West Germany 0; in Mexico City;
Wednesday 12th June 1985

1	Shilton	(Southampton)	1	Schumacher
2	Stevens	(Everton)	2	Berthold
3	Sansom	(Arsenal)	3	Herget
4	Hoddle	(Tottenham)	4	Jakobs
5	Wright	(Southampton)	5	Augenthaler
6	Butcher	(Ipswich Town)	6	Brehme
7	Robson*	(Man Utd) replaced by Bracewell	7	Matthaus
8	Reid	(Everton)	8	Magath
9	Dixon	(Chelsea)	9	Rahn
10	Lineker	(Everton) replaced by Barnes	10	Littbarski
11	Waddle	(Newcastle Utd)	11	Mill

Crowd: 8,000

England scorers: Robson, Dixon, (2)

Comments: A second-half double from Kerry Dixon ensured an uncharacteristically comfortable win over the West Germans. Paul Bracewell made his debut in this summer tournament triumph.

USA 0 ENGLAND 5; in Los Angeles;
Sunday 16th June 1985

1	Mausser	1	Woods	(Norwich City)
2	Crow	2	Anderson	(Notts Forest)
3	Windischmann	3	Sansom	(Arsenal) replaced by Watson
4	Canter	4	Hoddle	(Tottenham) replaced by Reid
5	Caligiuri	5	Fenwick	(QPR)
6	van der Beck	6	Butcher	(Ipswich Town)
7	Radwanski	7	Robson*	(Man Utd) replaced by Steven
8	Davis	8	Bracewell	(Everton)
9	Perez	9	Dixon	(Chelsea)
10	Murray	10	Lineker	(Everton)
11	Kerr	11	Waddle	(Newcastle Utd) replaced by Barnes

Crowd: 10,145

England scorers: Lineker (2), Dixon (2), Steven

Comments: Chris Woods made his debut between the sticks, but most of the action was at the other end as Kerry Dixon and Gary Lineker helped themselves to a pair of doubles.

ENGLAND 1 Romania 1; at Wembley;
Wednesday 11th September 1985 (World Cup qualifier)

1 Shilton	(Southampton)		1	Lung
2 Stevens	(Everton)		2	Negrila
3 Sansom	(Arsenal)		3	Iovan
4 Reid	(Everton)		4	Stefanescu
5 Wright	(Southampton)		5	Ungureanu
6 Fenwick	(QPR)		6	Rednic
7 Robson*	(Man Utd)		7	Boloni
8 Hoddle	(Tottenham)		8	Klein
9 Hateley	(AC Milan)		9	Hagi
10 Lineker	(Everton) replaced by Woodcock		10	Coras
11 Waddle	(Tottenham) replaced by Barnes		11	Camataru

Crowd: 59,500

England scorer: Hoddle

Comments: For the fourth successive time, England failed to beat Romania in a World Cup qualifying match, but the home team were still on course for the finals in Mexico the following summer.

ENGLAND 5 Turkey 0; at Wembley;
Wednesday 16th October 1985 (World Cup qualifier)

1 Shilton	(Southampton)		1	Duran
2 Stevens	(Everton)		2	Demiriz
3 Sansom	(Arsenal)		3	Altintas
4 Hoddle	(Tottenham)		4	Ozden
5 Wright	(Southampton)		5	Durmaz
6 Fenwick	(QPR)		6	Cetiner
7 Robson*	(Man Utd) replaced by Steven		7	Yetkiner
8 Wilkins	(AC Milan)		8	Corlu
9 Hateley	(AC Milan) replaced by Woodcock		9	Vezir
10 Lineker	(Everton)		10	Karaman
11 Waddle	(Tottenham)		11	Yula

Crowd: 52,500

England scorers: Waddle, Lineker (3), Robson

Comments: England stormed into a 4–0 half-time lead with Chris Waddle recording his first international goal. Gary Lineker added another after the interval to earn himself a hat-trick in this rout.

ENGLAND 0 Northern Ireland 0; at Wembley;
Wednesday 13th November 1985 (World Cup qualifier)

1 Shilton	(Southampton)	1 Jennings	
2 Stevens	(Everton)	2 Nicholl	
3 Sansom	(Arsenal)	3 Donaghy	
4 Hoddle	(Tottenham)	4 O'Neill	
5 Wright	(Southampton)	5 McDonald	
6 Fenwick	(QPR)	6 McCreery	
7 Bracewell	(Everton)	7 Penney	
8 Wilkins*	(AC Milan)	8 McIlroy	
9 Dixon	(Chelsea)	9 Quinn	
10 Lineker	(Everton)	10 Whiteside	
11 Waddle	(Tottenham)	11 Stewart	

Crowd: 70,500

Comments: The men in green joined England at the finals in Mexico as Pat Jennings collected a clean sheet in the twilight of his career. Suspicions were raised that both teams played for a draw.

Egypt 0 ENGLAND 4; in Cairo;
Wednesday 29th January 1986

1 El-Batal	1 Shilton	(Southampton) replaced by Woods	
2 Yassin	2 Stevens	(Everton)	
3 Sedki	3 Sansom	(Arsenal)	
4 Saleh	4 Cowans	(Bari)	
5 Omar	5 Wright	(Southampton)	
6 Mayhoub	6 Fenwick	(QPR)	
7 Abdel Ghani	7 Steven	(Everton) replaced by Hill	
8 Abouzaid	8 Wilkins*	(AC Milan)	
9 Abdou	9 Hateley	(AC Milan)	
10 Hazem	10 Lineker	(Everton) replaced by Beardsley	
11 Yehia	11 Wallace	(Southampton)	

Crowd: 20,000

England scorers: Steven, Omar (OG), Wallace, Cowans

Comments: 2 goals were scored in each half with Danny Wallace scoring in his only England appearance. Liverpool's Peter Beardsley also made his debut in this pre-World Cup warm-up match.

Israel 1 ENGLAND 2; in Tel Aviv;
Wednesday 26th February 1986

1	Ran	1	Shilton	(Southampton) replaced by Woods
2	Aharoni	2	Stevens	(Everton)
3	Shimonov	3	Sansom	(Arsenal)
4	Cohen	4	Hoddle	(Tottenham)
5	Davidi	5	Martin	(West Ham Utd)
6	Malmilian	6	Butcher	(Ipswich Town)
7	Ivanir	7	Robson*	(Man Utd)
8	Turk	8	Wilkins	(AC Milan)
9	Sinai	9	Dixon	(Chelsea) replaced by Woodcock
10	Armeli	10	Beardsley	(Liverpool)
11	Ohana	11	Waddle	(Tottenham) replaced by Barnes

Crowd: 30,000

England scorer: Robson (2)

Comments: Bryan Robson converted a late penalty after the tourists had been behind at half time. This was Tony Woodcock's last cap, as England wisely played another friendly in a hot climate.

USSR 0 ENGLAND 1; in Tbilisi;
Wednesday 26th March 1986

1	Daseyev	1	Shilton	(Southampton)
2	Bessonov	2	Anderson	(Notts Forest)
3	Chivadze	3	Sansom	(Arsenal)
4	Demianenko	4	Hoddle	(Tottenham)
5	Bubnov	5	Wright	(Southampton)
6	Kuznetsov	6	Butcher	(Ipswich Town)
7	Gotsmanov	7	Cowans	(Bari) replaced by Hodge
8	Zavarov	8	Wilkins*	(AC Milan)
9	Aleinikov	9	Beardsley	(Liverpool)
10	Kondratiev	10	Lineker	(Everton)
11	Rodionov	11	Waddle	(Tottenham) replaced by Steven

Crowd: 62,000

England scorer: Waddle

Comments: Chris Waddle scored the only goal halfway through the second half as England continued their impressive run of form. Aston Villa's Steve Hodge won his first cap as a substitute.

ENGLAND 2 Scotland 1; at Wembley; Wednesday 23rd April 1986 (the Rous Cup)

1	Shilton	(Southampton)	1	Rough
2	Stevens	(Everton)	2	Gough
3	Sansom	(Arsenal)	3	Malpas
4	Hoddle	(Tottenham)	4	Souness
5	Watson	(Norwich City)	5	McLeish
6	Butcher	(Ipswich Town)	6	Miller
7	Wilkins*	(AC Milan) replaced by Reid	7	Nicol
8	Francis	(Sampdoria)	8	Speedie
9	Hateley	(AC Milan)	9	Nicholas
10	Hodge	(Aston Villa) replaced by Stevens	10	Aitken
11	Waddle	(Tottenham)	11	Bannon

Crowd: 68,357

England scorers: Butcher, Hoddle

Comments: The home team were two goals ahead by half time, only for Graeme Souness to reply with a penalty for a team managed by Alex Ferguson. This was the last outing for Trevor Francis.

ENGLAND 3 Mexico 0; in Los Angeles; Saturday 17th May 1986

1	Shilton	(Southampton)	1	Larios
2	Anderson	(Notts Forest)	2	Trejo
3	Sansom	(Arsenal)	3	Barbosa
4	Hoddle	(Tottenham)	4	Manzo
5	Fenwick	(QPR)	5	Servin
6	Butcher	(Ipswich Town)	6	Munoz
7	Robson*	(Man Utd) replaced by Stevens	7	Espana
8	Wilkins	(AC Milan) replaced by Steven	8	Negrete
9	Hateley	(AC Milan) replaced by Dixon	9	Aguirre
10	Beardsley	(Liverpool)	10	Hermosillo
11	Waddle	(Tottenham) replaced by Barnes	11	Flores

Crowd: 63,770

England scorers: Hateley (2), Beardsley

Comments: Peter Beardsley netted his first England goal as his team raced into a 3–0 interval lead. England were again playing in a hot location to prepare for the temperature challenge of Mexico.

Canada 0 ENGLAND 1; in Vancouver;
Saturday 24th May 1986

1 Dolan	1 Shilton	(Southampton) replaced by Woods
2 Lenarduzzi	2 Stevens	(Everton)
3 Moore	3 Sansom	(Arsenal)
4 Samuel	4 Hoddle	(Tottenham)
5 Wison	5 Martin	(West Ham Utd)
6 James	6 Butcher	(Ipswich Town)
7 Ragan	7 Hodge	(Aston Villa)
8 Gray	8 Wilkins*	(AC Milan) replaced by Reid
9 Sweeney	9 Hateley	(AC Milan)
10 Valentine	10 Lineker	(Everton) replaced by Beardsley
11 Vrabic	11 Waddle	(Tottenham) replaced by Barnes

Crowd: 8,150

England scorer: Hateley

Comments: Mark Hateley's second-half winner extended England's unbeaten run to 11 matches, with all 6 fixtures this year having been won. The omens looked good for the imminent World Cup.

ENGLAND 0 Portugal 1; in Monterrey;
Tuesday 3rd June 1986 (World Cup finals)

1 Shilton	(Southampton)	1 Bento	
2 Stevens	(Everton)	2 Alvaro	
3 Sansom	(Arsenal)	3 Rosa	
4 Hoddle	(Tottenham)	4 Oliveira	
5 Fenwick	(QPR)	5 Inacio	
6 Butcher	(Ipswich Town)	6 Diamantino	
7 Robson*	(Man Utd) replaced by Hodge	7 Pacheco	
8 Wilkins	(AC Milan)	8 Andre	
9 Hateley	(AC Milan)	9 Sousa	
10 Lineker	(Everton)	10 Santos	
11 Waddle	(Tottenham) replaced by Beardsley	11 Gomes	

Crowd: 23,000

Comments: It was so typical of England to falter on the big stage against lesser ranked opponents. The late winner from Carlos Manuel Santos left Bobby Robson's team with a mountain to climb.

ENGLAND 0 Morocco 0; in Monterrey;
Friday 6th June 1986 (World Cup finals)

1	Shilton	(Southampton)	1	Zaki
2	Stevens	(Everton)	2	Khalifa
3	Sansom	(Arsenal)	3	El-Biaz
4	Hoddle	(Tottenham)	4	Bouyahiaoui
5	Fenwick	(QPR)	5	Lamriss
6	Butcher	(Ipswich Town)	6	Dolmy
7	Robson*	(Man Utd) replaced by Hodge	7	Merry
8	Wilkins	(AC Milan)	8	Bouderbala
9	Hateley	(AC Milan) replaced by Stevens	9	Timoumi
10	Lineker	(Everton)	10	Khairi
11	Waddle	(Tottenham)	11	Krimau

Crowd: 20,200

Comments: Having lost Bryan Robson through injury, Ray Wilkins then shot himself on the foot with a needless red card. England were now teetering on the brink of an embarrassing early exit.

ENGLAND 3 Poland 0; in Monterrey;
Wednesday 11th June 1986 (World Cup finals)

1	Shilton*	(Southampton)	1	Mlynarczyk
2	Stevens	(Everton)	2	Pawlak
3	Sansom	(Arsenal)	3	Wojcicki
4	Hoddle	(Tottenham)	4	Majewski
5	Fenwick	(QPR)	5	Ostrowski
6	Butcher	(Ipswich Town)	6	Dziekanowski
7	Hodge	(Aston Villa)	7	Matysik
8	Reid	(Everton)	8	Komornicki
9	Beardsley	(Liverpool) replaced by Waddle	9	Urban
10	Lineker	(Everton) replaced by Dixon	10	Boniek
11	Steven	(Everton)	11	Smolarek

Crowd: 22,700

England scorer: Lineker (3)

Comments: The ghosts of 1973 were exorcised as Poland were put to the sword in the first half. With the considerable help of Gary Lineker's hat-trick, England had squeezed into the next stages.

ENGLAND 3 Paraguay 0; in Mexico City; Wednesday 18th June 1986 (World Cup finals)

1 Shilton*	(Southampton)	1	Fernandez
2 Stevens	(Everton)	2	Torales
3 Sansom	(Arsenal)	3	Schettina
4 Hoddle	(Tottenham)	4	Delgado
5 Martin	(West Ham Utd)	5	Zabala
6 Butcher	(Ipswich Town)	6	Canete
7 Hodge	(Aston Villa)	7	Romero
8 Reid	(Everton) replaced by Stevens	8	Nunez
9 Beardsley	(Liverpool) replaced by Hateley	9	Ferreira
10 Lineker	(Everton)	10	Cabanas
11 Steven	(Everton)	11	Mendoza

Crowd: 98,728

England scorers: Lineker (2), Beardsley

Comments: Lineker scored a goal in each half, with an effort from Beardsley sandwiched in between, as England began to gather momentum. They now had a date with destiny against Argentina.

ENGLAND 1 Argentina 2; in Mexico City; Sunday 22nd June 1986 (World Cup finals)

1 Shilton*	(Southampton)	1	Pumpido
2 Stevens	(Everton)	2	Cuicuffo
3 Sansom	(Arsenal)	3	Luis Brown
4 Hoddle	(Tottenham)	4	Ruggeri
5 Fenwick	(QPR)	5	Olarticoechea
6 Butcher	(Ipswich Town)	6	Batista
7 Hodge	(Aston Villa)	7	Giusti
8 Reid	(Everton) replaced by Waddle	8	Burruchaga
9 Beardsley	(Liverpool)	9	Henrique
10 Lineker	(Everton)	10	Maradona
11 Steven	(Everton) replaced by Barnes	11	Valdano

Crowd: 114,580

England scorer: Lineker

Comments: Maradona scored in quick succession just after the interval with a brilliant effort and a farcical 'goal'. Lineker scored with ten minutes remaining, but England were undone by one man.

Sweden 1 ENGLAND 0; in Stockholm;
Wednesday 10th September 1986

1	Moller	1	Shilton*	(Southampton)
2	Nilsson	2	Anderson	(Notts Forest)
3	Hysen	3	Sansom	(Arsenal)
4	Larsson	4	Hoddle	(Tottenham)
5	Fredriksson	5	Martin	(West Ham Utd)
6	Prytz	6	Butcher	(Rangers)
7	Stromberg	7	Steven	(Everton) replaced by Waddle
8	Eriksson	8	Wilkins	(AC Milan)
9	Palmer	9	Dixon	(Chelsea)
10	Ekstrom	10	Hodge	(Aston Villa)
11	Nilsson	11	Barnes	(Watford) replaced by Cottee

Crowd: 15,640

Comments: The away team suffered their third defeat in six matches in this friendly. West Ham's Tony Cottee won his first cap while Alvin Martin and Kerry Dixon played in their last international.

ENGLAND 3 Northern Ireland 0; at Wembley;
Wednesday 15th October 1986 (European Championship)

1	Shilton	(Southampton)	1	Hughes
2	Anderson	(Notts Forest)	2	Fleming
3	Sansom	(Arsenal)	3	McDonald
4	Hoddle	(Tottenham)	4	Donaghy
5	Watson	(Everton)	5	McClelland
6	Butcher	(Rangers)	6	Worthington
7	Robson*	(Man Utd)	7	Penney
8	Hodge	(Aston Villa)	8	Campbell
9	Beardsley	(Liverpool) replaced by Cottee	9	Clarke
10	Lineker	(Barcelona)	10	Whiteside
11	Waddle	(Tottenham)	11	Stewart

Crowd: 35,300

England scorers: Lineker (2), Waddle

Comments: Two late goals eventually ensured a comfortable win as England began their European Championship qualifying group with maximum points against Billy Bingham's team.

ENGLAND 2 Yugoslavia 0; at Wembley;
Wednesday 12th November 1986 (European Championship)

1	Woods	(Rangers)	1	Ravnic
2	Anderson	(Notts Forest)	2	Vujovic
3	Sansom	(Arsenal)	3	Baljic
4	Hoddle	(Tottenham)	4	Sabandzovic
5	Wright	(Southampton)	5	Elsner
6	Butcher*	(Rangers)	6	Hadzibegic
7	Mabbutt	(Tottenham)	7	Skoro
8	Hodge	(Aston Villa) replaced by Wilkins	8	Katanec
9	Beardsley	(Liverpool)	9	Sliskovic
10	Lineker	(Barcelona)	10	Jankovic
11	Waddle	(Tottenham) replaced by Steven	11	Vujovic

Crowd: 60,000

England scorers: Anderson, Mabbutt

Comments: A goal in each half decided this fixture, with Gary Mabbutt scoring his only international goal to secure both points. Ray Wilkins made his final England appearance in this victory.

Spain 2 ENGLAND 4; in Madrid;
Wednesday 18th February 1987

1	Zubizarreta	1	Shilton	(Southampton) replaced by Woods
2	Chendo	2	Anderson	(Notts Forest)
3	Camacho	3	Sansom	(Arsenal)
4	Arteche	4	Hoddle	(Tottenham)
5	Victor	5	Adams	(Arsenal)
6	Gordillo	6	Butcher	(Rangers)
7	Carrasco	7	Robson*	(Man Utd)
8	Michel	8	Hodge	(Tottenham)
9	Butragueno	9	Beardsley	(Liverpool)
10	Gallego	10	Lineker	(Barcelona)
11	Vazquez	11	Waddle	(Tottenham) replaced by Steven

Crowd: 35,000

England scorer: Lineker (4)

Comments: Spain scored the first and last goals and Barcelona striker Gary Lineker scored four times at the home of his club's biggest rivals, Real Madrid. This was the debut for Tony Adams.

Northern Ireland o ENGLAND 2; in Belfast;
Wednesday 1st April 1987 (European Championship)

1	Dunlop	1 Shilton	(Southampton) replaced by Woods
2	Fleming	2 Anderson	(Notts Forest)
3	Donaghy	3 Sansom	(Arsenal)
4	McDonald	4 Mabbutt	(Tottenham)
5	McClelland	5 Wright	(Southampton)
6	Ramsey	6 Butcher	(Rangers)
7	McCreery	7 Robson*	(Man Utd)
8	Campbell	8 Hodge	(Tottenham)
9	Wilson	9 Beardsley	(Liverpool)
10	Worthington	10 Lineker	(Barcelona)
11	Whiteside	11 Waddle	(Tottenham)

Crowd: 20,578

England scorers: Robson, Waddle

Comments: Both goals were registered before half time as England completed the qualifying double over Northern Ireland and took a major step towards a place at the finals in West Germany.

Turkey o ENGLAND o; in Izmir;
Wednesday 29th April 1987 (European Championship)

1	Uraz	1 Woods	(Rangers)
2	Demiriz	2 Anderson	(Notts Forest)
3	Yuvakuran	3 Sansom	(Arsenal)
4	Coban	4 Hoddle	(Tottenham)
5	Onal	5 Adams	(Arsenal)
6	Calimbay	6 Mabbutt	(Tottenham)
7	Tutuneker	7 Robson*	(Man Utd)
8	Keser	8 Hodge	(Tottenham) replaced by Barnes
9	Vezir	9 Allen	(Tottenham) replaced by Hateley
10	Demiral	10 Lineker	(Barcelona)
11	Gunen	11 Waddle	(Tottenham)

Crowd: 25,000

Comments: This was England's fifteenth clean sheet in their last twenty-two matches. Seven players from the two north London clubs started this fixture, including five from Tottenham Hotspur .

ENGLAND 1 Brazil 1; at Wembley;
Tuesday 19th May 1987 (the Rous Cup)

1 Shilton	(Southampton)	1	Carlos
2 Stevens	(Everton)	2	Josimar
3 Pearce	(Notts Forest)	3	Geraldao
4 Reid	(Everton)	4	Rocha
5 Adams	(Arsenal)	5	Nelsinho
6 Butcher	(Rangers)	6	Douglas
7 Robson*	(Man Utd)	7	Silas
8 Barnes	(Watford)	8	Marangon
9 Beardsley	(Liverpool)	9	Muller
10 Lineker	(Barcelona) replaced by Hateley	10	Mirandinha
11 Waddle	(Tottenham)	11	Valdo

Crowd: 92,000

England scorer: Lineker

Comments: No sooner had Lineker given the home team the lead than Mirandinha equalised. The half-time score then remained unchanged. Stuart Pearce won his first cap in this encounter.

Scotland 0 ENGLAND 0; in Glasgow;
Saturday 23rd May 1987 (the Rous Cup)

1 Leighton	1 Woods	(Rangers)
2 Gough	2 Stevens	(Everton)
3 MacLeod	3 Pearce	(Notts Forest)
4 McStay	4 Hoddle	(Tottenham)
5 McLeish	5 Wright	(Southampton)
6 Miller	6 Butcher	(Rangers)
7 McCoist	7 Robson*	(Man Utd)
8 Aitken	8 Hodge	(Tottenham)
9 McClair	9 Beardsley	(Liverpool)
10 Simpson	10 Hateley	(AC Milan)
11 Wilson	11 Waddle	(Tottenham)

Crowd: 64,713

Comments: Chris Woods had still to concede a goal in four starts as an England goalkeeper as the oldest rivalry in football petered out into a rare draw. The Rous Cup would be won by Brazil.

West Germany 3 ENGLAND 1; in Dusseldorf; Wednesday 9th September 1987

1	Immel	1	Shilton*	(Derby County)
2	Herget	2	Anderson	(Notts Forest)
3	Brehme	3	Sansom	(Arsenal) replaced by Pearce
4	Kohler	4	Hoddle	(Monaco) replaced by Webb
5	Buchwald	5	Adams	(Arsenal)
6	Frontzeck	6	Mabbutt	(Tottenham)
7	Littbarski	7	Reid	(Everton)
8	Thon	8	Barnes	(Liverpool)
9	Dorfner	9	Beardsley	(Newcastle Utd)
10	Voller	10	Lineker	(Barcelona)
11	Allofs	11	Waddle	(Newcastle Utd) replaced by Hateley

Crowd: 50,000

England scorer: Lineker

Comments: Gary Lineker pulled a goal back before half-time after Pierre Littbarski had netted twice, but the West Germans sealed this 'friendly' triumph with a late goal. Neil Webb made his debut.

ENGLAND 8 Turkey 0; at Wembley; Wednesday 14th October 1987 (European Championship)

1	Shilton	(Derby County)	1	Uraz
2	Stevens	(Everton)	2	Calimbay
3	Sansom	(Arsenal)	3	Yuvakuran
4	Steven	(Everton) replaced by Hoddle	4	Coban
5	Adams	(Arsenal)	5	Onal
6	Butcher	(Rangers)	6	Gultiken
7	Robson*	(Man Utd)	7	Tutuneker
8	Webb	(Notts Forest)	8	Altintas
9	Beardsley	(Newcastle Utd) replaced by Regis	9	Kaynak
10	Lineker	(Barcelona)	10	Keser
11	Barnes	(Liverpool)	11	Gunen

Crowd: 45,528

England scorers: Barnes (2), Lineker (3), Robson, Beardsley, Webb

Comments: Barnes and Lineker each bagged two first-half goals as England annihilated Turkey again. Neil Webb also scored his first England goal and a recalled Cyrille Regis won his last cap.

Yugoslavia 1 ENGLAND 4; in Belgrade;
Wednesday 11th November 1987 (European Championship)

1	Ravnic	1	Shilton	(Derby County)
2	Vujovic	2	Stevens	(Everton)
3	Baljic	3	Sansom	(Arsenal)
4	Kaltanec	4	Steven	(Everton)
5	Elsner	5	Adams	(Arsenal)
6	Hadzibegic	6	Butcher	(Rangers)
7	Stojkovic	7	Robson*	(Man Utd) replaced by Reid
8	Mlinaric	8	Webb	(Notts Forest) replaced by Hoddle
9	Vokrri	9	Beardsley	(Newcastle Utd)
10	Bazdarevic	10	Lineker	(Barcelona)
11	Vujovic	11	Barnes	(Liverpool)

Crowd: 70,000

England scorer: Beardsley, Barnes, Robson, Adams

Comments: The visitors raced into a four-nil lead inside the first half hour as they rounded off their successful qualifying campaign with another rout. Tony Adams scored his first England goal.

Israel 0 ENGLAND 0; in Tel Aviv;
Wednesday 17th February 1988

1	Ginzburg	1	Woods	(Rangers)
2	Cohen II	2	Stevens	(Everton)
3	Cohen	3	Pearce	(Notts Forest)
4	Shimonov	4	Webb	(Notts Forest)
5	Alon	5	Watson	(Everton)
6	Cohen	6	Wright	(Derby County) replaced by Fenwick
7	Malmilian	7	Allen	(Tottenham) replaced by Harford
8	Klinger	8	McMahon	(Liverpool)
9	Ivanir	9	Beardsley*	(Newcastle Utd)
10	Tikva	10	Barnes	(Liverpool)
11	Driks	11	Waddle	(Tottenham)

Crowd: 5,000

Comments: A wretchedly tiny crowd attended this bore draw. Perhaps the absentees had anticipated a scoreless match. Anyhow, Mick Harford and Steve McMahon won their first caps.

ENGLAND 2 Holland 2; at Wembley;
Wednesday 23rd March 1988

1	Shilton	(Derby County)	1	van Breukelen
2	Stevens	(Everton)	2	Koeman
3	Sansom	(Arsenal)	3	van Aerle
4	Steven	(Everton)	4	Troost
5	Adams	(Arsenal)	5	Silooy
6	Watson	(Everton) replaced by Wright	6	Wouters
7	Robson*	(Man Utd)	7	Muhren
8	Webb	(Notts Forest) replaced by Hoddle	8	Vanenburg
9	Beardsley	(Newcastle Utd) replaced by Hateley	9	van't Schip
10	Lineker	(Barcelona)	10	Gullit
11	Barnes	(Liverpool)	11	Bosman

Crowd: 74,590

England scorers: Lineker, Adams

Comments: Tony Adams scored for both teams as the potential European champions England were held to a home draw by the eventual European champions, Holland.

Hungary 0 ENGLAND 0; in Budapest;
Wednesday 27th April 1988

1	Szendrei	1	Woods	(Rangers)
2	Kozma	2	Anderson	(Notts Forest)
3	Pinter	3	Pearce	(Notts Forest) replaced by Stevens
4	Sass	4	Steven	(Everton)
5	Balog	5	Adams	(Arsenal)
6	Roth	6	Pallister	(Middlesbrough)
7	Kiprich	7	Robson*	(Man Utd)
8	Garaba	8	McMahon	(Liverpool)
9	Fitos	9	Beardsley	(Newcastle Utd) replaced by Hateley
10	Detari	10	Lineker	(Barcelona) replaced by Cottee
11	Vincze	11	Waddle	(Tottenham) replaced by Hoddle

Crowd: 26,500

Comments: The goals had dried up again but Chris Woods had now earned yet another clean sheet. Big Gary Pallister made his debut in this pre-European Championship warm-up encounter.

ENGLAND 1 Scotland 0; at Wembley;
Saturday 21st May 1988 (the Rous Cup)

1 Shilton	(Derby County)	1 Leighton
2 Stevens	(Everton)	2 Gough
3 Sansom	(Arsenal)	3 Nicol
4 Webb	(Notts Forest)	4 Aitken
5 Watson	(Everton)	5 McLeish
6 Adams	(Arsenal)	6 Miller
7 Robson*	(Man Utd)	7 Simpson
8 Steven	(Everton) replaced by Waddle	8 McStay
9 Beardsley	(Newcastle Utd)	9 McCoist
10 Lineker	(Barcelona)	10 MacLeod
11 Barnes	(Liverpool)	11 Johnston

Crowd: 70,480

England scorer: Beardsley

Comments: Peter Beardsley scored inside the first fifteen minutes to decide this fixture. Both teams were competing with Columbia in the end of season Rous Cup competition.

ENGLAND 1 Columbia 1; at Wembley;
Tuesday 24th May 1988 (the Rous Cup)

1 Shilton	(Derby County)	1 Higuita
2 Anderson	(Notts Forest)	2 Herrera
3 Sansom	(Arsenal) replaced by Pearce	3 Escobar
4 McMahon	(Liverpool) replaced by Webb	4 Perea
5 Wright	(Derby County)	5 Hoyos
6 Adams	(Arsenal)	6 Garcia
7 Robson*	(Man Utd)	7 Valderrama
8 Waddle	(Tottenham) replaced by Hoddle	8 Redin
9 Beardsley	(Newcastle Utd) replaced by Hateley	9 Alvarez
10 Lineker	(Barcelona)	10 Arango
11 Barnes	(Liverpool)	11 Iguaran

Crowd: 25,756

England scorer: Lineker

Comments: The 2 goals from Gary Lineker and Andres Escobar both came in the first half. This was the last international appearance for Viv Anderson whose England career dated back to 1978.

Switzerland 0 ENGLAND 1; in Lausanne;
Saturday 28th May 1988

1 Corminboeuf	1 Shilton	(Derby County) replaced by Woods
2 Tschuppert	2 Stevens	(Everton)
3 Schallibaum	3 Sansom	(Arsenal)
4 Weber	4 Webb	(Notts Forest)
5 Geiger	5 Wright	(Derby County)
6 Perret	6 Adams	(Arsenal) replaced by Watson
7 Sutter	7 Robson*	(Man Utd) replaced by Reid
8 Hermann	8 Steven	(Everton) replaced by Waddle
9 Zwicker	9 Beardsley	(Newcastle Utd)
10 Bickel	10 Lineker	(Barcelona)
11 Bonvin	11 Barnes	(Liverpool)

Crowd: 10,000

England scorer: Lineker

Comments: The only goal inevitably came from Gary Lineker on the hour mark. This was Peter Reid's last international outing as the England defence helped themselves to another clean sheet.

ENGLAND 0 Republic of Ireland 1; in Stuttgart;
Sunday 12th June 1988 (European Championship)

1 Shilton	(Derby County)	1 Bonner	
2 Stevens	(Everton)	2 Morris	
3 Sansom	(Arsenal)	3 McCarthy	
4 Webb	(Notts Forest) replaced by Hoddle	4 Moran	
5 Wright	(Derby County)	5 Hughton	
6 Adams	(Arsenal)	6 Houghton	
7 Robson*	(Man Utd)	7 McGrath	
8 Waddle	(Tottenham)	8 Whelan	
9 Beardsley	(Newcastle Utd) replaced by Hateley	9 Galvin	
10 Lineker	(Barcelona)	10 Stapleton	
11 Barnes	(Liverpool	11 Aldridge	

Crowd: 55,500

Comments: Ray Houghton gave the Irish a very early lead and England failed to find a reply. This was a sweet triumph for their manager Jack Charlton who became Ireland's favourite Englishman.

ENGLAND 1 Holland 3; in Dusseldorf;
Wednesday 15th June 1988 (European Championship)

1 Shilton	(Derby County)	1 van Breukelen
2 Stevens	(Everton)	2 van Aerle
3 Sansom	(Arsenal)	3 Rijkaard
4 Hoddle	(Monaco)	4 Koeman
5 Wright	(Derby County)	5 van Tiggelen
6 Adams	(Arsenal)	6 Vanenburg
7 Robson*	(Man Utd)	7 Wouters
8 Steven	(Everton) replaced by Waddle	8 Muhren
9 Beardsley	(Newcastle Utd) replaced by Hateley	9 Koeman
10 Lineker	(Barcelona)	10 Gullit
11 Barnes	(Liverpool)	11 van Basten

Crowd: 68,400

England scorer: Robson

Comments: New sensation Marco van Basten commemorated the 100th cap for Peter Shilton by putting three goals past him. This was the first hat-trick scored against England since 1959.

ENGLAND 1 USSR 3; in Frankfurt;
Saturday 18th June 1988 (European Championship)

1 Woods	(Rangers)	1 Daseyev
2 Stevens	(Everton)	2 Bessonov
3 Sansom	(Arsenal)	3 Khidiatulin
4 Hoddle	(Monaco)	4 Kuznetsov
5 Watson	(Everton)	5 Rats
6 Adams	(Arsenal)	6 Aleinikov
7 Robson*	(Man Utd)	7 Litovchenko
8 Steven	(Everton)	8 Zavarov
9 McMahon	(Liverpool) replaced by Webb	9 Belanov
10 Lineker	(Barcelona) replaced by Hateley	10 Mikhailichenko
11 Barnes	(Liverpool)	11 Protasov

Crowd: 53,000

England scorer: Adams

Comments: For the second successive match, England came back from conceding the first goal, only to be overhauled 3–1. This defeat ended the England careers of Hoddle, Sansom, and Watson.

ENGLAND 1 Denmark 0; at Wembley; Wednesday 14th September 1988

1 Shilton	(Derby County) replaced by Woods	1 Rasmussen
2 Stevens	(Rangers)	2 Elstrup
3 Pearce	(Notts Forest)	3 Bartram
4 Rocastle	(Arsenal)	4 Hansen
5 Adams	(Arsenal) replaced by Walker	5 Helt
6 Butcher	(Rangers)	6 Laudrup
7 Robson*	(Man Utd)	7 Molby
8 Webb	(Notts Forest)	8 Vilfort
9 Harford	(Luton Town) replaced by Cottee	9 Jensen
10 Beardsley	(Newcastle Utd) replaced by Gascoigne	10 Nielsen
11 Hodge	(Notts Forest)	11 Olsen

Crowd: 25,837

England scorer: Webb

Comments: The home team returned to winning ways courtesy of Webb's goal just before the half-hour mark. This friendly marked the debuts for Paul Gascoigne, David Rocastle, and Des Walker.

ENGLAND 0 Sweden 0; at Wembley; Wednesday 19th October 1988 (World Cup qualifier)

1 Shilton	(Derby County)	1 Ravelli
2 Stevens	(Rangers)	2 Nilsson
3 Pearce	(Notts Forest)	3 Hysen
4 Webb	(Notts Forest)	4 Larsson
5 Adams	(Arsenal) replaced by Walker	5 Ljung
6 Butcher	(Rangers)	6 Thern
7 Robson*	(Man Utd)	7 Stromberg
8 Beardsley	(Newcastle Utd)	8 Prytz
9 Waddle	(Tottenham)	9 Nilsson
10 Lineker	(Barcelona)	10 Holmqvist
11 Barnes	(Liverpool) replaced by Cottee	11 Pettersson

Crowd: 65,628

Comments: It may have been the second successive shut-out for the England defence but it was hardly the most convincing start to the World Cup qualifying process for Bobby Robson's team.

Saudi Arabia 1 ENGLAND 1; in Riyadh;
Wednesday 16th November 1988

1	Al-Deayea	1	Seaman	(QPR)
2	Al-Nuaymah	2	Sterland	(Sheffield Wed)
3	Jameel	3	Pearce	(Notts Forest)
4	Al-Saleh	4	Thomas	(Arsenal) replaced by Gascoigne
5	Abdul Jawad	5	Adams	(Arsenal)
6	Al-Mussaibeeh	6	Pallister	(Middlesbrough)
7	Al-Mutlaq	7	Robson*	(Man Utd)
8	Al-Bishi	8	Rocastle	(Arsenal)
9	Mubarak	9	Beardsley	(Newcastle Utd) replaced by Smith
10	Al-Suwayed	10	Lineker	(Barcelona)
11	Abdullah	11	Waddle	(Tottenham) replaced by Marwood

Crowd: 8,000

England scorer: Adams

Comments: Adams provided a second-half equaliser which earned a draw. He was one of 5 Arsenal players involved in this match. Brian Marwood and Mel Sterland won their only caps in Riyadh.

Greece 1 ENGLAND 2; in Athens;
Wednesday 8th February 1989

1	Ikonomopoulos	1	Shilton	(Derby County)
2	Chatziathanasiou	2	Stevens	(Rangers)
3	Koutoulas	3	Pearce	(Notts Forest)
4	Kalitzakis	4	Webb	(Notts Forest)
5	Mavridis	5	Walker	(Notts Forest)
6	Tsalouchidis	6	Butcher	(Rangers)
7	Saravakos	7	Robson*	(Man Utd)
8	Lagonidis	8	Rocastle	(Arsenal)
9	Samaras	9	Smith	(Arsenal) replaced by Beardsley
10	Nioblias	10	Lineker	(Barcelona)
11	Tsiantakis	11	Barnes	(Liverpool)

Crowd: 4,000

England scorers: Barnes, Robson

Comments: The visitors went behind to a first-minute penalty before John Barnes quickly equalised and the captain Bryan Robson scored a late winner. This was the first start for Alan Smith.

Albania 0 ENGLAND 2; in Tirana;
Wednesday 8th March 1989 (World Cup qualifier)

1 Mercini	1 Shilton	(Derby County)
2 Zmijani	2 Stevens	(Rangers)
3 Josa	3 Pearce	(Notts Forest)
4 Hodja	4 Webb	(Notts Forest)
5 Gega	5 Walker	(Notts Forest)
6 Jera	6 Butcher	(Rangers)
7 Shehu	7 Robson*	(Man Utd)
8 Lekbello	8 Rocastle	(Arsenal)
9 Millo	9 Waddle	(Tottenham) replaced by Beardsley
10 Minga	10 Lineker	(Barcelona) replaced by Smith
11 Demollari	11 Barnes	(Liverpool)

Crowd: 30,000

England scorers: Barnes, Robson

Comments: A goal in each half provided the away team with both World Cup qualifying points. Peter Shilton and the England defence had also yet to concede a goal in their group matches.

ENGLAND 5 Albania 0; at Wembley;
Wednesday 26th April 1989 (World Cup qualifier)

1 Shilton	(Derby County)	1 Nallbani
2 Stevens	(Rangers) replaced by Parker	2 Zmijani
3 Pearce	(Notts Forest)	3 Bubeqi
4 Webb	(Notts Forest)	4 Hodja
5 Walker	(Notts Forest)	5 Gega
6 Butcher	(Rangers)	6 Jera
7 Robson*	(Man Utd)	7 Shehu
8 Rocastle	(Arsenal) replaced by Gascoigne	8 Lekbello
9 Beardsley	(Newcastle Utd)	9 Millo
10 Lineker	(Barcelona)	10 Hasanpapa
11 Waddle	(Tottenham)	11 Demollari

Crowd: 60,602

England scorers: Beardsley (2), Lineker, Waddle, Gascoigne

Comments: Gary Lineker ended a run of 7 matches without a goal while Paul Parker made his debut. However the show was stolen by four goals from three players from the north-east of England.

ENGLAND 0 Chile 0; at Wembley;
Tuesday 23rd May 1989 (the Rous Cup)

1	Shilton	(Derby County)	1 Rojas
2	Parker	(QPR)	2 Reyes
3	Pearce	(Notts Forest)	3 Contreras
4	Webb	(Notts Forest)	4 Gonzalez
5	Walker	(Notts Forest)	5 Pizarro
6	Butcher	(Rangers)	6 Rubio
7	Robson*	(Man Utd)	7 Ormeno
8	Gascoigne	(Tottenham)	8 Covarrubias
9	Clough	(Notts Forest)	9 Astengo
10	Fashanu	(Wimbledon) replaced by Cottee	10 Espinoza
11	Waddle	(Tottenham)	11 Hurtado

Crowd: 15,628

Comments: John Fashanu became the first Wimbledon player to represent England, while the other new cap Nigel Clough was one of four Nottingham Forest players involved in this stalemate.

Scotland 0 ENGLAND 2; in Glasgow;
Saturday 27th May 1989 (the Rous Cup)

1	Leighton	1	Shilton	(Derby County)	
2	McKimmie	2	Stevens	(Rangers)	
3	Malpas	3	Pearce	(Notts Forest)	
4	Aitken	4	Webb	(Notts Forest)	
5	McLeish	5	Walker	(Notts Forest)	
6	McPherson	6	Butcher	(Rangers)	
7	Nevin	7	Robson*	(Man Utd)	
8	McStay	8	Steven	(Everton)	
9	McCoist	9	Fashanu	(Wimbledon) replaced by Bull	
10	Connor	10	Cottee	(Everton) replaced by Gascoigne	
11	Johnston	11	Waddle	(Tottenham)	

Crowd: 63,282

England scorers: Waddle, Bull

Comments: Scotland failed to score against England for the third consecutive year in the Rous Cup as substitute and debutant Steve Bull added a late goal to Chris Waddle's first-half effort.

ENGLAND 3 Poland 0; at Wembley;
Saturday 3rd June 1989 (World Cup qualifier)

	England			Poland
1	Shilton	(Derby County)	1	Bako
2	Stevens	(Rangers)	2	Prusik
3	Pearce	(Notts Forest)	3	Wojcicki
4	Webb	(Man Utd)	4	Lukasik
5	Walker	(Notts Forest)	5	Wdowczyk
6	Butcher	(Rangers)	6	Warzycha
7	Robson*	(Man Utd)	7	Matysik
8	Waddle	(Tottenham) replaced by Rocastle	8	Wijas
9	Beardsley	(Newcastle Utd) replaced by Smith	9	Urban
10	Lineker	(Barcelona)	10	Furtok
11	Barnes	(Liverpool)	11	Lesniak

Crowd: 69,203

England scorers: Lineker, Barnes, Webb

Comments: In a repeat of the 1986 score, Gary Lineker again scored against the Poles. However it took two second-half goals from John Barnes and Neil Webb to make sure of both points.

Denmark 1 ENGLAND 1; in Copenhagen;
Wednesday 7th June 1989

	Denmark		England	
1	Schmeichel	1	Shilton	(Derby County) replaced by Seaman
2	Elstrup	2	Parker	(QPR)
3	Laudrup	3	Pearce	(Notts Forest)
4	Bartram	4	Webb	(Man Utd) replaced by McMahon
5	Helt	5	Walker	(Notts Forest)
6	Laudrup	6	Butcher	(Rangers)
7	Andersen	7	Robson*	(Man Utd)
8	Nielsen	8	Rocastle	(Arsenal)
9	Nielsen	9	Beardsley	(Newcastle Utd) replaced by Bull
10	Olsen	10	Lineker	(Barcelona)
11	Risom	11	Barnes	(Liverpool) replaced by Waddle

Crowd: 18,400

England scorer: Lineker

Comments: Gary Lineker gave the visitors the half-time lead, scoring against a relatively unknown Peter Schmeichel but the future European champions equalised in the second half.

Sweden 0 ENGLAND 0; in Stockholm;
Wednesday 6th September 1989 (World Cup qualifier)

1	Ravelli	1	Shilton	(Derby County)
2	Nilsson	2	Stevens	(Rangers)
3	Larsson	3	Pearce	(Notts Forest)
4	Hysen	4	Webb	(Man Utd) replaced by Gascoigne
5	Ljung	5	Walker	(Notts Forest)
6	Enqvist	6	Butcher*	(Rangers)
7	Thern	7	Beardsley	(Newcastle Utd)
8	Ingesson	8	McMahon	(Liverpool)
9	Nilsson	9	Waddle	(Marseille)
10	Ekstrom	10	Lineker	(Tottenham)
11	Magnusson	11	Barnes	(Liverpool) replaced by Rocastle

Crowd: 38,558

Comments: Both teams drew a blank against each other for the second successive year, but England still remained on course for qualification for the World Cup finals in Italy next year.

Poland 0 ENGLAND 0; in Chorzow;
Wednesday 11th October 1989 (World Cup qualifier)

1	Bako	1	Shilton	(Derby County)
2	Czachowski	2	Stevens	(Rangers)
3	Kaczmarek	3	Pearce	(Notts Forest)
4	Wdowczyk	4	McMahon	(Liverpool)
5	Warzycha	5	Walker	(Notts Forest)
6	Tarasiewicz	6	Butcher	(Rangers)
7	Nawrocki	7	Robson*	(Man Utd)
8	Ziober	8	Rocastle	(Arsenal)
9	Warzycha	9	Beardsley	(Newcastle Utd)
10	Dziekanowski	10	Lineker	(Tottenham)
11	Kosecki	11	Waddle	(Marseille)

Crowd: 35,000

Comments: A draw was enough to ensure World Cup qualification unlike 16 years earlier when a draw against Poland led to elimination. This was Peter Shilton's ninth clean sheet in 11 matches.

ENGLAND 0 Italy 0; at Wembley;
Wednesday 15th November 1989

1	Shilton	(Derby County) replaced by Beasant	1 Zenga
2	Stevens	(Rangers)	2 Bergomi
3	Pearce	(Notts Forest) replaced by Winterburn	3 Maldini
4	McMahon	(Liverpool) replaced by Hodge	4 Baresi
5	Walker	(Notts Forest)	5 Ferri
6	Butcher	(Rangers)	6 Berti
7	Robson*	(Man Utd) replaced by Phelan	7 Donadoni
8	Waddle	(Marseille)	8 de Napoli
9	Beardsley	(Newcastle Utd) replaced by Platt	9 Vialli
10	Lineker	(Tottenham)	10 Giannini
11	Barnes	(Liverpool)	11 Carnevale

Crowd: 67,500

Comments: Yet another goal-less draw was produced as Bobby Robson introduced four new players: Dave Beasant, David Platt, and Nigel Winterburn, while Mike Phelan won his only cap.

ENGLAND 2 Yugoslavia 1; at Wembley;
Wednesday 13th December 1989

1	Shilton	(Derby County) replaced by Beasant	1 Ivkovic
2	Parker	(QPR)	2 Stanojkovic
3	Pearce	(Notts Forest) replaced by Dorigo	3 Spasic
4	Thomas	(Arsenal) replaced by Hodge	4 Vulic
5	Walker	(Notts Forest)	5 Hadzibegic
6	Butcher	(Rangers)	6 Brnovic
7	Robson*	(Man Utd) replaced by McMahon	7 Skoro
8	Rocastle	(Arsenal) replaced by Platt	8 Susic
9	Bull	(Wolves)	9 Mihajlovic
10	Lineker	(Tottenham)	10 Stojkovic
11	Waddle	(Marseille)	11 Savevski

Crowd: 34,796

England scorer: Robson (2)

Comments: Bryan Robson re-introduced his old party trick of scoring inside the first minute. He then netted the winner in the second half to secure a narrow victory. Tony Dorigo made his debut.

ENGLAND 1 Brazil 0; at Wembley;
Wednesday 28th March 1990

1 Shilton	(Derby County) replaced by Woods	1	Taffarel
2 Stevens	(Rangers)	2	Jorginho
3 Pearce	(Notts Forest)	3	Mozer
4 McMahon	(Liverpool)	4	Gomes
5 Walker	(Notts Forest)	5	Galvao
6 Butcher*	(Rangers)	6	Branco
7 Platt	(Aston Villa)	7	Silas
8 Waddle	(Marseille)	8	Dunga
9 Beardsley	(Newcastle Utd) replaced by Gascoigne	9	Valdo
10 Lineker	(Tottenham)	10	Bebeto
11 Barnes	(Liverpool)	11	Careca

Crowd: 80,000

England scorer: Lineker

Comments: Gary Lineker recorded his thirtieth international goal just before half time as England carved out a morale-boosting friendly win ahead of the World Cup finals in Italy.

ENGLAND 4 Czechoslovakia 2; at Wembley;
Wednesday 25th April 1990

1 Shilton	(Derby County) replaced by Seaman	1	Miklosko
2 Dixon	(Arsenal)	2	Bielek
3 Pearce	(Notts Forest) replaced by Dorigo	3	Straka
4 Steven	(Rangers)	4	Haslek
5 Walker	(Notts Forest) replaced by Wright	5	Kocian
6 Butcher	(Rangers)	6	Kinier
7 Robson*	(Man Utd) replaced by McMahon	7	Bilek
8 Gascoigne	(Tottenham)	8	Kubik
9 Bull	(Wolves)	9	Knoflicek
10 Lineker	(Tottenham)	10	Skuhravy
11 Hodge	(Notts Forest)	11	Moravcik

Crowd: 21,342

England scorers: Bull (2), Pearce, Gascoigne

Comments: Expectations were being raised after this goals spree. Lee Dixon made his England debut, though it was a shame that an abysmally low crowd attended this commendable victory.

ENGLAND 1 Denmark 0; at Wembley; Tuesday 15th May 1990

1	Shilton	(Derby County) replaced by Woods	1	Schmeichel
2	Stevens	(Rangers)	2	Laudrup
3	Pearce	(Notts Forest) replaced by Dorigo	3	Poulsen
4	McMahon	(Liverpool) replaced by Platt	4	Bartram
5	Walker	(Notts Forest)	5	Jensen
6	Butcher*	(Rangers)	6	Laudrup
7	Hodge	(Notts Forest)	7	Vilfort
8	Gascoigne	(Tottenham)	8	Andersen
9	Waddle	(Marseille) replaced by Rocastle	9	Nielsen
10	Lineker	(Tottenham) replaced by Bull	10	Olsen
11	Barnes	(Liverpool)	11	Sivabaek

Crowd: 27,643

England scorer: Lineker

Comments: Gary Lineker was on target again against a Mr. Peter Schmeichel as England continued their pre-World Cup momentum. Another pitiful crowd figure came to view this spectacle.

ENGLAND 1 Uruguay 2; at Wembley; Tuesday 22nd May 1990

1	Shilton	(Derby County)	1	Parreira
2	Parker	(QPR)	2	Gutierrez
3	Pearce	(Notts Forest)	3	de Leon
4	Hodge	(Notts Forest) replaced by Beardsley	4	Herrera
5	Walker	(Notts Forest)	5	Perdomo
6	Butcher	(Rangers)	6	Dominguez
7	Robson*	(Man Utd)	7	Alzamendi
8	Gascoigne	(Tottenham)	8	Ostolaza
9	Waddle	(Marseille)	9	Francescoli
10	Lineker	(Tottenham) replaced by Bull	10	Sosa
11	Barnes	(Liverpool)	11	Paz

Crowd: 38,751

England scorer: Barnes

Comments: This was a wake-up call for Bobby Robson's team who had managed to beat Brazil and then lose to Uruguay. John Barnes at least managed to register his tenth England goal.

Tunisia 1 ENGLAND 1; in Tunis;
Saturday 2nd June 1990

1	Zitouni	1	Shilton	(Derby County)
2	Madjebi	2	Stevens	(Rangers)
3	Herichi	3	Pearce	(Notts Forest)
4	Ben Neji	4	Hodge	(Notts Forest) replaced by Beardsley
5	Mahjoubi	5	Walker	(Notts Forest)
6	Khemeri	6	Butcher	(Rangers) replaced by Wright
7	Sellimi	7	Robson*	(Man Utd)
8	Hergal	8	Waddle	(Marseille) replaced by Platt
9	Dhiab	9	Gascoigne	(Tottenham)
10	Rouissi	10	Lineker	(Tottenham) replaced by Bull
11	Ben Yahia	11	Barnes	(Liverpool)

Crowd: 25,000

England scorer: Bull

Comments: It took a goal from Steve Bull in the dying seconds to save England's blushes in this final pre-World Cup rehearsal. Matches against the Irish and the Dutch lay just around the corner.

ENGLAND 1 Republic of Ireland 1; in Cagliari;
Monday 11th June 1990 (World Cup finals)

1	Shilton	(Derby County)	1	Bonner
2	Stevens	(Rangers)	2	Morris
3	Pearce	(Notts Forest)	3	Staunton
4	Gascoigne	(Tottenham)	4	McCarthy
5	Walker	(Notts Forest)	5	Moran
6	Butcher	(Rangers)	6	Townsend
7	Robson*	(Man Utd)	7	McGrath
8	Waddle	(Marseille)	8	Houghton
9	Beardsley	(Newcastle Utd) replaced by McMahon	9	Cascarino
10	Lineker	(Tottenham) replaced by Bull	10	Aldridge
11	Barnes	(Liverpool)	11	Sheedy

Crowd: 35,238

England scorer: Lineker

Comments: This time Lineker scored in the first ten minutes, but England could not shake the men in green off and Kevin Sheedy netted a late equaliser. Both teams had gained a valuable point.

ENGLAND 0 Holland 0; in Cagliari;
Saturday 16th June 1990 (World Cup finals)

1 Shilton	(Derby County)	1	van Breukelen
2 Parker	(QPR)	2	van Aerle
3 Pearce	(Notts Forest)	3	Koeman
4 Wright	(Derby County)	4	van Tiggelen
5 Walker	(Notts Forest)	5	Wouters
6 Butcher	(Rangers)	6	Rijkaard
7 Robson*	(Man Utd) replaced by Platt	7	Gillhaus
8 Waddle	(Marseille) replaced by Bull	8	Witschge
9 Gascoigne	(Tottenham)	9	Gullit
10 Lineker	(Tottenham)	10	van Schip
11 Barnes	(Liverpool)	11	van Basten

Crowd: 35,267

Comments: England didn't quite exorcise the demons of 1988 but at least this time Shilton kept a clean sheet against van Basten. The group was delicately balanced after four drawn matches.

ENGLAND 1 Egypt 0; in Cagliari;
Thursday 21st June 1990 (World Cup finals)

1 Shilton*	(Derby County)	1	Shoubier
2 Parker	(QPR)	2	Hassan
3 Pearce	(Notts Forest)	3	Yaken
4 Gascoigne	(Tottenham)	4	Ramzy
5 Walker	(Notts Forest)	5	Yassin
6 Wright	(Derby County)	6	Ramzy
7 McMahon	(Liverpool)	7	Youssef
8 Waddle	(Marseille) replaced by Platt	8	Abdel Ghani
9 Bull	(Wolves) replaced by Beardsley	9	El-Kass
10 Lineker	(Tottenham)	10	Hassan
11 Barnes	(Liverpool)	11	Abdel Hamid

Crowd: 34,959

England scorer: Wright

Comments: Mark Wright chose an excellent time to head home his only international goal just short of the hour mark as England squeezed through to the knockout stages from a close group.

ENGLAND 1 Belgium 0 [After extra time]; in Bologna; Tuesday 26th June 1990 (World Cup finals)

1 Shilton	(Derby County)	1	Shoubier
2 Parker	(QPR)	2	Hassan
3 Pearce	(Notts Forest)	3	Yaken
4 Wright	(Derby County)	4	Ramzy
5 Walker	(Notts Forest)	5	Yassin
6 Butcher*	(Rangers)	6	Ramzy
7 McMahon	(Liverpool) replaced by Platt	7	Youssef
8 Waddle	(Marseille)	8	Abdel Ghani
9 Gascoigne	(Tottenham)	9	El-Kass
10 Lineker	(Tottenham)	10	Hassan
11 Barnes	(Liverpool) replaced by Bull	11	Abdel Hamid

Crowd: 34,520

England scorer: Platt

Comments: David Platt also chose an excellent time to volley home his first international goal in the dying moments of extra time as England squeezed through to face the unfancied Cameroon.

ENGLAND 3 Cameroon 2 [After extra time]; in Naples; Sunday 1st July 1990 (World Cup finals)

1 Shilton	(Derby County)	1	N'Kono
2 Parker	(QPR)	2	Massing
3 Pearce	(Notts Forest)	3	Ebwelle
4 Wright	(Derby County)	4	Kunde
5 Walker	(Notts Forest)	5	Pagal
6 Butcher*	(Rangers) replaced by Steven	6	Tataw
7 Platt	(Aston Villa)	7	M'Fede
8 Waddle	(Marseille)	8	Libiih
9 Gascoigne	(Tottenham)	9	Makanaky
10 Lineker	(Tottenham)	10	Mabang
11 Barnes	(Liverpool) replaced by Beardsley	11	Omam-Biyik

Crowd: 55,205

England scorers: Platt, Lineker (2 Pens)

Comments: In a bizarre match of 3 penalties, England came perilously near to defeat against the surprise package of Cameroon. Having led 1-0, England needed 2 Lineker penalties to rescue them.

ENGLAND 1 West Germany 1 [After extra time]; in Turin; Wednesday 4th July 1990 (World Cup finals)

1	Shilton	(Derby County)	1	Ilgner
2	Parker	(QPR)	2	Brehme
3	Pearce	(Notts Forest)	3	Kohler
4	Wright	(Derby County)	4	Augenthaler
5	Walker	(Notts Forest)	5	Buchwald
6	Butcher*	(Rangers) replaced by Steven	6	Hassler
7	Platt	(Aston Villa)	7	Voller
8	Waddle	(Marseille)	8	Matthaus
9	Gascoigne	(Tottenham)	9	Berthold
10	Lineker	(Tottenham)	10	Klinsmann
11	Beardsley	(Newcastle Utd)	11	Thon

Crowd: 62,628

England scorer: Lineker

Comments: If the last match had 3 penalties, this epic ended with 9, two of which were fatefully missed by Pearce and Waddle. It ended in tears for Gazza and Pearce. This was Butcher's last cap.

Italy 2 ENGLAND 1; in Bari; Saturday 7th July 1990 (World Cup finals)

1	Zenga	1	Shilton*	(Derby County)
2	Baresi	2	Stevens	(Rangers)
3	Bergomi	3	Dorigo	(Chelsea)
4	de Agostini	4	Parker	(QPR)
5	Ferrara	5	Walker	(Notts Forest)
6	Maldini	6	Wright	(Derby County) replaced by Webb
7	Vierchowod	7	Platt	(Aston Villa)
8	Ancelotti	8	Steven	(Rangers)
9	Giannini	9	McMahon	(Liverpool) replaced by Waddle
10	Baggio	10	Lineker	(Tottenham)
11	Schillachi	11	Beardsley	(Newcastle Utd)

Crowd: 62,628

England scorer: Platt

Comments: England had to settle for fourth place in a tournament that they could so easily have won. This defeat ended the Bobby Robson era and was the last of 125 caps for Peter Shilton.

ENGLAND 1 Hungary 0; at Wembley;
Wednesday 12th September 1990

1	Woods	(Rangers)	1	Petry
2	Dixon	(Arsenal)	2	Monos
3	Pearce	(Notts Forest) replaced by Dorigo	3	Disztl
4	Parker	(QPR)	4	Keller
5	Walker	(Notts Forest)	5	Limperger
6	Wright	(Derby County)	6	Garaba
7	Platt	(Aston Villa)	7	Kozma
8	Gascoigne	(Tottenham)	8	Bucs
9	Bull	(Wolves) replaced by Waddle	9	Gregor
10	Lineker*	(Tottenham)	10	Berczy
11	Barnes	(Liverpool)	11	Kovacs

Crowd: 51,459

England scorer: Lineker

Comments: New captain Gary Lineker scored almost on the stroke of half time to get the Graham Taylor era off to a flying start. A recalled Chris Woods also earned himself another shut-out.

ENGLAND 2 Poland 0; at Wembley;
Wednesday 17th October 1990 (European Championship)

1	Woods	(Rangers)	1	Wandzik
2	Dixon	(Arsenal)	2	Czachowski
3	Pearce	(Notts Forest)	3	Kaczmarek
4	Parker	(QPR)	4	Wdowczyk
5	Walker	(Notts Forest)	5	Warzycha
6	Wright	(Derby County)	6	Tarasiewicz
7	Platt	(Aston Villa)	7	Nawrocki
8	Gascoigne	(Tottenham)	8	Szewczyk
9	Bull	(Wolves) replaced by Waddle	9	Ziober
10	Lineker*	(Tottenham) replaced by Beardsley	10	Kosecki
11	Barnes	(Liverpool)	11	Furtok

Crowd: 77,040

England scorers: Lineker (Pen), Beardsley

Comments: The home team made a winning start to their European Championship campaign though it took a very late Beardsley goal to ensure victory after England had led 1–0 at the interval.

Republic of Ireland 1 ENGLAND 1; in Dublin;
Wednesday 14th November 1990 (European Championship)

1	Bonner	1	Woods	(Rangers)
2	Morris	2	Dixon	(Arsenal)
3	McCarthy	3	Pearce	(Notts Forest)
4	O'Leary	4	Adams	(Arsenal)
5	Staunton	5	Walker	(Notts Forest)
6	Houghton	6	Wright	(Derby County)
7	McGrath	7	Platt	(Aston Villa)
8	Whelan	8	Cowans	(Bari)
9	Townsend	9	Beardsley	(Newcastle Utd)
10	Aldridge	10	Lineker*	(Tottenham)
11	Quinn	11	McMahon	(Liverpool)

Crowd: 46,000

England scorer: Platt

Comments: For the second time in 1990 the Irish cancelled England's lead and rescued a point, courtesy of a Tony Cascarino goal. This was the last cap for Gordon Cowans and Steve McMahon.

ENGLAND 2 Cameroon 0; at Wembley;
Wednesday 6th February 1991

1	Seaman	(Arsenal)	1	Bell
2	Dixon	(Arsenal)	2	Ebwelle
3	Pearce	(Notts Forest)	3	Onana
4	Steven	(Rangers)	4	Kunde
5	Walker	(Notts Forest)	5	Tataw
6	Wright M	(Derby County)	6	M'Fede
7	Robson*	(Man Utd) replaced by Pallister	7	Mbouh-Mbouh
8	Gascoigne	(Tottenham) replaced by Hodge	8	Pagal
9	Wright I	(Crystal Palace)	9	Kana-Biyik
10	Lineker	(Tottenham)	10	Omam-Biyik
11	Barnes	(Liverpool)	11	Ekeke

Crowd: 61,075

England scorers: Lineker (2)

Comments: History repeated itself as Gary Lineker netted twice against Cameroon, including once from the penalty spot. His striking partner Ian Wright won his first cap in this friendly victory.

ENGLAND 1 Republic of Ireland 1; at Wembley; Wednesday 27th March 1991 (European Championship)

1	Seaman	(Arsenal)		1	Bonner
2	Dixon	(Arsenal)		2	Irwin
3	Pearce	(Notts Forest)		3	Staunton
4	Adams	(Arsenal) replaced by Sharpe		4	O'Leary
5	Walker	(Notts Forest)		5	Moran
6	Wright M	(Derby County)		6	Townsend
7	Robson*	(Man Utd)		7	McGrath
8	Platt	(Aston Villa)		8	Houghton
9	Beardsley	(Newcastle Utd)		9	Quinn
10	Lineker	(Tottenham) replaced by Wright I		10	Aldridge
11	Barnes	(Liverpool)		11	Sheedy

Crowd: 77,753

England scorer: Dixon

Comments: Lee Dixon scored his only England goal to give the hosts an early lead but big Niall Quinn equalised as both teams fought out their third consecutive 1–1. Lee Sharpe made his debut.

Turkey 0 ENGLAND 1; in Izmir; Wednesday 1st May 1991 (European Championship)

1	Demirbas	1	Seaman	(Arsenal)	
2	Calimbay	2	Dixon	(Arsenal)	
3	Temizkanoglu	3	Pearce	(Notts Forest)	
4	Keskin	4	Wise	(Chelsea)	
5	Cetin	5	Walker	(Notts Forest)	
6	Altintas	6	Pallister	(Man Utd)	
7	Karaman	7	Platt	(Aston Villa)	
8	Dilmen	8	Thomas	(Crystal Palace) replaced by Hodge	
9	Ozdilek	9	Smith	(Arsenal)	
10	Colak	10	Lineker*	(Tottenham)	
11	Gultiken	11	Barnes	(Liverpool)	

Crowd: 25,000

England scorer: Wise

Comments: Debutant Dennis Wise appeared to parry the ball into the net with his hand, but the goal was allowed to stand. Geoff Thomas also won his first cap and Steve Hodge won his last cap.

ENGLAND 3 USSR 1; at Wembley;
Tuesday 21st May 1991

1 Woods	(Rangers)	1	Uvarov
2 Stevens	(Rangers)	2	Chernyshov
3 Dorigo	(Chelsea)	3	Kulkov
4 Wise	(Chelsea) replaced by Batty	4	Tsveiba
5 Parker	(QPR)	5	Galiamin
6 Wright M*	(Derby County)	6	Shalimov
7 Platt	(Aston Villa)	7	Mikhailichenko
8 Thomas	(Crystal Palace)	8	Kanchelskis
9 Smith	(Arsenal)	9	Kolyvanov
10 Wright I	(Crystal Palace) replaced by Beardsley	10	Tatarchuk
11 Barnes	(Liverpool)	11	Kuznetsov

Crowd: 23,789

England scorers: Smith, Platt (2)

Comments: The USSR took an early lead but David Platt scored just before half time and converted a penalty just before full time. David Batty came on in the second half to win his first cap.

ENGLAND 2 Argentina 2; at Wembley;
Saturday 25th May 1991

1 Seaman	(Arsenal)	1	Goycochea
2 Dixon	(Arsenal)	2	Vazquez
3 Pearce	(Notts Forest)	3	Enrique
4 Batty	(Leeds United)	4	Basualdo
5 Walker	(Notts Forest)	5	Gamboa
6 Wright	(Derby County)	6	Ruggeri
7 Platt	(Aston Villa)	7	Garcia
8 Thomas	(Crystal Palace)	8	Franco
9 Smith	(Arsenal)	9	Simone
10 Lineker*	(Tottenham)	10	Martellotto
11 Barnes	(Liverpool) replaced by Clough	11	Boldrini

Crowd: 44,497

England scorers: Lineker, Platt

Comments: Although David Platt gave England a 2-0 advantage at the start of the second half, Argentina still managed to salvage a draw, even in the absence of the bete noir Diego Maradona.

Australia 0 ENGLAND 1; in Sydney;
Saturday 1st June 1991

1 Zabica	1 Woods	(Rangers)
2 Gray	2 Parker	(QPR)
3 Duraovic	3 Pearce	(Notts Forest)
4 Zelic	4 Batty	(Leeds United)
5 Tobin	5 Walker	(Notts Forest)
6 Vidmar	6 Wright	(Derby County)
7 Wade	7 Platt	(Aston Villa)
8 Petersen	8 Thomas	(Crystal Palace)
9 Vidmar	9 Clough	(Notts Forest)
10 Arnold	10 Lineker*	(Tottenham) replaced by Wise
11 Tapai	11 Hirst	(Sheffield Wed) replaced by Salako

Crowd: 35,472

England scorer: Gray (OG)

Comments: An Ian Gray own goal just before half time decided this 'Ashes' friendly. David Hirst made his debut. His half-time replacement John Salako duly collected his first cap too.

New Zealand 0 ENGLAND 1; in Auckland;
Monday 3rd June 1991

1 Gosling	1 Woods	(Rangers)
2 Ridenton	2 Parker	(QPR)
3 Gray	3 Pearce	(Notts Forest)
4 Dunford	4 Batty	(Leeds United) replaced by Deane
5 Evans	5 Walker	(Notts Forest)
6 Ironside	6 Barrett	(Oldham Athletic)
7 McGarry	7 Platt	(Aston Villa)
8 Halligan	8 Thomas	(Crystal Palace)
9 Edge	9 Wise	(Chelsea)
10 de Jong	10 Lineker*	(Tottenham)
11 Ferris	11 Walters	(Rangers) replaced by Salako

Crowd: 17,520

England scorer: Lineker

Comments: Gary Lineker scored in the final minute to secure a narrow friendly triumph. Earl Barrett and Brian Deane made their debut, while Mark Walters won his only cap.

New Zealand 0 ENGLAND 2; in Wellington;
Saturday 8th June 1991

1 Schofield	1 Woods	(Rangers)
2 Ridenton	2 Charles	(Notts Forest)
3 Gray	3 Pearce*	(Notts Forest)
4 Dunford	4 Wise	(Chelsea)
5 Evans	5 Walker	(Notts Forest)
6 Ironside	6 Wright M	(Derby County)
7 McGarry	7 Platt	(Aston Villa)
8 Halligan	8 Thomas	(Crystal Palace)
9 Edge	9 Deane	(Sheffield United) replaced by Hirst
10 de Jong	10 Wright I	(Crystal Palace)
11 Ferris	11 Salako	(Crystal Palace)

Crowd: 12,000

England scorers: Pearce, Hirst

Comments: David Hirst scored his only international goal early in the second half for an England team that fielded three Crystal Palace players and three Nottingham Forest players.

Malaysia 2 ENGLAND 4; in Kuala Lumpur;
Wednesday 12th June 1991

1 Hassan	1 Woods	(Rangers)
2 Singh	2 Charles	(Notts Forest)
3 Kin Hong	3 Pearce	(Notts Forest)
4 Zaid Jamil	4 Batty	(Leeds United)
5 Jayakanthan	5 Walker	(Notts Forest)
6 Siew Yai	6 Wright	(Derby County)
7 Ahmad Yusof	7 Platt	(Aston Villa)
8 Nazri Nasir	8 Thomas	(Crystal Palace)
9 Marjan	9 Clough	(Notts Forest)
10 Ab Hassan	10 Lineker*	(Tottenham)
11 Salleh	11 Salako	(Crystal Palace)

Crowd: 38,000

England scorer: Lineker (4)

Comments: In almost unbearable heat, Gary Lineker recorded a hat-trick inside the first half hour. Gary Charles won his final cap. He was one of four Nottingham Forest players in the line-up.

ENGLAND 0 Germany 1; at Wembley;
Wednesday 11th September 1991

1	Woods	(Sheffield Wed)		1	Ilgner
2	Dixon	(Arsenal)		2	Binz
3	Dorigo	(Leeds United)		3	Brehme
4	Batty	(Leeds United)		4	Kohler
5	Pallister	(Man Utd)		5	Effenberg
6	Parker	(Man Utd)		6	Buchwald
7	Platt	(Bari)		7	Moller
8	Steven	(Marseille) replaced by Stewart		8	Hassler
9	Smith	(Arsenal)		9	Riedle
10	Lineker*	(Tottenham)		10	Matthaus
11	Salako	(Crystal Palace) replaced by Merson		11	Doll

Crowd: 59,493

Comments: Karl-Heinz Riedle scored the only goal on the stroke of half time. This was the final cap for John Salako and the international debut for the substitutes Paul Merson and Paul Stewart.

ENGLAND 1 Turkey 0; at Wembley;
Wednesday 16th October 1991 (European Championship)

1	Woods	(Sheffield Wed)		1	Demirbas
2	Dixon	(Arsenal)		2	Cetin
3	Pearce	(Notts Forest)		3	Temizkanoglu
4	Batty	(Leeds United)		4	Keskin
5	Walker	(Notts Forest)		5	Tugay
6	Mabbutt	(Tottenham)		6	Sofuoglu
7	Robson	(Man Utd)		7	Ucar
8	Platt	(Bari)		8	Calimbay
9	Smith	(Arsenal)		9	Karaman
10	Lineker*	(Tottenham)		10	Cetin
11	Waddle	(Marseille)		11	Cikirikci

Crowd: 50,896

England scorer: Smith

Comments: In spite of completing a 1–0 double over Turkey in the qualifying group, this match marked the finish of the international careers of Bryan Robson and Chris Waddle.

Poland 1 ENGLAND 1; in Poznan;
Wednesday 13th November 1991 (European Championship)

1	Bako	1	Woods	(Sheffield Wed)
2	Soczynski	2	Dixon	(Arsenal)
3	Waldoch	3	Pearce	(Notts Forest)
4	Szewczyk	4	Gray	(Crystal Palace) replaced by Smith
5	Warzycha	5	Walker	(Notts Forest)
6	Czachowski	6	Mabbutt	(Tottenham)
7	Skrzypczak	7	Platt	(Bari)
8	Ziober	8	Thomas	(Crystal Palace)
9	Kosecki	9	Rocastle	(Arsenal)
10	Urban	10	Lineker*	(Tottenham)
11	Furtok	11	Sinton	(QPR) replaced by Daley

Crowd: 15,000

England scorer: Lineker

Comments: Lineker's late equaliser ensured that England would qualify for the finals in Sweden in 1992. Tony Daley and Andy Sinton won their first caps, while Andy Gray collected his only cap.

ENGLAND 2 France 0; at Wembley;
Wednesday 19th February 1992

1	Woods	(Sheffield Wed)	1	Rousset
2	Jones	(Liverpool)	2	Amoros
3	Pearce*	(Notts Forest)	3	Angloma
4	Keown	(Everton)	4	Boli
5	Walker	(Notts Forest)	5	Blanc
6	Wright	(Liverpool)	6	Casoni
7	Webb	(Man Utd)	7	Deschamps
8	Thomas	(Crystal Palace)	8	Fernandez
9	Clough	(Notts Forest)	9	Papin
10	Shearer	(Southampton)	10	Perez
11	Hirst	(Sheffield Wed) replaced by Lineker	11	Cantona

Crowd: 58,723

England scorers: Shearer, Lineker

Comments: Alan Shearer scored on his debut just before half time. Also collecting their first caps were Rob Jones and Martin Keown, while David Hirst and Geoff Thomas won their final caps.

Czechoslovakia 2 ENGLAND 2; in Prague;
Wednesday 25th March 1992

1 Miklosko	1 Seaman	(Arsenal)
2 Chovanec	2 Keown	(Everton)
3 Glonek	3 Pearce*	(Notts Forest)
4 Kadlec	4 Rocastle	(Arsenal) replaced by Dixon
5 Hapal	5 Walker	(Notts Forest)
6 Bilek	6 Mabbutt	(Tottenham) replaced by Lineker
7 Nemecek	7 Platt	(Bari)
8 Kubik	8 Merson	(Arsenal)
9 Kula	9 Clough	(Notts Forest) replaced by Stewart
10 Skuhravy	10 Hateley	(Rangers)
11 Knoflicek	11 Barnes	(Liverpool) replaced by Dorigo

Crowd: 6,000

England scorers: Merson, Keown

Comments: In front of a tiny crowd, the visitors came from behind twice. Mark Hateley and Gary Mabbutt made their final international appearances in this pre-European Championship warm-up.

CIS 2 ENGLAND 2; in Moscow;
Wednesday 29th April 1992

1 Kharine	1 Woods	(Sheffield Wed) replaced by Martyn
2 Chernyshov	2 Stevens	(Rangers)
3 Tskhadaze	3 Sinton	(QPR) replaced by Curle
4 Tsveiba	4 Palmer	(Sheffield Wed)
5 Ledyakov	5 Walker	(Notts Forest)
6 Shalimov	6 Keown	(Everton)
7 Mikhailichenko	7 Platt	(Bari)
8 Kanchelskis	8 Steven	(Marseille) replaced by Stewart
9 Kolyvanov	9 Shearer	(Southampton) replaced by Clough
10 Mostovoi	10 Lineker*	(Tottenham)
11 Yuran	11 Daley	(Aston Villa)

Crowd: 28,000

England scorers: Lineker, Steven

Comments: Gary Lineker and Trevor Steven scored their final goals, while Paul Stewart won his last cap, and Keith Curle, Nigel Martyn, and Carlton Palmer all made their debut in this friendly.

Hungary 0 ENGLAND 1; in Budapest;
Tuesday 12th May 1992

1 Brockhauser	1 Martyn	(Crystal Palace) replaced by Seaman
2 Simon	2 Stevens	(Rangers)
3 Telek	3 Dorigo	(Leeds United)
4 Szalma	4 Curle	(Man City) replaced by Sinton
5 Lorincz	5 Walker	(Notts Forest)
6 Limperger	6 Keown	(Everton)
7 Kiprich	7 Webb	(Man Utd) replaced by Batty
8 Kovacs	8 Palmer	(Sheffield Wed)
9 Pisont	9 Merson	(Arsenal) replaced by Smith
10 Lipcsei	10 Lineker*	(Tottenham) replaced by Wright
11 Vincze	11 Daley	(Aston Villa)

Crowd: 25,000

England scorer: Webb

Comments: Neil Webb scored his last England goal in the second half to separate the two teams as the away team stretched their unbeaten run to six internationals.

ENGLAND 1 Brazil 1; at Wembley;
Sunday 17th May 1992

1 Woods	(Sheffield Wed)	1 Carlos	
2 Stevens	(Rangers)	2 Winck	
3 Dorigo	(Leeds United) replaced by Pearce	3 Mozer	
4 Palmer	(Sheffield Wed)	4 Gomes	
5 Walker	(Notts Forest)	5 Branco	
6 Keown	(Everton)	6 Silva	
7 Daley	(Aston Villa) replaced by Merson	7 Henrique	
8 Steven	(Marseille) replaced by Webb	8 Rai	
9 Platt	(Bari)	9 Gaucho	
10 Lineker*	(Tottenham)	10 Bebeto	
11 Sinton	(QPR) replaced by Rocastle	11 Valdo	

Crowd: 53,428

England scorer: Platt

Comments: David Platt scored early in the second half to cancel out Bebeto's earlier goal. This was the last international appearance for David Rocastle who died nine years later, aged only 33.

Finland 1 ENGLAND 2; in Helsinki;
Wednesday 3rd June 1992

1	Huttunen	1	Woods	(Sheffield Wed)
2	Rinne	2	Stevens	(Rangers) replaced by Palmer
3	Jarvinen	3	Pearce	(Notts Forest)
4	Petaja	4	Keown	(Everton)
5	Holmgren	5	Walker	(Notts Forest)
6	Kinnunen	6	Wright	(Liverpool)
7	Litmanen	7	Platt	(Juventus)
8	Myyry	8	Steven	(Marseille) replaced by Daley
9	Hjelm	9	Webb	(Man Utd)
10	Tarkkio	10	Lineker*	(Tottenham)
11	Huhtamaki	11	Barnes	(Liverpool) replaced by Merson

Crowd: 16,101

England scorer: Platt (2)

Comments: After conceding the lead, England had to rely on a brace from David Platt to turn this friendly match in their favour. It would be the last international appearance for Gary Stevens.

ENGLAND 0 Denmark 0; in Malmo;
Thursday 11th June 1992 (European Championship)

1	Woods	(Sheffield Wed)	1	Schmeichel
2	Curle	(Man City) replaced by Daley	2	Christensen
3	Pearce	(Notts Forest)	3	Laudrup
4	Palmer	(Sheffield Wed)	4	Poulsen
5	Walker	(Notts Forest)	5	Jensen
6	Keown	(Everton)	6	Vilfort
7	Platt	(Juventus)	7	Andersen
8	Steven	(Marseille)	8	Christofte
9	Smith	(Arsenal)	9	Nielsen
10	Lineker*	(Tottenham)	10	Olsen
11	Merson	(Arsenal) replaced by Webb	11	Sivabaek

Crowd: 26,385

Comments: Peter Schmeichel and unfancied Denmark not only kept England at bay but they confounded all expectations by proceeding to win the tournament. This was Keith Curle's last cap.

ENGLAND 0 France 0; in Malmo;
Sunday 14th June 1992 (European Championship)

1 Woods	(Sheffield Wed)	1	Martini
2 Batty	(Leeds United)	2	Amoros
3 Pearce	(Notts Forest)	3	Boli
4 Palmer	(Sheffield Wed)	4	Blanc
5 Walker	(Notts Forest)	5	Casoni
6 Keown	(Everton)	6	Durand
7 Platt	(Juventus)	7	Sauzee
8 Steven	(Marseille)	8	Fernandez
9 Shearer	(Southampton)	9	Deschamps
10 Lineker*	(Tottenham)	10	Cantona
11 Sinton	(QPR)	11	Papin

Crowd: 26,535

Comments: For the second time in six months, Eric Cantona and his team failed to score against England, but Graham Taylor's outfit also drew a blank and now their hopes of success were flimsy.

Sweden 2 ENGLAND 1; in Stockholm;
Wednesday 17th June 1992 (European Championship)

1 Ravelli	1	Woods	(Sheffield Wed)
2 Nilsson	2	Batty	(Leeds United)
3 Eriksson	3	Pearce	(Notts Forest)
4 Andersson	4	Keown	(Everton)
5 Bjorklund	5	Walker	(Notts Forest)
6 Schwarz	6	Palmer	(Sheffield Wed)
7 Ingesson	7	Platt	(Juventus)
8 Thern	8	Webb	(Man Utd)
9 Limpar	9	Sinton	(QPR) replaced by Merson
10 Brolin	10	Lineker*	(Tottenham) replaced by Smith
11 Dahlin	11	Daley	(Aston Villa)

Crowd: 30,126

England scorer: Platt

Comments: Platt gave England an early lead but the wheels came off in the second half. This debacle ended the England careers of Daley, Smith, and Webb, whilst Gary Lineker chose to 'retire'.

Spain 1 ENGLAND 0; in Santander;
Wednesday 9th September 1992

1 Zubizarreta	1 Woods	(Sheffield Wed)
2 Ferrer	2 Dixon	(Arsenal) replaced by Bardsley
3 Toni	3 Pearce*	(Notts Forest)
4 Solozabal	4 Ince	(Man Utd)
5 Lopez	5 Walker	(Sampdoria)
6 Vizcaino	6 Wright	(Derby County)
7 Fonseca	7 White	(Man City) replaced by Merson
8 Michel	8 Platt	(Juventus)
9 Bakero	9 Clough	(Notts Forest)
10 Vazquez	10 Shearer	(Blackburn)
11 Amor	11 Sinton	(QPR) replaced by Deane

Crowd: 22,000

Comments: David Bardsley made his debut at half time, only to be substituted by Calton Palmer. Paul Ince also made his debut, while David White won his only cap and Deane won his final cap.

ENGLAND 1 Norway 1; at Wembley;
Wednesday 14th October 1992 (World Cup qualifier)

1 Woods	(Sheffield Wed)	1 Thorstvedt
2 Dixon	(Arsenal) replaced by Palmer	2 Nilsen
3 Pearce*	(Notts Forest)	3 Pedersen
4 Batty	(Leeds United)	4 Bratseth
5 Walker	(Sampdoria)	5 Bjornebye
6 Adams	(Arsenal)	6 Ingebrigtsen
7 Platt	(Juventus)	7 Mykland
8 Gascoigne	(Lazio)	8 Rekdal
9 Shearer	(Blackburn)	9 Halle
10 Wright	(Arsenal) replaced by Merson	10 Sorloth
11 Ince	(Man Utd)	11 Jakobsen

Crowd: 51,441

England scorer: Platt

Comments: England welcomed back Tony Adams and a fit-again Paul Gascoigne, but Rekdal scored a late equaliser as hapless England now recorded their fifth successive match without a win.

ENGLAND 4 Turkey 0; at Wembley;
Wednesday 18th November 1992 (World Cup qualifier)

1	Woods	(Sheffield Wed)	1	Demirbas
2	Dixon	(Arsenal)	2	Cetin
3	Pearce*	(Notts Forest)	3	Korkmaz
4	Palmer	(Sheffield Wed)	4	Keskin
5	Walker	(Sampdoria)	5	Temizkanoglu
6	Adams	(Arsenal)	6	Cikirikci
7	Platt	(Juventus)	7	Mandirali
8	Gascoigne	(Lazio)	8	Karaman
9	Shearer	(Blackburn)	9	Cetin
10	Wright	(Arsenal)	10	Ozdilek
11	Ince	(Man Utd)	11	Sukur

Crowd: 42,984

England scorers: Gascoigne (2), Shearer, Pearce

Comments: A pair of goals in each half put England's World Cup hopes back on track. Paul Gascoigne was the chief destroyer with two goals which helped to relieve the pressure on his manager.

ENGLAND 6 San Marino 0; at Wembley;
Wednesday 17th February 1993 (World Cup qualifier)

1	Woods	(Sheffield Wed)	1	Benedettini
2	Dixon	(Arsenal)	2	Muccioli
3	Dorigo	(Leeds United)	3	Gennari
4	Palmer	(Sheffield Wed)	4	Zanotti
5	Walker	(Sampdoria)	5	Canti
6	Adams	(Arsenal)	6	Guerra
7	Platt*	(Juventus)	7	Manzaroli
8	Gascoigne	(Lazio)	8	Mazza
9	Ferdinand	(QPR)	9	Bacciocchi
10	Barnes	(Liverpool)	10	Bonini
11	Batty	(Leeds United)	11	Francini

Crowd: 51,154

England scorers: Platt (4), Palmer, Ferdinand

Comments: Les Ferdinand scored on his debut while Carlton Palmer recorded his only England goal, though the home team only led 2–0 after an hour, until David Platt's efforts stole the show.

Turkey 0 ENGLAND 2; in Izmir;
Wednesday 31st March 1993 (World Cup qualifier)

1	Ipekoglu	1	Woods	(Sheffield Wed)
2	Cetin	2	Dixon	(Arsenal) replaced by Clough
3	Temizkanoglu	3	Sinton	(QPR)
4	Guncar	4	Palmer	(Sheffield Wed)
5	Kerimoglu	5	Walker	(Sampdoria)
6	Korkmaz	6	Adams	(Arsenal)
7	Ucar	7	Platt*	(Juventus)
8	Karaman	8	Gascoigne	(Lazio)
9	Cetin	9	Barnes	(Liverpool)
10	Ozdilek	10	Wright	(Arsenal) replaced by Sharpe
11	Cikirikci	11	Ince	(Man Utd)

Crowd: 60,000

England scorers: Platt, Gascoigne

Comments: The away team's goals came at the beginning and the end of the first half as Graham Taylor's outfit continued to gather momentum in their World Cup qualifying campaign.

ENGLAND 2 Holland 2; at Wembley;
Wednesday 28th April 1993 (World Cup qualifier)

1	Woods	(Sheffield Wed)	1	de Goey
2	Dixon	(Arsenal)	2	Blind
3	Keown	(Arsenal)	3	de Boer
4	Palmer	(Sheffield Wed)	4	Wouters
5	Walker	(Sampdoria)	5	Witschge
6	Adams	(Arsenal)	6	Winter
7	Platt*	(Juventus)	7	Bergkamp
8	Gascoigne	(Lazio) replaced by Merson	8	Rijkaard
9	Ferdinand	(QPR)	9	Bosman
10	Barnes	(Liverpool)	10	Gullit
11	Ince	(Man Utd)	11	Overmars

Crowd: 73,163

England scorers: Barnes, Platt

Comments: England raced into a 2–0 lead before Bergkamp pulled one back before half-time. Bergkamp was then fouled by Walker, enabling Van Vossen to convert a late penalty and steal a point.

Poland 1 ENGLAND 1; in Chorzow;
Saturday 29th May 1993 (World Cup qualifier)

1 Bako	1 Woods	(Sheffield Wed)
2 Czachowski	2 Bardsley	(QPR)
3 Szewczyk	3 Dorigo	(Leeds United)
4 Lesiak	4 Palmer	(Sheffield Wed) replaced by Wright
5 Adamczuk	5 Walker	(Sampdoria)
6 Kosecki	6 Adams	(Arsenal)
7 Brzeczek	7 Platt*	(Juventus)
8 Swierczewski	8 Gascoigne	(Lazio) replaced by Clough
9 Kozminski	9 Sheringham	(Tottenham)
10 Lesniak	10 Barnes	(Liverpool)
11 Furtok	11 Ince	(Man Utd)

Crowd: 60,000

England scorer: Wright

Comments: Ian Wright came off the bench to score a late equaliser and record his first goal at the ninth time of asking. This crucial draw marked the international debut of Teddy Sheringham.

Norway 2 ENGLAND 0; in Oslo;
Wednesday 2nd June 1993 (World Cup qualifier)

1 Thorstvedt	1 Woods	(Sheffield Wed)
2 Halle	2 Dixon	(Arsenal)
3 Pedersen	3 Pallister	(Man Utd)
4 Bratseth	4 Palmer	(Sheffield Wed)
5 Bjornebye	5 Walker	(Sampdoria) replaced by Clough
6 Leonhardsen	6 Adams	(Arsenal)
7 Rekdal	7 Platt*	(Juventus)
8 Mykland	8 Gascoigne	(Lazio)
9 Bohinen	9 Ferdinand	(QPR)
10 Flo	10 Sheringham	(Tottenham) replaced by Wright
11 Fjortoft	11 Sharpe	(Man Utd)

Crowd: 22,256

Comments: Norway scored either side of the interval to jeopardise England's chances of qualifying for the World Cup finals. "Can we not knock it?" Graham Taylor bemoaned from the bench.

USA 2 ENGLAND 0; in Boston;
Wednesday 9th June 1993

1	Meola	
2	Clavijo	
3	Lapper	
4	Doyle	
5	Agoos	
6	Dooley	
7	Armstrong	
8	Harkes	
9	Ramos	
10	Wegerle	
11	Wynalda	

1	Woods	(Sheffield Wed)
2	Dixon	(Arsenal)
3	Dorigo	(Leeds United)
4	Palmer	(Sheffield Wed) replaced by Walker
5	Pallister	(Man Utd)
6	Batty	(Leeds United)
7	Ince*	(Man Utd)
8	Clough	(Notts Forest)
9	Sharpe	(Man Utd)
10	Ferdinand	(QPR) replaced by Wright
11	Barnes	(Liverpool)

Crowd: 37,652

Comments: Graham Taylor's misery was compounded by a humiliation at the hands of Uncle Sam. Chris Woods's international career between the sticks did not survive this latest debacle.

ENGLAND 1 Brazil 1; in Washington;
Sunday 13th June 1993

1	Flowers	(Southampton)	1	Taffarel
2	Barrett	(Aston Villa)	2	Jorginho
3	Dorigo	(Leeds United)	3	Valber
4	Walker	(Sampdoria)	4	Santos
5	Pallister	(Man Utd)	5	Nonato
6	Batty	(Leeds United) replaced by Platt	6	Dunga
7	Ince*	(Man Utd) replaced by Palmer	7	Luisinho
8	Clough	(Notts Forest) replaced by Merson	8	Rai
9	Wright	(Arsenal)	9	Valdeir
10	Sinton	(QPR)	10	Careca
11	Sharpe	(Man Utd)	11	Elivelton

Crowd: 54,118

England scorer: Platt

Comments: David Platt came on at the start of the second half and scored almost immediately. However the debut of Tim Flowers was ruined by a late equaliser from Marcio Santos.

ENGLAND 1 Germany 2; in Detroit; Saturday 19th June 1993

1	Martyn	(Crystal Palace)	1	Ilgner
2	Barrett	(Aston Villa)	2	Helmer
3	Sinton	(QPR)	3	Buchwald
4	Walker	(Sampdoria)	4	Schulz
5	Pallister	(Man Utd) replaced by Keown	5	Strunz
6	Ince	(Man Utd)	6	Effenberg
7	Platt*	(Juventus)	7	Matthaus
8	Clough	(Notts Forest) replaced by Wright	8	Moller
9	Sharpe	(Man Utd) replaced by Winterburn	9	Ziege
10	Barnes	(Liverpool)	10	Riedle
11	Merson	(Arsenal)	11	Klinsmann

Crowd: 62,126

England scorer: Platt

Comments: Jurgen Klinsmann scored the only goal of the second half to extend England's winless sequence to 6 depressing matches. England finished last in the United States' Cup tournament.

ENGLAND 3 Poland 0; at Wembley; Wednesday 8th September 1993 (World Cup qualifier)

1	Seaman	(Arsenal)	1	Bako
2	Jones	(Liverpool)	2	Czachowski
3	Pearce*	(Notts Forest)	3	Kozminski
4	Ince	(Man Utd)	4	Lesiak
5	Pallister	(Man Utd)	5	Adamczuk
6	Adams	(Arsenal)	6	Kosecki
7	Platt	(Sampdoria)	7	Brzeczek
8	Gascoigne	(Lazio)	8	Warzycha
9	Ferdinand	(QPR)	9	Swierczewski
10	Wright	(Arsenal)	10	Furtok
11	Sharpe	(Man Utd)	11	Lesniak

Crowd: 71,220

England scorers: Ferdinand, Gascoigne, Pearce

Comments: Nerves were eased by an early goal from Ferdinand and two more at the start of the second half. It all rested now on a match in Holland which Gascoigne would be suspended from.

Holland 2 ENGLAND 0; in Rotterdam;
Wednesday 13th October 1993 (World Cup qualifier)

1 de Goey	1 Seaman	(Arsenal)
2 de Wolf	2 Parker	(Man Utd)
3 Koeman	3 Dorigo	(Leeds United)
4 de Boer	4 Ince	(Man Utd)
5 Rijkaard	5 Pallister	(Man Utd)
6 Wouters	6 Adams	(Arsenal)
7 Koeman	7 Platt*	(Sampdoria)
8 Bergkamp	8 Palmer	(Sheffield Wed) replaced by Sinton
9 Overmars	9 Shearer	(Blackburn)
10 de Boer	10 Merson	(Arsenal) replaced by Wright
11 Roy	11 Sharpe	(Man Utd)

Crowd: 48,000

Comments: Two second half goals from Koeman and Bergkamp ended England's World Cup hopes. This match finished the England careers of Tony Dorigo, Carlton Palmer, and Lee Sharpe.

San Marino 1 ENGLAND 7; in Bologna;
Wednesday 17th November 1993 (World Cup qualifier)

1 Benedettini	1 Seaman	(Arsenal)
2 Valentini	2 Dixon	(Arsenal)
3 Gennari	3 Pearce*	(Notts Forest)
4 Zanotti	4 Ince	(Man Utd)
5 Canti	5 Pallister	(Man Utd)
6 Guerra	6 Walker	(Sheffield Wed)
7 Manzaroli	7 Platt	(Sampdoria)
8 Della Valle	8 Ripley	(Blackburn)
9 Bacciocchi	9 Ferdinand	(QPR)
10 Bonini	10 Wright	(Arsenal)
11 Gualtieri	11 Sinton	(QPR)

Crowd: 2,378

England scorers: Ince (2), Wright (4), Ferdinand

Comments: For 20 embarrassing minutes, England were behind to a goal netted in the first 10 seconds! Then the floodgates opened. This match ended the careers of Sinton, Walker, and the boss.

ENGLAND 1 Denmark 0; at Wembley; Wednesday 9th March 1994

1	Seaman	(Arsenal)	1	Schmeichel
2	Parker	(Man Utd)	2	Christensen
3	Le Saux	(Blackburn)	3	Laudrup
4	Ince	(Man Utd) replaced by Batty	4	Jensen
5	Adams	(Arsenal)	5	Kjeldberg
6	Pallister	(Man Utd)	6	Larsen
7	Platt*	(Sampdoria)	7	Laudrup
8	Gascoigne	(Lazio) replaced by Le Tissier	8	Vilfort
9	Shearer	(Blackburn)	9	Dethlefsen
10	Beardsley	(Newcastle Utd)	10	Olsen
11	Anderton	(Tottenham)	11	Rieper

Crowd: 71,970

England scorer: Platt

Comments: The captain scored the only goal inside the first 20 minutes to give a winning start to the Terry Venables era. This match marked the debuts for Anderton, Le Saux, and Le Tissier.

ENGLAND 5 Greece 0; at Wembley; Tuesday 17th May 1994

1	Flowers	(Blackburn)	1	Karkamanis
2	Jones	(Liverpool) replaced by Pearce	2	Apostolakis
3	Le Saux	(Blackburn)	3	Kolisidakis
4	Richardson	(Aston Villa)	4	Kalitzakis
5	Bould	(Arsenal)	5	Karajiannis
6	Adams	(Arsenal)	6	Kofidis
7	Platt*	(Sampdoria)	7	Nioblias
8	Merson	(Arsenal)	8	Tsalouchidis
9	Shearer	(Blackburn)	9	Tsiantakis
10	Beardsley	(Newcastle Utd) replaced by Wright	10	Chatzidis
11	Anderton	(Tottenham) replaced by Le Tissier	11	Machlas

Crowd: 23,689

England scorers: Anderton, Beardsley, Platt (2), Shearer

Comments: The hosts led 3–0 at the interval on the debut of Steve Bould. Kevin Richardson also won his only cap while Darren Anderton opened the scoring with his first international goal.

ENGLAND 0 Norway 0; at Wembley;
Sunday 22nd May 1994

1 Seaman	(Arsenal)	1	Thorstvedt
2 Jones	(Liverpool)	2	Berg
3 Le Saux	(Blackburn)	3	Johnsen
4 Ince	(Man Utd) replaced by Wright	4	Bratseth
5 Bould	(Arsenal)	5	Nilsen
6 Adams	(Arsenal)	6	Flo
7 Platt*	(Sampdoria)	7	Berg
8 Wise	(Chelsea)	8	Bohinen
9 Shearer	(Blackburn)	9	Fjortoft
10 Beardsley	(Newcastle Utd)	10	Rekdal
11 Anderton	(Tottenham) replaced by Le Tissier	11	Jakobsen

Crowd: 64,327

Comments: For the third consecutive year, England failed to beat Norway. While the home team were having a low-key year, Norway were preparing for the World Cup finals in the USA in June.

ENGLAND 2 USA 0; at Wembley;
Wednesday 7th September 1994

1 Seaman	(Arsenal)	1	Friedel
2 Jones	(Liverpool)	2	Agoos
3 Le Saux	(Blackburn)	3	Balboa
4 Venison	(Newcastle Utd)	4	Lalas
5 Adams	(Arsenal)	5	Caligiuri
6 Pallister	(Man Utd)	6	Dooley
7 Platt*	(Sampdoria)	7	Sorber
8 Barnes	(Liverpool)	8	Reyna
9 Shearer	(Blackburn) replaced by Wright	9	Jones
10 Sheringham	(Tottenham) replaced by Ferdinand	10	Stewart
11 Anderton	(Tottenham)	11	Perez

Crowd: 38,629

England scorer: Shearer (2)

Comments: Two first-half goals from Alan Shearer avenged the humiliation of the previous summer. England had now achieved four successive shut-outs. It was also the debut of Barry Venison.

ENGLAND 1 Romania 1; at Wembley; Wednesday 12th October 1994

1 Seaman	(Arsenal)	1	Stelea
2 Jones	(Liverpool) replaced by Pearce	2	Petrescu
3 Le Saux	(Blackburn)	3	Popescu
4 Ince	(Man Utd)	4	Belodedici
5 Adams*	(Arsenal)	5	Prodan
6 Pallister	(Man Utd)	6	Hagi
7 Lee	(Newcastle Utd) replaced by Wise	7	Lupescu
8 Wright	(Arsenal) replaced by Sheringham	8	Dumitrescu
9 Shearer	(Blackburn)	9	Munteanu
10 Barnes	(Liverpool)	10	Lacatus
11 Le Tissier	(Southampton)	11	Raducioiu

Crowd: 48,754

England scorer: Lee

Comments: Rob Lee scored the equaliser on the stroke of half-time on his debut. England were in the midst of a phase of friendlies as they prepared to host the European Championships in 1996.

ENGLAND 1 Nigeria 0; at Wembley; Wednesday 16th November 1994

1 Flowers	(Blackburn)	1	Rufai
2 Jones	(Liverpool)	2	Okachukwu
3 Le Saux	(Blackburn)	3	Okafor
4 Lee	(Newcastle Utd) replaced by McManaman	4	Iroha
5 Howey	(Newcastle Utd)	5	Eguavon
6 Ruddock	(Liverpool)	6	Amokachi
7 Platt*	(Sampdoria)	7	Okocha
8 Beardsley	(Newcastle Utd) replaced by Le Tissier	8	Adepoju
9 Shearer	(Blackburn) replaced by Sheringham	9	George
10 Barnes	(Liverpool)	10	Amunike
11 Wise	(Chelsea)	11	Yekini

Crowd: 37,196

England scorer: Platt

Comments: The captain scored the only goal just before half time. Steve Howey and Steve McManaman made their debut while Neil Ruddock won his only cap against the fast-emerging Nigeria.

Republic of Ireland 1 ENGLAND 0; in Dublin;
Wednesday 15th February 1995

1	Kelly A		1	Seaman	(Arsenal)
2	Irwin		2	Barton	(Wimbledon)
3	Phelan		3	Le Saux	(Blackburn)
4	Kernaghan		4	Ince	(Man Utd)
5	McGrath		5	Adams	(Arsenal)
6	McGoldrick		6	Pallister	(Man Utd)
7	Townsend		7	Platt*	(Sampdoria)
8	Kelly D		8	Beardsley	(Newcastle Utd)
9	Quinn		9	Shearer	(Blackburn)
10	Sheridan		10	Le Tissier	(Southampton)
11	Staunton		11	Anderton	(Tottenham)

Crowd: 46,000

Comments: Caps were awarded even though this match was abandoned in the first half due to crowd trouble. David Kelly gave the hosts the lead before the match was rudely interrupted.

ENGLAND 0 Uruguay 0; at Wembley;
Wednesday 29th March 1995

1	Flowers	(Blackburn)		1	Ferro
2	Jones	(Liverpool)		2	Lopez
3	Le Saux	(Blackburn) replaced by McManaman	3	Aguirregaray
4	Venison	(Newcastle Utd)		4	Gutierrez
5	Adams	(Arsenal)		5	Montero
6	Pallister	(Man Utd)		6	Cedras
7	Platt*	(Sampdoria)		7	Dorta
8	Beardsley	(Newcastle Utd) replaced by Barmby	8	Bengoechea
9	Sheringham	(Tottenham) replaced by Cole		9	Francescoli
10	Barnes	(Liverpool)		10	Poyet
11	Anderton	(Tottenham)		11	Fonseca

Crowd: 34,849

Comments: This was the third consecutive clean sheet for Tim Flowers as new caps were awarded to Nicky Barmby and Andy Cole, while Rob Jones and Barry Venison won their last caps.

ENGLAND 2 Japan 1; at Wembley;
Saturday 3rd June 1995

1 Flowers	(Blackburn)	1	Maekawa
2 Neville	(Man Utd)	2	Tasaka
3 Pearce	(Notts Forest)	3	Hashiratani
4 Batty	(Blackburn) replaced by McManaman	4	Ihara
5 Scales	(Liverpool)	5	Narahashi
6 Unsworth	(Everton)	6	Morishima
7 Platt*	(Sampdoria)	7	Yamaguchi
8 Beardsley	(Newcastle Utd) replaced by Gascoigne	8	Kitazawa
9 Shearer	(Blackburn)	9	Soma
10 Collymore	(Notts Forest) replaced by Sheringham	10	Miura
11 Anderton	(Tottenham)	11	Nakayama

Crowd: 21,142

England scorers: Anderton, Platt (Pen)

Comments: All the goals came in the second half, with Platt converting a late penalty. New caps were awarded to Stan Collymore, Gary Neville, John Scales, and David Unsworth.

ENGLAND 3 Sweden 3; at Elland Road;
Thursday 8th June 1995

1 Flowers	(Blackburn)	1	Ravelli
2 Barton	(Newcastle Utd)	2	Sundgrun
3 Le Saux	(Blackburn)	3	Lucic
4 Barnes	(Liverpool) replaced by Gascoigne	4	Bjorklund
5 Cooper	(Notts Forest)	5	Kaamark
6 Pallister	(Man Utd) replaced by Scales	6	Alexandersson
7 Platt*	(Sampdoria)	7	Erlingmark
8 Beardsley	(Newcastle Utd) replaced by Barmby	8	Mild
9 Shearer	(Blackburn)	9	Gudmundsson
10 Sheringham	(Tottenham)	10	Larsson
11 Anderton	(Tottenham)	11	Andersson

Crowd: 32,008

England scorers: Sheringham, Platt, Anderton

Comments: The home team trailed 2–0 and 3–1 before Platt and Anderton scored in the last five minutes to earn a draw. Colin Cooper made his debut in this high-scoring spectacle in Leeds.

ENGLAND 1 Brazil 3; at Wembley;
Sunday 11th June 1995

1	Flowers	(Blackburn)	1	Zetti
2	Neville	(Man Utd)	2	Jorginho
3	Pearce	(Notts Forest)	3	Aldair
4	Batty	(Blackburn) replaced by Gascoigne	4	Santos
5	Cooper	(Notts Forest)	5	Carlos
6	Scales	(Liverpool) replaced by Barton	6	Sampaio
7	Platt*	(Sampdoria)	7	Dunga
8	Le Saux	(Blackburn)	8	Zinho
9	Shearer	(Blackburn)	9	Paulista
10	Sheringham	(Tottenham) replaced by Collymore	10	Edmundo
11	Anderton	(Tottenham)	11	Ronaldo

Crowd: 67,318

England scorer: Le Saux

Comments: Graeme Le Saux actually gave the hosts a half-time lead. He was one of 4 players selected from Blackburn Rovers in the line-up. This was the final cap for Barton, Cooper, and Scales.

ENGLAND 0 Columbia 0; at Wembley;
Wednesday 6th September 1995

1	Seaman	(Arsenal)	1	Higuita
2	Neville	(Man Utd)	2	Santa
3	Le Saux	(Blackburn)	3	Burmudez
4	Redknapp	(Liverpool) replaced by Barnes	4	Mendoza
5	Adams*	(Arsenal)	5	Perez
6	Howey	(Newcastle Utd)	6	Lozano
7	Barmby	(Middlesbrough)	7	Alvarez
8	Gascoigne	(Rangers) replaced by Lee	8	Valderrama
9	Shearer	(Blackburn) replaced by Sheringham	9	Rincon
10	McManaman	(Liverpool)	10	Asprilla
11	Wise	(Chelsea)	11	Valenciano

Crowd: 20,000

Comments: A small crowd at least witnessed a spectacular overhead kick from the Columbian goalkeeper. This was the debut of Jamie Redknapp and the end of John Barnes's 12-year career.

Norway 0 ENGLAND 0; in Oslo;
Wednesday 11th October 1995

1	Thorstvedt	1	Seaman	(Arsenal)
2	Loken	2	Neville	(Man Utd)
3	Johnsen	3	Pearce	(Notts Forest)
4	Berg	4	Redknapp	(Liverpool)
5	Bjornebye	5	Adams*	(Arsenal)
6	Bohinen	6	Pallister	(Man Utd)
7	Leonhardsen	7	Barmby	(Middlesbrough) replaced by Sheringham
8	Rekdal	8	Lee	(Newcastle Utd)
9	Jakobsen	9	Shearer	(Blackburn)
10	Flo	10	McManaman	(Liverpool)
11	Fjortoft	11	Wise	(Chelsea) replaced by Stone

Crowd: 21,006

Comments: For the third time in four years Erik Thorstvedt and his defence prevented England from scoring a single goal. Steve Stone made his debut for the toothless visitors.

ENGLAND 3 Switzerland 1; at Wembley;
Wednesday 15th November 1995

1	Seaman	(Arsenal)	1	Pascolo
2	Neville	(Man Utd)	2	Hottiger
3	Pearce	(Notts Forest)	3	Quentin
4	Redknapp	(Liverpool) replaced by Stone	4	Henchoz
5	Adams*	(Arsenal)	5	Geiger
6	Pallister	(Man Utd)	6	Fournier
7	Lee	(Newcastle Utd)	7	Sutter
8	Gascoigne	(Rangers)	8	Ohrel
9	Shearer	(Blackburn)	9	Sforza
10	Sheringham	(Tottenham)	10	Knup
11	McManaman	(Liverpool)	11	Turkyilmaz

Crowd: 29,874

England scorers: Pearce, Sheringham, Stone

Comments: After conceding the lead, England re-discovered their goalscoring form with Steve Stone coming off the bench to score. This was only England's second win of a disappointing year.

ENGLAND 1 Portugal 1; at Wembley;
Tuesday 12th December 1995

1 Seaman	(Arsenal)	1 Neno
2 Neville	(Man Utd)	2 Secretario
3 Pearce	(Notts Forest) replaced by Le Saux	3 Couto
4 Wise	(Chelsea) replaced by Southgate	4 Costa
5 Adams*	(Arsenal)	5 Dimas
6 Howey	(Newcastle Utd)	6 Souser
7 Barmby	(Middlesbrough) replaced by McManaman	7 Helder
8 Gascoigne	(Rangers)	8 Folha
9 Shearer	(Blackburn)	9 Figo
10 Ferdinand	(Newcastle Utd) replaced by Beardsley	10 Pinto
11 Stone	(Notts Forest)	11 Pinto

Crowd: 28,592

England scorer: Stone

Comments: Steve Stone gave the home team the interval lead but they had to settle for a draw after Paulo Alves equalised in the second half. Gareth Southgate made his international debut.

ENGLAND 1 Bulgaria 0; at Wembley;
Wednesday 27th March 1996

1 Seaman	(Arsenal)	1 Mihailov
2 Neville	(Man Utd)	2 Hubchev
3 Pearce*	(Notts Forest)	3 Ivanov
4 Ince	(Inter Milan)	4 Yankov
5 Southgate	(Aston Villa)	5 Kremenliev
6 Howey	(Newcastle Utd)	6 Lechkov
7 McManaman	(Liverpool)	7 Kirikov
8 Gascoigne	(Rangers) replaced by Lee	8 Guinchev
9 Ferdinand	(Newcastle Utd) replaced by Fowler	9 Yordanov
10 Sheringham	(Tottenham) replaced by Platt	10 Penev
11 Stone	(Notts Forest)	11 Kostadinov

Crowd: 29,708

England scorer: Ferdinand

Comments: Ferdinand scored the only goal in the first ten minutes as England prepared to host the European Championship in June. Robbie Fowler made his debut while Howey won his last cap.

ENGLAND 0 Croatia 0; at Wembley;
Wednesday 24th April 1996

1 Seaman	(Arsenal)	1 Mrmic
2 Neville	(Man Utd)	2 Pavlicic
3 Pearce	(Notts Forest)	3 Jarni
4 Ince	(Inter Milan)	4 Stimac
5 Wright	(Liverpool)	5 Jerkan
6 McManaman	(Liverpool)	6 Bilic
7 Platt*	(Arsenal)	7 Asanovic
8 Gascoigne	(Rangers)	8 Prosinecki
9 Fowler	(Liverpool)	9 Suker
10 Sheringham	(Tottenham)	10 Boban
11 Stone	(Notts Forest)	11 Boksic

Crowd: 33,650

Comments: David Seaman achieved his fourth shut-out in six matches but this was just the kind of match that England needed to be winning if they wanted to win the European Championship.

ENGLAND 3 Hungary 0; at Wembley;
Saturday 18th May 1996

1 Seaman	(Arsenal) replaced by Walker	1 Petry
2 Neville	(Man Utd)	2 Seebok
3 Pearce	(Notts Forest)	3 Banfi
4 Ince	(Inter Milan) replaced by Campbell	4 Plokai
5 Wright	(Liverpool) replaced by Southgate	5 Mracsko
6 Lee	(Newcastle Utd)	6 Urban
7 Platt*	(Arsenal) replaced by Wise	7 Hahn
8 Wilcox	(Blackburn)	8 Balog
9 Ferdinand	(Newcastle Utd) replaced by Shearer	9 Nagy
10 Sheringham	(Tottenham)	10 Horvath
11 Anderton	(Tottenham)	11 Vincze

Crowd: 34,184

England scorers: Anderton (2), Platt

Comments: The home team carved out a morale-boosting victory three weeks before 'Euro 96' was due to begin. First caps were awarded to Sol Campbell, Ian Walker, and Jason Wilcox.

China 0 ENGLAND 3; in Beijing;
Thursday 23rd May 1996

1	Chuliang	1	Flowers	(Blackburn) replaced by Walker
2	Hong	2	Neville G	(Man Utd)
3	Qun	3	Neville P	(Man Utd)
4	Zihyi	4	Redknapp	(Liverpool)
5	Hongjun	5	Adams*	(Arsenal) replaced by Ehiogu
6	Yuxing	6	Southgate	(Aston Villa)
7	Bing	7	Barmby	(Middlesbrough) replaced by Beardsley
8	Feng	8	Gascoigne	(Rangers)
9	Mingu	9	Shearer	(Blackburn) replaced by Fowler
10	Feng	10	McManaman	(Liverpool) replaced by Stone
11	Haidong	11	Anderton	(Tottenham)

Crowd: 65,000

England scorers: Barmby (2), Gascoigne

Comments: Nicky Barmby scored his first and then second England goals on the debut of Ugo Ehiogu and Phil Neville. This match was the final international appearance for Peter Beardsley.

ENGLAND 1 Switzerland 1; at Wembley;
Saturday 8th June 1996 (European Championship)

1	Seaman	(Arsenal)	1	Pascolo
2	Neville	(Man Utd)	2	Jeanneret
3	Pearce	(Notts Forest)	3	Vega
4	Ince	(Inter Milan)	4	Henchoz
5	Adams*	(Arsenal)	5	Quentin
6	Southgate	(Aston Villa)	6	Vogel
7	McManaman	(Liverpool) replaced by Stone	7	Geiger
8	Gascoigne	(Rangers) replaced by Platt	8	Sforza
9	Shearer	(Blackburn)	9	Bonvin
10	Sheringham	(Tottenham) replaced by Barmby	10	Grassi
11	Anderton	(Tottenham)	11	Turkyilmaz

Crowd: 76,567

England scorer: Shearer

Comments: Shearer gave the hosts an early lead but they conceded a late penalty, scored by Turkyilmaz. England's ability to shoot themselves in the foot in major finals was rearing its ugly head.

ENGLAND 2 Scotland 0; at Wembley;
Saturday 15th June 1996 (European Championship)

1	Seaman	(Arsenal)	1	Goram
2	Neville	(Man Utd)	2	McKimmie
3	Pearce	(Notts Forest) replaced by Redknapp	3	Boyd
4	Ince	(Inter Milan) replaced by Stone	4	McKinlay
5	Adams*	(Arsenal)	5	Hendry
6	Southgate	(Aston Villa)	6	Calderwood
7	McManaman	(Liverpool)	7	Spencer
8	Gascoigne	(Rangers)	8	McCall
9	Shearer	(Blackburn)	9	Durie
10	Sheringham	(Tottenham)	10	McAllister
11	Anderton	(Tottenham)	11	Collins

Crowd: 76,864

England scorers: Shearer, Gascoigne

Comments: Paul Gascoigne sealed victory with a sweet strike past his Rangers' team-mate Andy Goram, prompting a flamboyant act of celebrating the goal, much to Goram's dismay.

ENGLAND 4 Holland 1; at Wembley;
Tuesday 18th June 1996 (European Championship)

1	Seaman	(Arsenal)	1	van der Sar
2	Neville	(Man Utd)	2	Reiziger
3	Pearce	(Notts Forest)	3	Blind
4	Ince	(Inter Milan) replaced by Platt	4	Bogarde
5	Adams*	(Arsenal)	5	Winter
6	Southgate	(Aston Villa)	6	de Boer
7	McManaman	(Liverpool)	7	Seedorf
8	Gascoigne	(Rangers)	8	Witschge
9	Shearer	(Blackburn) replaced by Fowler	9	Cruyff
10	Sheringham	(Tottenham) replaced by Barmby	10	Bergkamp
11	Anderton	(Tottenham)	11	Hoekstra

Crowd: 76,798

England scorers: Shearer (2), Sheringham (2)

Comments: This was the Shearer and Sheringham show as England put the Dutch to the sword, thus exorcising the demons of 1988 and 1993. Patrick Kluivert's late consolation flattered his team.

**ENGLAND o Spain o [After extra time]; at Wembley;
Saturday 22nd June 1996 (European Championship)**

1	Seaman	(Arsenal)	1	Zubizarreta	
2	Neville	(Man Utd)	2	Alkorta	
3	Pearce	(Notts Forest)	3	Nadal	
4	McManaman	(Liverpool) replaced by Stone	4	Aberlardo	
5	Adams*	(Arsenal)	5	Belsue	
6	Southgate	(Aston Villa)	6	Manjarin	
7	Platt	(Arsenal)	7	Hierro	
8	Gascoigne	(Rangers)	8	Amor	
9	Shearer	(Blackburn)	9	Sergi	
10	Sheringham	(Tottenham) replaced by Barmby	10	Salinas	
11	Anderton	(Tottenham) replaced by Fowler	11	Kiko	

Crowd: 75,440

Comments: This was a collector's item – an England victory in a penalty shoot-out. Stuart Pearce even scored from the spot as England progressed to the semi-finals. This was Stone's last cap.

**ENGLAND 1 Germany 1 [After extra time]; at Wembley;
Wednesday 26th June 1996 (European Championship)**

1	Seaman	(Arsenal)	1	Kopke	
2	McManaman	(Liverpool)	2	Babbel	
3	Pearce	(Notts Forest)	3	Sammer	
4	Ince	(Inter Milan)	4	Helmer	
5	Adams*	(Arsenal)	5	Reuter	
6	Southgate	(Aston Villa)	6	Freund	
7	Platt	(Arsenal)	7	Scholl	
8	Gascoigne	(Rangers)	8	Eilts	
9	Shearer	(Blackburn)	9	Ziege	
10	Sheringham	(Tottenham)	10	Moller	
11	Anderton	(Tottenham)	11	Kuntz	

Crowd: 75,862

England scorer: Shearer

Comments: Shearer gave the hosts a flying start before they were pegged back by a goal from Kuntz. It took penalties to separate them and Southgate was the unfortunate villain of the piece.

Moldova o ENGLAND 3; in Chisinau;
Sunday 1st September 1996 (World Cup qualifier)

1	Romanenco	1	Seaman	(Arsenal)
2	Secu	2	Neville	(Man Utd)
3	Nani	3	Pearce	(Notts Forest)
4	Testimitanu	4	Ince	(Inter Milan)
5	Gaidamasciuc	5	Pallister	(Man Utd)
6	Shishkin	6	Southgate	(Aston Villa)
7	Epureanu	7	Beckham	(Man Utd)
8	Curteanu	8	Gascoigne	(Rangers) replaced by Batty
9	Clesenco	9	Shearer*	(Newcastle Utd)
10	Miterev	10	Barmby	(Middlesbrough) replaced by Le Tissier
11	Popovici	11	Hinchcliffe	(Everton)

Crowd: 9,500

England scorers: Barmby, Gascoigne, Shearer

Comments: Terry Venables had bowed out, so Glenn Hoddle took the managerial baton. This World Cup qualifier was also the debut of young David Beckham and Andy Hinchcliffe.

ENGLAND 2 Poland 1; at Wembley;
Wednesday 9th October 1996 (World Cup qualifier)

1	Seaman	(Arsenal)	1	Wozniak
2	Neville	(Man Utd)	2	Wojtala
3	Pearce	(Notts Forest)	3	Zielinski
4	Ince	(Inter Milan)	4	Jozwiak
5	Southgate	(Aston Villa) replaced by Pallister	5	Hajto
6	Hinchcliffe	(Everton)	6	Michalski
7	Beckham	(Man Utd)	7	Nowak
8	Gascoigne	(Rangers)	8	Waldoch
9	Shearer*	(Newcastle Utd)	9	Baluszynski
10	Ferdinand	(Newcastle Utd)	10	Warzycha
11	McManaman	(Liverpool)	11	Citko

Crowd: 74,663

England scorer: Shearer (2)

Comments: The Poles took an early lead but the home captain responded with a pair of first-half goals. This qualifying group triumph was the last international appearance for Gary Pallister.

Georgia 0 ENGLAND 2; in Tbilisi;
Saturday 9th November 1996 (World Cup qualifier)

1	Zoidze	1	Seaman	(Arsenal)
2	Lobianidze	2	Campbell	(Tottenham)
3	Shelia	3	Hinchcliffe	(Everton)
4	Tshkadadze	4	Ince	(Inter Milan)
5	Gogichaishvili	5	Adams*	(Arsenal)
6	Kinkladze	6	Southgate	(Aston Villa)
7	Nemsadze	7	Beckham	(Man Utd)
8	Jamarauli	8	Gascoigne	(Rangers)
9	Kobiashvili	9	Ferdinand	(Newcastle Utd) replaced by Wright
10	Ketsbaia	10	Sheringham	(Tottenham)
11	Arveladze	11	Batty	(Newcastle Utd)

Crowd: 48,000

England scorers: Sheringham, Ferdinand

Comments: Both goals came in the first half as the visitors made it three wins out of three in their qualifying group. David Seaman earned his ninth clean sheet from his last fifteen matches.

ENGLAND 0 Italy 1; at Wembley;
Wednesday 12th February 1997 (World Cup qualifier)

1	Walker	(Tottenham)	1	Peruzzi
2	Neville	(Man Utd)	2	Ferrara
3	Pearce	(Notts Forest)	3	Costacurta
4	Ince	(Inter Milan)	4	Cannavaro
5	Campbell	(Tottenham)	5	di Livio
6	Le Saux	(Blackburn)	6	Maldini
7	Beckham	(Man Utd)	7	Albertini
8	Batty	(Newcastle Utd) replaced by Wright	8	di Matteo
9	Shearer*	(Newcastle Utd)	9	Baggio
10	Le Tissier	(Southampton) replaced by Ferdinand	10	Zola
11	McManaman	(Liverpool) replaced by Merson	11	Casiraghi

Crowd: 75,055

Comments: Little Chelsea striker Gianfranco Zola scored the only goal of this contest inside the first twenty minutes. Matthew Le Tissier was substituted and never played for England again.

ENGLAND 2 Mexico 0; at Wembley;
Saturday 29th March 1997

1	James	(Liverpool)		1	Rios
2	Keown	(Arsenal)		2	Pardo
3	Pearce	(Notts Forest)		3	Davino
4	Batty	(Newcastle Utd) replaced by Redknapp		4	Ramirez
5	Southgate	(Aston Villa)		5	Alfaro
6	Le Saux	(Blackburn)		6	Coyote
7	Lee	(Newcastle Utd)		7	Galindo
8	Ince*	(Inter Milan)		8	Aspe
9	Fowler	(Liverpool)		9	Hermosillo
10	Sheringham	(Tottenham) replaced by Wright		10	Alves
11	McManaman	(Liverpool) replaced by Butt		11	Suarez

Crowd: 48,076

England scorers: Sheringham (Pen), Fowler

Comments: The hosts recorded a goal in each half on the debut of Nicky Butt and David James. England finished this friendly encounter with four Liverpool players in the team.

ENGLAND 2 Georgia 0; at Wembley;
Wednesday 30th April 1997 (World Cup qualifier)

1	Seaman	(Arsenal)		1	Zoidze
2	Neville	(Man Utd)		2	Chikhradze
3	Campbell	(Tottenham)		3	Shekiladze
4	Batty	(Newcastle Utd)		4	Tshkadadze
5	Adams	(Arsenal) replaced by Southgate		5	Shelia
6	Le Saux	(Blackburn)		6	Machavariani
7	Beckham	(Man Utd)		7	Nemsadze
8	Ince	(Inter Milan) replaced by Redknapp		8	Jamarauli
9	Shearer*	(Newcastle Utd)		9	Ketsbaia
10	Sheringham	(Tottenham)		10	Kinkladze
11	Lee	(Newcastle Utd)		11	Arveladze

Crowd: 71,206

England scorers: Sheringham, Shearer

Comments: The deadly duo of Sheringham and Shearer netted at the end of each half as England secured more precious qualifying points en route to a possible entry into the World Cup finals.

ENGLAND 2 South Africa 1; at Old Trafford;
Saturday 24th May 1997

1 Martyn	(Leeds United)	1	Arendse
2 Neville	(Man Utd)	2	Fish
3 Pearce*	(Notts Forest)	3	Tovey
4 Keown	(Arsenal)	4	Radebe
5 Southgate	(Aston Villa)	5	Motuang
6 Le Saux	(Blackburn) replaced by Beckham	6	Tinkler
7 Redknapp	(Liverpool) replaced by Batty	7	Moeti
8 Gascoigne	(Rangers) replaced by Campbell	8	Moshoeu
9 Wright	(Arsenal)	9	Khumalo
10 Sheringham	(Tottenham) replaced by Scholes	10	Masinga
11 Lee	(Newcastle Utd) replaced by Butt	11	Augustine

Crowd: 52,676

England scorers: Lee, Wright

Comments: Nigel Martyn became the fourth different goalkeeper in 4 successive matches. He conceded an equaliser to Phil Masinga just before the interval, but Ian Wright grabbed a winner.

Poland 0 ENGLAND 2; in Chorzow;
Saturday 31st May 1997 (World Cup qualifier)

1 Wozniak	1 Seaman	(Arsenal)
2 Jozwiak	2 Neville G	(Man Utd)
3 Zielinski	3 Campbell	(Tottenham)
4 Kaluszny	4 Ince	(Inter Milan)
5 Ledwon	5 Southgate	(Aston Villa)
6 Bukalski	6 Le Saux	(Blackburn)
7 Nowak	7 Beckham	(Man Utd) replaced by Neville P
8 Dembinski	8 Gascoigne	(Rangers) replaced by Batty
9 Majak	9 Shearer*	(Newcastle Utd)
10 Waldoch	10 Sheringham	(Tottenham)
11 Juskowiak	11 Lee	(Newcastle Utd)

Crowd: 35,000

England scorers: Shearer, Sheringham

Comments: Shearer and Sheringham scored at the beginning and end of this qualifier to secure all the points for the visitors as England looked set to win a place at the World Cup finals in France.

ENGLAND 2 Italy 0; in Nantes;
Wednesday 4th June 1997

1 Flowers	(Blackburn)	1 Peruzzi
2 Neville G	(Man Utd)	2 Ferrara
3 Pearce	(Notts Forest)	3 Costacurta
4 Keown	(Arsenal)	4 Cannavaro
5 Southgate	(Aston Villa)	5 di Livio
6 Le Saux	(Blackburn) replaced by Neville P	6 Baggio
7 Beckham	(Man Utd)	7 Albertini
8 Ince*	(Inter Milan)	8 di Matteo
9 Wright	(Arsenal) replaced by Cole	9 Benarrivo
10 Sheringham	(Tottenham) replaced by Gascoigne	10 Zola
11 Scholes	(Man Utd)	11 Casiraghi

Crowd: 30,000

England scorers: Wright, Scholes

Comments: Tim Flowers was the fifth England goalkeeper to be chosen this year. Paul Scholes scored on his first start for England. He was one of five Red Devils involved in this fixture.

France 0 ENGLAND 1; in Montpellier;
Saturday 7th June 1997

1 Barthez	1 Seaman	(Arsenal)
2 Thuram	2 Neville G	(Man Utd)
3 Blanc	3 Campbell	(Tottenham)
4 N'Gotty	4 Neville P	(Man Utd)
5 Laigle	5 Southgate	(Aston Villa)
6 Djorkaeff	6 Le Saux	(Blackburn)
7 Vieira	7 Beckham	(Man Utd) replaced by Lee
8 Deschamps	8 Gascoigne	(Rangers)
9 Dugarry	9 Shearer*	(Newcastle Utd)
10 Ouedec	10 Wright	(Arsenal) replaced by Sheringham
11 Keller	11 Batty	(Newcastle Utd) replaced by Ince

Crowd: 28,000

England scorer: Shearer

Comments: The England captain netted a late winner in this Tournoi de France match, but France had the last laugh as it was them who would go on to win the World Cup a year later.

ENGLAND 0 Brazil 1; in Paris;
Tuesday 10th June 1997

1	Seaman	(Arsenal)		1	Taffarel
2	Keown	(Arsenal) replaced by Neville G		2	Cafu
3	Campbell	(Tottenham)		3	Celio Silva
4	Ince	(Inter Milan)		4	Aldair
5	Southgate	(Aston Villa)		5	Carlos
6	Le Saux	(Blackburn)		6	Dunga
7	Neville P	(Man Utd)		7	Conceicao
8	Gascoigne	(Rangers)		8	Leonardo
9	Shearer*	(Newcastle Utd)		9	Denilson
10	Sheringham	(Tottenham) replaced by Wright		10	Romario
11	Scholes	(Man Utd) replaced by Lee		11	Ronaldo

Crowd: 50,000

Comments: Romario scored the winner just after the hour mark, but it did not prevent England from winning the Tournoi de France, finishing first ahead of such giants as Brazil, France, and Italy.

ENGLAND 4 Moldova 0; at Wembley;
Wednesday 10th September 1997 (World Cup qualifier)

1	Seaman*	(Arsenal)		1	Romanenco
2	Neville G	(Man Utd)		2	Fistican
3	Neville P	(Man Utd)		3	Testimitanu
4	Batty	(Newcastle Utd)		4	Kulibaba
5	Campbell	(Tottenham)		5	Spyriu
6	Southgate	(Aston Villa)		6	Stroenco
7	Beckham	(Man Utd) replaced by Ripley		7	Curteanu
8	Gascoigne	(Rangers)		8	Shishkin
9	Ferdinand	(Tottenham) replaced by Collymore		9	Miterev
10	Wright	(Arsenal)		10	Rebeja
11	Scholes	(Man Utd)		11	Rogachev

Crowd: 74,102

England scorers: Scholes, Wright (2), Gascoigne

Comments: The hosts only led 1–0 at half time but in the second half, Gascoigne and Wright scored thier final England goals. Meanwhile, Stan Collymore and Stuart Ripley claimed their final caps.

Italy 0 ENGLAND 0; in Rome;
Saturday 11th October 1997 (World Cup qualifier)

1 Peruzzi	1 Seaman	(Arsenal)
2 Nesta	2 Campbell	(Tottenham)
3 Maldini	3 Le Saux	(Chelsea)
4 Albertini	4 Ince*	(Liverpool)
5 Cannavaro	5 Adams	(Arsenal)
6 Costacurta	6 Southgate	(Aston Villa)
7 di Livio	7 Beckham	(Man Utd)
8 Baggio	8 Gascoigne	(Rangers) replaced by Butt
9 Vieri	9 Wright	(Arsenal)
10 Zola	10 Sheringham	(Tottenham)
11 Inzaghi	11 Batty	(Newcastle Utd)

Crowd: 81,200

Comments: David Seaman earned his fourteenth clean sheet in his last 21 internationals as a rock solid England obtained revenge for 1977 by qualifying for the World Cup finals at Italy's expense.

ENGLAND 2 Cameroon 0; at Wembley;
Saturday 15th November 1997

1 Martyn	(Leeds United)	1 Ongandzi
2 Campbell	(Tottenham)	2 Song
3 Neville	(Man Utd)	3 Wome
4 Ince*	(Liverpool)	4 Mimoe
5 Southgate	(Aston Villa) replaced by Ferdinand	5 Kalla
6 Hinchcliffe	(Everton)	6 Desire Job
7 Beckham	(Man Utd)	7 Mboma
8 Gascoigne	(Rangers) replaced by Lee	8 Etchi
9 Fowler	(Liverpool)	9 Mayer
10 Scholes	(Man Utd) replaced by Sutton	10 Foe
11 McManaman	(Liverpool)	11 Ipoua

Crowd: 46,176

England scorers: Scholes, Fowler

Comments: England scored twice for the eighth time in 13 matches with both goals coming immediately before the interval. Rio Ferdinand made his debut while Chris Sutton won his only cap.

ENGLAND 0 Chile 2; at Wembley;
Wednesday 11th February 1998

1 Martyn	(Leeds United)	1 Tapia
2 Neville G	(Man Utd)	2 Villaoel
3 Campbell	(Tottenham)	3 Reyes
4 Batty	(Newcastle Utd) replaced by Ince	4 Fentes
5 Adams*	(Arsenal)	5 Margas
6 Neville P	(Man Utd) replaced by Le Saux	6 Rojas
7 Lee	(Newcastle Utd)	7 Parrguez
8 Butt	(Man Utd)	8 Acunda
9 Dublin	(Coventry City)	9 Sierra
10 Sheringham	(Man Utd) replaced by Shearer	10 Barrera
11 Owen	(Liverpool)	11 Salas

Crowd: 65,228

Comments: Marcelo Salas scored in each half to secure victory. England weren't helped by the constant change of personnel. Dion Dublin and Michael Owen were the 2 latest recruits to the team.

Switzerland 1 ENGLAND 1; in Berne;
Wednesday 25th March 1998

1 Corminboeuf	1 Flowers	(Blackburn)
2 Vega	2 Keown	(Arsenal)
3 Yakin	3 Hinchcliffe	(Sheffield Wed)
4 Henchoz	4 Ince	(Liverpool)
5 Vogel	5 Southgate	(Aston Villa)
6 Sforza	6 Ferdinand	(West Ham Utd)
7 Wicky	7 McManaman	(Liverpool)
8 Fournier	8 Merson	(Middlesbrough) replaced by Batty
9 Sesa	9 Shearer*	(Newcastle Utd)
10 Grassi	10 Owen	(Liverpool) replaced by Sheringham
11 Chapuisat	11 Lee	(Newcastle Utd)

Crowd: 17,100

England scorer: Merson

Comments: Ramon Vega gave the hosts the interval lead before Paul Merson equalised with twenty minutes remaining. Only two of the chosen eleven had started in England's previous match.

ENGLAND 3 Portugal 0; at Wembley;
Wednesday 22nd April 1998

1 Seaman	(Arsenal)	1	Baia
2 Neville G	(Man Utd) replaced by Neville P	2	Xavier
3 Le Saux	(Chelsea)	3	Dimas
4 Ince	(Liverpool)	4	Beto
5 Adams	(Arsenal)	5	Couto
6 Campbell	(Tottenham)	6	Sousa
7 Beckham	(Man Utd) replaced by Merson	7	Figo
8 Batty	(Newcastle Utd)	8	Pinto
9 Shearer*	(Newcastle Utd)	9	Calado
10 Sheringham	(Man Utd) replaced by Owen	10	Santos
11 Scholes	(Man Utd)	11	Cadete

Crowd: 63,463

England scorers: Shearer (2), Sheringham

Comments: The old double act of Alan Shearer and Teddy Sheringham inflicted all the damage here as England recorded a morale-boosting victory ahead of the World Cup finals in France.

ENGLAND 0 Saudi Arabia 0; at Wembley;
Saturday 23rd May 1998

1 Seaman	(Arsenal)	1	Al-Deayea
2 Neville G	(Man Utd)	2	Al-Jahani
3 Hinchcliffe	(Sheffield Wed) replaced by Neville P	3	Al-Khilaiwi
4 Batty	(Newcastle Utd)	4	Zebramawi
5 Adams	(Arsenal)	5	Solaimani
6 Southgate	(Aston Villa)	6	Amin
7 Beckham	(Man Utd) replaced by Gascoigne	7	Al-Shahrani
8 Anderton	(Tottenham)	8	Al-Owairan
9 Shearer*	(Newcastle Utd) replaced by Ferdinand	9	Al-Jaber
10 Sheringham	(Man Utd) replaced by Wright	10	Al-Owairan
11 Scholes	(Man Utd)	11	Al-Muwallid

Crowd: 63,733

Comments: This toothless display from the home team was scarcely a good omen ahead of the imminent World Cup tournament. At least David Seaman and his defence earned another shut-out.

Morocco 0 ENGLAND 1; in Casablanca;
Wednesday 27th May 1998

1 Benzekri	1 Flowers	(Blackburn)
2 Saber	2 Keown	(Arsenal)
3 Rossi	3 Le Saux	(Chelsea)
4 Neqrouz	4 Ince*	(Liverpool)
5 El-Hadrioui	5 Campbell	(Tottenham)
6 Chiba	6 Southgate	(Aston Villa)
7 El-Khalej	7 Anderton	(Tottenham)
8 Chippo	8 Gascoigne	(Middlesbrough)
9 Ouakili	9 Dublin	(Coventry City) replaced by Ferdinand
10 Bassir	10 Wright	(Arsenal) replaced by Owen
11 Rokki	11 McManaman	(Liverpool)

Crowd: 80,000

England scorer: Owen

Comments: Michael Owen came on as a first-half substitute and won this World Cup warm-up with his first England goal. Tim Flowers kept a clean sheet but never played for England again.

ENGLAND 0 Belgium 0; in Casablanca;
Friday 29th May 1998

1 Martyn	(Leeds United)	1 van der Walle	
2 Neville G	(Man Utd) replaced by Ferdinand R	2 Deflandre	
3 Neville P	(Man Utd) replaced by Owen	3 van Meir	
4 Butt	(Man Utd)	4 Verstraeten	
5 Campbell*	(Tottenham) replaced by Dublin	5 Borkelmans	
6 Keown	(Arsenal)	6 de Boeck	
7 Lee	(Newcastle Utd)	7 Verheyen	
8 Gascoigne	(Middlesbrough) replaced by Beckham	8 M'Penza	
9 Ferdinand L	(Tottenham)	9 Goossens	
10 Merson	(Arsenal)	10 Scifo	
11 Le Saux	(Chelsea)	11 Boffin	

Crowd: 18,000

Comments: This match went straight to penalties after 90 minutes of stalemate. Not for the first time (nor the last), England proceeded to lose the spot kicks contest. This was Gascoigne's last cap.

ENGLAND 2 Tunisia 0; in Marseille;
Monday 15th June 1998 (World Cup finals)

1	Seaman	(Arsenal)	1	El-Ouaer
2	Campbell	(Tottenham)	2	Badra
3	Le Saux	(Chelsea)	3	Boukadida
4	Ince	(Liverpool)	4	Trabelsi
5	Adams	(Arsenal)	5	Trabelsi
6	Southgate	(Aston Villa)	6	Chihi
7	Anderton	(Tottenham)	7	Souayeh
8	Batty	(Newcastle Utd)	8	Godhbane
9	Shearer*	(Newcastle Utd)	9	Clayton
10	Sheringham	(Man Utd) replaced by Owen	10	Sellimi
11	Scholes	(Man Utd)	11	Ben Slimane

Crowd: 54,587

England scorers: Shearer, Scholes

Comments: Shearer and Scholes scored at the end of each half to get England's World Cup challenge off to the best possible start. However, the dangerous Romania were next on the agenda.

ENGLAND 1 Romania 2; in Toulouse;
Monday 22nd June 1998 (World Cup finals)

1	Seaman	(Arsenal)	1	Stelea
2	Neville	(Man Utd)	2	Petrescu
3	Le Saux	(Chelsea)	3	Ciobotariu
4	Ince	(Liverpool) replaced by Beckham	4	Popescu
5	Adams	(Arsenal)	5	Filipescu
6	Campbell	(Tottenham)	6	Munteanu
7	Anderton	(Tottenham)	7	Hagi
8	Batty	(Newcastle Utd)	8	Galca
9	Shearer*	(Newcastle Utd)	9	Popescu
10	Sheringham	(Man Utd) replaced by Owen	10	Moldovan
11	Scholes	(Man Utd)	11	Ilie

Crowd: 33,500

England scorer: Owen

Comments: Michael Owen netted a vital equaliser shortly after coming on as a substitute, but England's hearts were then broken by a last minute strike from Chelsea's Dan Petrescu.

ENGLAND 2 Columbia 0; in Lens; Friday 26th June 1998 (World Cup finals)

1	Seaman	(Arsenal)	1	Mondragon
2	Neville	(Man Utd)	2	Cabrera
3	Le Saux	(Chelsea)	3	Burmudez
4	Ince	(Liverpool) replaced by Batty	4	Palacios
5	Adams	(Arsenal)	5	Moreno
6	Campbell	(Tottenham)	6	Rincon
7	Beckham	(Man Utd)	7	Serna
8	Anderton	(Tottenham) replaced by Lee	8	Lozano
9	Shearer*	(Newcastle Utd)	9	Valderrama
10	Owen	(Liverpool)	10	Preciado
11	Scholes	(Man Utd) replaced by McManaman	11	de Avila

Crowd: 41,275

England scorers: Anderton, Beckham

Comments: David Beckham scored his first England goal as England safely reached the knockout stages. However, having finished second to Romania, they were now confronted with Argentina.

ENGLAND 2 Argentina 2 [After extra time]; in Saint-Etienne; Tuesday 30th June 1998 (World Cup finals)

1	Seaman	(Arsenal)	1	Roa
2	Neville	(Man Utd)	2	Vivas
3	Le Saux	(Chelsea) replaced by Southgate	3	Ayala
4	Ince	(Liverpool)	4	Chamot
5	Adams	(Arsenal)	5	Zanetti
6	Campbell	(Tottenham)	6	Almeyda
7	Beckham	(Man Utd)	7	Simone
8	Anderton	(Tottenham) replaced by Batty	8	Veron
9	Shearer*	(Newcastle Utd)	9	Ortega
10	Owen	(Liverpool)	10	Batistuta
11	Scholes	(Man Utd) replaced by Merson	11	Lopez

Crowd: 30,600

England scorers: Shearer (Pen), Owen

Comments: Shearer's penalty cancelled out a spot kick from Batistuta before Owen scored his wonder goal. Beckham then got sent off and England then typically lost the penalty shoot-out.

Sweden 2 ENGLAND 1; in Stockholm;
Saturday 5th September 1998 (European Championship)

1	Hedman	1	Seaman	(Arsenal)
2	Nilsson	2	Campbell	(Tottenham) replaced by Merson
3	Andersson	3	Le Saux	(Chelsea)
4	Bjorklund	4	Ince	(Liverpool)
5	Kaamark	5	Adams	(Arsenal)
6	Schwarz	6	Southgate	(Aston Villa)
7	Andersson	7	Anderton	(Tottenham) replaced by Lee
8	Mjallby	8	Redknapp	(Liverpool)
9	Ljungberg	9	Shearer*	(Newcastle Utd)
10	Larsson	10	Owen	(Liverpool)
11	Pettersson	11	Scholes	(Man Utd) replaced by Sheringham

Crowd: 35,394

England scorer: Shearer

Comments: Andersson and Mjallby scored in quick succession to cancel out Shearer's second-minute goal. This time it was Paul Ince's turn to get sent off, halfway through the second half.

ENGLAND 0 Bulgaria 0; at Wembley;
Saturday 10th October 1998 (European Championship)

1	Seaman	(Arsenal)	1	Zdavkov
2	Neville	(Man Utd)	2	Kirilov
3	Hinchcliffe	(Sheffield Wed) replaced by Le Saux	3	Zagorchich
4	Lee	(Newcastle Utd)	4	Yordanov
5	Campbell	(Tottenham)	5	Naidenov
6	Southgate	(Aston Villa)	6	Kishishev
7	Anderton	(Tottenham) replaced by Batty	7	Petkov
8	Redknapp	(Liverpool)	8	Yankov
9	Shearer*	(Newcastle Utd)	9	Hristov
10	Owen	(Liverpool)	10	Stoichkov
11	Scholes	(Man Utd) replaced by Sheringham	11	Iliev

Crowd: 72,794

Comments: Hapless England drew a blank as they had now failed to win in eight of their twelve matches in this year. Andy Hinchcliffe never won another cap after this scoreless encounter.

Luxembourg 0 ENGLAND 3; in Luxembourg City;
Wednesday 14th October 1998 (European Championship)

1	Koch	1	Seaman	(Arsenal)	
2	Ferron	2	Ferdinand	(West Ham Utd)	
3	Funck	3	Neville	(Man Utd)	
4	Deville	4	Batty	(Newcastle Utd)	
5	Strasser	5	Campbell	(Tottenham)	
6	Saibene	6	Southgate	(Aston Villa)	
7	Theis	7	Beckham	(Man Utd)	
8	Deville	8	Anderton	(Tottenham) replaced by Lee	
9	Christophe	9	Shearer*	(Newcastle Utd)	
10	Cardoni	10	Owen	(Liverpool)	
11	Posing	11	Scholes	(Man Utd) replaced by Wright	

Crowd: 8,054

England scorers: Owen, Shearer (Pen), Southgate

Comments: England survived an early scare when the home team missed a penalty to go on and achieve maximum points. This would be the last international appearance for substitute Rob Lee.

ENGLAND 2 Czech Republic 0; at Wembley;
Wednesday 18th November 1998 (European Championship)

1	Martyn	(Leeds United)	1	Kouba	
2	Keown	(Arsenal)	2	Latal	
3	Campbell*	(Tottenham)	3	Votava	
4	Butt	(Man Utd)	4	Novotny	
5	Ferdinand	(West Ham Utd)	5	Repka	
6	Le Saux	(Chelsea)	6	Berger	
7	Beckham	(Man Utd)	7	Nemec	
8	Anderton	(Tottenham)	8	Poborsky	
9	Dublin	(Coventry City)	9	Kuka	
10	Wright	(West Ham Utd) replaced by Fowler	10	Smicer	
11	Merson	(Aston Villa) replaced by Hendrie	11	Bejbl	

Crowd: 38,535

England scorers: Anderton, Merson

Comments: Paul Merson doubled England's lead before half time in his last international. His replacement Lee Hendrie won his only cap, while it was the last cap for Dion Dublin and Ian Wright.

ENGLAND 0 France 2; at Wembley;
Monday 1st February 1999

1	Seaman	(Arsenal) replaced by Martyn	1	Barthez
2	Dixon	(Arsenal) replaced by Ferdinand	2	Thuram
3	Le Saux	(Chelsea)	3	Lizarazu
4	Ince	(Liverpool)	4	Desailly
5	Adams	(Arsenal)	5	Blanc
6	Keown	(Arsenal) replaced by Wilcox	6	Deschamps
7	Beckham	(Man Utd)	7	Petit
8	Redknapp	(Liverpool) replaced by Scholes	8	Zidane
9	Shearer*	(Newcastle Utd)	9	Djorkaeff
10	Owen	(Liverpool) replaced by Cole	10	Pires
11	Anderton	(Tottenham)	11	Anelka

Crowd: 74,111

Comments: Only 4 players who started the previous match were chosen for this tussle. Both goals were netted by Nicolas Anelka. Even Glenn Hoddle had to resign after making tactless remarks.

ENGLAND 3 Poland 1; at Wembley;
Wednesday 27th March 1999 (European Championship)

1	Seaman	(Arsenal)	1	Matysek
2	Neville G	(Man Utd)	2	Bak
3	Le Saux	(Chelsea)	3	Lapinski
4	Sherwood	(Tottenham)	4	Ratajczyk
5	Keown	(Arsenal)	5	Zielinski
6	Campbell	(Tottenham)	6	Hajto
7	Beckham	(Man Utd) replaced by Neville P	7	Swierczewski
8	Scholes	(Man Utd) replaced by Redknapp	8	Iwan
9	Shearer*	(Newcastle Utd)	9	Siadaczka
10	Cole	(Man Utd)	10	Brzeczek
11	McManaman	(Liverpool) replaced by Parlour	11	Trzecziak

Crowd: 73,836

England scorer: Scholes (3)

Comments: Kevin Keegan had now succeeded as England coach after Howard Wilkinson's one-match stint as caretaker. Paul Scholes got the Keegan era off to a flying start with a hat-trick.

Hungary 1 ENGLAND 1; in Budapest;
Wednesday 28th April 1999

1 Kiraly	1 Seaman	(Arsenal)
2 Hrutka	2 Brown	(Man Utd) replaced by Gray
3 Korsos	3 Neville	(Man Utd)
4 Matyus	4 Batty	(Newcastle Utd)
5 Sebok	5 Ferdinand	(West Ham Utd) replaced by Carragher
6 Halmai	6 Keown	(Arsenal)
7 Dombi	7 Butt	(Man Utd)
8 Dardai	8 Sherwood	(Tottenham)
9 Pisont	9 Shearer*	(Newcastle Utd)
10 Illes	10 Phillips	(Sunderland) replaced by Heskey
11 Korsos	11 McManaman	(Liverpool) replaced by Redknapp

Crowd: 20,000

England scorer: Shearer (Pen)

Comments: Alan Shearer's first-half penalty was cancelled out by a second-half equaliser. New caps were awarded to Wes Brown, Jamie Carragher, Michael Gray, Emile Heskey, and Kevin Phillips.

ENGLAND 0 Sweden 0; at Wembley;
Saturday 5th June 1999 (European Championship)

1 Seaman	(Arsenal)	1 Hedman
2 Neville	(Man Utd) replaced by Gray	2 Nilsson
3 Le Saux	(Chelsea)	3 Andersson
4 Sherwood	(Tottenham)	4 Bjorklund
5 Keown	(Arsenal) replaced by Ferdinand	5 Kaamark
6 Campbell	(Tottenham)	6 Schwarz
7 Beckham	(Man Utd) replaced by Parlour	7 Mild
8 Batty	(Newcastle Utd)	8 Mjallby
9 Shearer*	(Newcastle Utd)	9 Ljungberg
10 Cole	(Man Utd)	10 Larsson
11 Scholes	(Man Utd)	11 Andersson

Crowd: 75,824

Comments: Scholes went from hero to villain as he became the second player to be sent off against Sweden in two matches. He was also the first English player to be sent off in a home fixture.

Bulgaria 1 ENGLAND 1; in Sofia;
Wednesday 9th June 1999 (European Championship)

1 Ivankov	1 Seaman	(Arsenal)
2 Kishishev	2 Neville	(Man Utd)
3 Zagorchich	3 Gray	(Sunderland)
4 Stoilov	4 Woodgate	(Leeds) replaced by Parlour
5 Markov	5 Southgate	(Aston Villa)
6 Kirilov	6 Campbell	(Tottenham)
7 Petrov	7 Redknapp	(Liverpool)
8 Stoichkov	8 Batty	(Newcastle Utd)
9 Yovov	9 Shearer*	(Newcastle Utd)
10 Petkov	10 Sheringham	(Man Utd)
11 Iliev	11 Fowler	(Liverpool) replaced by Heskey

Crowd: 22,000

England scorer: Shearer

Comments: Shearer scored after fifteen minutes but the Bulgars soon equalised. England's hopes of qualification were now in jeopardy. This was the last cap for Gray and the debut for Woodgate.

ENGLAND 6 Luxembourg 0; at Wembley;
Saturday 4th September 1999 (European Championship)

1 Martyn	(Leeds United)	1 Felgen
2 Dyer	(Newcastle Utd) replaced by Neville G	2 Ferron
3 Pearce	(West Ham Utd)	3 Schauls
4 Batty	(Newcastle Utd)	4 Birsens
5 Adams	(Arsenal) replaced by Neville P	5 Funck
6 Keown	(Arsenal)	6 Saibene
7 Beckham	(Man Utd) replaced by Owen	7 Theis
8 Parlour	(Arsenal)	8 Vanek
9 Shearer*	(Newcastle Utd)	9 Christophe
10 Fowler	(Liverpool)	10 Schneider
11 McManaman	(Real Madrid)	11 Posing

Crowd: 68,772

England scorers: Shearer (3), McManaman (2), Owen

Comments: The home team led 5–0 at half time. Steve McManaman had failed to score in his previous 24 caps, but now he scored twice in 15 minutes! This was the first start for Dyer and Parlour.

Poland 0 ENGLAND 0; in Warsaw;
Wednesday 8th September 1999 (European Championship)

1 Matysek	1 Martyn	(Leeds United)
2 Klos	2 Neville G	(Man Utd) replaced by Neville P
3 Waldoch	3 Pearce	(West Ham Utd)
4 Siadaczka	4 Batty	(Newcastle Utd)
5 Zielinski	5 Adams	(Arsenal)
6 Hajto	6 Keown	(Arsenal)
7 Michalski	7 Beckham	(Man Utd)
8 Iwan	8 Scholes	(Man Utd)
9 Trzecziak	9 Shearer*	(Newcastle Utd)
10 Nowak	10 Fowler	(Liverpool) replaced by Owen
11 Gilewicz	11 McManaman	(Real Madrid) replaced by Dyer

Crowd: 17,000

Comments: David Batty is sent off late in the match and never plays for England again. This is also the last cap for Stuart Pearce. England are now forced to play Scotland in a two-legged play-off.

ENGLAND 2 Belgium 1; at Sunderland;
Sunday 10th October 1999

1 Seaman	(Arsenal) replaced by Martyn	1 de Vlieger
2 Dyer	(Newcastle Utd) replaced by Neville	2 Deflandre
3 Southgate	(Aston Villa)	3 Peeters
4 Lampard	(West Ham Utd) replaced by Wise	4 van Meir
5 Adams	(Arsenal)	5 Oyen
6 Keown	(Arsenal)	6 Vanderhaeghe
7 Redknapp	(Liverpool)	7 Wilmots
8 Ince	(Middlesbrough)	8 van Kerkhoven
9 Shearer*	(Newcastle Utd) replaced by Heskey	9 de Bilde
10 Phillips	(Sunderland) replaced by Owen	10 Strupar
11 Guppy	(Leicester City)	11 Tanghe

Crowd: 40,987

England scorers: Shearer, Redknapp

Comments: After both teams had scored within the first fifteen minutes, Jamie Redknapp restored England's lead in the second half with his only goal for his country. This was also the only cap for Steve Guppy.

Scotland 0 ENGLAND 2; in Glasgow;
Saturday 13th November 1999 (European Championship)

	Scotland			England	
1	Sullivan		1	Seaman	(Arsenal)
2	Weir		2	Campbell	(Tottenham)
3	Ritchie		3	Neville	(Man Utd)
4	Dailly		4	Ince	(Middlesbrough)
5	Hendry		5	Adams	(Arsenal)
6	Ferguson		6	Keown	(Arsenal)
7	Dodds		7	Beckham	(Man Utd)
8	Burley		8	Scholes	(Man Utd)
9	Gallacher		9	Shearer*	(Newcastle Utd)
10	Hutchinson		10	Owen	(Liverpool) replaced by Cole
11	Collins		11	Redknapp	(Liverpool)

Crowd: 50,132

England scorer: Scholes (2)

Comments: It was June 1996 all over again as England broke Scottish hearts in a vital European Championship qualifier. The hero was Paul Scholes who bagged himself a double in the first half.

ENGLAND 0 Scotland 1; at Wembley;
Wednesday 17th November 1999 (European Championship)

	England			Scotland
1	Seaman	(Arsenal)	1	Sullivan
2	Campbell	(Tottenham)	2	Weir
3	Neville	(Man Utd)	3	Davidson
4	Ince	(Middlesbrough)	4	Dailly
5	Adams	(Arsenal)	5	Hendry
6	Southgate	(Aston Villa)	6	Ferguson
7	Beckham	(Man Utd)	7	Dodds
8	Scholes	(Man Utd) replaced by Parlour	8	Burley
9	Shearer*	(Newcastle Utd)	9	McCann
10	Owen	(Liverpool) replaced by Heskey	10	Hutchinson
11	Redknapp	(Liverpool)	11	Collins

Crowd: 75,848

Comments: Craig Brown's Scotland enjoyed a bitter-sweet victory as they humbled England in their own backyard but still exited 2–1 on aggregate. Don Hutchinson scored the only goal.

ENGLAND 0 Argentina 0; at Wembley;
Wednesday 23rd February 2000

1 Seaman	(Arsenal)	1	Cavallero
2 Dyer	(Newcastle Utd) replaced by Neville	2	Ayala
3 Southgate	(Aston Villa)	3	Sensini
4 Wise	(Chelsea)	4	Chamot
5 Campbell	(Tottenham)	5	Simone
6 Keown	(Arsenal) replaced by Ferdinand	6	Zanetti
7 Beckham	(Man Utd) replaced by Parlour	7	Gonzalez
8 Scholes	(Man Utd)	8	Arrubarrena
9 Shearer*	(Newcastle Utd) replaced by Phillips	9	Ortega
10 Heskey	(Leicester City) replaced by Cole	10	Veron
11 Wilcox	(Leeds United)	11	Batistuta

Crowd: 74,008

Comments: David Beckham was faced with his nemesis Diego Simone, but there was no repeat of the drama of St. Etienne. This match was an anti-climax and also the last cap for Jason Wilcox.

ENGLAND 1 Brazil 1; at Wembley;
Saturday 27th May 2000

1 Seaman	(Arsenal)	1	Dida
2 Neville G	(Man Utd)	2	Cafu
3 Neville P	(Man Utd)	3	Carlos
4 Ince	(Middlesbrough) replaced by Parlour	4	Aldair
5 Campbell	(Tottenham)	5	Silvinho
6 Keown	(Arsenal)	6	Emerson
7 Beckham	(Man Utd)	7	Sampaio
8 Scholes	(Man Utd)	8	Ze Roberto
9 Shearer*	(Newcastle Utd) replaced by Phillips	9	Rivaldo
10 Owen	(Liverpool) replaced by Fowler	10	Amoroso
11 Wise	(Chelsea)	11	Franca

Crowd: 73,956

England scorer: Owen

Comments: Michael Owen's goal was soon cancelled out by Franca shortly before half time as Kevin Keegan's troops warmed up for the European Championship finals with this friendly.

ENGLAND 2 Ukraine 0; at Wembley;
Wednesday 31st May 2000

1	Martyn	(Leeds United)	1 Kernozenko
2	Gerrard	(Liverpool) replaced by Dyer	2 Luzhny
3	Neville	(Man Utd) replaced by Barry	3 Holovko
4	Southgate	(Aston Villa)	4 Vaschuk
5	Adams	(Arsenal)	5 Dumitrulin
6	Campbell	(Tottenham)	6 Popov
7	Beckham	(Man Utd)	7 Tymoshchuk
8	Scholes	(Man Utd) replaced by Barmby	8 Husin
9	Shearer*	(Newcastle Utd)	9 Kandourov
10	Fowler	(Liverpool) replaced by Heskey	10 Shevchenko
11	McManaman	(Real Madrid)	11 Rebrov

Crowd: 55,975

England scorers: Fowler, Adams

Comments: Tony Adams scored his last England goal to add to one netted by Robbie Fowler just before half time. This home win was the debut appearance of Gareth Barry and Steven Gerrard.

Malta 1 ENGLAND 2; in Valletta;
Saturday 3rd June 2000

1	Barry	1	Wright	(Ipswich Town)
2	Said	2	Neville G	(Man Utd)
3	Spiteri	3	Neville P	(Man Utd)
4	Vella	4	Wise	(Chelsea) replaced by McManaman
5	Debono	5	Campbell	(Tottenham)
6	Buttigieg	6	Keown	(Arsenal) replaced by Southgate
7	Busuttil	7	Beckham	(Man Utd) replaced by Barry
8	Carabott	8	Scholes	(Man Utd) replaced by Ince
9	Turner	9	Shearer*	(Newcastle Utd) replaced by Heskey
10	Brincat	10	Phillips	(Sunderland) replaced by Fowler
11	Agius	11	Barmby	(Everton)

Crowd: 10,023

England scorers: Keown, Heskey

Comments: Richard Wright had to face three penalties on his debut. Only one was actually scored. Meanwhile Emile Heskey scored his first England goal in this final Euro' 2000 warm-up match.

ENGLAND 2 Portugal 3; in Eindhoven;
Monday 12th June 2000 (European Championship)

1 Seaman	(Arsenal)	1	Baia
2 Neville G	(Man Utd)	2	Xavier
3 Neville P	(Man Utd)	3	Dimas
4 Ince	(Middlesbrough)	4	Bento
5 Adams	(Arsenal) replaced by Keown	5	Couto
6 Campbell	(Tottenham)	6	Costa
7 Beckham	(Man Utd)	7	Figo
8 Scholes	(Man Utd)	8	Costa
9 Shearer*	(Newcastle Utd)	9	Gomes
10 Owen	(Liverpool) replaced by Heskey	10	Pinto
11 McManaman	(Real Madrid) replaced by Wise	11	Vidigal

Crowd: 30,000

England scorers: Scholes, McManaman

Comments: England got off to a flying start with two goals inside the first 20 minutes, but Portugal stunned their opponents with a remarkable comeback, inspired by a Luis Figo wonder goal.

ENGLAND 1 Germany 0; in Charleroi;
Saturday 17th June 2000 (European Championship)

1 Seaman	(Arsenal)	1	Kahn
2 Neville G	(Man Utd)	2	Babbel
3 Neville P	(Man Utd)	3	Ziege
4 Ince	(Middlesbrough)	4	Hamann
5 Campbell	(Tottenham)	5	Matthaus
6 Keown	(Arsenal)	6	Nowotny
7 Beckham	(Man Utd)	7	Deisler
8 Scholes	(Man Utd) replaced by Barmby	8	Scholl
9 Shearer*	(Newcastle Utd)	9	Jancker
10 Owen	(Liverpool) replaced by Gerrard	10	Kirsten
11 Wise	(Chelsea)	11	Jeremies

Crowd: 30,000

England scorer: Shearer

Comments: The ghosts of 1970, 1972, 1990, and 1996 were finally laid to rest when the captain scored early in the second half against a German team that flopped at this tournament.

ENGLAND 2 Romania 3; in Charleroi;
Tuesday 20th June 2000 (European Championship)

1 Martyn	(Leeds United)	1	Stelea
2 Neville G	(Man Utd)	2	Contra
3 Neville P	(Man Utd)	3	Filipescu
4 Ince	(Middlesbrough)	4	Popescu
5 Campbell	(Tottenham)	5	Chivu
6 Keown	(Arsenal)	6	Petrescu
7 Beckham	(Man Utd)	7	Galca
8 Scholes	(Man Utd) replaced by Southgate	8	Mutu
9 Shearer*	(Newcastle Utd)	9	Munteanu
10 Owen	(Liverpool) replaced by Heskey	10	Moldovan
11 Wise	(Chelsea) replaced by Barmby	11	Ilie

Crowd: 30,000

England scorers: Shearer, Owen

Comments: Having trailed 1–0, England scored twice just before half time only to concede a penalty in the dying seconds. Not for the first time, a premature exit was the consequence.

France 1 ENGLAND 1; in Paris;
Saturday 2nd September 2000

1 Lama	1 Seaman	(Arsenal)
2 Thuram	2 Campbell	(Tottenham)
3 Blanc	3 Adams*	(Arsenal) replaced by Southgate
4 Desailly	4 Keown	(Arsenal)
5 Lizarazu	5 Barry	(Aston Villa)
6 Deschamps	6 Anderton	(Tottenham) replaced by Dyer
7 Petit	7 Beckham	(Man Utd)
8 Djorkaeff	8 Scholes	(Man Utd) replaced by Owen
9 Zidane	9 Cole	(Man Utd)
10 Anelka	10 Barmby	(Liverpool) replaced by McManaman
11 Henry	11 Wise	(Chelsea)

Crowd: 76,318

England scorer: Owen

Comments: Michael Owen came off the bench to record a late equalizer after Arsenal's Emmanuel Petit had given the world champions the lead halfway through the second half of this friendly.

ENGLAND o Germany 1; at Wembley;
Saturday 7th October 2000 (World Cup qualifier)

1 Seaman	(Arsenal)	1	Kahn
2 Neville	(Man Utd) replaced by Dyer	2	Rehmer
3 Le Saux	(Chelsea) replaced by Barry	3	Nowotny
4 Keown	(Arsenal)	4	Linke
5 Adams*	(Arsenal)	5	Deisler
6 Southgate	(Aston Villa)	6	Ramelow
7 Beckham	(Man Utd) replaced by Parlour	7	Ballack
8 Scholes	(Man Utd)	8	Hamann
9 Cole	(Man Utd)	9	Bode
10 Owen	(Liverpool)	10	Scholl
11 Barmby	(Liverpool)	11	Bierhoff

Crowd: 76,377

Comments: Dietmar Hamann scored the last goal at the old Wembley Stadium. Tony Adams and Graeme Le Saux never played for England again while Kevin Keegan resigned after the match.

Finland o ENGLAND o; in Helsinki;
Wednesday 11th October 2000 (World Cup qualifier)

1 Niemi	1	Seaman	(Arsenal)
2 Tihinen	2	Neville	(Man Utd)
3 Hyypia	3	Barry	(Aston Villa) replaced by Brown
4 Saarinen	4	Wise	(Chelsea)
5 Helin	5	Southgate	(Aston Villa)
6 Valakari	6	Keown*	(Arsenal)
7 Wiss	7	Parlour	(Arsenal)
8 Nurmela	8	Scholes	(Man Utd)
9 Johansson	9	Cole	(Man Utd)
10 Litmanen	10	Sheringham	(Man Utd) replaced by McManaman
11 Forssell	11	Heskey	(Liverpool)

Crowd: 26,310

Comments: Howard Wilkinson was again drafted in as a caretaker manager and England failed to score in his second match in temporary charge. This stalemate was the last cap for Dennis Wise.

Italy 1 ENGLAND 0; in Turin;
Wednesday 15th November 2000

1 Buffon	1 James	(Aston Villa)
2 Coco	2 Neville	(Man Utd)
3 Maldini	3 Barry	(Aston Villa) replaced by Johnson
4 Albertini	4 Butt	(Man Utd) replaced by Carragher
5 Cannavaro	5 Ferdinand	(West Ham Utd)
6 Nesta	6 Southgate	(Aston Villa)
7 di Livio	7 Beckham*	(Man Utd)
8 Gattuso	8 Parlour	(Arsenal) replaced by Anderton
9 Inzaghi	9 Heskey	(Liverpool) replaced by Phillips
10 Fiore	10 Barmby	(Liverpool)
11 Delvecchio	11 Dyer	(Newcastle Utd) replaced by Fowler

Crowd: 22,714.

Comments: The Italian bulldog Gennaro Gattuso scored the only goal just after the hour mark. Peter Taylor was now the caretaker boss. This was the only cap for Derby County's Seth Johnson.

ENGLAND 3 Spain 0; at Villa Park;
Wednesday 28th February 2001

1 James	(Aston Villa) replaced by Martyn	1 Cassillas
2 Neville P	(Man Utd) replaced by Neville G	2 Pablo
3 Powell	(Charlton Athletic) replaced by Ball	3 Romero
4 Butt	(Man Utd) replaced by McCann	4 Guardiola
5 Ferdinand	(Leeds United) replaced by Ehiogu	5 Aberlardo
6 Campbell	(Tottenham)	6 Mendieta
7 Beckham*	(Man Utd) replaced by Lampard	7 Raul
8 Scholes	(Man Utd) replaced by Heskey	8 Enrique
9 Cole	(Man Utd)	9 Urzaiz
10 Owen	(Liverpool)	10 Helguera
11 Barmby	(Liverpool)	11 Unai

Crowd: 42,129

England scorers: Barmby, Heskey, Ehiogu

Comments: The Eriksson era made an impressive start with this fine win. Chris Powell made his debut while Everton's Michael Ball and Sunderland's Gavin McCann earned their only caps.

ENGLAND 2 Finland 1; at Anfield;
Saturday 24th March 2001 (World Cup qualifier)

1	Seaman	(Arsenal)		1	Niemi
2	Neville	(Man Utd)		2	Pasanen
3	Powell	(Charlton Athletic)		3	Hyypia
4	Gerrard	(Liverpool)		4	Tihinen
5	Ferdinand	(Leeds United)		5	Ylonen
6	Campbell	(Tottenham)		6	Nurmela
7	Beckham*	(Man Utd)		7	Wiss
8	Scholes	(Man Utd)		8	Riihilahti
9	Cole	(Man Utd) replaced by Fowler		9	Kolkka
10	Owen	(Liverpool) replaced by Butt		10	Litmanen
11	McManaman	(Real Madrid) replaced by Heskey		11	Johansson

Crowd: 44,262

England scorers: Owen, Beckham

Comments: The home team conceded the lead but goals on either side of half time from Owen and then Beckham managed to revive their chances of qualifying for the World Cup finals next year.

Albania 1 ENGLAND 3; in Tirana;
Wednesday 28th March 2001 (World Cup qualifier)

1	Strakosha		1	Seaman	(Arsenal)
2	Lala		2	Neville	(Man Utd)
3	Cipi		3	Cole	(Arsenal)
4	Xhumba		4	Butt	(Man Utd)
5	Fakaj		5	Ferdinand	(Leeds United)
6	Hasi		6	Campbell	(Tottenham) replaced by Brown
7	Bellai		7	Beckham*	(Man Utd)
8	Kola		8	Scholes	(Man Utd)
9	Vata		9	Cole	(Man Utd)
10	Bushi		10	Owen	(Liverpool) replaced by Sheringham
11	Tare		11	McManaman	(Real Madrid) replaced by Heskey

Crowd: 18,000

England scorers: Owen, Scholes, Cole

Comments: This game was still 0–0 with 20 minutes left. England finished the match with 7 Manchester United players, including Andy Cole who scored his only international goal. Ashley Cole made his debut.

ENGLAND 4 Mexico 0; at Derby;
Friday 25th May 2001

1 Martyn	(Leeds United) replaced by James	1 Sanchez
2 Neville	(Man Utd)	2 Beltran
3 Cole A	(Arsenal) replaced by Powell	3 Suarez
4 Gerrard	(Liverpool) replaced by Butt	4 Oteo
5 Ferdinand	(Leeds United) replaced by Southgate	5 Chavez
6 Keown	(Arsenal) replaced by Carragher	6 Ruiz
7 Beckham*	(Man Utd) replaced by Cole J	7 Coyote
8 Scholes	(Man Utd) replaced by Carrick	8 Ruiz
9 Fowler	(Liverpool) replaced by Sheringham	9 Rodriguez
10 Owen	(Liverpool) replaced by Smith	10 de Negris
11 Heskey	(Liverpool) replaced by Mills	11 Abundis

Crowd: 33,597

England scorers: Scholes, Fowler, Beckham, Sheringham

Comments: The home team were 3–0 ahead inside the first half hour. New caps were awarded to Michael Carrick, Joe Cole, Danny Mills, and Alan Smith. Only Phil Neville played the full match.

Greece 0 ENGLAND 2; in Athens;
Wednesday 6th June 2001 (World Cup qualifier)

1 Nikopolidis	1 Seaman	(Arsenal)	
2 Mavrogenidis	2 Neville	(Man Utd)	
3 Eyssas	3 Cole	(Arsenal)	
4 Dabizas	4 Gerrard	(Liverpool)	
5 Ouzonidis	5 Ferdinand	(Leeds United)	
6 Goumas	6 Keown	(Arsenal)	
7 Basinas	7 Beckham*	(Man Utd)	
8 Zagorakis	8 Scholes	(Man Utd) replaced by Butt	
9 Machlas	9 Fowler	(Liverpool) replaced by Smith	
10 Karagounis	10 Owen	(Liverpool)	
11 Vryzas	11 Heskey	(Liverpool) replaced by McManaman	

Crowd: 29,300

England scorers: Scholes, Beckham

Comments: Two goals in the final half hour put England firmly back on track for the World Cup finals. Only four English clubs were represented in the team that achieved a hard-fought victory.

ENGLAND 0 Holland 2; at Tottenham;
Wednesday 15th August 2001

1 Martyn	(Leeds United) replaced by James	1 van der Sar
2 Neville	(Man Utd) replaced by Mills	2 Reiziger
3 Cole	(Arsenal) replaced by Powell	3 Stam
4 Carragher	(Liverpool)	4 Hofland
5 Brown	(Man Utd) replaced by Southgate	5 van Bronckhorst
6 Keown	(Arsenal) replaced by Ehiogu	6 Cocu
7 Beckham*	(Man Utd) replaced by Lampard	7 van Bommel
8 Scholes	(Man Utd) replaced by Barmby	8 Zenden
9 Fowler	(Liverpool) replaced by Owen	9 van Nistelrooy
10 Cole	(Man Utd) replaced by Smith	10 Kluivert
11 Hargreaves	(Bayern Munich) replaced by Carrick	11 Overmars

Crowd: 35,238

Comments: Van Bommel and van Nistelrooy did the damage just before half time. This was the debut of Owen Hargreaves. Richard Wright also came on to replace the replacement, David James!

Germany 1 ENGLAND 5; in Munich;
Saturday 1st September 2001 (World Cup qualifier)

1 Kahn	1 Seaman	(Arsenal)
2 Worms	2 Neville	(Man Utd)
3 Bohme	3 Cole	(Arsenal)
4 Linke	4 Gerrard	(Liverpool) replaced by Hargreaves
5 Nowotny	5 Ferdinand	(Leeds United)
6 Hamann	6 Campbell	(Arsenal)
7 Rehmer	7 Beckham*	(Man Utd)
8 Ballack	8 Scholes	(Man Utd) replaced by Carragher
9 Jancker	9 Heskey	(Liverpool)
10 Deisler	10 Owen	(Liverpool)
11 Neuville	11 Barmby	(Liverpool) replaced by McManaman

Crowd: 63,000

England scorers: Owen (3), Gerrard, Heskey

Comments: The visitors may have feared the worst when Jancker scored an early goal, but thereafter England ran riot with three Liverpool players plundering the goals in this sensational triumph.

ENGLAND 2 Albania 0; at Newcastle;
Wednesday 5th September 2001 (World Cup qualifier)

1 Seaman	(Arsenal)	1	Strakosha
2 Neville	(Man Utd)	2	Dede
3 Cole	(Arsenal)	3	Cipi
4 Gerrard	(Liverpool) replaced by Carragher	4	Xhumba
5 Ferdinand	(Leeds United)	5	Fakaj
6 Campbell	(Arsenal)	6	Hasi
7 Beckham*	(Man Utd)	7	Mutari
8 Scholes	(Man Utd)	8	Bellai
9 Heskey	(Liverpool) replaced by Fowler	9	Vata
10 Owen	(Liverpool)	10	Rraklli
11 Barmby	(Liverpool) replaced by McManaman	11	Bogdani

Crowd: 51,046

England scorers: Owen, Fowler

Comments: After the most successful invasion of Germany since 1945, England were not surprisingly unchanged. However it took a late goal in each half to see off the resistance of Albania.

ENGLAND 2 Greece 2; at Old Trafford;
Saturday 6th October 2001 (World Cup qualifier)

1 Martyn	(Leeds United)	1	Nikopolidis
2 Neville	(Man Utd)	2	Patsatzoglu
3 Cole	(Arsenal) replaced by McManaman	3	Dabizas
4 Gerrard	(Liverpool)	4	Vokolos
5 Ferdinand	(Leeds United)	5	Konstandinidis
6 Keown	(Arsenal)	6	Fyssas
7 Beckham*	(Man Utd)	7	Zagorakis
8 Scholes	(Man Utd)	8	Kassapis
9 Heskey	(Liverpool)	9	Karagounis
10 Fowler	(Liverpool) replaced by Sheringham	10	Charisteas
11 Barmby	(Liverpool) replaced by Cole	11	Nikolaidis

Crowd: 66,009

England scorers: Sheringham, Beckham

Comments: England only needed a point to qualify but they made hard work of obtaining it. Sheringham scored immediately as a substitute but it took a Beckham free kick to save the home team.

ENGLAND 1 Sweden 1; at Old Trafford;
Saturday 10th November 2001

1 Martyn	(Leeds United)	1	Hedman
2 Neville G	(Man Utd) replaced by Mills	2	Andersson
3 Carragher	(Liverpool) replaced by Neville P	3	Svensson
4 Butt	(Man Utd) replaced by Murphy	4	Mjallby
5 Ferdinand	(Leeds United)	5	Edman
6 Southgate	(Middlesbrough)	6	Linderoth
7 Beckham*	(Man Utd)	7	Alexandersson
8 Scholes	(Man Utd) replaced by Lampard	8	Mild
9 Heskey	(Liverpool) replaced by Fowler	9	Svensson
10 Phillips	(Sunderland) replaced by Sheringham	10	Allback
11 Sinclair	(West Ham Utd) replaced by Anderton	11	Ibrahimovic

Crowd: 64,413

England scorer: Beckham (Pen)

Comments: Both goals came in the first half as Danny Murphy and Trevor Sinclair made their debut. This friendly match was the last international appearance for Darren 'Sicknote' Anderton.

Holland 1 ENGLAND 1; in Amsterdam;
Wednesday 13th February 2002

1 van der Sar	1 Martyn	(Leeds United) replaced by James
2 Reiziger	2 Neville G	(Man Utd) replaced by Neville P
3 Ricksen	3 Bridge	(Southampton) replaced by Powell
4 de Boer	4 Gerrard	(Liverpool) replaced by Butt
5 van Bronckhorst	5 Ferdinand	(Leeds United)
6 Cocu	6 Campbell	(Arsenal) replaced by Southgate
7 van Bommel	7 Beckham*	(Man Utd)
8 de Boer	8 Scholes	(Man Utd) replaced by Lampard
9 van Nistelrooy	9 Heskey	(Liverpool)
10 Kluivert	10 Ricketts	(Bolton Wanderers) replaced by Phillips
11 Overmars	11 Vassell	(Aston Villa) replaced by Cole

Crowd: 48,500

England scorer: Vassell

Comments: Patrick Kluivert gave the Dutch a half-time lead but debutant Darius Vassell equalised. Wayne Bridge won his first cap, while Michael Ricketts made his only England appearance.

ENGLAND 1 Italy 2; at Leeds;
Wednesday 27th March 2002

1 Martyn	(Leeds United) replaced by James	1 Buffon
2 Mills	(Leeds United) replaced by Neville P	2 Panucci
3 Bridge	(Southampton) replaced by Neville G	3 Materazzi
4 Butt	(Man Utd) replaced by Hargreaves	4 Zanetti
5 Southgate	(Middlesbrough) replaced by Ehiogu	5 Cannavaro
6 Campbell	(Arsenal) replaced by King	6 Nesta
7 Beckham*	(Man Utd) replaced by Murphy	7 Zambrotta
8 Lampard	(Chelsea) replaced by Cole	8 di Biagio
9 Heskey	(Liverpool) replaced by Fowler	9 Delvecchio
10 Owen	(Liverpool) replaced by Vassell	10 Totti
11 Sinclair	(West Ham Utd) replaced by Sheringham	11 Doni

Crowd: 36,635

England scorer: Fowler

Comments: Robbie Fowler gave England the lead halfway through the second half but then a double from the substitute Montella stole the show. This was the international debut of Ledley King.

ENGLAND 4 Paraguay 0; at Anfield;
Wednesday 17th April 2002

1 Seaman	(Arsenal)	1 Tavarelli
2 Neville G	(Man Utd) replaced by Neville P	2 Arca
3 Bridge	(Southampton) replaced by Lampard	3 Ayala
4 Gerrard	(Liverpool) replaced by Murphy	4 Gamarra
5 Southgate	(Middlesbrough) replaced by Carragher	5 Caniza
6 Keown	(Arsenal) replaced by Mills	6 Gavilan
7 Butt	(Man Utd) replaced by Hargreaves	7 Bonet
8 Scholes	(Man Utd) replaced by Cole	8 Struway
9 Vassell	(Aston Villa) replaced by Sheringham	9 Paredes
10 Owen*	(Liverpool) replaced by Fowler	10 Cardozo
11 Dyer	(Newcastle Utd) replaced by Sinclair	11 Santa Cruz

Crowd: 42,713

England scorers: Owen, Murphy, Vassell, Ayala (OG)

Comments: The new captain Michael Owen gave the home team the lead inside five minutes which was added to by three second half efforts, including Danny Murphy's only international goal.

South Korea 1 ENGLAND 1; in Seogwipo;
Tuesday 21st May 2002

1	Woon-jae	1	Martyn	(Leeds United) replaced by James
2	Jong-gook	2	Mills	(Leeds United) replaced by Brown
3	Myung-bo	3	Cole A	(Arsenal) replaced by Bridge
4	Jin-cheul	4	Hargreaves	(Bayern Munich)
5	Nam-il	5	Ferdinand	(Leeds United) replaced by Keown
6	Tae-uk	6	Campbell	(Arsenal) replaced by Southgate
7	Young-pyo	7	Murphy	(Liverpool) replaced by Sinclair
8	Sang-cheol	8	Scholes	(Man Utd) replaced by Cole J
9	Ji-sung	9	Heskey	(Liverpool)
10	Ki-hyun	10	Owen*	(Liverpool) replaced by Sheringham
11	Cheon-soo	11	Vassell	(Aston Villa)

Crowd: 39,876

England scorer: Owen

Comments: The skipper gave his team the interval lead again, but Eriksson's troops had to settle for a draw as they continued their pre-World Cup finals preparations with a fixture in the Far East.

ENGLAND 2 Cameroon 2; in Kobe;
Sunday 26th May 2002

1	Martyn	(Leeds United) replaced by James	1	Alioum
2	Brown	(Man Utd)	2	Kalla
3	Bridge	(Southampton)	3	Wome
4	Hargreaves	(Bayern Munich)	4	Tchato
5	Ferdinand	(Leeds United) replaced by Keown	5	Lauren
6	Campbell	(Arsenal) replaced by Southgate	6	Geremi
7	Cole	(West Ham Utd)	7	Song
8	Scholes	(Man Utd) replaced by Mills	8	Foe
9	Vassell	(Aston Villa) replaced by Fowler	9	Olembe
10	Owen*	(Liverpool) replaced by Sheringham	10	Mboma
11	Heskey	(Liverpool) replaced by Sinclair	11	Eto'o

Crowd: 42,000

England scorers: Vassell, Fowler

Comments: England twice came from behind to salvage a draw after Eto'o and Geremi had scored for the Africans. England now entered the World Cup finals on the back of one win in 7 matches.

ENGLAND 1 Sweden 1; in Saitama;
Sunday 2nd June 2002 (World Cup finals)

1	Seaman	(Arsenal)	1	Hedman
2	Mills	(Leeds United)	2	Mellberg
3	Cole A	(Arsenal)	3	Mjallby
4	Hargreaves	(Bayern Munich)	4	Linderoth
5	Ferdinand	(Leeds United)	5	Jakobsson
6	Campbell	(Arsenal)	6	Lucic
7	Beckham*	(Man Utd) replaced by Dyer	7	Alexandersson
8	Scholes	(Man Utd)	8	Ljungberg
9	Vassell	(Aston Villa) replaced by Cole J	9	Allback
10	Owen	(Liverpool)	10	Larsson
11	Heskey	(Liverpool)	11	Svensson

Crowd: 52,721

England scorer: Campbell

Comments: Sol Campbell chose an excellent time to register his only England goal to give his team a half-time lead, but the Swedes typically fought back to earn a share of the points.

ENGLAND 1 Argentina 0; in Sapporo;
Friday 7th June 2002 (World Cup finals)

1	Seaman	(Arsenal)	1	Cavallero
2	Mills	(Leeds United)	2	Placente
3	Cole	(Arsenal)	3	Pochettino
4	Hargreaves	(Bayern Munich) replaced by Sinclair	4	Samuel
5	Ferdinand	(Leeds United)	5	Simone
6	Campbell	(Arsenal)	6	Zanetti
7	Beckham*	(Man Utd)	7	Gonzalez
8	Scholes	(Man Utd)	8	Sorin
9	Heskey	(Liverpool) replaced by Sheringham	9	Ortega
10	Owen	(Liverpool) replaced by Bridge	10	Veron
11	Butt	(Man Utd)	11	Batistuta

Crowd: 35,927

England scorer: Beckham (Pen)

Comments: The England captain overcame a pre-World Cup metatarsal injury to settle an old score with his Argentine foes. Eriksson's team were now on course for the knockout stages.

ENGLAND 0 Nigeria 0; in Osaka;
Wednesday 12th June 2002 (World Cup finals)

1 Seaman	(Arsenal)	1	Enyeama
2 Mills	(Leeds United)	2	Yobo
3 Cole	(Arsenal) replaced by Bridge	3	Okoronkwo
4 Butt	(Man Utd)	4	Udeze
5 Ferdinand	(Leeds United)	5	Christopher
6 Campbell	(Arsenal)	6	Sodje
7 Beckham*	(Man Utd)	7	Okocha
8 Scholes	(Man Utd)	8	Opabunmi
9 Heskey	(Liverpool) replaced by Sheringham	9	Akwuegbu
10 Owen	(Liverpool) replaced by Vassell	10	Obiorah
11 Sinclair	(West Ham Utd)	11	Aghahowa

Crowd: 44,864

Comments: Two clean sheets in consecutive matches for David Seaman was encouraging, but two wins in twelve matches didn't suggest England were credible candidates for World Cup glory.

ENGLAND 3 Denmark 0; in Niigata;
Saturday 15th June 2002 (World Cup finals)

1 Seaman	(Arsenal)	1	Sorensen
2 Mills	(Leeds United)	2	Tofting
3 Cole	(Arsenal)	3	Henriksen
4 Butt	(Man Utd)	4	Laursen
5 Ferdinand	(Leeds United)	5	Helveg
6 Campbell	(Arsenal)	6	Gravesen
7 Beckham*	(Man Utd)	7	Gronkjaer
8 Scholes	(Man Utd) replaced by Dyer	8	Tomasson
9 Heskey	(Liverpool) replaced by Sheringham	9	Sand
10 Owen	(Liverpool) replaced by Fowler	10	Jensen
11 Sinclair	(West Ham Utd)	11	Rommedahl

Crowd: 40,582

England scorers: Ferdinand, Owen, Heskey

Comments: Rio Ferdinand opened his England goals account and gave England a flying start. By half time, this knock-out contest was no longer a contest. This was Robbie Fowler's last cap.

ENGLAND 1 Brazil 2; in Shizuoka;
Friday 21st June 2002 (World Cup finals)

1 Seaman	(Arsenal)	1	Marcos
2 Mills	(Leeds United)	2	Lucio
3 Cole	(Arsenal) replaced by Sheringham	3	Edmilson
4 Butt	(Man Utd)	4	Junior
5 Ferdinand	(Leeds United)	5	Cafu
6 Campbell	(Arsenal)	6	Silva
7 Beckham*	(Man Utd)	7	Kleberson
8 Scholes	(Man Utd)	8	Carlos
9 Heskey	(Liverpool)	9	Ronaldinho
10 Owen	(Liverpool) replaced by Vassell	10	Rivaldo
11 Sinclair	(West Ham Utd) replaced by Dyer	11	Ronaldo

Crowd: 47,436

England scorer: Owen

Comments: Michael Owen gave England the lead, but then they shot themselves in the foot as David Seaman conceded a stupendous goal from Ronaldinho in another quarter-finals exit.

ENGLAND 1 Portugal 1; at Leeds;
Saturday 7th September 2002

1 James	(West Ham Utd)	1	Baia
2 Mills	(Leeds United) replaced by Hargreaves	2	Beto
3 Cole A	(Arsenal) replaced by Bridge	3	Meira
4 Gerrard	(Liverpool) replaced by Dunn	4	Couto
5 Ferdinand	(Man Utd) replaced by Woodgate	5	Conceicao
6 Southgate	(Middlesbrough)	6	Petit
7 Bowyer	(Leeds United) replaced by Sinclair	7	Costa
8 Butt	(Man Utd) replaced by Murphy	8	Jorge
9 Smith	(Man Utd)	9	Figo
10 Owen*	(Liverpool) replaced by Cole J	10	Simao
11 Heskey	(Liverpool)	11	Pauleta

Crowd: 40,058

England scorer: Smith

Comments: Alan Smith scored his only England goal while Lee Bowyer and Blackburn's David Dunn won their only caps as England maintained their winless ways.

Slovakia 1 ENGLAND 2; in Bratislava;
Saturday 12th October 2002 (European Championship)

1	Konig	1 Seaman	(Arsenal)
2	Petras	2 Neville	(Man Utd)
3	Karhan	3 Cole	(Arsenal)
4	Hlinka	4 Gerrard	(Liverpool) replaced by Dyer
5	Dzurik	5 Woodgate	(Leeds United)
6	Zeman	6 Southgate	(Middlesbrough)
7	Pinte	7 Beckham*	(Man Utd)
8	Nemeth	8 Scholes	(Man Utd)
9	Leitner	9 Heskey	(Liverpool) replaced by Smith
10	Janocko	10 Owen	(Liverpool) replaced by Hargreaves
11	Vittek	11 Butt	(Man Utd)

Crowd: 30,000

England scorers: Beckham, Owen

Comments: Having trailed at the interval, the visitors relied on their captain and his understudy captain to rescue them and bag maximum points in this opening qualifying encounter.

ENGLAND 2 Macedonia 2; at Southampton;
Wednesday 16th October 2002 (European Championship)

1	Seaman	(Arsenal)	1	Milosevski
2	Neville	(Man Utd)	2	Popov
3	Cole	(Arsenal)	3	Petrov
4	Gerrard	(Liverpool) replaced by Butt	4	Sedloski
5	Woodgate	(Leeds United)	5	Vasoski
6	Campbell	(Arsenal)	6	Sumulikosko
7	Beckham*	(Man Utd)	7	Trajanov
8	Scholes	(Man Utd)	8	Mitreski
9	Smith	(Leeds United)	9	Toleski
10	Owen	(Liverpool)	10	Sakiri
11	Bridge	(Southampton) replaced by Vassell	11	Grozdanovski

Crowd: 32,095

England scorers: Beckham, Gerrard

Comments: The away team twice took the lead as all goals came in the first half. Alan Smith got himself sent off. This match brought to an end David Seaman's England career, after 75 caps.

ENGLAND 1 Australia 3; at Upton Park;
Wednesday 12th February 2003

1	James	(West Ham Utd) replaced by Robinson	1	Schwarzer
2	Neville	(Man Utd) replaced by Mills	2	Moore
3	Cole	(Arsenal) replaced by Konchesky	3	Neill
4	Lampard	(Chelsea) replaced by Murphy	4	Okon
5	Ferdinand	(Man Utd) replaced by Brown	5	Popovic
6	Campbell	(Arsenal) replaced by King	6	Emerton
7	Beckham*	(Man Utd) replaced by Hargreaves	7	Kewell
8	Scholes	(Man Utd) replaced by Jenas	8	Lazaridis
9	Beattie	(Southampton) replaced by Jeffers	9	Skoko
10	Owen	(Liverpool) replaced by Rooney	10	Chipperfield
11	Dyer	(Newcastle Utd) replaced by Vassell	11	Viduka

Crowd: 34,590

England scorer: Jeffers

Comments: Franny Jeffers scored on his debut but this was an embarrassing setback for England. New caps were also awarded to Beattie, Jenas, Konchesky, Robinson, and Wayne Rooney.

Liechtenstein 0 ENGLAND 2; in Vaduz;
Saturday 29th March 2003 (European Championship)

1	Jehle	1	James	(West Ham Utd)
2	Tesler	2	Neville	(Man Utd)
3	D'Elia	3	Bridge	(Southampton)
4	Hasler	4	Gerrard	(Liverpool) replaced by Butt
5	Stocklasa	5	Ferdinand	(Man Utd)
6	Stocklasa	6	Southgate	(Middlesbrough)
7	Zech	7	Beckham*	(Man Utd) replaced by Murphy
8	Buchel	8	Scholes	(Man Utd)
9	Beck	9	Heskey	(Liverpool) replaced by Rooney
10	Frick	10	Owen	(Liverpool)
11	Gerster	11	Dyer	(Newcastle Utd)

Crowd: 3,548

England scorers: Owen, Beckham

Comments: One goal in each half yielded a far from convincing scoreline, but England at least returned to winning ways, albeit in a mismatch that doubled as a qualifying fixture.

ENGLAND 2 Turkey 0; at Sunderland;
Wednesday 2nd April 2003 (European Championship)

1	James	(West Ham Utd)	1	Recber	
2	Neville	(Man Utd)	2	Belozoglou	
3	Bridge	(Southampton)	3	Korkmaz	
4	Gerrard	(Liverpool)	4	Arkyel	
5	Ferdinand	(Man Utd)	5	Ozalan	
6	Campbell	(Arsenal)	6	Penbe	
7	Beckham*	(Man Utd)	7	Buruk	
8	Scholes	(Man Utd)	8	Kerimoglou	
9	Rooney	(Everton) replaced by Dyer	9	Mansiz	
10	Owen	(Liverpool) replaced by Vassell	10	Basturk	
11	Butt	(Man Utd)	11	Kahveci	

Crowd: 47,667

England scorers: Vassell, Beckham (Pen)

Comments: Two goals in the last fifteen minutes decided the outcome of this group match. Turkey were no longer England's whipping boys, having recently reached the World Cup semi-finals.

South Africa 1 ENGLAND 2; in Durban;
Thursday 22nd May 2003

1	Baloyi	1	James	(West Ham Utd) replaced by Robinson
2	Mabizela	2	Mills	(Leeds United)
3	Radebe	3	Neville	(Man Utd)
4	Mokoena	4	Gerrard	(Liverpool) replaced by Barry
5	Molefe	5	Ferdinand	(Man Utd) replaced by Upson
6	Sibaya	6	Southgate	(Middlesbrough)
7	Buckley	7	Beckham*	(Man Utd) replaced by Jenas
8	Mokoena	8	Scholes	(Man Utd) replaced by Cole
9	Frederiks	9	Heskey	(Liverpool) replaced by Vassell
10	Bartlett	10	Owen	(Liverpool)
11	McCarthy	11	Sinclair	(West Ham Utd) replaced by Lampard

Crowd: 48,000

England scorers: Southgate, Heskey

Comments: In the twilight of his career, Gareth Southgate managed to score inside 40 seconds of this friendly! Although Benni McCarthy equalised from a penalty, Heskey later restored the lead.

ENGLAND 2 Serbia & Montenegro 1; at Leicester; Tuesday 3rd June 2003

1 James	(West Ham Utd)	1	Jevric
2 Mills	(Leeds United) replaced by Carragher	2	Mirkovic
3 Cole A	(Arsenal) replaced by Bridge	3	Vidic
4 Gerrard	(Liverpool) replaced by Hargreaves	4	Stefanovic
5 Upson	(Birmingham City) replaced by Barry	5	Markovic
6 Southgate	(Middlesbrough) replaced by Terry	6	Duljac
7 Lampard	(Chelsea) replaced by Cole J	7	Kovacevic
8 Scholes	(Man Utd) replaced by Jenas	8	Dmitrovic
9 Heskey	(Liverpool) replaced by Vassell	9	Ilic
10 Owen*	(Liverpool) replaced by Rooney	10	Vukic
11 Neville	(Man Utd) replaced by Beattie	11	Jestrovic

Crowd: 30,900

England scorers: Gerrard, Cole J

Comments: Joe Cole netted a late winner after both sides had scored in the first half. This friendly was the debut for John Terry and the first home appearance for Matthew Upson.

ENGLAND 2 Slovakia 1; at Middlesbrough; Wednesday 11th June 2003 (European Championship)

1 James	(West Ham Utd)	1	Konig
2 Mills	(Leeds United) replaced by Hargreaves	2	Petras
3 Cole	(Arsenal)	3	Hanek
4 Gerrard	(Liverpool)	4	Zeman
5 Upson	(Birmingham City)	5	Zabavnik
6 Southgate	(Middlesbrough)	6	Demo
7 Lampard	(Chelsea)	7	Labant
8 Scholes	(Man Utd)	8	Nemeth
9 Rooney	(Everton) replaced by Vassell	9	Michalik
10 Owen*	(Liverpool)	10	Janocko
11 Neville	(Man Utd)	11	Vittek

Crowd: 35,000

England scorer: Owen (2)

Comments: This was a repeat of the scoreline from the previous year as England relied on a second half double from their captain to rescue them after they had conceded the half time lead.

ENGLAND 3 Croatia 1; at Ipswich;
Wednesday 20th August 2003

1 James	(West Ham Utd) replaced by Robinson	1 Pletikosa
2 Neville	(Man Utd) replaced by Mills	2 Simic
3 Cole A	(Arsenal) replaced by Bridge	3 Simunic
4 Gerrard	(Liverpool) replaced by Murphy	4 Kovac
5 Ferdinand	(Man Utd) replaced by Upson	5 Zivkovic
6 Terry	(Chelsea)	6 Tomas
7 Beckham*	(Real Madrid) replaced by Cole J	7 Rapaic
8 Scholes	(Man Utd) replaced by Dyer	8 Leko
9 Heskey	(Liverpool) replaced by Beattie	9 Kovac
10 Owen	(Liverpool) replaced by Sinclair	10 Maric
11 Butt	(Man Utd) replaced by Lampard	11 Olic

Crowd: 28,700

England scorers: Beckham (Pen), Owen, Lampard

Comments: Frank Lampard recorded his first England goal when he restored the home team's two goal advantage with less than ten minutes remaining. This was Trevor Sinclair's last cap.

Macedonia 1 ENGLAND 2; in Skopje;
Saturday 6th September 2003 (European Championship)

1 Milosevski	1 James	(West Ham Utd)	
2 Stavrevski	2 Neville G	(Man Utd)	
3 Grozdanovski	3 Cole	(Arsenal)	
4 Pandev	4 Hargreaves	(Bayern Munich)	
5 Mitreski	5 Terry	(Chelsea)	
6 Stojanski	6 Campbell	(Arsenal)	
7 Trajanov	7 Beckham*	(Real Madrid)	
8 Sumulikoski	8 Lampard	(Chelsea) replaced by Heskey	
9 Hristov	9 Rooney	(Everton) replaced by Neville P	
10 Sakiri	10 Owen	(Liverpool) replaced by Dyer	
11 Naumoski	11 Butt	(Man Utd)	

Crowd: 20,500

England scorers: Rooney, Beckham (Pen)

Comments: Yet again England were in arrears at half time. However, Wayne Rooney equalised with his first international goal before David Beckham slotted home a penalty for maximum points.

ENGLAND 2 Liechtenstein 0; at Old Trafford;
Wednesday 10th September 2003 (European Championship)

1	James	(West Ham Utd)		1	Jehle
2	Neville G	(Man Utd)		2	Tesler
3	Bridge	(Chelsea)		3	Stocklasa
4	Gerrard	(Liverpool) replaced by Hargreaves		4	Hasler
5	Terry	(Chelsea)		5	Ritter
6	Upson	(Birmingham City)		6	Stocklasa
7	Beckham*	(Real Madrid) replaced by Neville P		7	Beck
8	Lampard	(Chelsea)		8	Gerster
9	Rooney	(Everton) replaced by Cole		9	D'Elia
10	Owen	(Liverpool)		10	Frick
11	Beattie	(Southampton)		11	Burgmeier

Crowd: 64,931

England scorers: Owen, Rooney

Comments: The home team again made hard work of the minnows of Liechtenstein who kept a clean sheet in the first half, but they had now scored at least twice in eight successive matches.

Turkey 0 ENGLAND 0; in Istanbul;
Saturday 11th October 2003 (European Championship)

1	Recber	1	James	(West Ham Utd)
2	Uzulmez	2	Neville	(Man Utd)
3	Korkmaz	3	Cole	(Arsenal)
4	Arkyel	4	Gerrard	(Liverpool)
5	Ozalan	5	Terry	(Chelsea)
6	Belozoglou	6	Campbell	(Arsenal)
7	Buruk	7	Beckham*	(Real Madrid)
8	Kerimoglou	8	Scholes	(Man Utd) replaced by Lampard
9	Sukur	9	Rooney	(Everton) replaced by Dyer
10	Kahveci	10	Heskey	(Liverpool) replaced by Vassell
11	Yalcin	11	Butt	(Man Utd)

Crowd: 45,000

Comments: A second successive shut-out from David James helped to ensure England's safe passage to the European Championship finals in spite of a missed penalty from Beckham.

ENGLAND 2 Denmark 3; at Old Trafford;
Sunday 16th November 2003

1	James	(West Ham Utd) replaced by Robinson	1	Sorensen
2	Neville G	(Man Utd) replaced by Johnson	2	Wieghorst
3	Cole A	(Arsenal) replaced by Bridge	3	Henriksen
4	Butt	(Man Utd) replaced by Neville P	4	Nielsen
5	Terry	(Chelsea)	5	Jensen
6	Upson	(Birmingham City)	6	Helveg
7	Beckham*	(Real Madrid) replaced by Jenas	7	Gravesen
8	Lampard	(Chelsea)	8	Gronkjaer
9	Rooney	(Everton) replaced by Parker	9	Rommedahl
10	Heskey	(Liverpool) replaced by Beattie	10	Jorgensen
11	Cole J	(Chelsea) replaced by Murphy	11	Sand

Crowd: 64,159

England scorers: Rooney, Cole J

Comments: Erratic England scored twice in the first 10 minutes but Denmark were able to avenge their World Cup defeat of last year. Glen Johnson and Charlton's Scott Parker won their first caps.

Portugal 1 ENGLAND 1; in Faro;
Wednesday 18th February 2004

1	Ricardo	1	James	(Man City)
2	Ferreira	2	Neville	(Man Utd) replaced by Mills
3	Rui Jorge	3	Cole A	(Arsenal) replaced by Bridge
4	Andrade	4	Butt	(Man Utd) replaced by Hargreaves
5	Couto	5	King	(Tottenham)
6	Costinha	6	Southgate	(Middlesbrough)
7	Figo	7	Beckham*	(Real Madrid) replaced by Jenas
8	Petit	8	Scholes	(Man Utd) replaced by Cole J
9	Pauleta	9	Rooney	(Everton) replaced by Smith
10	Costa	10	Owen	(Liverpool) replaced by Heskey
11	Simao	11	Lampard	(Chelsea) replaced by Dyer

Crowd: 27,000

England scorer: King

Comments: Both teams were preparing for the European Championship finals, hosted by Portugal. Ledley King gave England the lead before Pauleta equalised. This was Danny Mills's last cap.

Sweden 1 ENGLAND 0; in Gothenburg;
Wednesday 31st March 2004

1 Isaksson	1 James	(Man City)
2 Lucic	2 Carragher	(Liverpool)
3 Mellberg	3 Neville	(Man Utd)
4 Mjallby	4 Gerrard*	(Liverpool) replaced by Heskey
5 Edman	5 Terry	(Chelsea) replaced by Southgate
6 Andersson	6 Woodgate	(Newcastle Utd) replaced by Gardner
7 Nilsson	7 Hargreaves	(Bayern Munich) replaced by Jenas
8 Svensson	8 Butt	(Man Utd) replaced by Parker
9 Elmander	9 Rooney	(Everton) replaced by Smith
10 Ibrahimovic	10 Vassell	(Aston Villa) replaced by Defoe
11 Wilhelmsson	11 Thompson	(Glasgow Celtic) replaced by Cole

Crowd: 40,464

Comments: Ibrahimovic scored the only goal just after half time. This was the debut of Jermain Defoe and the last cap for Gareth Southgate, while Gardner and Thompson won their only caps.

ENGLAND 1 Japan 1; at Manchester City;
Tuesday 1st June 2004

1 James	(Man City)	1 Narazaki
2 Neville G	(Man Utd) replaced by Neville P	2 Nakazawa
3 Cole A	(Arsenal)	3 Tsuboi
4 Gerrard	(Liverpool) replaced by Hargreaves	4 Miyamoto
5 Terry	(Chelsea) replaced by King	5 Kaji
6 Campbell	(Arsenal)	6 Inamoto
7 Beckham*	(Real Madrid) replaced by Butt	7 Ono
8 Scholes	(Man Utd) replaced by Heskey	8 Santos
9 Rooney	(Everton) replaced by Vassell	9 Kubo
10 Owen	(Liverpool) replaced by Dyer	10 Tamada
11 Lampard	(Chelsea) replaced by Cole J	11 Nakamura

Crowd: 38,581

England scorer: Owen

Comments: Michael Owen gave the home team a half-time lead, but Shinji Ono equalised soon after the break. This was hardly the most impressive of pre-tournament warm-up results.

ENGLAND 6 Iceland 1; at Manchester City; Saturday 5th June 2004

1	Robinson	(Tottenham) replaced by Walker	1 Arason
2	Neville G	(Man Utd) replaced by Neville P	2 Ingimarsson
3	Cole A	(Arsenal) replaced by Bridge	3 Sigurdsson
4	Gerrard	(Liverpool) replaced by Hargreaves	4 Gudjonsson
5	Carragher	(Liverpool) replaced by Defoe	5 Marteinsson
6	Campbell	(Arsenal) replaced by King	6 Helguson
7	Beckham*	(Real Madrid) replaced by Butt	7 Hreidarsson
8	Scholes	(Man Utd) replaced by Heskey	8 Gretarsson
9	Rooney	(Everton) replaced by Vassell	9 Gudjohnsen
10	Owen	(Liverpool) replaced by Dyer	10 Gudjonsson
11	Lampard	(Chelsea) replaced by Cole J	11 Sigurdssson

Crowd: 43,500

England scorers: Lampard, Rooney (2), Vassell (2), Bridge

Comments: The hosts cruised into a 3–1 interval lead courtesy of a Wayne Rooney double. Wayne Bridge also recorded his only England goal as Eriksson's team produced a goals spree.

ENGLAND 1 France 2; in Lisbon; Sunday 13th June 2004 (European Championship)

1	James	(Man City)	1 Barthez
2	Neville	(Man Utd)	2 Lizarazu
3	Cole	(Arsenal)	3 Silvestre
4	Gerrard	(Liverpool)	4 Vieira
5	King	(Tottenham)	5 Gallas
6	Campbell	(Arsenal)	6 Makelele
7	Beckham*	(Real Madrid)	7 Pires
8	Scholes	(Man Utd) replaced by Heskey	8 Thuram
9	Rooney	(Everton) replaced by Hargreaves	9 Zidane
10	Owen	(Liverpool) replaced by Vassell	10 Henry
11	Lampard	(Chelsea)	11 Trezeguet

Crowd: 62,487

England scorer: Lampard

Comments: Frank Lampard headed England into a half-time lead but after Beckham's penalty was saved, Zidane spoiled the party with two goals in the dying minutes including a decisive penalty.

ENGLAND 3 Switzerland 0; in Coimbra; Thursday 17th June 2004 (European Championship)

#	England	Club	#	Switzerland
1	James	(Man City)	1	Stiel
2	Neville	(Man Utd)	2	Haas
3	Cole	(Arsenal)	3	Yakin
4	Gerrard	(Liverpool)	4	Muller
5	Terry	(Chelsea)	5	Spycher
6	Campbell	(Arsenal)	6	Huggel
7	Beckham*	(Real Madrid)	7	Wicky
8	Scholes	(Man Utd) replaced by Hargreaves	8	Celestini
9	Rooney	(Everton) replaced by Dyer	9	Yakin
10	Owen	(Liverpool) replaced by Vassell	10	Frei
11	Lampard	(Chelsea)	11	Chapuisat

Crowd: 28,214

England scorers: Rooney (2), Gerrard

Comments: Wayne Rooney scored in each half in stifling heat as England made sure there would be no repeat of their 1996 slip-up against the Swiss. Steven Gerrard added the third goal.

ENGLAND 4 Croatia 2; in Lisbon; Monday 21st June 2004 (European Championship)

#	England	Club	#	Croatia
1	James	(Man City)	1	Butina
2	Neville G	(Man Utd)	2	Simunic
3	Cole	(Arsenal)	3	Tudor
4	Gerrard	(Liverpool)	4	Zivkovic
5	Terry	(Chelsea)	5	Rapajic
6	Campbell	(Arsenal)	6	Prso
7	Beckham*	(Real Madrid)	7	Kovac
8	Scholes	(Man Utd) replaced by King	8	Sokota
9	Rooney	(Everton) replaced by Vassell	9	Simic
10	Owen	(Liverpool)	10	Rosso
11	Lampard	(Chelsea) replaced by Neville P	11	Kovac

Crowd: 57,047

England scorers: Scholes, Rooney (2), Lampard

Comments: England were galvanised by conceding an early goal. They responded with two shortly before half time. Rooney scored in each half again as England progressed to a quarter final.

Portugal 2 ENGLAND 2 [After extra time]; in Lisbon; Thursday 24th June 2004 (European Championship)

1	Ricardo	1	James	(Man City)
2	Miguel	2	Neville G	(Man Utd)
3	Andrade	3	Cole	(Arsenal)
4	Carvalho	4	Gerrard	(Liverpool) replaced by Hargreaves
5	Valente	5	Terry	(Chelsea)
6	Deco	6	Campbell	(Arsenal)
7	Costinha	7	Beckham*	(Real Madrid)
8	Maniche	8	Scholes	(Man Utd) replaced by Neville P
9	Ronaldo	9	Rooney	(Everton) replaced by Vassell
10	Figo	10	Owen	(Liverpool)
11	Gomes	11	Lampard	(Chelsea)

Crowd: 62,564

England scorers: Owen, Lampard

Comments: England led for 80 minutes after Owen's early goal. Helga Postiga came off the bench to net a late equaliser. It took penalties to separate the teams. England again were second best.

ENGLAND 3 Ukraine 0; at Newcastle; Wednesday 18th August 2004

1	James	(Man City)	1	Shovkovsky
2	Neville	(Man Utd) replaced by Johnson	2	Nesmachny
3	Cole	(Arsenal) replaced by Carragher	3	Federov
4	Gerrard	(Liverpool) replaced by Dyer	4	Tymoschuk
5	Terry	(Chelsea)	5	Yezerskyi
6	King	(Tottenham)	6	Shelayev
7	Beckham*	(Real Madrid)	7	Shevchenko
8	Lampard	(Chelsea) replaced by Jenas	8	Rusol
9	Smith	(Man Utd) replaced by Defoe	9	Husev
10	Owen	(Real Madrid)	10	Rotan
11	Butt	(Newcastle Utd) replaced by Wright-Phillips	11	Vorobey

Crowd: 35,387

England scorers: Beckham, Owen, Wright-Phillips

Comments: Shaun Wright-Phillips came off the bench to score within 20 minutes of his debut as free-scoring England maintained their impressive form from their exploits in Portugal.

Austria 2 ENGLAND 2; in Vienna;
Saturday 4th September 2004 (World Cup qualifier)

1	Manninger	1	James	(Man City)
2	Standfest	2	Neville	(Man Utd)
3	Hiden	3	Cole A	(Arsenal)
4	Stranzl	4	Gerrard	(Liverpool) replaced by Carragher
5	Pogatetz	5	Terry	(Chelsea)
6	Aufhauser	6	King	(Tottenham)
7	Sick	7	Beckham*	(Real Madrid)
8	Kuhbauer	8	Lampard	(Chelsea)
9	Haas	9	Smith	(Man Utd) replaced by Defoe
10	Ivanschitz	10	Owen	(Real Madrid)
11	Glieder	11	Bridge	(Chelsea) replaced by Cole J

Crowd: 48,500

England scorers: Lampard, Gerrard

Comments: David 'Calamity' James conceded two goals which cancelled out the lead which Steven Gerrard had extended just after the hour mark, following after Frank Lampard's first-half effort.

Poland 1 ENGLAND 2; in Chorzow;
Wednesday 8th September 2004 (World Cup qualifier)

1	Dudek	1	Robinson	(Tottenham)
2	Mila	2	Neville	(Man Utd) replaced by Carragher
3	Rzasa	3	Cole	(Arsenal)
4	Zewlakow	4	Gerrard	(Liverpool)
5	Glowacki	5	Terry	(Chelsea)
6	Bak	6	King	(Tottenham)
7	Rasiak	7	Beckham*	(Real Madrid) replaced by Hargreaves
8	Krzynowek	8	Lampard	(Chelsea)
9	Zurawski	9	Defoe	(Tottenham) replaced by Dyer
10	Lewandowski	10	Owen	(Real Madrid)
11	Kosowski	11	Bridge	(Chelsea)

Crowd: 38,000

England scorers: Defoe, Glowacki (OG)

Comments: Jermain Defoe registered his first England goal to give the visitors the interval lead. Although Poland soon equalised after the break, England went on to accumulate maximum points.

ENGLAND 2 Wales 0; at Old Trafford;
Saturday 9th October 2004 (World Cup qualifier)

1	Robinson	(Tottenham)	1	Jones
2	Neville	(Man Utd)	2	Delaney
3	Cole	(Arsenal)	3	Thatcher
4	Butt	(Newcastle Utd)	4	Pembridge
5	Ferdinand	(Man Utd)	5	Gabbidon
6	Campbell	(Arsenal)	6	Koumas
7	Beckham*	(Real Madrid) replaced by Hargreaves	7	Davies
8	Lampard	(Chelsea)	8	Bellamy
9	Rooney	(Man Utd) replaced by King	9	Hartson
10	Owen	(Real Madrid)	10	Speed
11	Defoe	(Tottenham) replaced by Smith	11	Giggs

Crowd: 65,224

England scorers: Lampard, Beckham

Comments: Frank Lampard netted an early goal against the neighbours, but it took a David Beckham effort fifteen minutes from time to break the Welsh resistance.

Azerbaijan 0 ENGLAND 1; in Baku;
Wednesday 13th October 2004 (World Cup qualifier)

1	Hasanzade	1	Robinson	(Tottenham)
2	Amirbekov	2	Neville	(Man Utd)
3	Hajiyev	3	Cole A	(Arsenal)
4	Shukurov	4	Butt	(Newcastle Utd)
5	Guliyev	5	Ferdinand	(Man Utd)
6	Guliyev	6	Campbell	(Arsenal)
7	Sadygov	7	Jenas	(Newcastle Utd) replaced by Wright-Phillips
8	Kerimov	8	Lampard	(Chelsea)
9	Aliyev	9	Rooney	(Man Utd) replaced by Cole J
10	Ponomarev	10	Owen*	(Real Madrid)
11	Nabiyev	11	Defoe	(Tottenham) replaced by Smith

Crowd: 15,000

England scorer: Owen

Comments: Michael Owen scored the only goal halfway through the first half. He was captain in the enforced absence of Beckham who appeared to engineer his suspension in the Wales match.

Spain 1 ENGLAND 0; in Madrid;
Wednesday 17th November 2004

1	Casillas		
2	Salgado		
3	del Horno		
4	Alonso		
5	Marchena		
6	Juanito		
7	Raul		
8	Xavi		
9	Torres		
10	Joaquin		
11	Reyes		

1	Robinson	(Tottenham)
2	Neville	(Man Utd)
3	Cole	(Arsenal) replaced by Defoe
4	Butt	(Newcastle Utd)
5	Ferdinand	Man Utd) replaced by Carragher
6	Terry	(Chelsea) replaced by Upson
7	Beckham*	(Real Madrid) replaced by Jenas
8	Lampard	(Chelsea) replaced by Wright-Phillips
9	Rooney	(Man Utd) replaced by Smith
10	Owen	(Real Madrid)
11	Bridge	(Chelsea)

Crowd: 48,000

Comments: Perhaps distracted by the racist abuse from the Spanish fans, England were thoroughly outplayed. The hosts were rewarded with an early lead from Asier del Horno.

ENGLAND 0 Holland 0; at Villa Park;
Wednesday 9th February 2005

1	Robinson	(Tottenham)
2	Neville	(Man Utd)
3	Cole	(Arsenal)
4	Gerrard	(Liverpool) replaced by Dyer
5	Carragher	(Liverpool)
6	Brown	(Man Utd)
7	Beckham*	(Real Madrid) replaced by Jenas
8	Lampard	(Chelsea) replaced by Hargreaves
9	Rooney	(Man Utd) replaced by Johnson
10	Owen	(Real Madrid)
11	Wright-Phillips	(Man City) replaced by Downing

1	van der Sar
2	Kromkamp
3	Boulahrouz
4	Mathijsen
5	van Bronckhorst
6	Heitinga
7	Castelen
8	Landzaat
9	Makaay
10	van der Vaart
11	Kuyt

Crowd: 40,705

Comments: Substitutes Stewart Downing of Middlesbrough and Andy Johnson of Crystal Palace made their debut in this winter stalemate against the highly-rated Dutch.

ENGLAND 4 Northern Ireland 0; at Old Trafford; Saturday 26th March 2005 (World Cup qualifier)

1 Robinson	(Tottenham)	1 Taylor
2 Neville	(Man Utd)	2 Baird
3 Cole A	(Arsenal)	3 Capaldi
4 Gerrard	(Liverpool) replaced by Dyer	4 Hughes
5 Ferdinand	(Man Utd)	5 Murdock
6 Terry	(Chelsea)	6 Johnson
7 Beckham*	(Real Madrid) replaced by Hargreaves	7 Gillespie
8 Lampard	(Chelsea)	8 Doherty
9 Rooney	(Man Utd) replaced by Defoe	9 Healy
10 Owen	(Real Madrid)	10 Whitley
11 Cole J	(Chelsea)	11 Elliott

Crowd: 65,239

England scorers: Cole J, Owen, Baird (OG), Lampard

Comments: Maik Taylor managed to keep England at bay until half time, but then the floodgates opened with four goals in 15 minutes. Lawrie Sanchez's team sought revenge in September.

ENGLAND 2 Azerbaijan 0; at Newcastle; Wednesday 30th March 2005 (World Cup qualifier)

1 Robinson	(Tottenham)	1 Kramarenko
2 Neville	(Man Utd)	2 Amirbekov
3 Cole A	(Arsenal)	3 Hajiyev
4 Gerrard	(Liverpool)	4 Hashimov
5 Ferdinand	(Man Utd) replaced by King	5 Bahshiyev
6 Terry	(Chelsea)	6 Abdurakhmanov
7 Beckham*	(Real Madrid) replaced by Defoe	7 Melikov
8 Lampard	(Chelsea)	8 Kerimov
9 Rooney	(Man Utd) replaced by Dyer	9 Gurbanov
10 Owen	(Real Madrid)	10 Sadygov
11 Cole J	(Chelsea)	11 Nabiyev

Crowd: 49,046

England scorers: Gerrard, Beckham

Comments: Both goals came early in the second half as an unchanged England team continued to cruise towards qualification for the World Cup finals in Germany the following year.

USA 1 ENGLAND 2; in Chicago;
Saturday 28th May 2005

1 Keller	1 James	(Man City)
2 Cherundolo	2 Johnson G	(Chelsea)
3 Gibbs	3 Cole A	(Arsenal) replaced by Defoe
4 Pope	4 Carrick	(Tottenham)
5 Vanney	5 Brown	(Man Utd)
6 Ralston	6 Campbell*	(Arsenal) replaced by Knight
7 Zavagnin	7 Jenas	(Newcastle Utd)
8 Dempsey	8 Richardson	(Man Utd) replaced by Neville
9 McBride	9 Smith	(Man Utd)
10 Donovan	10 Johnson A	(Crystal Palace) replaced by Young
11 Wolff	11 Cole J	(Chelsea)

Crowd: 47,637

England scorer: Richardson (2)

Comments: Kieran Richardson netted two first-half goals on his debut, then Dempsey scored a consolation goal. First caps were also awarded to Fulham's Zat Knight and Charlton's Luke Young.

ENGLAND 3 Columbia 2; in New York;
Tuesday 31st May 2005

1 James	(Man City) replaced by Green	1 Mondragon
2 Neville	(Man Utd)	2 Benitez
3 Cole A	(Arsenal)	3 Palacio
4 Carrick	(Tottenham)	4 Yepes
5 Johnson	(Chelsea)	5 Restrepo
6 Knight	(Fulham)	6 Viafara
7 Beckham*	(Real Madrid) replaced by Richardson	7 Soto
8 Jenas	(Newcastle Utd)	8 Rey
9 Crouch	(Southampton) replaced by Defoe	9 Hurtado
10 Owen	(Real Madrid) replaced by Smith	10 Angel
11 Cole J	(Chelsea) replaced by Young	11 Perea

Crowd: 58,000

England scorer: Owen (3)

Comments: Michael Owen stole the show with a hat-trick on the debut of big Peter Crouch. This was the last cap for Zat Knight and the only appearance for Norwich City's Robert Green thus far.

Denmark 4 ENGLAND 1; in Copenhagen;
Wednesday 17th August 2005

1 Sorensen	1 Robinson	(Tottenham) replaced by James
2 Poulsen	2 Neville	(Man Utd) replaced by Johnson
3 Agger	3 Cole A	(Arsenal)
4 Nielsen	4 Gerrard	(Liverpool) replaced by Jenas
5 Jensen	5 Ferdinand	(Man Utd)
6 Priske	6 Terry	(Chelsea) replaced by Carragher
7 Gravesen	7 Beckham*	(Real Madrid)
8 Gronkjaer	8 Lampard	(Chelsea) replaced by Hargreaves
9 Tomasson	9 Rooney	(Man Utd)
10 Jorgensen	10 Defoe	(Tottenham) replaced by Owen
11 Jensen	11 Cole J	(Chelsea)

Crowd: 41,438

England scorer: Rooney

Comments: The hapless David James came on at half time and then proceeded to concede four goals. It wasn't his fault. England were poor. It was their heaviest defeat since Wales in 1980.

Wales 0 ENGLAND 1; in Cardiff;
Saturday 3rd September 2005 (World Cup qualifier)

1 Coyne	1 Robinson	(Tottenham)
2 Duffy	2 Young	(Charlton Athletic)
3 Ricketts	3 Cole A	(Arsenal)
4 Gabbidon	4 Gerrard	(Liverpool) replaced by Richardson
5 Page	5 Ferdinand	(Man Utd)
6 Partridge	6 Carragher	(Liverpool)
7 Fletcher	7 Beckham*	(Real Madrid)
8 Robinson	8 Lampard	(Chelsea)
9 Hartson	9 Rooney	(Man Utd)
10 Davies	10 Wright-Phillips	(Chelsea) replaced by Defoe
11 Giggs	11 Cole J	(Chelsea) replaced by Hargreaves

Crowd: 70,715

England scorer: Cole J

Comments: Joe Cole scored shortly after half time to decide the outcome at the Millennium Stadium. This was Paul Robinson's sixth clean sheet in his last seven full internationals.

Northern Ireland 1 ENGLAND 0; in Belfast;
Wednesday 7th September 2005 (World Cup qualifier)

1 Taylor	1 Robinson	(Tottenham)
2 Baird	2 Young	(Charlton Athletic)
3 Capaldi	3 Cole A	(Arsenal)
4 Hughes	4 Gerrard	(Liverpool) replaced by Defoe
5 Craigan	5 Ferdinand	(Man Utd)
6 Davis	6 Carragher	(Liverpool)
7 Gillespie	7 Beckham*	(Real Madrid)
8 Johnson	8 Lampard	(Chelsea) replaced by Hargreaves
9 Healy	9 Rooney	(Man Utd)
10 Quinn	10 Owen	(Real Madrid)
11 Elliott	11 Wright-Phillips	(Chelsea) replaced by ColeJ

Crowd: 14,000

Comments: Clueless England were all at sea in the unique atmosphere of Windsor Park. Eventually the prolific David Healy raced forward to thump home Northern Ireland's most famous goal.

ENGLAND 1 Austria 0; at Old Trafford;
Saturday 8th October 2005 (World Cup qualifier)

1 Robinson	(Tottenham)	1 Macho
2 Young	(Charlton Athletic)	2 Dober
3 Carragher	(Liverpool)	3 Stranzl
4 Gerrard	(Liverpool)	4 Scharner
5 Terry	(Chelsea)	5 Ibertsberger
6 Campbell	(Arsenal) replaced by Ferdinand	6 Aufhauser
7 Beckham*	(Real Madrid)	7 Schopp
8 Lampard	(Chelsea)	8 Keisenebner
9 Crouch	(Liverpool)	9 Linz
10 Owen	(Newcastle Utd) replaced by Richardson	10 Ivanschitz
11 Cole	(Chelsea) replaced by King	11 Weissenberger

Crowd: 66,482

England scorer: Lampard (Pen)

Comments: Frank Lampard slotted home a first-half penalty but David Beckham made life difficult for his team by earning the second red card of his chequered international career.

ENGLAND 2 Poland 1; at Old Trafford;
Wednesday 12th October 2005 (World Cup qualifier)

1 Robinson	(Tottenham)	1	Boruc
2 Young	(Charlton Athletic)	2	Jop
3 Carragher	(Liverpool)	3	Zewlakow
4 King	(Tottenham)	4	Baszczynski
5 Ferdinand	(Man Utd)	5	Kosowski
6 Terry	(Chelsea)	6	Bak
7 Wright-Phillips	(Chelsea) replaced by Crouch	7	Sobolewski
8 Lampard	(Chelsea)	8	Smolarek
9 Rooney	(Man Utd)	9	Zurawski
10 Owen*	(Newcastle Utd) replaced by Jenas	10	Lewandowski
11 Cole	(Chelsea) replaced by Smith	11	Rasiak

Crowd: 65,467

England scorers: Owen, Lampard

Comments: No sooner had Owen given his team the lead than the Poles equalised. It took a late winner from Lampard to secure the win. He was one of 4 Chelsea players in the starting eleven.

ENGLAND 3 Argentina 2; in Geneva;
Saturday 12th November 2005

1 Robinson	(Tottenham)	1	Abbondanzieri
2 Young	(Charlton Athletic) replaced by Crouch	2	Ayala
3 Bridge	(Chelsea) replaced by Konchesky	3	Sorin
4 Gerrard	(Liverpool)	4	Zanetti
5 Ferdinand	(Man Utd)	5	Demichelis
6 Terry	(Chelsea)	6	Samuel
7 Beckham*	(Real Madrid)	7	Rodriguez
8 Lampard	(Chelsea)	8	Riquelme
9 Rooney	(Man Utd)	9	Crespo
10 Owen	(Newcastle Utd)	10	Cambiasso
11 King	(Tottenham) replaced by Cole	11	Tevez

Crowd: 29,000

England scorers: Rooney, Owen (2)

Comments: England trailed twice to goals from Crespo and Samuel but Michael Owen pulled 2 rabbits out of the hat in the final minutes. This was the last cap for Konchesky and Young thus far.

ENGLAND 2 Uruguay 1; at Anfield;
Wednesday 1st March 2006

1 Robinson	(Tottenham)	1	Carini
2 Neville	(Man Utd)	2	Lugano
3 Bridge	(Chelsea) replaced by Carragher	3	Godin
4 Gerrard	(Liverpool) replaced by Jenas	4	Pouso
5 Ferdinand	(Man Utd)	5	Diogo
6 Terry	(Chelsea) replaced by King	6	Lima
7 Beckham*	(Real Madrid) replaced by Crouch	7	Varela
8 Carrick	(Tottenham)	8	Perez
9 Rooney	(Man Utd) replaced by Wright-Phillips	9	Vargas
10 Bent	(Charlton Athletic) replaced by Defoe	10	Forlan
11 Cole	(Chelsea)	11	Regueiro

Crowd: 40,013

England scorers: Crouch, Cole

Comments: Peter Crouch came off the bench to net his first goal after the home team had trailed at half time. Joe Cole then scored the winner in added on time. This was the debut for Darren Bent.

ENGLAND 3 Hungary 1; at Old Trafford;
Tuesday 30th May 2006

1 Robinson	(Tottenham)	1	Kiraly
2 Neville	(Man Utd) replaced by Hargreaves	2	Feher
3 Cole A	(Arsenal)	3	Komlosi
4 Carragher	(Liverpool)	4	Halmosi
5 Ferdinand	(Man Utd)	5	Eger
6 Terry	(Chelsea) replaced by Campbell	6	Molnar
7 Beckham*	(Real Madrid)	7	Szabics
8 Lampard	(Chelsea)	8	Dardai
9 Gerrard	(Liverpool) replaced by Walcott	9	Toth
10 Owen	(Newcastle Utd) replaced by Crouch	10	Gera
11 Cole J	(Chelsea)	11	Huszti

Crowd: 56,323

England scorers: Gerrard, Terry, Crouch

Comments: All the goals came in the second half, including John Terry's first successful effort. Earlier, Lampard had uncharacteristically failed from a spot kick. This was Theo Walcott's first cap.

ENGLAND 6 Jamaica 0; at Old Trafford ;
Saturday 3rd June 2006

1 Robinson	(Tottenham) replaced by James	1 Ricketts
2 Carragher	(Liverpool)	2 Reid
3 Cole A	(Arsenal) replaced by Bridge	3 Stewart
4 Gerrard	(Liverpool) replaced by Downing	4 Taylor
5 Ferdinand	(Man Utd)	5 Davis
6 Terry	(Chelsea) replaced by Campbell	6 Daley
7 Beckham*	(Real Madrid) replaced by Lennon	7 Euell
8 Lampard	(Chelsea) replaced by Carrick	8 Hue
9 Crouch	(Liverpool)	9 Campbell-Ryce
10 Owen	(Newcastle Utd)	10 Fuller
11 Cole J	(Chelsea)	11 Shelton

Crowd: 70,373

England scorers: Lampard, Taylor (OG), Crouch (3), Owen

Comments: The West Indians were put to the sword as England stormed into a 4–0 lead in the first half. Crouch added two more after the break to complete his hat-trick on Aaron Lennon's debut.

ENGLAND 1 Paraguay 0; in Frankfurt;
Saturday 10th June 2006 (World Cup finals)

1 Robinson	(Tottenham)	1 Villar
2 Neville	(Man Utd)	2 Caniza
3 Cole A	(Arsenal)	3 Toledo
4 Gerrard	(Liverpool)	4 Gamarra
5 Ferdinand	(Man Utd)	5 Caceres
6 Terry	(Chelsea)	6 Bonet
7 Beckham*	(Real Madrid)	7 Paredes
8 Lampard	(Chelsea)	8 Valdez
9 Crouch	(Liverpool)	9 Santa Cruz
10 Owen	(Newcastle Utd) replaced by Downing	10 Acuna
11 Cole J	(Chelsea) replaced by Hargreaves	11 Riveros

Crowd: 48,000

England scorer: Gamarra (OG)

Comments: A David Beckham free kick was responsible for the only goal which arrived inside five minutes. Highly fancied England could not build on this great start as they wilted in the heat.

ENGLAND 2 Trinidad & Tobago 0; in Nurenberg;
Thursday 15th June 2006 (World Cup finals)

1	Robinson	(Tottenham)		1	Hislop
2	Carragher	(Liverpool) replaced by Lennon		2	Jones
3	Cole A	(Arsenal)		3	Lawrence
4	Gerrard	(Liverpool)		4	Gray
5	Ferdinand	(Man Utd)		5	Sancho
6	Terry	(Chelsea)		6	Edwards
7	Beckham*	(Real Madrid)		7	Birchill
8	Lampard	(Chelsea)		8	Theobold
9	Crouch	(Liverpool)		9	Whitley
10	Owen	(Newcastle Utd) replaced by Rooney	10	Yorke
11	Cole J	(Chelsea) replaced by Downing	11	John

Crowd: 41,000

England scorers: Crouch, Gerrard

Comments: England made hard work of overcoming the Carribbean minnows. It took two goal in the last ten minutes from the Liverpool duo of Crouch and Gerrard to spare Eriksson's blushes.

ENGLAND 2 Sweden 2; in Koln;
Tuesday 20th June 2006 (World Cup finals)

1	Robinson	(Tottenham)		1	Isaksson
2	Carragher	(Liverpool)		2	Alexandersson
3	Cole A	(Arsenal)		3	Mellberg
4	Hargreaves	(Bayern Munich)		4	Lucic
5	Ferdinand	(Man Utd) replaced by Campbell	5	Edman
6	Terry	(Chelsea)		6	Linderoth
7	Beckham*	(Real Madrid)		7	Kallstrom
8	Lampard	(Chelsea)		8	Jonson
9	Rooney	(Man Utd) replaced by Gerrard	9	Ljungberg
10	Owen	(Newcastle Utd) replaced by Crouch	10	Allback
11	Cole J	(Chelsea)		11	Larsson

Crowd: 45,000

England scorers: Cole J, Gerrard

Comments: England could not shake the Swedes off, despite leading twice. Henrik Larsson netted a last minute equaliser 5 minutes after Gerrard's goal. Joe Cole had earlier scored a wonder volley.

ENGLAND 1 Ecuador 0; in Stuttgart;
Sunday 25th June 2006 (World Cup finals)

1	Robinson	(Tottenham)	1	Mora	
2	Hargreaves	(Bayern Munich)	2	de la Cruz	
3	Cole A	(Arsenal)	3	Hurtado	
4	Carrick	(Tottenham)	4	Espinoza	
5	Ferdinand	(Man Utd)	5	Reasco	
6	Terry	(Chelsea)	6	Valencia	
7	Beckham*	(Real Madrid) replaced by Lennon	7	Tenorio	
8	Lampard	(Chelsea)	8	Castillo	
9	Rooney	(Man Utd)	9	Mendez	
10	Gerrard	(Liverpool) replaced by Downing	10	Delgado	
11	Cole J	(Chelsea) replaced by Carragher	11	Tenorio	

Crowd: 52,000

England scorer: Beckham

Comments: England nudged into the quarter-finals with another unconvincing win. Hero of the hour was the captain, David Beckham, whose second half goal ultimately separated the two teams.

ENGLAND 0 Portugal 0 [After extra time]; in Gelsenkirchen;
Saturday 1st July 2006 (World Cup finals)

1	Robinson	(Tottenham)	1	Ricardo	
2	Neville	(Man Utd)	2	Carvalho	
3	Cole A	(Arsenal)	3	Miguel	
4	Hargreaves	(Bayern Munich)	4	Valente	
5	Ferdinand	(Man Utd)	5	Meira	
6	Terry	(Chelsea)	6	Maniche	
7	Beckham*	(Real Madrid) replaced by Lennon	7	Figo	
8	Lampard	(Chelsea)	8	Petit	
9	Rooney	(Man Utd)	9	Pauleta	
10	Gerrard	(Liverpool)	10	Ronaldo	
11	Cole J	(Chelsea) replaced by Crouch	11	Tiago	

Crowd: 52,000

Comments: It was a case of deja-vu as England exited the World Cup undefeated over 90 minutes. Wayne Rooney was sent off and then Carragher, Gerrard and Lampard all missed their penalties.

Appendix I: Most capped players, 1946–2006

Peter Shilton (1970–1990), 125 caps
Bobby Moore (1962–1973), 108 caps
Bobby Charlton (1958–1970), 106 caps
Billy Wright (1946–1959), 105 caps
David Beckham (1996–2006), 94 caps
Bryan Robson (1980–1991), 90 caps
Kenny Sansom (1979–1988), 85 caps
Ray Wilkins (1976–1986), 84 caps
Gary Neville (1995–2006), 81 caps
Gary Lineker (1984–1992), 80 caps
Michael Owen (1998–2006), 80 caps
John Barnes (1983–1995), 79 caps
Stuart Pearce (1987–1999), 78 caps
Terry Butcher (1980–1990), 77 caps
Tom Finney (1946–1958), 76 caps
David Seaman (1988–2002), 75 caps
Gordon Banks (1963–1972), 73 caps
Alan Ball (1965–1975), 72 caps
Sol Campbell (1996–2006), 69 caps
Martin Peters (1966–1974), 67 caps

Appendix II: England Managers, 1946–2006

Walter Winterbottom, 1946–1962
Alf Ramsey, 1963–1974
Joe Mercer, 1974
Don Revie, 1974–1977
Ron Greenwood, 1977–1982
Bobby Robson, 1982–1990
Graham Taylor, 1990–1993
Terry Venables, 1994–1996
Glenn Hoddle, 1996–1998
Howard Wilkinson, 1999 and 2000
Kevin Keegan, 1999–2000
Peter Taylor, 2000
Sven Goran Eriksson, 2001–2006

Appendix III: England's Hat-trick Heroes, 1946–2006

APPENDIX IV: ENGLAND'S GOALKEEPERS, 1946–2006

Frank Swift, 1946–1949, 19 caps
Ted Ditchburn, 1948–1956, 6 caps
Bert Williams, 1949–1955, 24 caps
Bernard Streten, 1949, 1 cap
Gil Merrick, 1951–1954, 23 caps
Ray Wood, 1954–1956, 3 caps
Ron Baynham, 1955, 3 caps
Reg Matthews, 1956, 5 caps
Alan Hodgkinson, 1957–1960, 5 caps
Eddie Hopkinson, 1957–1959, 14 caps
Colin McDonald, 1958, 8 caps
Ron Springett, 1959–1966, 33 caps
Gordon Banks, 1963–1972, 73 caps
Tony Waiters, 1964, 5 caps
Peter Bonetti, 1966–1970, 7 caps
Alex Stepney, 1968, 1 cap
Gordon West, 1968–1969, 3 caps
Peter Shilton, 1970–1990, 125 caps
Ray Clemence, 1972–1983, 61 caps
Phil Parkes, 1974, 1 cap
Jimmy Rimmer, 1976, 1 cap
Joe Corrigan, 1976–1982, 9 caps
Nigel Spink, 1983, 1 cap
Gary Bailey, 1985, 2 caps
Chris Woods, 1985–1993, 43 caps
David Seaman, 1988–2002, 74 caps
Dave Beasant, 1989, 2 caps
Nigel Martyn, 1992–2002, 23 caps
Tim Flowers, 1993–1998, 11 caps
Ian Walker, 1996–2004, 4 caps
David James, 1997_, 34 caps
Richard Wright, 2000–2001, 2 caps
Paul Robinson, 2003_, 26 caps
Robert Green, 2005, 1 cap

Appendix V: Leading goalscorers, 1946–2006

Bobby Charlton, 49 goals from 105 starts
Gary Lineker, 48 goals from 74 starts
Jimmy Greaves, 44 goals from 57 starts
Michael Owen, 36 goals from 69 starts
Tom Finney, 30 goals from 76 starts
Nat Lofthouse, 30 goals from 33 starts
Alan Shearer, 30 goals from 61 starts
David Platt, 27 goals from 55 starts
Bryan Robson, 26 goals from 90 starts
Geoff Hurst, 24 goals from 47 starts

Appendix VI: English Football League Champions, 1946–2006

Arsenal: 1948, 1953, 1971, 1989, 1991, 1998, 2002, 2004
Aston Villa: 1981
Blackburn Rovers: 1995
Burnley: 1960
Chelsea: 1955, 2005, 2006
Derby County: 1972, 1975
Everton: 1963, 1970, 1985, 1987
Ipswich Town: 1962
Leeds United: 1969, 1974, 1992
Liverpool: 1947, 1964, 1966, 1973, 1976–7, 1979–80, 1982–4, 1986, 1988, 1990
Manchester City: 1968
Manchester United: 1952, 1956–7, 1965, 1967, 1993–4, 1996–7, 1999–2001, 2003
Nottingham Forest: 1978
Portsmouth: 1949–50
Tottenham Hotspur: 1951, 1961
Wolverhampton Wanderers: 1954, 1958–9

Appendix VII: English FA Cup Champions, 1946–2006

Arsenal: 1950, 1971, 1979, 1993, 1998, 2002–3, 2005
Aston Villa: 1957
Blackpool: 1953
Bolton Wanderers: 1958
Charlton Athletic: 1947
Chelsea: 1970, 1997, 2000
Coventry City: 1987
Derby County: 1946
Everton: 1966, 1984, 1995
Ipswich Town: 1978
Leeds United: 1972
Liverpool: 1965, 1974, 1986, 1989, 1992, 2001, 2006
Manchester City: 1956, 1969
Manchester United: 1948, 1963, 1977, 1983, 1985, 1990, 1994, 1996, 1999, 2004
Newcastle United: 1951–2, 1955
Nottingham Forest: 1959
Southampton: 1976
Sunderland: 1973
Tottenham Hotspur: 1961–2, 1967, 1981–2, 1991
West Bromwich Albion: 1954, 1968
West Ham United: 1964, 1975, 1980
Wimbledon: 1988
Wolverhampton Wanderers: 1949,1960

Appendix VIII: English football clubs' European triumphs

1963: Tottenham Hotspur win the European Cup-Winners' Cup
1965: West Ham United win the European Cup-Winners' Cup
1968: Manchester United win the European Champions' Cup
1968: Leeds United win the Fairs' Cup
1969: Newcastle United win the Fairs' Cup
1970: Manchester City win the European Cup-Winners' Cup
1970: Arsenal win the European Fairs' Cup
1971: Chelsea win the European Cup-Winners' Cup
1971: Leeds United win the European Fairs' Cup
1972: Tottenham Hotspur win the UEFA Cup
1973: Liverpool win the UEFA Cup
1976: Liverpool win the UEFA Cup
1977: Liverpool win the European Champions' Cup
1978: Liverpool win the European Champions' Cup
1979: Nottingham Forest win the European Champions' Cup
1980: Nottingham Forest win the European Champions' Cup
1981: Liverpool win the European Champions' Cup
1981: Ipswich Town win the UEFA Cup
1982: Aston Villa win the European Champions' Cup
1983: Liverpool win the European Champions' Cup
1984: Liverpool win the European Champions' Cup
1984: Tottenham Hotspur win the UEFA Cup
1985: Everton win the European Cup-Winners' Cup
1991: Manchester United win the European Cup-Winners' Cup
1994: Arsenal win the European Cup-Winners' Cup
1998: Chelsea win the European Cup-Winners' Cup
1999: Manchester United win the European Champions' League
2001: Liverpool win the UEFA Cup
2005: Liverpool win the European Champions' League

Appendix IX: England in the two major tournaments, 1946–2006

1950 World Cup: Eliminated at the finals' group stage
1954 World Cup: Reached the quarter-finals
1958 World Cup: Eliminated at the finals' group stage
1960 European Nations' Cup: Did not compete
1962 World Cup: Reached the quarter-finals
1964 European Nations' Cup: Eliminated in the First Round
1966 World Cup: Tournament winners
1968 European Championship: Reached the semi-finals
1970 World Cup: Reached the quarter-finals
1972 European Championship: Reached the quarter-finals
1974 World Cup: Did not qualify for the finals
1976 European Championship: Did not qualify for the quarter-finals
1978 World Cup: Did not qualify for the finals
1980 European Championship: Eliminated at the finals' group stage
1982 World Cup: Reached the finals' second group phase
1984 European Championship: Did not qualify for the finals
1986 World Cup: Reached the quarter-finals
1988 European Championship: Eliminated at the finals' group stage
1990 World Cup: Reached the semi-finals
1992 European Championship: Eliminated at the finals' group stage
1994 World Cup: Did not qualify for the finals
1996 European Championship: Reached the semi-finals
1998 World Cup: Reached the last sixteen
2000 European Championship: Eliminated at the finals' group stage
2002 World Cup: Reached the quarter-finals
2004 European Championship: Reached the quarter-finals
2006 World Cup: Reached the quarter-finals

APPENDIX X: ENGLAND'S HIGHS AND LOWS, 1946–2006

1946: England 7 Northern Ireland 2
1950: England 0 USA 1
1953: England 3 Hungary 6
1954: Hungary 7 England 1; Uruguay 4 England 2
1957: England 2 Northern Ireland 3
1961: England 9 Scotland 3
1962: Brazil 3 England 1
1963: England 2 Rest Of The World 1; England 8 Northern Ireland 3
1966: England 2 Portugal 1; England 4 West Germany 2
1967: England 2 Scotland 3
1969: England 5 France 0; England 4 Scotland 1
1970: England 2 West Germany 3
1972: England 1 West Germany 3
1973: England 1 Poland 1
1975: England 5 Scotland 1
1976: England 3 Italy 2
1977: Italy 2 England 0
1980: Wales 4 England 1; Italy 1 England 0
1981: Norway 2 England 1
1982: England 3 France 1
1984: Brazil 0 England 2
1986: England 3 Poland 0; England 1 Argentina 2
1988: England 0 Republic Of Ireland 1
1990: England 3 Cameroon 2; England 1 West Germany 1
1992: Sweden 2 England 1
1993: Holland 2 England 0
1996: England 2 Scotland 0; England 4 Holland 1
1998: England 2 Argentina 2
2000: England 1 Germany 0; England 2 Romania 3
2001: Germany 1 England 5
2002: England 1 Argentina 0; England 1 Brazil 2
2004: England 4 Croatia 2; England 2 Portugal 2
2005: Northern Ireland 1 England 0
2006: England 0 Portugal 0